Clio in Oceania

Clio in Oceania

Toward a Historical Anthropology

Edited by Aletta Biersack

Smithsonian Institution Press • Washington and London

Editor: Joanne Reams
Designer: Janice Wheeler

Library of Congress Cataloging-in-Publication Data

Clio in Oceania : toward a historical anthropology / edited by Aletta
   Biersack.
       p.   cm.
   Includes bibliographical references (p.).
   ISBN 0-87474-304-4 (alk. paper)

   1. Ethnohistory — Oceania.   2. Oceania — Historiography.
   3. Ethnology — Oceania.   4. Oceania — History.   I. Biersack, Aletta.
   GN662.C57   1990

   995 — dc20   90-9765

British Library Cataloging-in-Publication Data available
Manufactured in the United States of America
97 96 95 94 93 92 91 90   5 4 3 2 1

For permission to reproduce the illustrations appearing in this
book, please correspond directly with the sources; the
Smithsonian Institution Press does not retain reproduction
rights for these illustrations or maintain a file of addresses for
sources.

⊚ The paper used in this publication meets the minimum requirements of the
American National Standard for Permanence of Paper for Printed Library
Materials
Z39.48–1984.

Contents

Acknowledgments

An earlier version of Valerio Valeri's article "The Transformation of a Transformation" was published in *Social Analysis* in 1982. Our thanks to that journal for permitting us to reprint the article with minor revisions here.

My thanks to Jocelyn Linnekin for her assistance in the initial stages of preparing this volume. Various people have read various versions of the introduction. Thanks go to members of the History Department at the University of Oregon; also Peter Bellwood, Marie Reay, Nicholas Thomas, Valerio Valeri, Roy Wagner, and an anonymous reviewer. The volume was finalized while I was a visiting fellow in the Department of Anthropology, Research School of Pacific Studies, Australian National University, participating in the Comparative Austronesian Project convened by Dr. James J. Fox. My thanks to Dr. Fox and my colleagues at C.A.P. The book has benefited from the technical assistance of Chris Stole and Laura Couture in Eugene and Ria Van de Zandt and Margaret Tyrie in Canberra. Sylvia L. Thrupp first introduced me to anthropology-history interfaces when I was a masters candidate in medieval history at the University of Michigan, and to her I continue to be grateful.

Clio in Oceania

1. Introduction

History and Theory in Anthropology

Aletta Biersack

hough the intensity of interdisciplinary excitement is especially sharp today, the enthusiasm for historicizing anthropological inquiry is not unprecedented. In a 1950 critique that still seems fresh, Evans-Pritchard defended historicism against Radcliffe-Brown's assaults, writing that "what social anthropologists have in fact chiefly been doing is to write cross-sections of history, integrative descriptive accounts . . . at a moment of time" (Evans-Pritchard 1950:122). In one stroke, he dismissed the myth of the "ethnographic present" and the synchronic investigation that myth charters. Although Leach's *Political Systems of Highland Burma* boldly assailed the equilibrium assumptions of structural analysis (Evans-Pritchard's among them [Leach 1954:282]) and writers like Eric Wolf and Sidney Mintz explained cultural features historically (focusing upon the colonial experience) rather than synchronically (Roseberry 1988), attempts to join anthropology and history were more often than not devoid of theoretical interest. Claiming as its preserve the history of culture contact, particularly in North America, ethnohistory combined the two fields, drawing from history its methodology, its "careful evaluation of sources" (Carmack 1972:23), and from anthropology "the generalizing aspects of ethnology" (ibid.). The labor thus divided, the twain could all too easily meet, without transforming either field (see Dirks 1987:12, 1988; Thomas 1989:3)—in particular, without theorizing culture history as such.

Until recently, either/or choices and the antinomies supporting them —globe/locality, political economy/systems of meaning, objectivism/subjectivism, materialism/idealism, and structure/history—have proliferated, fracturing anthropology. The novelty today lies in the way this agonistic theoretical praxis yields ground. In the name of reclaiming for synthetic projects what older frameworks exclude, paradigms are relaxed to enable a "free play with concepts and methods" (Marcus and Fischer 1986:81) and an attention to various mediations. Historical anthropology in particular holds "the middle ground between poles of every kind" (Dening, this volume) to found a more dynamic view of social life upon the mobilities of energized and productive borderlands. Such synthetic efforts are empowered by the broader context. In the social and human sciences at large, the mood is not merely interdisciplinary but postdisciplinary, governed by a politics of inclusion rather than exclusion and by the play of texts across topically diverse terrains.

Operating against a backdrop of historical and cultural studies, historical anthropology has implications for anthropology's interdisciplinary position and also for the linkages between and among the discipline's subfields, as well as for its theory and methodology. Taking as its point of departure Marshall Sahlins's *Historical Metaphors and Mythical Realities*, this introduction explores these implications. Where relevant, attention will be paid to the Paris-based Annales school—a shifting configuration of scholars associated with the famous journal *Annales: Économies, Sociétés, Civilisations* founded by Marc Bloch and Lucien Febvre in 1929 and identified most strongly today with Fernand Braudel (1902–85), author of *The Mediterranean and the Mediterranean World in the Age of Philip II* (1972 [1949]).

Historical Metaphors and Mythical Realities

The slenderest of volumes, *Historical Metaphors and Mythical Realities* is theoretically ambitious. The book focuses on what Anthony Giddens has called a "central problem" in social theory: how to overcome the antinomy of system/action so as to account for "structuration." Structuration is a structure-transforming process in which action— however much the "instantiation" of structure—nonetheless triggers change through its own products. Structure is both the medium and the outcome of practices: participant in and precipitate of a dialectic founded on structure's "duality" (Giddens 1979:ch. 2; see Karp 1986). In the second chapter of his *Outline of a Theory of Practice*, Pierre Bourdieu develops essentially the same model. There Bourdieu argues that structural constraints are brought to bear not on action as such —which in any case cannot be treated as a mere mechanical enactment of "pre-established assemblies, 'models' or 'rôles'" (Bourdieu 1977:73) —but on action's productivity, as a regulation of the improvisations of practice (ibid.:78).

As is by now well known, Sahlins's interpretation of Captain Cook's death is one of the linchpins in his argument that history is ordered by structures of signification (1981:ch. 1, 1985:ch. 4, 1989a). (The other is the empowerment of Hawaiian chiefs in the context of intercultural trade.) Classified as the Hawaiian peace-and-fertility god Lono, participant in a religious-cum-political pantheon (see Valeri, this volume), Cook became a Saussurean sign, a historical metaphor of a mythical reality, for in his arrival, departure, and eventual demise, Cook's actions were governed by the logic of the structures they un-wittingly reproduced.

But structure thus instantiated became vulnerable to the surround-ing circumstances; reproduction always entails the possibility of trans-formation. To make this point, Sahlins develops his concept of the "structure of the conjuncture." The "structure of the conjuncture" is a class of phenomena of which intercultural trade in the early history of the Sandwich Islands is one example. In *Historical Metaphors* the "structure of the conjuncture" refers specifically to the dynamism of intercultural commerce and in particular to the sandalwood trade between Hawaiian and foreign enclaves in nineteenth-century Hawaii. Equipped from ancient times with the taboo (*kapu*), by socially constituted right Hawaiian chiefs could monopolize valuables. When foreign traders seeking sandalwood arrived in the archipelago, the chiefs exercised their *kapu* privileges and monopolized the sandalwood supply. But they did so for reasons of personal gain rather than to finance chiefly largesse. Hence the conjuncture: chiefs capitalized upon circumstances as chiefs (structure); but they did so with respect to specific historical circumstances (the novel demand for sandalwood), which they exploited to further their own interests (action).

In "The Return of the Event, Again" (this volume), Sahlins defines the "structure of the conjuncture" rather abstractly as "the way the cultural categories are actualized in a specific context through the interested action of the historic agents and the pragmatics of their interaction." The gloss is similarly abstract in *Islands of History*: "the practical realization of the cultural categories in a specific historical context, as expressed in the interested actions of the historic agents, including the microsociology of their interaction" (1985:xiv). The terms calls attention to the complexity of the order of determinations in play: how structure mediates a practice that even so *could have been different*. In principle irreducible, the event is "a *relation* between a happening and a structure (or structures)" (ibid.). There is no friction between this claim and the claim that the "'event is the empirical form of the system'" (Friedman 1988:32, quoted from Sahlins 1985:153), which merely implies (à la Giddens [1979]) that structure "enables" action, which then instantiates structure, or (à la Ricoeur and apropos of the *langue/parole* dichotomy [1974:chs. 3, 4]) that speech "takes up" *langue*, making "the system occur as an act and the structure as an event" (ibid.:85).

Ricoeur goes on to argue (as does Sahlins) that in taking up *langue*, speech overcomes "the closure of the universe of signs" (ibid.) as novel values accrue to the sign-in-play and that these values, when sedimented within the system, give the *system* a *history* (ibid.:92–93). Exercising a privilege that emanates from a totality—the right to levy a *kapu*—Hawaiian chiefs nevertheless transformed that totality through their actions. Today the *kapu* sign protects private property, not the store of surpluses and valuables chiefs traditionally deployed as leaders of kin-based polities. "In action . . . the cultural categories acquire new functional values. Burdened with the world, the cultural meanings are thus altered. It follows that the relationships between categories change: the structure is transformed" (Sahlins 1985:138).

Here Sahlins identifies three moments of his dialectic: "instantiation wherein the larger cultural categories of the history are represented by particular persons, objects, and acts" (this volume, italics removed); denouement, the interplay of structure, action, interest, and circumstances in a "structure of the conjuncture"; and the totalization of the consequences "or the return of the act to the system by the attribution of general meanings to particular incidents" (ibid.). The dialectic—with all the paradoxes it supports ("Man . . . is *at once both* the product of his own product *and a historical agent who can under no circumstances be taken as a product,*" Sartre wrote [1963:87])— locates anthropological inquiry beyond the problematic antinomies of yesterday. Neither synchrony or diachrony, Braudel's long or short *durée*, the history Sahlins isolates is exactly both, artifact of the complexity of the dialect itself. As in structuralism, so in Sahlins's "evenemential history" (this volume), the empirical (the stream of events) remains a surface to be penetrated. Beneath the surface lies not Lévi-Strauss's "order of structure," however, but the regularities of the dialectic and its conjunctural logic.

Event-Centered Anthropology

In his contribution to this volume, Sahlins rehearses the imagery that held a generation of Annalists and structural anthropologists in thrall, inhibiting the development of event-centered analysis. Both Annalists and structuralists experienced a kind of metaphysical dread of the event, for whether seen as "external" to the "order of structure" or as an instantiation of it, the event *as such* lacked systematicity and eluded analysis. In integrating the problem of order with the problem of change, Sahlins renders events intelligible in terms of the dialectic's shaping power. His shift from regularities of stasis to regularities of change—

or, at least, of flow—is signaled at the outset in the monograph's motto: not the familiar structuralist claim that "the more things change, the more they remain the same," but the assertion that "the more things remain the same, the more they change" (Sahlins 1981:7). This accounts for the central paradox of the monograph: that discontinuities always entail significant continuities.

Focusing upon the "world" a community of speakers signifies and experiences, phenomenological frameworks, including Geertzian "interpretation" (1973, 1983), have found the event—as sign or "text," an index of that "world"—far more congenial. Not surprisingly, Geertz's (phenomenological) "cultural analysis" has inspired historians to rehabilitate the event by way of redefining the alliance between history and the social sciences (Braudel 1980), this time as a kind of symbolic anthropology (Biersack 1989:74–78). The event is embraced as an opportunity to probe popular culture, construed in symbolic anthropological terms. Robert Darnton's depiction of a "great cat massacre" in eighteenth-century Paris (1984), Carlo Ginzburg's charming account of the sixteenth-century miller who was tried for the heretical character of his cheese-and-worms cosmology (1980), and the second part of Le Roy Ladurie's account of a fourteenth-century village in the Pyrenees, *Montaillou* (1979), are all examples of a new interest in an exotic, popular "local knowledge" (Geertz 1983)—*mentalité*, as it is called (Darnton 1984: introduction and conclusion; LaCapra 1985: chs. 2 and 3; Stone 1981).

Other frameworks as well are event centered. Developing out of symbolic interactionism, performance theory devotes itself to the event-performances and event-experiences in and through which signs are embodied and acquire efficacy and new meaning. Life history has always been event focused; and a new "biographical" approach to objects documents their "social life" through transformations of context and construction, within and across cultural boundaries (Appadurai 1984; Clifford 1988: pt. 2; Stocking, Jr., 1985).

Sahlins's recuperation of the event (1981, 1985, and this volume) arguably generalizes the orientation within the field. Although it would be premature to attempt an exhaustive inventory of the agenda of an event-oriented anthropology, some matters are already at hand that will no doubt preoccupy historical anthropology, as they do the contributors to this volume.

World and Text

Sahlins makes explicit his contribution to symbolic anthropology in the closing section of *Islands of History*, which is titled "the phenomenology of the social life." The classic phenomenology renders the public meanings that endow persons and things with significance. The extrasymbolic—nature, for example, or the signs of a foreign "horizon" of meaning—remains "bracketed" as a self-enclosing, self-generating *symbolic* space is presented to analysis. Sahlins removes the brackets and examines the interplay of world and "world." As used, signs may reference a world-beyond-"world," a world that evades their signifying power. Symbol use brings the symbolic and the extrasymbolic into relation, allowing each to condition the other. Cook has historical efficacy as Lono, but he also has historical efficacy as Cook.

> In action, people put their concepts and categories into ostensive relations to the world. Such referential uses bring into play other determinations of the signs, besides their received sense, namely the actual world and the people concerned. *Praxis* is, then, a risk to the sense of signs in the culture-as-constituted, precisely as the sense is arbitrary in its capacity as reference. Having its own properties, the world may then prove intractable. . . . [R]eferential action, by placing a priori concepts in correspondence with external objects, will imply some unforeseen effects that cannot be ignored (Sahlins 1985:149).

In removing the brackets and joining world and "world" by way of synthesizing structure and action, Sahlins defines the event as a moment in which symbolic, political, and economic planes converge.

Parallel approaches to symbolic production blossom in adjacent fields. Among Annalists, Braudel's rejection of political history has been overturned as politics has been rehabilitated (Sahlins, this volume) but also linked to knowledge, discourse, and symbolic practices under the inspiration of Foucault and Bourdieu and sometimes in the name of a cultural Marxism (Dirks 1988; Hunt 1986, 1989). Seeking a merger between intellectual and social history, Roger Chartier summons his own generation of Annalists to recast the study of representation in less rarefied ways, by means of "opening up a working-space between texts and readings so as to grasp the complex, multiple and highly differentiated practices ["political, social and discursive" (Chartier 1988:14)] that construct the world of representation" (ibid.). In literary studies, a "new historicism" develops an insight of Marxist criticism—that the text, in its production and consumption, is embedded in social and political realties; and a new "literary sociology" contests "the hypostatization of 'literature' into a pure essence uncontaminated by the dross of history and modernity" (Felperin 1985:14). Affirming neither the autonomy of the text nor its reduction to extratextual ("contextual") factors, the new historicism insists on the interpenetration of text and world, the necessity of viewing each from the perspective of the other. "History is not simply discovered in the precincts surrounding the literary text or the performance of the image," Stephen Greenblatt writes (1987:vii); "it is found in the artworks themselves, as enabling condition, shaping force, forger of meaning, censor, community of patronage and reception" (ibid.). Not merely reflectionist in its claims, the "new historicism" goes on to assert the impact of the text upon the world as an event among events. "The world of art is not the passive surface on which this historical experience leaves its stamp but one of the creative agents in the fashioning and re-fashioning of experience" (ibid.).

In these approaches, and also in *Historical Metaphors* and *Islands of History*, a dialectic of the world-in-the-text and the text-in-the-world (or world-in-the-"world" and "world"-in-the-world) displaces the classic phenomenological concern with the "world" *of* the text, establishing a terrain for investigating the way in which the ideal and the material, the symbolic and the political, condition each other. Here the goal is to supplant the reductions of base/superstructure models and also purely symbolic ones with frameworks that accommodate the multifaceted complexity of actual, historical reality. Such efforts set the stage for reconciling Marxist and non-Marxist approaches by bonding hermeneutical preoccupations with an awareness of political and material factors. In developing such a synthesis, the writings of Pierre Bourdieu, Fredric Jameson, Raymond Williams, and E. P. Thompson become crucial resources.

The Question of Totalities

In anthropology as well as in history, a modified holism persists. However many voices Sahlins raises—whether of chiefs or commoners, men or women, Captain Cook or Lono—together, even in the moments of their sharpest discord, these constitute an ensemble, albeit one in transition (see Sahlins, this volume).

For some, however, the mood of the moment is anti-Durkheimian as belief in the society-god wanes. Culture is said to be decomposed into "seriously contested codes and representations" (Clifford 1986:2; see also Keesing 1987, M. Strathern, in press, and Thomas, this volume). The demand for polyphonic representational practices that allow for atonality and cacophany and not just harmony—or even dissonance, which still requires totalization—is spurred by the feminist critique of androcentrism, with its suppression of alternate, even oppositional, voices (M. Strathern 1988:ch. 2). Marcus recommends a shift from "the trope of structure" to "the perspective of voice" to capture the heterogeneity of a fragmented social "fabric" (Marcus 1989a and in press; see also Thomas 1989:43–50 and this volume). Indeed, particularly as a result of feminism's impact, Pacific ethnography has increasingly concentrated upon internal heterogeneities (Godelier 1986, Herdt 1982, Linnekin 1990a, A. Strathern 1982a, and M. Strathern 1988), although totalizing concepts such as hierarchy and stratification tend to undercut any "deconstructive" thrust in this literature (see Kapferer 1988). Event-centeredness provides occasions (the Fijian coup, for example [Thomas, this volume]) for exploring the utility of a postconfigurational anthropology.

Totalizing concepts have met with a similar fate in history. In *The Mediterranean*, Braudel stratified history according to a tripartite polyrhythmic scheme, each level representing a distinctive tempo or relative "immobility" (Braudel 1980:passim; Hexter 1979; Ricoeur 1984: 101–11; Sahlins, this volume). This "total history" is a history "written in three different registers . . . , the writer's aim being to bring together in all their multiplicity the different measures of time past. . . . My favourite vision of history is as a song for many voices" (Braudel 1972, 2:1238). Rabelaisian in its tendency to sprawl boundlessly in time and space, "total history" is (according to the historian J. H. Hexter) "history that aspires to embrace the whole of human activity, bringing to bear upon it all the knowledge that the sciences of man can provide" (1979:133). Despite the influence of *The Mediterranean* and the remarkable historiographic ideas underwriting it, Braudel's "total history" has either yielded ground to local history (Stone 1981:94) or been "radically contested in the name of a 'splintered' or decentered history" (LaCapra 1985:118) striving to reflect a fragmented world.

In place of more familiar totalizing concepts such as community, society, collectivity, or world-system—possibly even culture—James Clifford and George Marcus substitute art-cultural epochs such as "modernism," "postmodernism," and Clifford's "twentieth century" in recognition of the "deterritorialized," "rootless," and "homeless" character of cultural production in modern and postmodern times (Clifford 1988, Marcus in press). Identity today is "conjunctural, not essential" (Clifford 1988:11); traveling is a mode of dwelling (ibid.:13); and "the roots of tradition are cut and retied, collective symbols appropriated from external influences" (ibid.:15; see also M. Strathern, in press). Rather than ethnographies of people and place, depending as these do upon notions of a "transcendent regime of authenticity" (ibid.:10), Clifford proffers a "poetics of displacement" (1988:pt. 2).

Except for the fact that Clifford and Marcus both show discomfort with configurational language (M. Strathern, in press), their art-cultural epochs could be described as semitotalities. The world is at once centered and decentered, "increasingly connected, though not unified, economically and culturally" (Clifford 1988:17); people are both dispersed and aggregated; diversity is generated paradoxically from the very forces promoting global homogenization (Marcus 1989a and in press).

The ambiguities and paradoxes of this literature raise a number of questions, regional and general. If the present epoch of cultural production is adequately classified as "late capitalist," what is the relationship between art-cultural formations and Clifford's poetics, on the one hand, and global sociohistorical formations, on the other? How important are class and class culture for Pacific communities today (Hau'ofa 1987; Linnekin, this volume, and what would an adequate account of the emergence of class in the Pacific look like? How are class, gender, ethnicity, and nationalism related? The "break with the trope of settled community" Marcus recommends (1989a:14) is tailored for the study of creolized "interculture" developing on a global scale (Clifford 1988:15; Marcus, in press) and has clear relevance for the study of Pacific overseas communities and processes of urbanization. But can such a strategy illuminate the Melpa of the Papua New Guinea highlands, who continue to "make *moka*" in our twentieth century (A. Strathern 1982b and this volume)? What role will an ethnography of cosmopolitanism play in historical anthropology, and how will it disturb prevailing paradigms?

World History, Local History

Braudel eventually sought to realize his ambitions for a "total history" in a world history tracking the development and advance of capitalism. Inspired initially by the dependency theory of Andre Gunder Frank and more recently by the world-system theory of Immanuel Wallerstein (whose research institute at the State University of New York at Binghamton is called the Fernand Braudel Center for the Study of Economies, Historical Systems, and Civilizations), the political-economy or world-system approach challenges the claim that the local unit of analysis (anthropology's "culture") is an autonomous, self-organizing entity and concentrates instead upon axes of domination and subordination linking the local unit and the global system impinging upon it (see Wolf 1982 and the discussion in Roseberry 1988:173). Centrist and metropolitan in perspective, world-system theory taken to its extreme formulates a single, self-regulating whole whose subordinate elements are determined by processes engendered at the global level. History is unified and universal (Ortner 1984 and Roseberry 1988). Although this extreme position is seldom adopted, anthropological debate still pivots on the issue of which level in the final instance is the determining one. Thus, Friedman writes (against Sahlins) that in the history of the Sandwich Islands outcomes were governed in the short run as well as in the long by the world-system (1985).

Those who would defend an "islands of history" approach point out in reply that the so-called periphery is culturally diverse, variable in its forms (John Comaroff 1982:145, Ragin and Chirot 1984:303–4, Sahlins 1985:viii). The historical outcome of colonialism and imperialism has not been "ruin and cultural decay" (Clifford 1988:14) but a world in which the other has found "new ways to be different" (ibid.:338), suggesting pressure from below as well as from above. "The world system is not a physics of proportionate relationships between economic 'impacts' and cultural 'reactions'. The specific effects of the global-material forces depend on the various ways they are mediated in local cultural schemes" (Sahlins 1989b:5; see also Biersack, Linnekin, and Strathern, this volume). Pacific island historians have also insisted upon the two-sidedness of metropolitan-periphery encounters and accorded local groups a measure of self-determination (Davidson 1966, Howe 1979; see also Thomas 1990b).

World-system and culturalist approaches alike tacitly corroborate (or fail to challenge) the assumption that non-Western societies are inherently static. Yet the pages of an important anthology, *Big Men and Great Men*, are replete with examples of Melanesian indigenous turbulence (Godelier and M. Strathern, in press); and usurpation is a regular feature of highly stratified Polynesian kingdoms (Bott 1982; Sahlins 1981, 1985; Valeri 1985a, 1985b, 1989, 1990, in press). The "heroism" of Sahlins's "heroic history" (1985:ch.2 and this volume) resides in part in the boldness of the projects spawned by a ubiquitous fraternal and cross-cousin rivalry fed by "hatred and violence" and a jockeying for position that the "gift economy" did nothing to allay but instead exacerbated as insult was added to insult (Sahlins, this volume; see also Whitehead 1987). In Hawaii, at least, the fact that paramountcy was often achieved through war meant that war could not be arrested, even though settled governance depended on peace and prosperity (Valeri, this volume; see also Parmentier 1987 and Peterson 1982 for evidence of instability in Micronesia).

The presence of internecine strife in certain Oceanic societies suggests the significance an anthropology devoted to conflict has for historical anthropology. In this context, since exchange is crucial to the resolution of conflict but paradoxically also a central cause of it, Bourdieu's critique of exchange theory acquires its specific areal interest. In that critique

Bourdieu faults deterministic models for their failure to recognize that a cultural scheme "works itself out only in and through time" (1977:6), through the strategies of particular actors as these are temporally motivated, devised, and implemented. Exchange is thus inextricable from practice. Sahlins (this volume) transforms "alliance" into praxis (see also Sahlins 1985:ch.1); and Andrew Strathern's microhistory of a series of Melpa transactions in this volume—together with the film *Ongka's Big Moka*, for which Strathern served as consultant—also illustrate Bourdieu's point ethnographically (see also Biersack, this volume).

The instabilities of highly stratified Polynesian systems are linked to the duality of chieftaincy itself—a theme first enunciated by Hocart (1970) and taken up recently by Sahlins (1985:ch. 3 and this volume) and others (Biersack in press a and b; Friedman 1985; Gunson 1979; Howard 1985, 1986; Marcus 1989b; Valeri 1985a, 1985b, 1989, 1990, in press, and this volume). The fact that the chief–commoner relationship was phrased in terms of foreigner–native suggests that the inside/outside boundary identified a point of openness rather than closure and that some Pacific societies at least were *constitutionally* open to peoples lying beyond their territorial borders. Paiela society exhibits a similar lack of closure for a Melanesian community (Biersack, this volume). Given the existence of long-distance trade and *kula*-like "rings," barter across cultural borders (Thomas in press), and interethnic marriages prior to contact, the possibility that Pacific societies have *always* participated in regional systems, surviving "only by changing in interaction with one another through time" (Gewertz 1983:2), should be considered (Trigger 1984:284–86). To the extent that this proves true, contact and commerce, along with the emergence of regional identities in the postcolonial era (Linnekin 1990b:166–68, Thomas n.d.), may provide special cases of the regionalization of history in the area and even illustrate how existing protocols for transcultural sociality have been creatively deployed under changing circumstances (Thomas in press). In the event, "there is no overriding distinction between causes which are intrinsic to the anthropological object, and those which stem from what are construed as intrusions or irruptions" (Thomas 1989:97); and the way is opened toward developing a dialectical analysis of contact and its aftermath as full-fledged *intersocietal* processes (Jean Comaroff 1985; John Comaroff 1982; Friedman 1985; Valeri, this volume).

In the name of a "free play with concept and methods," Marcus and Fischer recommend an "attention to microprocesses without denying the importance of retaining some vision of larger world-historical trends" (1986:81); and Clifford advocates an analytical style that "migrates between local and global perspectives, constantly recontextualizing its topic" (1988:10). What appears to be required is nuanced accounts of interrhythmic, interstructural, and/or intercultural open-ended processes that take into consideration power asymmetries and their vicissitudes along with the shaping force of local inertias, aspirations, and/or dynamics. Ideally longitudinal, such studies would establish the locally and possibly regionally constituted historical field that missionaries, colonizers, and traders penetrated upon first contact by way of examining how local and global levels of organization conditioned each other over a series of phases (Linnekin, this volume; Thomas 1989:ch. 7). Such longitudinal studies would productively join the work of historical reconstruction with fieldwork (Howard and Borofsky 1989).

Finally, whereas emphasizing the global level has in practice meant privileging issues of political economy while emphasizing the locality has tended instead to inspire symbolic analysis, a burgeoning literature on the culture of colonialism destabilizes these associations, demonstrating the feasibility of synthetic approaches at the global level itself (Dening 1980; Gates, Jr., 1986; Genovese 1974; Gunson 1978; Keesing n.d.; Said 1978a; Smith 1985; Thomas 1990a, 1990b; I thank Nicholas Thomas for this point).

Rethinking the Ethnographic Present

In his introduction to *The Invention of Tradition*, Eric Hobsbawm distinguishes "tradition"—formalized, ritualistic, legitimated through an appeal (often spurious) to the practices of the past, invented as a lever against novel and problematic circumstances—from "custom"—living, genuine, flexible (Hobsbawm 1983:3–4), the anthropologist's culture. The literature on identity formation in the contemporary Pacific preserves this distinction. Here, "tradition"—a "conscious model of past lifeways" (Linnekin 1983:241, 1990b:150) developed in the present and as a political instrument in colonial and postcolonial contexts—is contrasted to "culture," which—because it is not "objectified," "externalized," "reified," or "substantivized" (ibid.; Keesing 1982a, 1989; Thomas n.d.)—is not an ideological resource. The emergence of tradition is thus inextricable from colonial and other contact processes. Constructs such as *fa'a Samoa*, 'the Samoan way', for example, "have been completely revalorized around meanings which are mostly specifically in opposition to 'foreign' values (themselves selectively understood)" (Thomas, this volume, n. 37) and in this are "traditional." "'Customs', 'traditional culture', and related labels do not refer merely to a set of beliefs and practices that happens to have persisted over a long period but to a selective construct defined partly in opposition to foreign ways or intrusions" (ibid.).

Addressing matters of cultural production, the invention-of-tradition literature leaves plenty of scope for fruitful discussion and debate. In a recent statement, Nicholas Thomas challenges a tendency to explain features of "modern," "neotraditional" Pacific communities with respect to their positional values (à la Saussure) and advocates instead that these be referred to colonial and historical processes to avoid misrecognizing the "consequences of colonial penetration as elements of a timeless 'culture'" (Thomas n.d.). Dismissing the Maussian vision of exchange as "total social fact," Thomas interprets customs such as the Fijian *kerekere* as a rhetorical lever in a project of self-reconstruction that is primarily politically motivated (ibid.). For Thomas, the Fijian practice of *kerekere* acquires saliency specifically as a response to colonialism. However, Andrew Strathern envisions *moka* exchanges among the Melpa as traditional. *Moka* persists because, as a "major preoccupation or focal institution," it "does not fade away easily" (this volume; see also Wagner, this volume). Similarly, though Keesing attributes the presence of Manichaean symbolism in the Pacific to the deployment of colonial tropes in the fashioning of counterhegemonic discourse for purposes of political struggle (1989:27), others identify such symbolism as the key to *indigenous* ideology (Biersack, this volume and 1990, for example). The options thus posed—identifying the constituents of the ethnographic present as residuals of a prior configuration or interpreting them as the products of colonial and neocolonial history—threaten to reinstate the structure/history antinomy, if they do not also imply an irreconcilable conflict between historical and anthropological approaches.

Attempts at implementing the distinction between tradition and culture are handicapped by the paucity of sorting criteria offered. This inadequacy reflects a failure to theorize the relationship between cultural precedent and cultural emergence, which would enable historically and theoretically informed discriminations. Some would demur that such a theory is irrelevant. "Twentieth-century identities no longer presuppose continuous cultures or traditions" (Clifford 1988:14); there is a radical break between past and present. But analysis then becomes tautological, for the failure to discover traces of prior configurations in the present follows from the lack of sorting criteria the premise of rupture justifies. As elsewhere in the human and social sciences (see Jameson 1988:ch. 5), this premise, along with the Eurocentric character of the periodization with which it is associated, are bound to be controversial.

Alternate readings of the ethnographic present—product of a response to colonialism and/or self-fashioning in a "neotraditional" order, on the one hand, a self-conscious conservation of the configured elements of the past, on the other—provide further occasion for exploring the friction between political-economy and culturalist perspectives (Ortner 1984). But to the extent that they do, new issues may emerge and new alliances form. Although dialectical models can reconcile political economy and culturalist approaches, easing one source of tension in the current theoretical spectrum, they are themselves at odds with the "deconstructionist" and postmodernist view that present-day conditions of cultural production defy totalization (Kapferer 1988). The future may witness an eventual polarization between those who continue to pursue a "logic of historical and cultural forms" (Jameson 1988:172) and for whom history remains a developmental process unfolding in geocultural space, on the one hand, and, on the other, those who regard historical and cultural reality as dispersed, discontinuous, fragmented, irregular, a matter of depthless "pastiche," and for whom organicism of any kind is suspicious.

Finally, it should be noted that in the name of historicizing anthropological inquiry, the invention-of-tradition literature nevertheless leaves intact the Geertzian view that culture is a system of symbols (Biersack 1989, Keesing 1987). Thus, Keesing distinguishes culture from "tradition" as local knowledge from political symbol (1982a, 1982b, 1989). The kingship literature makes abundantly clear, however, that Pacific symbolism is saturated with political values and that at least some Pacific societies are organized in the first instance as polities—suggesting not only the inadequacy of the dichotomization but the place for political-cum-symbolic analysis in ethnography (Marcus and Fischer 1986; see also Keesing 1989:30).

Consciousness

The historicism of figures such as Wilhelm Dilthey rests upon the philosophical claims that human essence is not fixed but produces itself in time and also that the species necessarily exists in contemplation of its past. These claims are rather different from Sahlins's dictum that structures emerge, persist, and are transformed only in and through time, which stresses inertias no less than mobilities.

Several contributions (most certainly Dening's, soon to be discussed) imply that the stronger historicism has its place in Pacific studies. Among the Paiela of the Papua New Guinea highlands, reproduction —in the ordinary sense of the term, as the transgenerational persistence of groups (Evans-Pritchard 1940)—does not occur. Categories and hierarchies (divine/human, male/female) do persist. But these are best understood as structures *of* practice, structures *of* agency, and as apparatuses deployed with respect to a culture *of* practical reason. Consequently, their intelligibility rests upon a hermeneutics *of* praxis, not system, for they are organizational dimensions of a millenarian project. Attention is thus focused directly on self-production, self-transformation, self-temporalization, and on local consciousness and the future it imagines (Biersack 1990; see also Munn 1986).

Roy Wagner's special theme is the inexhaustibility of human creativity as culture's source. "The creation of human society is still in progress, however remote in time its inception may have been" (Wagner 1972:168). This doctrine is applied specifically to the symbolic realm.

Used, the symbol is "turned" (tropically) from its original meaning ("obviated"); and the original meaning is "fragmented or 'differentiated' into something 'new'" as the range of any one symbol polysemically expands (1978:24). Wagner goes on to develop the relationship between convention and invention in dialectical terms. Novel meaning is "drawn through the meshes of the conventional" (Wagner 1981:52) to "integrate an act into a collectivity" (ibid.:53) and systematize action's deposits. Though Wagner's language is reminiscent of Sahlins's, his writings are closer in spirit to those of Victor Turner, who also insisted that "the social world is a world in becoming, not a world in being" (1974:24), a historicist sentiment he stressed in several posthumously published essays (1985). In his contribution to this volume, Wagner condenses and sharpens the argument of the closing chapters of *Asiwinarong*, illustrating how in ritual a symbolic system can destroy ("consume") itself as a preliminary to its own self-recreation ("production"). Culture is thus located in the time of self-invention and the event-rituals of self-reflection and self-transformation.

Within hermeneutics, an event (Wagner's *kaba*, for example [1986 and this volume]) is construed as an "objectification" of thought (as Dilthey put it), as thought's expression or "outside" (as Collingwood expressed it [1946]), or as a "text" the observer reads over the shoulders of native participants (Geertz's famous metaphor). Greg Dening's *Islands and Beaches* merges these two hermeneutical streams, the one associated with the philosophy of history and the other with anthropological inquiry (see also Turner and Bruner 1986). Targeting for the study of symbolic production Sahlins's own chosen site, cultural margins, *Islands and Beaches* develops a refurbished "ethnohistory" (Dening 1980:35–44)—or, more recently, an "ethnographic history" (1988:99)— focused upon historical moments of intercultural encounter as these disclose the consciousness of the actors party to it. The "island" of the title is a metaphor for the phenomenological world, the culture of a particular people conceived in quasi-Geertzian terms as the "webs of significance" human groups "spin" (Geertz 1973:5) and objectify in "texts" of various kinds, quotidian lifeways. "To know a culture is to know its system of expressed meanings" (Dening 1980:6). "Beach" is the boundary that divides "worlds," the phenomenological horizon Captain Cook, for example, punctured, a point of openness in a world of constraint. Engaged in Geertzian "cultural analysis," Dening combines the remoteness of the historian from his or her other with the remoteness of the anthropologist from his or her other, a feat Geertz also accomplishes in *Negara*.

Merging hermeneutical and structural frameworks by way of integrating structure and action, Sahlins arrives at an interest in the psychic dimensions of history by a different route. If structure is embodied in the event (Bourdieu 1977:ch. 2, Sahlins 1981), practice is at once an individual initiative assumed with respect to ephemeral circumstances *and* an instantiation of structure. Something psychic— but at once conscious *and* unconscious, subjective *and* objective, a set of collective predispositions *and* an individualized ground of circumstance-sensitive action—becomes central. In his contribution to this volume, Sahlins elaborates upon what he has called elsewhere "heroic history" (1985:35–44) by way of developing a notion of the "social-historical individual" and his or her consequential actions. Not all individuals are "social-historical"; only those who—by virtue of their systemic position "personify the clan or the land" (this volume) and thus serve as "a kind of living ancestor" (ibid.)—are. The consequences of the actions of social-historical individuals reverberate throughout the totality and are universalized. Subverting in equal measure the reductions of a "great man" theory of history *and* structuralism in its indifference to action and its protagonists, Sahlins's notion of "heroic history" authorizes a reconstructed psychohistory (this volume), retrieving political history (which the Annales school originally discarded) but as "genealogy rather than chronology" (Friedman 1988:18). History is thus dialectically incarnated in *mentalité* at the top: royal biography (cf. Ricoeur's rereading of *The Mediterranean* [1984:209–17]).

Sahlins's "heroic history" resonates with other efforts to center the dialectic, as a "moving unity of subjectivity and objectivity" (Sartre 1963:97), upon strategically positioned players—whether the intelligentsia, the proletariat, or, as here in this anthropological contribution, Polynesian chiefs—and their experience, consciousness, habitus, or praxis (see, for example, Bourdieu 1977, Jay 1984, Sartre 1963, and Thompson 1978). Sahlins's "heroic history" differs only in the monolithic nature of the historical entity it posits. Conflict is restricted to the topmost echelon rather than being located more pervasively across strata, in class or caste struggle and in structures of domination and subordination. "Heroic history" authorizes elite history as a kind of "total history."

For obvious reasons, consciousness is central to the postmodernist focus upon identity formation and to the related invention-of-tradition literature, with its emphasis on the self-conscious modeling and deployment of the past.

Historical Consciousness, Narrative, and Issues of Representation

In his contribution to this volume, Dening recasts ethnohistory as the study of historical consciousness per se. No longer the past as "consciousness externalized" (Dening 1980:6), history is "a conscious relationship between past and present" (Dening 1988:3), a matter of historical representation. Inscribed or "texted," the traces of some past cross a cultural threshold no less than a temporal one and are constructed (Clifford would say collected) out of the "local knowledge" of some present. "The relics of the past are always cargo to the present. Things that cross cultural boundaries lose the meaning encapsulated in them and are reconstituted in meaning by the cultures that receive them" (this volume; see also A. Strathern, this volume). Local philosophies of history, meters of time, and the manner of their expression (see, for example, Biersack, this volume; Evans-Pritchard 1940:ch.3; Munn 1986; Parmentier 1987), along with the cultural politics of collection (Clifford 1988:pt. 3, Stocking 1985), are relevant to a historical anthropology.

The anthropologist learns of events in part through the narrations of others, and narratives are as culturally particular as anything else (Dening, this volume; see Bohannan 1966 for a delightful illustration of this fact). In the interpretive mode, renarration requires coming to terms with the events *as narrated*; and understanding and explanation become alike windows on historical consciousness. Andrew Strathern's story (this volume) joins pigs, money, women, goddesses, and land in a plot that contributes to narratology and invites further reflection on the relationship between myth and history (see also Wagner, this volume).

Thomas's "Alejandro Mayta in Fiji" reminds us that *how* history is recounted and *what* is recounted, by whom, to whom, and for what purpose, may be political and not merely symbolic. In its partiality historical narrative can be argumentative and contestatory; it may also be quite conservative, a defense of the status quo in response to dissidence (see Biersack in press a; Clifford 1986; Firth 1961; Parmentier 1987:ch. 6; Thomas, this volume). As a result, chronicles and narratives may themselves have a partisan impact upon local dynamics; and ipso facto they may afford insight into the interpenetration of the symbolic and the extrasymbolic at the local level.

Returning to narrative by way of returning to the event, anthropology invigorates and enlarges the terms of the debate concerning representational practices and the truth value of certain fictions (Clifford 1986, Clifford and Marcus 1986, Marcus and Fischer 1986). Any attempt to render the subjectivity of actors blurs the distinction, always shaky at best, between fact and fiction, science and art, not only for the time-worn reason that epistemology is inevitably subjective, but because historical events remain opaque and their protagonists one-dimensional without some unbridling of the historical imagination (see the preface and introduction of Natalie Zemon Davis's *The Return of Martin Guerre*, for example, and compare the book to the film). Telling history's stories always requires some configuring or plotting of the events and a mythification of history (Dening, this volume; Ricoeur 1984; White 1978). Historical narratives are "verbal fictions, the contents of which are as much invented as found and the forms of which have more in common with their counterparts in literature than they have with those in the social sciences" (White 1978:82). Deploying narratives for one reason or another, historical anthropology tests the limits of analytic discourse and offers opportunities for experimenting with filmic and fictional modes (MacDougall 1978, Nichols 1981:ch. 8; see Marcus 1989a for an exploration of filmic strategies for representing the postmodern condition).

For anthropologists, Edward Said's illustration of the dialectic of world-in-the-text and text-in-the-world discussed earlier, *Orientalism*, holds the greatest interest. Like Greenblatt and Chartier, Said contests the claim that "there is nothing outside the text" of any relevance to it (Said 1978b:673), along with its implication that textuality becomes "the exact antithesis and displacement of what might be called history" (Said 1983:3–4), for these isolate the text from "the circumstances, the events, the physical senses that made it possible and render it intelligible as the result of human work" (ibid.:4). Any analysis of texts must affirm the connection between textual representations and "the existential actualities of human life, politics, societies, and events" (ibid.:5). And the other side of the coin: texts also participate in the production of those "existential actualities." They have an "implemented, effective power" (Said 1978b:705). In *Orientalism*, Said attempts to bridge "the gap between the superstructural and the base levels in a textual, historical scholarship" (1978a:13). Integral to colonialism, Orientalist discourse has a "material effectiveness" (Said 1978a:23) as an event among events.

The focus of interest in Orientalism for me has been the partnership between a discursive and archival textuality and worldly power, one as an index and refraction of the other. As a systematic discourse Orientalism is written knowledge, but because it is in the world and directly about the world, it is more than knowledge; it is power since, so far as the Oriental is concerned, Orientalism is the operative and effective knowledge by which he was delivered textually to the West, occupied by the West, milked by the West for his resources, humanly quashed by the West (Said 1976:41).

Though anthropology was exempted from criticism in *Orientalism*, Said later denounced anthropological representations for their complicity with colonialism (1989). Anthropologists have long conceded the point that anthropological texts, in their production and consumption, are not only embedded in wider political and historical realities but themselves impact such realities. "There is no knowledge of the Other which is not also a temporal, historical, a political act" (Fabian 1983:1). Anthropology's participation in more general "orientalizing" processes clamors for a history of anthropology that is also a meta-anthropology (George Stocking, Jr.'s, H.O.A. series at the University of Wisconsin Press, for example, and Borofsky 1987, Clifford 1982, and Thomas

1989:chs. 3–6 for the Pacific in particular), a reflexive critique of the material, political, and discursive foundations of our own textual and filmic practices and strategies (Clifford 1988, Clifford and Marcus 1986, Geertz 1988).

Present proclamations of a "crisis in representation" (Clifford 1988: introduction, ch. 1; Marcus and Fischer 1986:ch.1) are triggered by the publication of works in which the "other" "writes back" (Clifford 1988:ch. 11 and the paperback cover) as an uninvited interlocutor. "The West can no longer present itself as the unique purveyor of anthropological knowledge about others" (ibid.:22); "it has become necessary to imagine a world of generalized ethnography" (ibid.). Historical anthropology is a branch of Western historiography; and anthropology's historiography is in principle no less contestable than its ethnography. In questioning teleological narratives that ground the other in our own "progress" and bury the other there as its victim—obscuring "specific paths through modernity" (ibid.:5)—Clifford impugns the one as much as the other. Such narratives assume a "questionable Eurocentric position at the 'end' of a unified human history, gathering up, memorializing the world's local historicities" (ibid.:14–15). Clifford's "world of generalized ethnography" is thus a world of generalized *historiography* (Dening, this volume) in which the representation of the past no less than of the present becomes open to contestation and issues of authority are historiographically no less than ethnographically posed (see Clifford 1988:ch. 1; Thomas this volume, 1990b). Since in such a general historiography colonial history itself would become subject to the criticism of "subaltern" voices (Guha 1982), the voice of the other would carry an unprecedented *theoretical, critical,* and *moral* authority that would promote the decolonization of anthropology by indigenizing and internationalizing its theory.

Ethnology and Archaeology

If cultural anthropology is rethinking its earlier rejection of historical inquiry, archaeology—which, to a certain extent, has developed in tandem with it—is as well. In America in the sixties and seventies, the "New Archaeology" or "Processual Archaeology" marked the culmination of decades of antihistorical sentiment. Archaeology would be *anthropological*—nomothetic, a science in pursuit of general law—and *not* historical—idiographic, descriptive, nontheoretic (Trigger 1978, 1984). Events and the real time in which they unfolded were presumed to be largely irrelevant to the taxonomic project of classifying known societies according to their level of evolutionary achievement and to the synchronic project of modeling evolutionary stages. An empirical variation in space was thus converted into a speculative one in time (Fabian 1983). (In cultural anthropology the same logic motivated Sahlins's and Service's distinction between "general evolution" and "specific evolution" [1960], along with Radcliffe-Brown's [among others'] rejection of history in the name of developing a science of cultures.) Without historical investigation, however, there could be no empirically grounded theory of the transition between levels of "sociocultural integration"—a deficiency that continues to plague evolutionary theory.

From the midseventies on, partly in response to the critique of positivism associated with "interpretive" approaches, archaeology has been nudged in a variety of "postprocessual" and "radical critical" directions —structuralist, poststructuralist, symbolic, contextualist, and Marxist (see Earle and Preucel 1987 and Hodder 1986 for overviews); and it has been urged to reinstate history. Bruce Trigger, for one, envisions archaeology's empirical contribution as being specifically historical (or "prehistorical"), "providing detailed information about the actual course of socio-cultural development" (1978:36; see also Hodder 1987).

Patrick Kirch's and Roger Green's recent article "History, Phylogeny, and Evolution in Polynesia" provides the most substantial contribution to the reconstruction of archaeology along historical-cum-anthropological (and historical-cum-evolutionary) lines for the Pacific. Developing a method for purifying the archaeological record of non-"phylogenetic" elements, Kirch and Green strive to establish "a historical sequence which can be precisely defined in both time and space" (1987:433) so that evolutionary theory might have the empirical resources to model transformations. It is worthwhile noting that Kirch's and Green's program parallels Sahlins's in identifying historical knowledge as the prerequisite for theory-building and comparison (see in particular Sahlins 1985:72). Archaeologists have already acknowledged the utility of Sahlins's model, along with those of Giddens and Bourdieu, in developing evolutionary theory (Hodder 1986:85).

Judging by the responses to this *Current Anthropology* article, the effort to produce a historical archaeology (Hodder's term is "ethnoarchaeology" [1986:117 and 1987]) will prove as theoretically and methodologically challenging and as fraught with contention as the parallel effort in cultural anthropology has proved. But to good effect. It has become common (if not commonplace) for ethnographers, who increasingly place the ethnographic present in longitudinal perspective, to acknowledge the relevance of archaeological data for their own analytical projects (for example, Thomas 1989:122 and Weiner 1988). The more historical cultural anthropology and archaeology become, the "less sectarian within the broader context of anthropology" (Trigger 1984:275) each will be. Linguistics, too, seems to be rethinking its synchronic investments as its weight shifts toward the historical pole. In varying degrees, the issues of history and theory rehearsed herein bear on other branches of anthropology and serve as core issues around which the subfields of anthropology may coalesce and enter into collaboration.

Attempts at synthesis bring together those who, whether from habit or by inclination, approach empirical tasks from different angles. The battle line no longer drawn, debate becomes less acrimonious and more productive (ibid.). Positioned among historical and cultural studies and at a powerful confluence of subdisciplines within anthropology, historical anthropology provides a forum within which to perpetuate the debates of the last two decades but on new and less parochial terrain. To historical anthropology is thus transferred the theoretical commissions of the discipline: past, present, and future.

References Cited

Appadurai, Arjun, ed.
1984   *The Social Life of Things.* Cambridge: Cambridge University Press.

Biersack, Aletta
1989   Local Knowledge, Local History: Geertz and Beyond. In *The New Cultural History,* ed. Lynn Hunt. Berkeley and Los Angeles: University of California Press.
1990   Histories in the Making: Paiela and Historical Anthropology. *History and Anthropology* 5.
In press a   Under the *Toa* Tree: The Genealogy of the Tongan Chiefs. In *Culture and History in the Pacific,* ed. Jukka Siikala. Transactions of the Finnish Anthropological Society. Helsinki: The Society.
In press b   Kava'onau and the Tongan Chiefs. *Journal of the Polynesian Society.*

Bohannan, Laura
1966   Shakespeare in the Bush. *Natural History* 75:28–33.

Borofsky, Robert
1987   *Making History: Pukapukan and Anthropological Constructions of Knowledge.* Cambridge: Cambridge University Press.

Bott, Elizabeth, with the assistance of Tavi
1982   *Tongan Society at the Time of Captain Cook's Visits: Discussions with Her Majesty Queen Sālote Tupou.* Memoir no. 44. Wellington: The Polynesian Society.

Bourdieu, Pierre
1977   *Outline of a Theory of Practice.* Cambridge: Cambridge University Press.
1984   *Distinction: A Social Critique of the Judgement of Taste.* Tr. Richard Nice. Cambridge, Mass.: Harvard University Press.

Braudel, Fernand
1972–73[1949]
        The Mediterranean and the Mediterranean World of the Age of Philip II. 2d rev. ed. 2 vols. Tr. Sian Reynolds. 1st ed. 1949. London: Collins.
1980   *On History.* Tr. S. Matthews. Chicago: University of Chicago Press.

Carmack, Robert M.
1972   Ethnohistory: A Review of Its Development, Definitions,

Methods, and Aims. In *Annual Review of Anthropology*, ed. B. J. Siegal et al. Palo Alto: Annual Reviews, Inc.

Chartier, Roger
1988 Introduction. In *Cultural History: Between Practices and Representations*. Tr. Lydia G. Cochrane. Cambridge: Polity Press.

Clifford, James
1982 *Person and Myth: Maurice Leenhardt in the Melanesian World*. Berkeley and Los Angeles: University of California Press.
1986 Introduction: Partial Truths. In *Writing Culture: The Poetics and Politics of Ethnography*, ed. James Clifford and George E. Marcus. Berkeley and Los Angeles: University of California Press.
1988 *The Predicament of Culture: Twentieth-Century Ethnography, Literature, and Art*. Cambridge, Mass.: Harvard University Press.

Clifford, James, and George E. Marcus, eds.
1986 *Writing Culture: The Poetics and Politics of Ethnography*. Berkeley and Los Angeles: University of California Press.

Collingwood, R. G.
1946 *The Idea of History*. Oxford: Clarendon Press.

Comaroff, Jean
1985 *Body of Power, Spirit of Resistance: The Culture and History of a South African People*. Chicago: University of Chicago Press.

Comaroff, John
1982 Dialectical Systems, History, and Anthropology: Units of Study and Questions of Theory. *Journal of Southern African Studies* 8:143–72.

Darnton, Robert
1984 *The Great Cat Massacre and Other Episodes in French Cultural History*. New York: Basic Books.

Davidson, J. W.
1966 Problems of Pacific History. *Journal of Pacific History* 1:5–21.

Davis, Natalie Zemon
1983 *The Return of Martin Guerre*. Cambridge, Mass.: Harvard University Press.

Dening, Greg
1980 *Islands and Beaches: Discourse on a Silent Land, Marquesas 1774–1880*. Honolulu: University Press of Hawaii.
1988 *History's Anthropology: The Death of William Gooch*. A.S.A.O. Special Publication no. 2. Lanham, Md.: University Press of America.

Dirks, Nicholas B.
　1987　　　*The Hollow Crown: Ethnohistory of an Indian Kingdom*. Cambridge: Cambridge University Press.
　1988　　　Does Social Theory Need History? The Case of the Culture Concept. Paper given at the Social Science History Association meetings, Chicago, 4 November 1988.
Earle, Timothy K., and Robert W. Preucel
　1987　　　Processual Archaeology and the Radical Critique. *Current Anthropology* 28:501–38.
Evans-Pritchard, E. E.
　1940　　　*The Nuer*. Oxford: Oxford University Press.
　1950　　　Social Anthropology: Past and Present. *Man* 50:118–24.
Fabian, Johannes
　1983　　　*Time and the Other: How Anthropology Makes Its Object*. New York: Columbia University Press.
Felperin, Howard
　1985　　　*Beyond Deconstruction: The Uses and Abuses of Literary Theory*. Oxford: Clarendon Press.
Firth, Raymond
　1961　　　*History and Traditions of Tikopia*. Wellington: The Polynesian Society.
Friedman, Jonathan
　1985　　　Captain Cook, Culture and World System. *Journal of Pacific History* 20:191–201.
　1988　　　No History Is an Island: An Exchange between Jonathan Friedman and Marshall Sahlins. *Critique of Anthropology* 8 (no. 3):7–39.
Gates, Henry Louis, Jr., ed.
　1986　　　*"Race," Writing, and Difference*. Chicago: University of Chicago Press.
Geertz, Clifford
　1973　　　*The Interpretation of Cultures*. New York: Basic Books.
　1980　　　*Negara: The Theatre State in Nineteenth-Century Bali*. Princeton: Princeton University Press.
　1983　　　*Local Knowledge*. New York: Basic Books.
　1988　　　*Works and Lives: The Anthropologist as Author*. Stanford: Stanford University Press.
Genovese, Eugene D.
　1974　　　*Roll, Jordan, Roll: The World the Slaves Made*. New York: Random House (Pantheon Books).

Gewertz, Deborah
1983   *Sepik River Societies: A Historical Ethnography of the Chambri
            and Their Neighbors.* New Haven: Yale University Press.
Giddens, Anthony
1979   Central Problems in Social Theory: Action, Structure, and
            Contradiction in Social Analysis. Berkeley and Los Angeles:
            University of California Press.
Ginzburg, Carlo
1980   *The Cheese and the Worms: The Cosmos of a Sixteenth-Century
            Miller.* Tr. J. and A. Tedeschi. Baltimore: Johns Hopkins
            University Press.
Godelier, Maurice
1986   *The Making of Great Men: Male Domination and Power among
            the New Guinea Baruya.* Tr. R. Swyer. Cambridge: Cam-
            bridge University Press.
Godelier, Maurice, and Marilyn Strathern, eds.
In press   *Big Men and Great Men: The Development of a Comparison in
            Melanesia.* Cambridge: Cambridge University Press.
Greenblatt, Stephen
1987   Introduction. In *Representing the English Renaissance*, ed. S.
            Greenblatt. Berkeley and Los Angeles: University of Califor-
            nia Press.
Guha, Ranajit
1982   Historiography of Colonial India. In *Subaltern Studies I:
            Writings on South Asian History and Society.* Delhi: Oxford
            University Press.
Gunson, Niel
1978   *Messengers of Grace: Evangelical Missionaries in the South Seas,
            1797–1869.* Melbourne: Oxford University Press.
1979   The *Hau* Concept of Leadership in Western Polynesia. *Jour-
            nal of Pacific History* 14:28–49.
Hau'ofa, Epeli
1987   The New South Pacific Society: Integration and Indepen-
            dence. In *Class and Culture in the South Pacific*, ed. A. Hooper
            et al. Auckland: Centre for Pacific Studies /Institute for Pa-
            cific Studies.
Herdt, Gilbert, ed.
1982   *Rituals of Manhood.* Berkeley and Los Angeles: University of
            California Press.

Hexter, J. H.

1979   Braudel and The Monde Braudellien. In *On Historians*. Cambridge, Mass.: Harvard University Press.

Hobsbawm, Eric

1983   Introduction. In *The Invention of Tradition*, ed. E. Hobsbawm and T. Ranger. Cambridge: Cambridge University Press.

Hocart, A. M.

1970   *Kings and Councillors: An Essay in the Comparative Anatomy of Human Society*. Ed. Rodney Needham. Chicago: University of Chicago Press.

Hodder, Ian

1986   *Reading the Past: Current Approaches in Interpretation in Archaeology*. Cambridge: Cambridge University Press.

1987   Preface. In *Archaeology as Long-Term History*, ed. I. Hodder. Cambridge: Cambridge University Press.

Howard, Alan

1985   History, Myth and Polynesian Chieftainship: The Case of Rotuman Kings. In *Transformations of Polynesian Culture*, ed. A. Hooper and J. Huntsman. Memoir no. 45. Auckland: The Polynesian Society.

1986   Cannibal Chiefs and Rebellion in Rotuman Myth. *Pacific Studies* 10:1–27.

Howard, Alan, and Robert Borofsky

1989   Introduction. In *Developments in Polynesian Ethnology*, ed. A. Howard and R. Borofsky. Honolulu: University of Hawaii Press.

Howe, Kerry

1979   Pacific History in the 1980s: New Directions or Monograph Myopia? *Pacific Studies* 3:81–90.

Hunt, Lynn

1986   French History in the Last Twenty Years: The Rise and Fall of the *Annales* Paradigm. *Journal of Contemporary History* 21:209–24.

1989   Introduction: History, Text, and Culture. In *The New Cultural History*, ed. L. Hunt. Berkeley and Los Angeles: University of California Press.

Jameson, Fredric

1988   *The Ideologies of Theory: Essays, 1971–1986*, vol. 2. Minneapolis: University of Minnesota Press.

Jay, Martin

1984   *Marxism and Totality: The Adventures of a Concept from Lukacs to Habermas.* Berkeley and Los Angeles: University of California Press.

Kapferer, Bruce
1988   The Anthropologist as Hero: Three Exponents of Post-
         Modernist Anthropology. *Critique of Anthropology* 8:77–104.

Karp, Ivan
1986   Agency and Social Theory: A Review of Anthony Giddens.
         American Ethnologist 13:131–37.

Keesing, Roger
1982a   Kastom in Melanesia: An Overview. In, Reinventing Tradi-
         tional Culture: The Politics of Kastom in Island Melanesia,
         ed. R. M. Keesing and R. Tonkinson. *Mankind* 13:297–305.

1982b   Kastom and Anticolonialism in Malaita: 'Culture' as Politi-
         cal Symbol. *Mankind* 13:357–73.

1987   Anthropology as Interpretive Quest. *Current Anthropology*
         28:161–76.

1989   Creating the Past: Custom and Identity in the Contempo-
         rary Pacific. *Contemporary Pacific* 1:19–42.

n.d.   Colonial Discourse and Codes of Discrimination in the Pa-
         cific. Unpublished manuscript.

Kirch, Patrick V., and Roger C. Green
1987   History, Phylogeny, and Evolution in Polynesia. *Current An-
         thropology* 28:431–56.

LaCapra, Dominick
1985   *History and Criticism.* Ithaca: Cornell University Press.

Le Roy Ladurie, Emmanuel
1979   *Montaillou: The Promised Land of Error.* Tr. Barbara Bray.
         New York: Vintage Books.

Leach, Edmund
1954   *Political Systems of Highland Burma.* Boston: Beacon Press.

Linnekin, Jocelyn
1983   Defining Tradition: Variations on the Hawaiian Identity.
         American Ethnologist 10:241–52.

1990a   *Sacred Queens and Women of Consequence: Rank, Gender, and
         Colonialism in the Hawaiian Islands.* Ann Arbor: University of
         Michigan Press.

1990b   The Politics of Culture in the Pacific. In *Cultural Identity and
         Ethnicity in the Pacific,* ed. J. Linnekin and L. Poyer. Hono-
         lulu: University of Hawaii Press.

MacDougall, David
1978   Ethnographic Film: Failure and Promise. *Annual Review of
         Anthropology* 7:405–25.

Marcus, George E.

1989a   The Modernist Sensibility in Recent Ethnographic Writing and the Cinematic Metaphor of Montage. Paper given at the conference "Coming to Terms with the Photographic Image," Humanities Research Centre, Australian National University, 6 July 1989.

1989b   Chieftaincy. In *Developments in Polynesian Ethnology*, ed. A. Howard and R. Borofsky. Honolulu: University of Hawaii Press.

In press   Requirements for Ethnographies of Late Twentieth Century Modernity Worldwide. In *Modernity and Identity*, ed. Jonathan Friedman and Scott Lash. London: Hutchinson.

Marcus, George E., and Michael M. J. Fischer

1986   *Anthropology as Cultural Critique: An Experimental Moment in the Human Sciences*. Chicago: University of Chicago Press.

Munn, Nancy

1986   *The Fame of Gawa: A Symbolic Study of Value Transformation in a Massim (Papua New Guinea) Society*. Cambridge: Cambridge University Press.

Nichols, Bill

1981   *Ideology and the Image: Social Representation in the Cinema and Other Media*. Bloomington: Indiana University Press.

Ortner, Sherry B.

1984   Theory in Anthropology since the Sixties. *Comparative Studies in Society and History* 26:126–66.

Parmentier, Richard J.

1987   *The Sacred Remains: Myth, History, and Polity in Belau*. Chicago: University of Chicago Press.

Petersen, Glenn

1982   *One Man Cannot Rule a Thousand: Fission in a Ponapean Chiefdom*. Ann Arbor: University of Michigan Press.

Ragin, Charles, and Daniel Chirot

1984   The World System of Immanuel Wallerstein: Sociology and Politics as History. In *Vision and Method in Historical Sociology*, ed. Theda Skocpol. New York: Cambridge University Press.

Ricoeur, Paul

1974   *Conflict of Interpretations*. Evanston: Northwestern University Press.

1984   *Time and Narrative*, vol. 1. Chicago: University of Chicago Press.

Roseberry, William
    1988   Political Economy. *Annual Review of Anthropology* 7:161–85.
Sahlins, Marshall
    1981   *Historical Metaphors and Mythical Realities: Structure in the Early History of the Sandwich Islands Kingdom.* A.S.A.O. Special Publication no. 1. Ann Arbor: University of Michigan Press.
    1985   *Islands of History.* Chicago: University of Chicago Press.
    1989a   Captain Cook at Hawaii. *Journal of the Polynesian Society* 98:371–423.
    1989b   Cosmologies of Capitalism: The Trans-Pacific Sector of the World-System. Radcliffe-Brown Lecture in Social Anthropology for 1988. *Proceedings of the British Academy for 1988.* London: Oxford University Press.
Sahlins, Marshall, and Elman Service, eds.
    1960   *The Evolution of Culture.* Ann Arbor: University of Michigan Press.
Said, Edward
    1976   Interview. *Diacritics* 6:30–47.
    1978a   *Orientalism.* New York: Random House (Vintage Books).
    1978b   The Problem of Textuality: Two Exemplary Positions. *Critical Inquiry* 4:673–714.
    1983   *The World, the Text, and the Critic.* Cambridge: Harvard University Press.
    1989   Representing the Colonized: Anthropology's Interlocutors. *Critical Inquiry* 15:205–25.
Sartre, Jean Paul
    1963   *Search for a Method.* Tr. H. Barnes. New York: Alfred A. Knopf.
Smith, Bernard
    1985   *European Vision and the South Pacific.* 2d ed. New Haven: Yale University Press.
Stocking, George, Jr., ed.
    1985   Objects and Others: Essays on Museums and Material Culture. *History of Anthropology,* vol. 3. Madison: University of Wisconsin Press.
Stone, Lawrence
    1981   The Revival of Narrative: Reflections on a New Old History. In *The Past and the Present.* Boston: Routledge and Kegan Paul.
Strathern, Andrew
    1982a   *Inequality in New Guinea Highland Societies.* Ed. A. Strathern. Cambridge: Cambridge University Press.

1982b   Tribesman or Peasants? In *Inequality in New Guinea Highland Societies*, ed. A. Strathern. Cambridge: Cambridge University Press.

Strathern, Marilyn
1988   *The Gender of the Gift.* Berkeley and Los Angeles: University of California Press.

In press
Or, Rather, on Not Collecting Clifford. *Social Analysis.*

Thomas, Nicholas
1989   *Out of Time: History and Evolution in Anthropological Discourse.* Cambridge: Cambridge University Press.

1990a   Sanitation and Seeing: The Creation of State Power in Early Colonial Fiji. *Comparative Studies in Society and History* 32:149–70.

1990b   Partial Texts: Representation, Colonialism, and Agency in Pacific History. *Journal of Pacific History* 25.

n.d.   Substantivization and Anthropological Discourse: The Transformation of Practices into Institutions in Neotraditional Pacific Societies. In *History and Tradition in Melanesian Anthropology*, ed. J. Carrier.

In press   Politicized Values: The Cultural Dynamics of Peripheral Exchanges. In *Barter, Exchange and Value*, ed. C. Humphrey and S. Hugh-Jones. Cambridge: Cambridge University Press.

Thompson, E. P.
1978   *The Poverty of Theory, & Other Essays.* London: Merlin Press.

Trigger, Bruce G.
1978   *Time and Traditions: Essays in Archaeological Interpretation.* Edinburgh: Edinburgh University Press.

1984   Archaeology at the Crossroads: What's New? *Annual Review of Anthropology* 13:275–300.

Turner, Victor
1974   *Dramas, Fields, and Metaphors: Symbolic Action in Human Society.* Ithaca: Cornell University Press.

1985   *On the Edge of the Bush.* Ed. E. Turner. Tucson: University of Arizona Press.

Turner, Victor W., and Edward M. Bruner, eds.
1986   *The Anthropology of Experience.* Urbana: University of Illinois Press.

Valeri, Valerio
1985a   The Conqueror Becomes King: A Political Analysis of the Hawaiian Legend of 'Umi. In *Transformations of Polynesian*

Culture, ed. A. Hooper and J. Huntsman. Memoir no. 45.
Auckland: The Polynesian Society.

1985b   *Kingship and Sacrifice: Ritual and Society in Ancient Hawaii.*
Tr. Paula Wissing. Chicago: University of Chicago Press.

1989   Death in Heaven: Myths and Rites of Kinship in Tongan
Kingship. *History and Anthropology* 4:209–47.

1990   Constitutive History: Genealogy and Narrative in the Legitimation of Hawaiian Kingship. In *Culture through Time*, ed.
Emiko Ohnuki-Tierney. Stanford: Stanford University Press.

In press   Diarchy and History in Hawaii and Tonga. In *Culture and
History in the Pacific*, ed. Jukka Siikala. Transactions of the
Finnish Anthropological Society. Helsinki: The Society.

Wagner, Roy

1972   *Habu: The Innovation of Meaning in Daribi Religion.* Chicago:
University of Chicago Press.

1978   *Lethal Speech: Daribi Myth as Symbolic Obviation.* Ithaca: Cornell University Press.

1981   *The Invention of Culture.* 2d ed. Chicago: University of Chicago Press.

1986   *Asiwinarong: Ethos, Image, and Social Power among the Usen
Barok of New Ireland.* Princeton: Princeton University Press.

Weiner, James, ed.

1988   *The Mountain Papuans: Historical and Comparative Perspectives
from New Guinea Fringe Highlands Societies.* Ann Arbor:
University of Michigan Press.

White, Hayden V.

1978   *Tropics of Discourse: Essays in Cultural Criticism.* Baltimore:
Johns Hopkins University Press.

Whitehead, Harriet

1987   Fertility and Exchange in New Guinea. In *Gender and Kinship: Essays toward a Unified Analysis*, ed. J. F. Collier and S.
Yanagisako. Stanford: Stanford University Press.

Wolf, Eric

1982   *Europe and the People without History.* Berkeley and Los Angeles: University of California Press.

Films

The Kawelka: Ongka's Big Moka (55 minutes, 16 mm, color). Great Britain:
Granada Television.

The Return of Martin Guerre (111 minutes, 35 mm, color). A film by

Daniel Vigne; screenplay by Jean-Claude Carriere and Daniel Vigne. Société français de production cinematographique.

Trobriand Cricket: An Indigenous Response to Colonialism (53 minutes, 16 mm, color). Jerry W. Leach, director; Gary Kildea, filmmaker. Papua New Guinea: Office of Information.

2. The Return of the Event, Again;

With Reflections on the Beginnings of the Great Fijian War of 1843 to 1855 between the Kingdoms of Bau and Rewa

Marshall Sahlins

T he general aim of this paper is to say something not too banal about the nature of historical events and their relations to cultural orders. It is difficult not to be banal because one can hardly do more than say explicitly what good historians have been doing for a long time. There are two things, however, that make the attempt seem worthwhile. One is the history I deal with, the early modern history of the Fiji Islands. Culturally exotic from the perspective of most academic history, Fiji may nevertheless be a revelatory case, if the unusual structural features then make it easier for us to see their play in the course of events. (At the same time, to keep certain issues comparable, the events I focus on fall into a classic historiographic category: the contingent incidents that set off a great war.) The second reason why this effort at an anthropological history is perhaps worthwhile is the lingering presence, in the disciplines of anthropology and history both, of an exaggerated opposition between "structure" and "event." This antithesis has had too long a run. Probably it is already vestigial in scholarly practice, although in abstract talk it still seems to be the current word. And there is still a problem with practice.

The problem with practice, at least in classic narrative history, is that it rarely gives an account of itself. As one philosopher complains, "no historian spends sleepless nights over the question, 'What is an historical event?'" (Gruner 1969:141).[1] Apart from the metaphysical elusiveness of historical "causality," this reticence may be because explanation is built into the form itself, the narrative being "one thing because of another" (cf. Ricoeur 1984). Ruth Benedict says somewhere that if deep-sea fish could speak the last thing they would name is water. On the other hand, historians who do not live in the narrative element, notably those who move with the Annales school, must have spent a lot of waking hours puzzling over events in order to invent all those ways of putting them down. I refer of course to those who have followed Lucien Febvre and Fernand Braudel in devaluing "evenemential history"—to domestic the phrase, *enfin*.[2]

The terms of this dismissal of the event make it irreconcilable with "structure" and therefore with a supposedly better history that deals with the latter or at least with "series," phenomena comparable and quantifiable over time (cf. Furet 1982). Braudel's metaphorical turns are well known. Events are merely surface disturbances, foam on the great tides of history. They shine like fireflies whose feeble glow still leaves the surrounding world in darkness; or else like flames that can scarcely be perceived but whose "delusive smoke" fills the minds of the onlookers (Braudel 1980:3, 10–11, 27, etc.).[3] The language is almost equalled in the early structural-anthropological wound literature, with its descriptions of the logical disfigurements inflicted by history on archaic systems of classification. The big difference is that in the anthropological versions the contingent events were the flood tides of history, leaving the disassembled jetsam of once-coherent cultural schemes floating in time's wake (Lévi-Strauss:1966; 1963:101f.). But this was only an inversion of the same structure. More important, for a certain anthropology, as for a certain history, it seemed that "event" and "structure" could not occupy the same epistemological space. The event was conceived as antistructural, the structure as nullifying the event.

The antithesis could not last; it is giving way to synthesis. The exile of the event was only temporary, partly because (in good Hegelian fashion) it was taking refuge all the time in its opposite. Unless it is totally immobile, a history of the long run has rather the form of a narrative history—in slow motion. "Can the historian detest the event," Ricoeur asks in making this point, "without detesting himself?" (1980:11). Then in France came "The Events"—of 1968. Within a few years two important articles appeared under the same title of "The Return of the Event," one by a historian (Nora 1974), one by a sociologist (Morin 1972a).[4] It was not simply a return to the event. It was a call for the synthesis of event and system. Said Morin: *"Système et événement ne devraient-ils pas enfin être conçus de façon couplée?"* (1972a:19).[5]

I would like to associate this essay with the project of synthesis. First by briefly rehearsing the received antithesis of "structure" and "event," to see where the problems lie.

Structure and Event

Reviewing some sympathetic reviews of *The Mediterranean*, Hexter remarks on the sense they all convey of Braudel's inability to achieve a satisfactory liaison between the structural levels— structures of the long run, as imposed geographically, or conjunctural phenomena such as economic cycles—between these and the more conventional political history of the third part (Hexter 1979:134f.). The book "does not solve the historiographical problem that it poses: how to deal with the perennial historiographic difficulty of linking the durable phenomena of history with those that involve rapid change" (ibid.:137). Perhaps because the book also recreates the problem. Once *structure* and *event* are defined in mutually exclusive ways, the one cannot be made intelligible in the terms of the other; all King Philip's men will not be able to put them together again. How shall we reconcile structures that are logical and durable with events that are emotional and ephemeral? The first somehow belong in the order of the real and the efficacious, whereas the apparent potency of events is only illusory. "To the smoke of events," Ricoeur comments, "is opposed the rock of endurance" (1984:105). Indeed the table of oppositions that could be constructed from Annales texts would be worthy almost of the cosmological dualisms of certain Amazonian peoples. Structure is to event as the social to the individual, the essential to the accidental, the recurrent to the idiosyncratic, the invisible to the visible, the lawful to the aleatory, the quotidian to the extraordinary, the silent to the audible, the anonymous to the authored, the normal to the traumatic, the comparable to the unique, and so on (Braudel 1972:4, 21; 1980:passim; LeGoff 1988; Nora 1974; Furet 1982; cf. Ricoeur 1980, 1984; Stone 1981).

Sometimes the ontological oppositions are backed up by ideological contradictions. Contradictions arise out of the scrambling for the moral high ground in politics and attitudes toward "positivism."[6] Evenemential history is condemned as "merely political." Concerned singularly with the doings of the elite, as if they were the sole movers and shakers, this kind of history carries within itself a hierarchical idea of society—with its cult of power, its idealization of the state, and its implication of a future, as of a past, incarnated by the directors. Whereas the structural histories, in privileging mass, general and institutional phenomena, can pretend to be populist, at least by comparison (Burguière 1988). This is to say that evenemential history is "merely political," but structural history is truly political. Ironic that in an age where nothing can escape being "political," where everything that is said has a value in terms of "power," which is supposed to be its "meaning," as witness this very criticism of evenemential history, it is ironic then that it should be criticized as "merely political." The paradoxes are matched by the suspicions Annales history may reserve for the experiences of the people. Taken too seriously, their lives and hopes could imperil a historical understanding, just as much as the narrow ideas of Philip II himself:

We must learn to distrust this history with its still burning passions, as it was felt, described and lived by contemporaries whose lives were as short and as short-sighted as ours. It has the dimensions of their anger, dreams, or illusions. In the sixteenth century, after the true Renaissance, came the Renaissance of the poor, the humble, eager to write, to talk of themselves and of others. This precious mass of paper distorts, filling up the lost hours and assuming a false importance (Braudel 1972:21).[7]

Moral high-grounding in methodology consists of adopting the stance toward natural science explanations currently fashionable in the human sciences. Here it seems that some new historians have been caught by the changing of the avant-garde. They would now stick evenemential history with the unpopular pretensions of "scientism"—by a certain slide in the older criticism of its "positivism" (Burguière 1988:139–40; cf. Ricoeur 1980:9).[8] Originally, however, the structuralist position claimed to be the scientific one, in invidious contrast to mere chronicles of haphazard events. Most of the familiar antinomies of structure and event go back to turn-of-the-century social science. They are to be found in François Simiand's (1903) article "Methode historique et science sociale," often invoked as a theoretical charter by Annales historians. But Simiand denounced the event in the name of a generalizing social science, which an obsession with the unique and the individual would render impossible. Today the same concern for the event, taken as a form of atomistic empiricism —the event is to history as the atom to physics or the cell to biology —this concern makes evenemential history the bastion of an old-fashioned science. *Autres temps, autres moeurs.*

On the other hand, as taken up in the Durkheim group of which Simiand was a member, his arguments about the unintelligibility of the contingent enjoyed a long success in structural anthropologies. Notably in Radcliffe-Brown's "natural science of society," a project for developing comparative and lawful statements about social relations, which seemed to require that one ignore the historical accidents of their expression.[9] The important comparative point was not that some donned their hats and some doffed their hats in a house of god, but that either way one showed respect. Considered as the account merely of the accidents, historical knowledge was as unessential in principle as it was, for nonliterate peoples, unattainable in practice. Or again, by another line of development, Durkheimian ideas were crossed with Saussurean to produce the radical opposition of structure and history we have noted in the early French structural anthropology. As an analysis of pure values in which the significance of any sign depended solely on its differential relations to coexisting signs, the linguistics of Saussure had made simultaneity a condition of its scientific possibility (Saussure 1966 [1915]; cf. Sahlins 1981:3–6). Language (*la langue*) could be a systematic object if and only if its concepts were synchronically determined. From this vantage, history appears as an imposition from outside in the form of contingent and dislocating events, a sense of discontinuity amplified by Saussure's treatment of diachrony as the intersection of phonetic change and syntactic relations. Transposed then into continental anthropology, "structure" and "history" became contending forces on the field of society, locked in a "constant struggle," a "repeated battle," between order and disorder. Here is structure always valiantly but never altogether successfully trying to repair the damages to its ancient harmonies inflicted by untoward events (cf. Lévi-Strauss 1966:155, 157, 232, etc.).[10]

Paradoxically, however, from the same structuralisms that would make "system" and "event" into contraries, that have the one precluding the other, from these structuralisms it follows that there is no event without system. For the definition of a "something-happened" as an event, as well as its specific historic consequences, must depend on the structure in place. All it takes to see this is a little goodwill. If as Saussure says there is no "inner bond" between the nature of a phonetic change and the effect it may have on the system (1966: 87), it follows that the evenemential character of the change, as opposed simply to its phonetic properties, is the work of the system. The same kind of thing is implied by Lévi-Strauss's dictum that

there is always a mediator between *praxis* and practices, namely the conceptual scheme by the operation of which matter and form, neither with any independent existence, are realized as structures, that is as entities which are both empirical and intelligible (1966:130).

It does not seem to stretch this idea too far to make it out as a description of the constitution of historical events by cultural structures. For it speaks to the transformation of sui generis happenings, having their own properties and reasons, to the order of culture in which these properties acquire a determinate mode of existence. And the implication of the one and the other, Saussure and Lévi-Strauss, is that events become such by the meaningful integration of material circumstances:

> The event is at once produced and received by the community in which it happens and to understand its existence and modalities it is necessary to know the cognitive and symbolic system of this community. . . . It is not a question of some extreme relativism, according to which events would be purely ideal or symbolic, but rather of seriously taking the symbolic into account: one cannot separate something in the event that would be "what really, materially happened" from something else that would be the meaning the actors and spectators attributed to it; the two are indissociable (Molino 1986:264).

No event without system. Consider the radical case of exogenous events, phenomena that erupt in a given society from nature or another society, such as an earthquake or Captain Cook sailing into some Hawaiian bay. What kind of event this may be, what historic significance it has, cannot be predicated simply from the "objective properties" of the happening. The specific historical effects turn on the way those properties are taken up in the culture in question, a way that is never the only one possible. I am rehearsing here some ideas more fully expressed elsewhere, with the aim of developing further an anthropological concept of the historical event (Sahlins 1981, 1985, 1988). For that matter, I am merely putting into another context Evans-Pritchard's reflections on why the Azande, who know very well that it is a natural disposition of elephants to trample people's gardens, nevertheless when it happens will hold some neighbor or affine responsible and accuse him of witchcraft (Evans-Pritchard 1937). Evans-Pritchard said the response was intelligible, one placed the blame on a personal enemy, for although it might be a property of elephants to trample gardens, it is not a property of elephants to trample *your* garden. To which one might add, neither is it a property of elephants to trample *property*. Once introduced into the human domain, given a definite cultural value, the natural phenomenon will assume some particular effect, as orchestrated by the relations of the particular cultural scheme. The natural properties of the phenomenon are clearly necessary conditions for the effect, but they do not account for its historical form. There is no adequate relation between an elephant trampling a garden and an accusation of witchcraft: the latter does not follow logically from the former—except by way of Azande culture.

In the same way, the Thessalians held that Poseidon made the gorge through which the Peneus River runs; and so would anyone, Herodotus says, who believed Poseidon was responsible for earthquakes (*Hist.* 7.129). The famous Lisbon earthquake of 1757 had a different theological significance. But if these Iberian tremors shook the *philosophes'* panglossian confidence in Divine Providence, is this because they differed from the shocks of Poseidon by their intensity on the Richter scale? Of course the cultural effects of earthquakes are not confined to mental perturbations. The scale of the social catastrophe likewise varies according to the structures in place, as was literally true of Mexico City in 1985:

While many buildings, both large and small, performed well during the earthquake, 5,728 buildings in the city were damaged. . . . The report noted that a high percentage of damage occurred in buildings 6 to 17 stories high. It said the natural period of motion—the time to complete a vibration—of such buildings was amplified by the ground motion of the drained lake bed on which Mexico City lies. Those buildings and the earth's movement had periods of motion that were roughly equal, about two seconds, resulting in serious damage. Taller and shorter buildings were less likely to be affected, the study found (*New York Times*, 27 September 1987).

Then again, an upheaval of exactly the same force in the same place would have had other consequences when it was inhabited by Chichamec hunters and gatherers. "Does the physical ever affect the social," Marc Bloch asked, "unless its operations have been prepared, abetted, and given scope by factors which themselves have already derived from man?" (1953:24).

Notice that the too-simple dualism of "event" and "structure" is causing conceptual problems. What is generally called "event" is itself complex: at once a sui generis phenomenon with its own force, shape, and causes, and the significance these qualities acquire in the cultural context, significance in the double sense of meaning and importance. In fact, this is an argument in three terms—happenings, structures, and events—in which the event is the relation between the other two (Sahlins 1985:xiv, 153).[11] And while events emanating from natural or foreign causes can show this complexity *en clair*, endogenous events, developing within a given historical order, are constructed in the same general way. They likewise involve a work of cultural signification, which can be similarly described as the appropriation of local phenomena that have their own reasons *in* and *as* an existing cultural-historical scheme. Let us simply substitute *incident* for *happening* in the above argument about exogenous events: an endogenous event is a relation between an incident and a structure. And again, the same kind of incident arising in different societies will have different historical consequences—think of Chinese, French, and American student protests of recent decades. The historical significance of a given incident—its determinations and effects as "event" —depends on the cultural context.

We shall be dealing here with such internally generated events, events that developed out of incidents involving certain Fijian chiefs into the greatest war the islands had ever seen. Yet from the perspective of the larger structure or the system of relations between the kingdoms whose destinies were put at stake, the decisive actions and subjective dispositions of these chiefs were at least relatively autonomous. They were not simply expressions or (in Bourdieu's term) "executions" of the larger system. Indeed in common historiographic practice what makes an act or incident an event is precisely its contrast to the going order of things, its disruption of that order.

Here at least is a broad area of agreement among historians, philosophers, anthropologists, sociologists: the event is "a difference," as Paul Veyne says, "something that stands out against a background of uniformity . . . a thing we could not know *a priori*" (1984:5). It is a difference and it makes a difference. The event is a *"coupure"* (Bastide 1980: 822)—and not merely an "epistemological break" this time; for we know the event by the change that ensues in the existing order (cf. Teggart 1960:18; Morin 1972a:18; Jayawardena 1987:41; Gruner

1969; Moles 1972:90). "Once the event is produced, nothing is any more as before" (Molino 1986:55). All the scholars I have cited and many others would consent to distinguish events from actions or happenings that repeat themselves, from reproduction of the order. Not every action is a historical event. In a physical sense, of course, every human act qualifies as an event. But this is not physics. A human action is a meaningful value, having existence and effect that cannot be determined from its physical-empirical properties. Let us recall famous examples: the difference between a wink and a blink or between moving from point A to point B and "going home." And although they may be equally physical happenings, actions are not all alike historically, insofar as they have greater or less effect on a state of affairs. "History is historical," Ricoeur puts it, "because there are unparalleled actions which count and others which do not count; men who carry weight and others who do not; a lost battle, a leader who dies too soon . . . the result being a changed destiny" (1965:90; cf. Veyne 1984:31). In the general category of human actions, historical events are a subclass only, consisting of those actions that change the order of things.[12]

We see how endogenous events resemble the exogenous since both arise in circumstances eccentric to the structural schemes they affect. By inference from recent reflections of historians, one might say that events articulate phenomena of different levels or registers, such as the individual and the social, actions and institutions, the short term and the long term, the local and the global (Nora 1974; Vovelle 1988; Pomian 1988; cf. Gallie 1968; Ricoeur 1984:131, 193). Alternatively, social scientists speak of the intersection of different systems or subsystems: Edgar Morin, for example, for whom modifying events are those "which result from meetings or interactions between a principle of order or an organized system, on one side, and on the other, another principle of order or organized system, or any sort of perturbation" (1972a:17). Such interacting systems may be independent of one another—as culture and nature (earthquakes again)—or they may be only relatively autonomous—as individual talents and class relations (cf. Sartre 1968). But what then marks all these ways of conceiving the event are the discontinuities in the properties and the determinants of the phenomena so articulated. Hence the Big

Question. How are these incommensurables related to produce the historical process? How can a momentary incident, for example, resume and carry forth a whole historical trajectory of the relations between nations? How can these social totalities be reduced to individualities, thus allowing personal fates to shape the collective destinies? Such are fundamental enigmas of the event.

The problem is precisely that the one cannot be reduced to the other, the structure to the event nor vice versa, and yet each is somehow determining the other. The structures and relations of higher order whose history this may be—the warring kingdoms in our Fijian example—their characteristics as such do not specify the unique circumstances or individual biographies through which their history is worked out. If the destiny of the totality is subjected to the dispositions of the individual, still there is no adequate relation in either direction between the politics and the persons in the sense that neither can satisfactorily motivate the description of the other. Sartre said it was true that Valéry was a petit bourgeois intellectual, but not every petit bourgeois intellectual is a Valéry (1968). Or in the terms of another discourse: neither the nominalist argument that there are only individuals nor the realist respect for the coercive powers of the cultural order turns out to be a good historical explanation. To paraphrase Ricoeur, history unfolds as a synthesis of the heterogeneous (1984:216).

Just so in the history we are about to consider, the fates of Fijian kingdoms are integrated in the ambitions and disputes of certain ruling chiefs, a story that will hinge moreover on critical escapades of adultery and the roaming of a fat pig through a particular village at a particular time. Here is a history of war with all the inevitabilities of Cleopatra's nose and the geese that saved Rome. One could even speak of a dialectic of the heterogeneous. A higher order of structure —the relations between kingdoms—momentarily devolves upon certain circumstantial relations between particular chiefs, to be reconfigured in the terms and dynamics of this lower level, where it is besides subject to various accidents including those of personality, to emerge finally from the "structure of the conjuncture" in the changed state of an all-out war. The event develops as a reciprocal movement between higher and lower orders, a translation of each into the register of the other. Clearly this is a work of signification. The metamorphoses are tropes. The equation between the action of a person and the fate of a group, for instance, is a logic of synecdoche: the claim of the chief to embody his people. Or again, in the Fijian system, adultery with a chief's wife is a metaphor of usurpation. But if history is thus a kind of poetics, it is again structurally grounded. Without certain logical relations in the cultural order such tropes would neither be formulable nor intelligible. The key problem will be to find the structural motivations of the transpositions.

Finally, our Fijian history will reveal another kind of "synthesis of the heterogeneous." It concerns what historians call the intersection of different causal series in the event, the coincidence of different chains of determination. Without denying this element of "chance," the argument here will be that something more than "intersection" is involved in the historical relations between series. These series are themselves put into relations by the thinking subjects in whom they intersect so as to form complex structures that then may have synergetic effects. In the incidents about to be described, hostilities between rival kingdoms get linked into a fraternal struggle for succession to one of the kingships, so that in prosecuting his personal ambitions in the latter field a certain prince exacerbates the oppositions of the former. Effecting a correlation between different conflicts, the incident adds the interests of the one to the energies of the other. Such structures of synergy, revealing the invisible significances of an event that "testifies less to what it is than to what it sets off" (Nora 1974:299 –300), thereby help us understand the disproportions so commonly observed between the incident and the consequent—historiographic hallmark of the event, which is another formulation of its enigmas.

The Incidents

The cryptic entry for 12 January 1841 in the diary of the Methodist missionary Thomas Jaggar reads, "Q. driven away & other chiefs." Normally stationed upriver at Rewa (Lomanikoro), Jaggar happened to be visiting the town of Suva on the Viti Levu coast and so was able to record a fateful insult suffered by the high Rewa chief Ratu Qaraniqio, by all accounts the first in a series of events that issued in the great war of 1843–55 between the kingdoms of Rewa and Bau.[13] Since the efficacy of such events consists in what they led to—as reciprocally the magnitude of the sequel gives them notoriety in historical memory —a word should be said about the organization and dimensions of the war.

In the midnineteenth century Bau and Rewa were the most powerful states in the Fiji Islands (Map 1).[14] Although the war they fought engaged allies from far and wide and seemed to have the rule of all Fiji at stake, the main arena of battle was the populous Rewa Delta that lay between them (Map 2). The Bau confederacy was centered in the small islet of that name just off the coast to the northeast. Encircled by stone-lined jetties sheltering large ocean-going canoes, with much of its 23 acres covered by the houses of some three thousand inhabitants, Bau was not much more than an offshore naval base on the flank of the fertile Rewa Delta. Yet for at least a century its great fleets

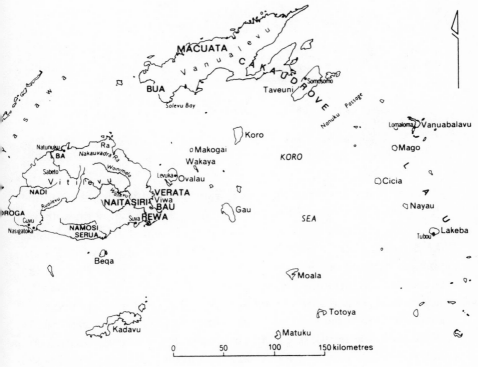

Map 1. Fiji Islands.

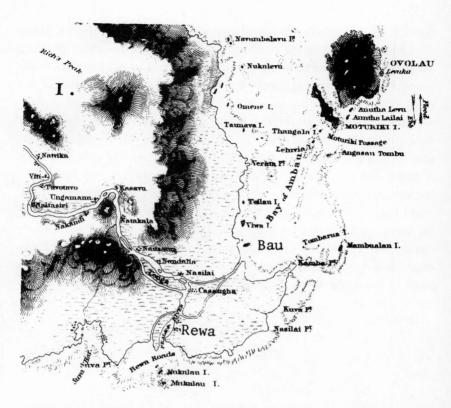

Map 2. Detail of southeast Viti Levu, from "Chart of the Viti Group or Feejee Islands" (Wilkes 1844).

of warriors had been terrorizing Fiji from one end to the other: from the Lau Islands in the east to the west coast of Viti Levu, with notable forays also along the north and south coasts of Vanua Levu and through the channels of the Rewa Delta. The terror had successfully spread Bau's political writ. By the beginning of the war, the Bau confederacy could be reckoned as including the islands of the central Koro Sea (Lomaiviti), several lands in and around the northern and eastern sides of the delta, the neighboring island of Viwa, certain important warrior peoples called Waimarō in the northeast of Viti Levu, as well as outlying places such as Suva and Nausori. The foods, wealth, and men of these subordinate lands, transported in Bau's famous canoe fleets, were put to the service of her increasingly hegemonic ambitions. Unlike the other main eastern Fijian states, but more like the mountain lands, Bau was indeed led by warrior-kings, those of the title Vunivalu, 'Root of War' (or 'God of War'), men for whom violence was a condition of their being—according to Fijian conceptions, it ran in their blood. Such a man was Tanoa, the war king of Bau who initiated the conflict with Rewa, as also his famous son Cakobau, who actively plotted and led it (cf. Scarr 1970).[15]

In double contrast to Bau, Rewa was a kingdom of established status and of agricultural rather than maritime orientation. Its ruling sacerdotal king, the Roko Tui Dreketi, descended in the collateral line from the ancient rulers of Verata on the east coast of Viti Levu, and Verata was the homeland of high nobility in eastern Fiji. The Rewa confederacy was concentrated in the delta, in low-lying swampy lands well known for the production of the giant 'horse taro' (*via kana*, F; *Crystosperma chamissionis*). Connected by causeways and river channels, the numerous villages of the confederacy were strongly fortified. Their surrounding moats, earthworks, and timber palisades made them virtually impregnable. Most of these Rewa villages were within 5–10 kilometers of the Rewa capital (Lomanikoro), a town also of about three thousand inhabitants in the midnineteenth century (Parry 1977).

To compare little things with great ones, this Polynesian war, like the Peloponnesian war, thus joined a major land power in prolonged struggle with a major sea power, each at the head of a considerable league of allied states—although in the Fijian case the sea power won out. Bau won, but not before the bloodiest and most destructive war Fiji had ever known, in the opinion of the Wesleyan missionaries who were witnesses to its sufferings. In scale, duration, and casualties it was probably the greatest war ever fought by any island people of this ocean. And it all began when the Rewa chief Ratu Qaraniqio attempted to requisition a pig—an act he could justify as a kinship right—in Suva, a Bauan village of no great account.

There is a large area of agreement in the principal documents about what happened in Suva that day in January 1841, as well as about the attacks on Suva by Rewa that followed. The primary sources are also in accord about the significance of these incidents in setting off the long war between Bau and Rewa, or at least these incidents plus one other: the flight of the ranking wife of Tanoa, the Bau war king, to Rewa in 1843, together with certain secondary wives, all of whom were distributed among the chiefs of Rewa.

I should note that the sources I am relying on are of several kinds:

(1) Reports of missionaries at or near the scene of the events, at or near the time they occurred. These are principally the letters and journals of John Hunt and Thomas Jaggar (Hunt, Journal; Jaggar, Diaries; MMS, Letters).

(2) Accounts of other Europeans living elsewhere in Fiji during the period, including missionaries such as James Calvert (Williams and Calvert 1859, vol. 2; Calvert, Journals) and Joseph Waterhouse (1978 [1866]) as well as people associated with the bêche de mer trade such as Mary Wallis (1983 [1851]). Not all these sources are independent: Wallis got a lot from Hunt, and other missionaries from Hunt and Jaggar both.

(3) Fijian oral traditions of the war recorded several decades later in the vernacular (Anonymous 1891, Toganivalu n.d., NLC/TR) or in English (Hocart FN:2507–13, 2564–71; Wall 1919). Toganivalu appears to get his information from the anonymous account in *Na Mata* (Anonymous 1891) and may be responsible in turn for the Bau Lands Commission history (NLC/TR). In general the Fijian traditions, including those collected by Hocart and Wall from Suva people, are consistent with the earlier European chronicles—but much more detailed and interesting.

Ratu Qaraniqio—hereafter Ratu Qara—the Rewa chief driven off by the Suvans, was the younger brother of Kania, the ruling king (Roko Tui Dreketi; Figure 1).[16] Often contending with his royal brother, whose principal wife he had recently slept with, Ratu Qara was the greatest fighter among the Rewa chiefs: a 'man of war' (*tamata ni valu*) as the Rewans said, whose bellicose disposition was clearly related to his political ambition.[17] What happened to him at Suva in 1841 was something as follows. Accompanied by a retinue of other chiefs and followers, he was making his way homeward from a journey to Nadrogā in southwestern Viti Levu. It is said the Rewans were at first feasted by the Suva people and only afterward did Ratu Qara spy the large pig wandering about the village and demand it be seized. (Such is the historical fame of this pig that its name, "Tamavua," has come down to us, along with its description as a prize red porker, *vuaka damu*.) Inasmuch as Suva was a Bauan land, Ratu Qara's demand was not arbitrary but within his rights as a uterine nephew (*vasu*) of the Roko Tui Bau, the sacerdotal king of Bau. On the other hand, Ravulo, the young ruler of Suva (Roko Tui Suva), the owner of the pig according to some, was likewise a uterine nephew to Bau (*vasu ki Bau*), but to the paramount king Tanoa (Figure 2). Ravulo resented and resisted the Rewa chief's attempt to take the pig. There followed a fracas in which clubs and spears were used and some Rewans were injured. According to Suva tradition, the one Rewa fatality occurred late that night when a Suva scouting party fell on Ratu Qara's people encamped at Laucala Bay. Tradition also has it that Ratu Qara was personally insulted when, escaping from the fight, he climbed up the mast of his canoe, whence a comb fell from his head, which was picked up and broken by a Suva warrior—an insult, this, because of the association with the chief's head, to which the Suvans added the injury of offering him a piece of firewood and daring him to come down and burn down their village (Hocart FN:2507–8; Wall 1919; Jaggar, Diaries:25 June 1842; MMS, Letters, Hunt:6 November 1846; Hunt, Journal:following 19 October 1845; Waterhouse 1978 [1866]:110–12; Wallis 1983 [1851]:162f.).

In months to come Ratu Qara would have revenge by destroying Suva, thus parlaying the quarrel over the porker to a major crisis in the relations between the kingdoms of Rewa and Bau. But even by itself the affair of the pig may have contributed to a deterioration in these relations. Months before Suva was actually attacked, Jaggar was reporting from Rewa that all sailing between that place and Bau was prohibited (Diaries:7 February 1842). Some days later came the more ominous note in his journal of, "rumour of war with Bau being near" (ibid.:15 February 1842). The rumor was premature. However, twice in the next fourteen months Ratu Qara mounted major assaults on Suva, the second resulting in a massacre.

The first time the Rewans were beaten off, despite that they mobilized fighting men from all over the delta. Hocart's informants (seventy years after the event) listed many of the traditional lands of the Rewa confed-

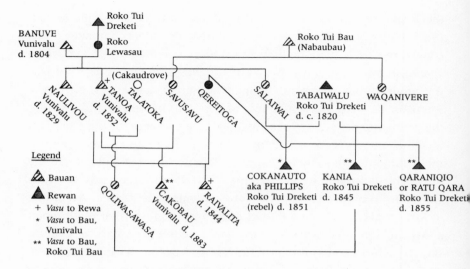

Fig. 1. Relations of Bau and Rewa ruling families.

eracy in the attacking force (Noco, Dreketi, Toga, Burebasaga, Vutia, Naselai, Nakelo, and Tokatoka; Hocart FN:2508, 2564). This late tradition might seem elaborated were it not for Jaggar's contemporary notice of an army of "perhaps 2000" leaving Rewa to attack Suva on 23 June 1842 (Jaggar, Diaries). Jaggar was still there two days later to record the return of the embarrassed Rewan host. Unable to penetrate the enemy town, they had suffered five dead and some wounded. Suva had been too well fortified, too well supplied with ammunition—and too well resolved to defend itself:

The Suva people said to the chiefs [of Rewa], "We shall not run away or be driven away, for where shall we run to?—to the reef? We are not fish but men, this is our land, and if we die we will die in our town. We have but one burial ground and it is this, our town" (Jaggar, Diaries:25 June 1842).[18]

The sequel reveals something Fijian about whose war it was anyhow. Chagrined at the defeat, Ratu Qara was anxious to return to the attack immediately, but, says Jaggar, "he does not seem to be seconded or encouraged by any (ibid.)." It took the Rewa chief almost a year to

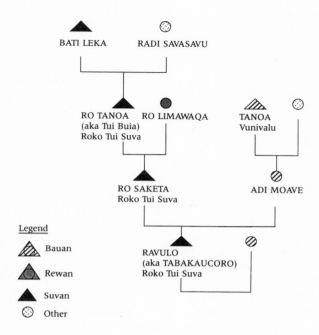

BATI LEKA   RADI SAVASAVU

RO TANOA   RO LIMAWAQA   TANOA
(aka Tui Buia)   Vunivalu
Roko Tui Suva

RO SAKETA   ADI MOAVE
Roko Tui Suva

RAVULO
(aka TABAKAUCORO)
Roko Tui Suva

Legend

Bauan

Rewan

Suvan

Other

Fig. 2. Suva ruling line.*

regroup the Rewan forces.[19] Just as the cause of the conflict appears as an insult to the chief's person, so the effective interests in the war were the interests of ruling chiefs.

Another incident during the lull between the battles of Suva affords further insights into the aristocratic politics of war. This was in August 1842. The Rewa first king, Roko Tui Dreketi, asked formal permission of his brother-in-law, the Bau war king Tanoa, to attack the Naitasiri people, who were remotely allied to Bau (*vanua vaka Bau*). Such was the customary 'chiefly practice' (*tovo vakatūraga*). In this instance Tanoa refused to sanction the attack and it never came off (Jaggar, Diaries:21 August 1842). But then the scrupulousness of the Rewa king, his observance of the proprieties, makes a nice contrast to the behavior of his

*After Hocart FN 2509–10; Wall 1919; Cargill (1977:179).

younger brother Ratu Qara. The contrast expresses the broad Fijian opposition between constituted authority and the pretensions of violence, which these brothers would demonstrate several times over in the events that followed. Ratu Qara had already ignored chiefly custom by not asking leave of the Bau rulers to attack Suva—thus defying the extension of their power in the lower delta.

Arriving at Suva on the morning of 7 April 1843, Jaggar's missionary colleague John Hunt found the town had been reduced to ashes by a large Rewan force the day before (MMS Letters, Hunt:12 June 1843). The negotiations and rituals required to mount an attack of this scale may help account for the many months it took to bring it off. In addition to recognized lands of the Rewan confederacy, tradition has it that the attacking army was bolstered by warriors from Soloira and Viria to the north, by former allies of Suva from the south coast who had been seduced by Ratu Qara's "gifts and promises," and by a cannon from *L'Aimable Josephine*—a French ship taken off Bau in 1834 manned by Charlie Pickering, a white friend of the Rewa chiefs (Wall 1919; Hocart FN:2508–9). The cannon had no particular effect. Or at least nowhere near the effect of a conspiracy between the Rewans and the Lomaivuna people who were in Suva at the time attending a feast and turned upon their hosts at a decisive moment. They are supposed to have opened the fortifications to the besieging army. The survivors of the ensuing slaughter fled upland and inland to an old village site. A day or two later they sent a whale tooth of submission (*i soro*), asking for safe passage for the women and children (*nai katikati*). The request was granted. But the Suva noncombatants were set upon as they were making their way to safety—a violation of the surrender rituals that at least one commentator believed unprecedented in Fijian warfare (Wall 1919). The total casualties suffered by the Suvans were also unusually heavy; estimates vary from four hundred killed in the retreat alone (ibid.) to Jaggar's figure, probably more reliable, of one hundred dead in all (MMS Letters, Jaggar:29 May 1843). In the same context Jaggar tells of a new "rumour of war between Rewa and Bau, because of the destruction of Suva by the Rewa people" (ibid.).

Within two or three years, while the war was raging full out, the opinion that it had originated in the destruction of Suva was settling into the status of a historical tradition. Jaggar's report of this opinion, however, is marked by the italics of his own skepticism: "Tanoa, who is carrying on this war, is exceedingly attached to the Chief of Suva, whose town the Rewa people destroyed, and on which account *it is said* the war was commenced" (MMS Letters, Jaggar:5 July 1845; cf. Hocart FN:2509–10). Still, contemporary documents confirm that Tanoa and his son Cakobau were furious about the attacks on Suva, the more so since the Rewans embellished their defiance of Bau with other little treacheries (MMS Letters, Jaggar:29 May 1843; Williams and Calvert 1858, 2:175). It seems that the Rewans sent their envoy to Bau—a formal title, Mata ki Bau, held by the Navolau clan—to officially report the destruction of the town to Tanoa, while assuring him that the women and children had been spared. The envoy was himself deceived and embarrassed by the subsequent news of the slaughter of the Suva innocents. According to traditions current to the present day, this was the reason for his betrayal of Rewa (Lomanikoro) to the besieging Bau army in December 1845. But we are not there yet. In fact Bau did not open the war with Rewa until late November 1843, nearly eight months after the destruction of Suva that was presumably the cause of war.[20] Suva was indeed a cause, but not sufficient to move the Bau king.

Reverend Hunt recalled Tanoa's hesitations, despite that the Suva massacre had made "a deep impression on Bau":

I remember having a conversation with Tanoa on the subject about this time, and he assured me that something further must be done by Rewa before hostilities would commence. He observed with his characteristic calmness: They have destroyed one town, but never mind, let them destroy another, and then we will fight (Hunt, Journal:following 19 October 1845).

Likewise, according to wide report, Cakobau, who was already acting as war king for his father, left Bau for Lakeba (Lau) at this time in order to avoid opening hostilities with Rewa (ibid., cf. Calvert 1858, 2:175–76). Hunt's colleagues Thomas Williams and James Calvert duly record the arrival of the Bau fleet at Lakeba on 21 May 1843, "to receive the homage and riches of [the Lau paramount] Tuinayau and his people" (Williams 1931, 1:162–63). Here let it be noted that Lau, which was tributary to Bau, was a great source of Fijian wealth, especially of the maritime goods the Bauans could use in Viti Levu to reward their fighting allies and "turn" the allies of their enemies to their own cause. In view of the strategy Cakobau later employed in the Rewa Delta, which was to undermine the towns of the Rewa confederacy by a combination of force and bribery until the Rewa capital Lomanikoro was bereft of all support, this voyage to Lau could be interpreted as something more than a political respite.[21]

All the same there were good reasons why the Bau warrior-rulers should show customary forebearance (*vosota ga*) with Rewa. Himself a *vasu* or privileged uterine nephew of the royal house of Rewa, even as his wife was the sister of the Rewa ruler, Tanoa represented the party of Rewa within Bau (Figure 1). In 1832, Tanoa had been deposed as war king and sent into exile by a faction that included certain paternal half-brothers (whose mother was from the island of Nairai) and the clan of the former war kings of Bau—rebels who could give as the reason for their usurpation the favoritism that Tanoa had openly and secretly shown for Rewa, especially in the distribution of wealth (Wilkes 1845, 3:63–64; Cross, Extracts:3 May 1838; Eagleston UD 1: 439). The rebels held power until 1837, using it to launch several attacks on Rewa towns. Whereas Tanoa himself took refuge in Rewa (after Cakaudrove), whence he was carried in triumph back to Bau after his son Cakobau had routed his enemies.[22] In sum, the relations subsisting between the Bau war king and his kinsman the Rewa ruler Kania were running against an outbreak of hostilities between them.

Reverend Hunt picked up another reason for Bau's unwillingness to avenge Suva:

A Bau chief told me the people of Bau do not wish to fight as they shall gain nothing by it. If they fight at Somosomo [Cakaudrove] or Lakemba [Lau] they obtain riches, but Rewa being another kingdom [like Bau] they have nothing to expect from them. So covetousness has a lot to do with Fijian wars (Hunt, Journal:13 November 1843).

Nevertheless, for weeks Hunt had been noting the palpable tension and the preparations for war in Bau (Lyth, Letters [Hunt to Lyth]:21 October

1843, 9 November 1843). And within the month the Bauans, or more precisely the ruling house of warrior-kings, had found good reason to declare total war on Rewa. Moreover for the next twelve years Cakobau had good enough reason to keep it going: indeed covetousness of a kind, though rather a lust for domination (*libido dominandi*) in the Augustinian sense. Soon after the war began, Hunt was reporting that "the idea of universal domination of the Fiji islands" was growing in Bau (following 19 October 1845).

This is one of those historical moments that are easily imagined otherwise (cf. Aron 1981). Desultory war had been going on with Rewa for decades—or at least a kind of warfare that, if not exactly desultory, was always terminable in a relatively short time and short too of total victory and defeat. But now something occurred that not only exacerbated the tensions over Suva but completely ruptured the kinship of Bau and Rewa ruling families and led to war in the worst form known to Fiji: a "war of the chiefs . . . in which the leading chiefs on either side [that is, on one side or the other] must be killed before it can terminate" (Hunt, Journal:following 19 October 1845). We need not be too cynical then about Cakobau's vaulting ambition of "universal domination," supposing it was the true cause of the all-out war on Rewa. The converse is equally plausible: total war fueled the chief's total ambitions, made them conceivable; whereas, the war itself developed from an all-out insult. The turn toward a war of chiefs came when Tanoa's principal wife Qereitoga, accused of adultery in Bau, fled along with several secondary wives to refuge with her brother Kania, first king of Rewa. We do not know with whom Qereitoga contracted this (reputed) liaison, or why. There is only reason to suspect that she took the initiative, as her own son by Tanoa, Raivalita, was losing ground as potential successor to his half-brother Cakobau. The sequel to her flight was even more significant: Qereitoga and her co-wives were redistributed among Rewan notables (Hunt, ibid.; MMS Letters, Hunt:6 November 1846; Williams and Calvert 1859, 2:175–76; Waterhouse 1978 [1866]:110–12; Wallis 1983 [1851]:165–66). The claim of John Hunt —our principal source in the matter—that the Rewan appropriation of the women "was contrary to all customs of Fiji" may be misleading inasmuch as the seduction of royal women was a recurrent sign of usurpation. Hence the sequitur in the Hunt text: "this was too gross an insult" for Tanoa.

Indeed insult as it may have been, the sacerdotal king of Rewa was generally more measured in his conduct than these warrior-kings of Bau, whose functions took them beyond the boundaries and proprieties of their fellow men (Sahlins 1987). When Bau sent a message taking leave of Rewa, breaking off all relations, the Rewans answered by offering to ceremonially atone (*i soro*) for their wrongs. The Rewa move was appropriate and normal according to custom. But it was too late, observed Reverend Hunt. Tanoa and Cakobau

had passed [*sic*] the Rubicon, and the malignant perseverance of the father, the ambitious perseverance of the son, to say nothing of the abilities and re-sources of each, rendered it quite unlikely that anything less than the blotting out of Rewa from the list of independent states in Fiji could satisfy them. Such was the origin and commencement of this destructive war (Hunt, Journal:following 19 October 1845).

Interpretations

As is true of more famous wars, the causes of this Polynesian war did not lie so much in the particular incidents that set it off as in the larger and longer situation, the global relations of hostility already existing between Bau and the great Fijian states of noble lineage, Rewa notably. In the same way, the truce between Athens and Sparta had been broken by a series of local disputes, disputes in which their interests clashed, "but the real reason for the war," Thucydides said, "is most likely to be disguised by such an argument. What made the war inevitable was the growth of Athenian power and the fear which this caused in Sparta" (*Peloponnesian War* I.23). For a long time Bau likewise had been expanding against the established Fijian kingdoms. If the Rewa rulers insisted on provoking the Bau war king, if they chose to make a demonstration of their own might by reducing Suva, which was after all a Bauan town in their own backyard, was it not in reaction to the historic growth of Bauan power? Fear of Bau, yes, but also envy, exasperation, and contempt for these parvenu kings whose treacherous methods were fair testimony to their dubious ancestry.

The growth of Bauan power had been going on longer than the introduction of muskets into Fijian wars in 1808 by the notorious Charlie Savage, to whom Westerners beginning with the early Methodist missionaries have been too quick to attribute Bau's successes (cf. France 1969:21, Campbell 1980). This is not the place to document the antiquity of Bau's expansion. Perhaps it will be enough to note that years before Savage, Bau was controlling the main islands of the Koro Sea (Lomaiviti) and large Bauan armies were fighting along the coast of Vanua Levu. Sometime in the latter half of the eighteenth century one such army, complemented by warriors from northeast Viti Levu (Nakorotubu), had successfully stormed the inland fortress of Kedekede at Lakeba, Lau. Indeed, in the list of Fijian place names collected by Captain Cook from Tongans in 1777—perhaps the earliest European notice of Fijian politics—only two are mentioned from the area in and around the main island of Viti Levu: Bau and Rewa.[23] Notably not mentioned is Verata. The ancient hearth of Fijian aristocracy, including the ruling clan of Rewa, Verata once enjoyed a hegemony of a certain kind over much of eastern Fiji. The kind in question was legitimate descent, in contrast to hegemony by conquest. Verata people still say theirs was a 'government of [the] blood' (*matanitū ni dra*), owing to the descent of their sacred king (Rātū) in the senior line of high Fijian nobility, by contrast to Bauans who know only a 'government of force' or a 'government of war' (*matanitū ni kaukauwa; matanitū ni valu*). We shall see that Bau royalty was the issue of a misalliance of a woman of the Verata noble stock—thus a bastard sister's son (*vasu*). The genealogical irregularity is the counterpart of a customary political conduct that likewise transcends the established norms. Bau is famous for treachery: *vere vaka-Bau*, 'conspiracy à la Bau', is a proverbial phrase in Fiji.

The war between Bau and Rewa was thus generations old before it began. The great Fijian kingdoms "have shown no disposition to submit to Bau rule," observed an American trader in1832, "consequently war with them is going on and has been for years" (Eagleston UD, 1:385). If war was still imminent in 1843, a Thucydidian view of its causes would seem appropriate: that it could not be sufficiently explained by the relatively minor events that unleashed it. And although the like has been said of many great wars since the Peloponnesian, it is not always recognized that neither would the general correlation of the social forces explain the events. Nothing so specific as history follows from the state of hostilities prevailing between Bau and Rewa. It does not follow that in January 1841, Ratu Qara would be insulted in Suva on his way home from Nadrogā, that he would persist in seeking revenge, that in April 1843, Suva would be betrayed by Lomaivuna visitors to a besieging Rewa army, that soon after, the wife of the Bau war king would commit adultery, flee to Rewa, and take up another liaison there. Conversely, it is not self-evident from the nature or sequence of these events why they had such remarkable consequences. The effect on the larger relations between states was distinctive as well as decisive: a "war of chiefs," war to the end, unlike all the previous wars.[24] System and event seem indissolubly joined in the kind of double indeterminacy remarked earlier. Each is responsible for the existence of the other, yet neither can account for the characteristics of the other. Therefore to say that the situation was ripe for war does not do away with the event. On the contrary it opens an issue of even greater scope than at first appears, because the whole historic course of the war, not just its beginnings, but every strategic movement and engagement, will likewise turn on the contingencies of person and action. Clearly we need to know how the higher order relations, as of Bau and Rewa, are relayed into practice, in a way that allows the actions of certain persons, such as Ratu Qara and Tanoa, to represent the larger system —and thereby configure its destiny.

It may help to have some names. Let us call these relays between the larger system and action *mediations*. Mediations would be the covering term for both the reductions from system to action or *instantiation* and the amplifications from action to system or *totalization*. Instantiation refers to the embodiment of generals in particulars, as of social groups or categories in specific persons, places, objects, or acts.[25] Totalization is the converse movement by which specific beings, objects, or acts achieve systematic significance, as by constituting relations between groups. Mediations are clearly complex processes, processes involving the engagement of compelling social relations—as the powers of Fijian chiefs—which are at the same time significant cultural meanings. But this is getting too abstract: let us look at some of the mediations by which the apparently trivial incidents at Suva turned into the worst Fijian war.

Social-Historical Individuals

The appropriation of a pig at Suva in 1841 could have been an unremarkable incident, the normal exercise of the uterine nephew (*vasu*) privilege, not even an "event" by the definition adopted here, were it not that the persons concerned represented certain lands whose historic relations were entailed in this otherwise mundane act. The instantiation of the land in and as the chief is of course a meaning-formation, but it is not an abstract play of signs. It is also well described as "power." The heroic capacity of Ratu Qara to signify Rewa and so incarnate its fate is built into the structures of the people's domination. The chief's power, then, does not simply reflect something outside itself, as a dividend on the control of real-coercive force, but it is itself this symbolic magnification of the person.

People so endowed with the power to embody a larger social order become *social-historical individuals*. The paraphrase is intended to resemble Hegel's world-historical individuals in part only. By *world-historical individuals* Hegel meant the "best men" (though not women) of their times: those whose own goals—perhaps only obliquely, through the cunning of reason—corresponded best to the progressive-dialectic movement of the World Spirit, which movement they made manifest. We can retain the notion of persons whose own acts unfold a collective history. But not because they incarnate an inevitable march of the Idea. Rather because they personify the clan or the land and because their acts, universalized through the acquiescence of the historic group, then signify its dispositions. Of course everybody's actions signify, are meaningful. But what distinguishes social-historical individuals is that their acts transcend self-reference—by far and in a twofold way. Their acts engage social totalities, in the first place by virtue of structures of hierarchy in which as chiefs they encompass the others. This is logical as well as sociological; the chief represents the logical class of which the people are members (Dumont 1970). Secondly, then, the acts of the chief acquire a sense equally social, in the Polynesian case a sense that is always political and cosmological in import, though the intention may be substantially personal. If Tanoa responds to the loss of his wives —of which, incidentally, he had plenty more—by a declaration of total war, it is because the liaisons they contracted showed contempt of the aging king's powers of fertility and thereby his claim on the sovereignty. And notice that this movement from instantiation to totalization is also a sequence from metonymy to metaphor, as the acts of the person who stands for the historic group become icons of concepts that pertain to the totality as such, to structures of that higher level.

Hence a final contrast to the Hegelian world-historical individual: where the project of the latter is the realization of a necessary and progressive historical course, here history may appear as a contingent realization of an individual project. True that Fijian chiefs are social beings. They make up a more-or-less uniform sociological class, with inclinations often alike, and their actions are generally skilled or knowledgeable (in Giddens's sense [1976,1984]). All of this implies that how they act is often a predictable working out of the social categories and forces. Yet nothing guarantees that the king is the best of men, or even much of one. And although his status may multiply his intelligence by supplying it with the power of society—thus making him a genius—it could also amplify every defect, pettiness of disposition, or weakness of spirit into a historical debacle. At decisive moments the collective fate is at the mercy of the individual psyche. Which is probably why the course of true history never did run smooth.

To include the existence of others in one's own person: this classic concept of hierarchy is curiously reminiscent of Polynesian ideas of *mana*. Speaking of Maori, Johansen suggests that *mana* can be thought of as a kind of 'fellowship', implying a life-power of the chief that extends to and activates others, whether people or objects (Johansen 1954:85f.; Valeri 1985:95f.). Thus the sometime dangers of the chief's *mana* as a life more powerful than one's own, which could invade and cancel one's own. Not to claim that Fijian concepts of chiefly *mana* are identical to the Maori. But they are in this respect similar and share the common implication that the chief lives the life of the group. He is the principle of the group's existence, a kind of living ancestor, and accordingly its history is his own. He recounts this history in the first person singular. Consider the following argument between the sacred ruler of Verata (Na Rātū) and a Bauan representing the war king (Vunivalu) at a government hearing on fishing rights in 1947, each challenging the other's version of eighteenth- and nineteenth-century history:

The Ratu of Verata (responding to question by the Bau representative [*mata*]): "I never heard of our meeting at Naivonini in 1750. . . . I don't know any Tunitoga [Bau herald] named Sainisakalo that you say I killed at the beach at Walu [late 1830s]. . . . I don't know when you burned Natavatolo [this was 1839; Cross, Diary:30 October 1839]. . . . I know of no such set of 10 whale teeth that you say were offered on my behalf by Nagalu to Ratu Cakobau and Ratu Mara [probably in the 1850s]. I only know we are true kinsmen, myself and both these chiefs [Cakobau and Ratu Mara]" (VQ:243–44).

The Bau *mata* (responding to questions of the Verata ruler): "From long ago until 1750 you were the owner of all the reefs we are disputing here, but I seized them from you in 1750 when I defeated you in our war at Naivonini. . . . I know that I destroyed you [literally, 'clubbed you', *mokuti iko*] the third time I took your town. . . . I never heard that you were able to take or destroy a single land in all of Fiji. You never captured a single place in Fiji because of your weakness: the reason you have never made war on another state is not [as you say] because you are the first born [i.e., the senior line of Fijian ruling aristocracies; see above] (VQ:284–88).

Elsewhere I have discussed the "heroic" organization of the Fijians and societies of the like (Sahlins 1985:35f.). Here it is necessary only to stress that the heroic system involves a certain mode of historical production, a kind of historical practice. One aspect of this practice —of which these uses of the "heroic I" give such clear testimony—is the sense of history as incorporated in the chiefly person and expressed in his current action. It follows that not everything in the event is evenemential. The presence of the chief brings forth political relations of ancient memory, carries them into the organization of current experience and actions. This is an instance of the transposition of registers, here temporal, that characterizes important events: a long trajectory of the relations between states is brought to bear in a given incident and a single instant. When Ratu Qara of Rewa is refused a pig in Suva, this is no mere injury to a great noble's amour propre; it evokes the whole course of deteriorating relations between Rewa and Bau (to whom Suva gives allegiance and whence no doubt it gets its cheekiness). All of a sudden, in a village marginal to both and of no vital economic importance to either, the issue between two great kingdoms is joined. Surging out of the depths comes all that notorious history of the growth of Bauan power and the fear it inspires in Rewa. The event, as Pierre Nora says, is "the site of social projections and latent conflicts and the most important of events is that which invokes the most archaic heritage" (1974:303).

Embodying and making history, ruling chiefs thus practice socially the capacities they are given cosmologically, for in the great kingdoms the holders of the highest titles are 'human gods' (*kalou tamata*).[26] History thus appears as the continuation of the creation by human means, and making society as the sublunar version of making the cosmos. In Bau, Cakaudrove, and, in all probability, the other major states—for Rewa we have no information on this— the sacred king ritually recreates the social world every day. Until kava is ceremonially offered to him in the early morning, no noise or work is permitted in the village: human society is suspended. A loud cry reverberating through the community indicates the king has drunk the offering, which moreover he shares with—dedicates to—the unseen gods. Thereupon, the life of the people may begin (Lyth T/F, 1:61–63; Wilkes 1845, 3:157–58; Lester 1941–42:113–14).

Following Hocart, the Fijian state (*matanitū*) can be described as a ritual polity, organized as a system of worship of the king (Hocart 1950, 1969, 1970). The several clans (*mataqali*) of the kingdom are defined by the specialized services they perform for the divine ruler—fishers, heralds, priests, warriors—even as the word for such service (*veiqaravi*) also means 'to worship'. Hence the principle of heroic generalization we have seen at work in events, the structural extension of the king's acts and concerns to the people in general. The marriages of Fijian rulers are not domestic affairs merely but political alliances, their kinship prestations turn into massive exchanges of local products, and their personal disputes—the wars of states. "As for the common people," the historian comments, "the chief's cause was their cause" (Derrick

1946:78). Reverend Hunt explains how, early in the Bau-Rewa war, nearly half the Rewans readily defected to the enemy: "one of their own chiefs [Cokanauto] having joined Bau made the disgrace connected with joining that place but trifling, as whichever party they fought for they were fighting for their own chief" (Journal:following 19 October 1845). Something similar might be said of the whole war, insofar as it developed from the incidents that have been recounted:

The most important [of the new wars of conquest of the nineteenth century] —the Bau-Rewa War of 1843–1855, for example—grew out of family feuds or the quarrels of blood relations in a few leading families. The common people fought to avenge the wrongs, real or fancied, of their high chiefs; sons of one father were to be found on opposite sides (Derrick 1946:48, cf. p. 83).

Making history this way is a function of the system of hierarchy, but by the principles of that system it is not the exclusive privilege of the king. The titled heads of clans and villages have similar powers in the space given by affairs of their own people. But more important, in any such constituted group, inasmuch as the chief's being includes the whole, so reciprocally the other people participate in his person and thus retain the right, in proportion to their rank, to represent him. In any ceremonial prestation—which is also to say any important negotiation because the affair will have to be marked by the ritual offering of kava (*i sevusevu*)—if the chief is absent his place is taken by the person next senior. The latter is accorded the chiefly title in the exchange of honors. This principle of substitution is important, as it implies the presence of the collective whenever high-ranking people, such as Ratu Qara of Rewa, are involved.

When Ratu Qara was denied a pig in Suva, it was an offense as well against his royal brother the Roko Tui Dreketi and the revenge accordingly engaged the whole Rewan confederacy. Yet at the same time this devolution of powers to the younger brother submitted the affairs of Rewa to certain personal ambitions that magnified the collective-political consequences. For the quarrel with Suva was then articulated with the fierce rivalry over the kingship, the history of parricide, fratricide, intrigue, and betrayal, for which the Rewa ruling house was already too well known (Lyth T/F, 1:126–28; Wilkes 1845, 3:131f.;

Waterhouse 1978[1866]:42). Ratu Qara's attempt to seduce a wife of his brother the king was a prolongation of these battles royal: an apparently mild thrust, yet the most terrible carnage had been set off by a similar episode of adultery a generation back. Ratu Qara's other evident passion—for violence—may be understood in the same connection. A well-spent youth spreading terror and mayhem was a qualification for succession, especially recommended for younger brothers or the sons of junior wives. (In Bau, the careers of both Tanoa and his son Cakobau would illustrate the point.) Well into the 1830s and 1840s, the several brothers of the Rewa king, Kania, were outdoing him and each other in feats of atrocity, as in their respective punitive expeditions to the islands of Beqa and Kadavu, not to neglect their conspiracies against one another. If the response of Ratu Qara to the refusal of a pig at Suva seems out of proportion—I mean his persistent ambition to annihilate the place—it was in part due to the insertion of the affair in other heroic projects. This is also to say that the larger historic relations of Rewa, Suva, and Bau were implicated in other structures, importing to these relations new dimensions of hatred and violence. The instantiation of larger systems in chiefly individuals brought the former into a field of interpersonal conflict, itself marked by an intensity worthy of the greater glory at stake—the kingship.

We shall meet this kind of structural palimpsest again, where relations of one sphere are inscribed on those of another. Of course it is merely another way of describing what historians customarily remark about events, that they stand at the intersection of different casual series. Yet there is more here than "intersection," a meeting. There is a *synthesis* of heterogeneities, with the effect of a *structural synergy*. The combination of relations from different fields—here relations between states and between brothers contending for kingship—thus transforms local incidents into global crises.

Sovereignty, Marriage, and the Uterine Nephew (*Vasu*)

Insofar as the destiny of kingdoms is displaced onto certain social-historical individuals, their acts assume meanings of proportionate universality. Ratu Qara's quarrel at Suva and Tanoa's marital misfortunes metaphorically figured the general balance of forces among Fijian kingdoms. These were structural connotations, grounded in the Fijian scheme of sovereignty, involving the famous privileges of the *vasu*, the sacred uterine nephew (cf. Sahlins 1983, 1985:ch. 3).

The ruling line in the great Fijian kingdoms typically comes from elsewhere. "'The chiefs came from overseas'," a Lauan said to Hocart; "'it is so in all countries of Fiji'" (Hocart 1929:129). An immigrant prince who leaves his homeland because of some contention, and whose character and circumstances suggest violence, even cannibalism, this stranger founds a dynasty by marrying a ranking woman (or women) of the indigenous people, a union that domesticates him and sets up an ordered and productive society. As the indigenous people are known as 'the owners' (*i taukei*) and 'the land' (*na vanua*), the constituting union has the qualities of a Frazerian sacred marriage. It is the union of the king (the sea) with the land, from the issue of which —the ruling line— the society will continue to enjoy fertility and tranquility (*sautū*). The Cakaudrove people go so far as to explicitly articulate a Frazerian theory, for when the sacred king (Tui Cakau) is installed, he is said to marry the land:

After the new Tui Cakau has drunk the installation cup of *yaqona* [kava], a member of the [former rulers] Mataikoro ties the *vesa i sole mana* on his upper right arm. As it is being tied the Mataikoro *turaga* [chief] calls out that he is marrying the Tui Cakau to the *vanua* [land] Cakaudrove (*vakamautaka kina na vanua kei na turaga Tui Cakau*). When a people gave themselves and their land to a paramount, it was said that they married, or betrothed, him to their land (*musuka vua na vanua*) (Sayes 1982:204–5).[27]

Marriage to the land sublimates the powers of the stranger-king. (Indeed it remains the function of the chieftains of the indigenous people, the 'mature ones' [or 'elders', *matua*] to control the proverbial anger of the king.) The king's cannibal disposition is directed outward, turning royal violence into reproductive benefits through the provision of sacrificial victims to the gods of the land. The ruling king has charge of the sacrificial and fertility ritual. The sovereign powers of violence devolve upon an active, second king, such as I have here called the war king. "War is his part," Fijians say. Traditionally the war king is the successor in the lineage of the indigenous rulers. And since his victims are of the nature of the stranger-king—in the best case famous enemy warriors and chiefs— this warfare is a recursive form of the legendary events that founded the dynasty. For in war, the terrible stranger, captured and made an offering to the god and sacred food to the people, has been metamorphosed into the prosperity of the land. Again, the installation rites of the ruling king have the same general structure, as they entail his symbolic death as an outsider and his rebirth as a domestic god. Indeed in formal speech the ruler, as the issue of the indigenous woman, is the 'child chief' (gone tūraga). More precisely, by the initial sacred marriage, the chiefly line is sister's son to the land, the sacred uterine nephew (vasu).

Here is a Lauan version of the theory of sovereignty, as recently told to anthropologist Steven Hooper:

When there is a place [vanua] and they have their chief, or customary leader, if a greater chief comes along he will lead them. The thing that will be done — the chief will marry a woman of the land. In their marriage, when they have issue, he/she [o koya] will be chief in the land. Formerly the ladies [marama], the first-born ladies, were the ones who married the chief. . . . If a lady is married to a chief who has arrived, gardening land will be given to the chief. . . . It is possible for the chief of the land to give all the gardening land to the chief who has come by sea. His child [land chief's daughter] is given . . . the lady of this land comes and resides with the chief. Every thing is his. The first fruits can be done—then will come the first fruits of the earth to the chief and the lady, because their child, when their child is born, will be the great chief in this land. Because the mother [is] the land, the father [is] the chief (Baleta a jinana: a vanua, a tamana: a tūraga). They are mutually facing, bound together. So the things which come from the sea, the chief will bring, the valuables of the chief (Hooper 1982:153).

We come to a point most pertinent to the Bau-Rewa war. As the king is the male element in the reproduction of the land, so his control of women is an essential icon of the sovereignty itself. When a defeated land formally submits (i soro) to its conqueror, it presents to the latter a basket of earth symbolic of the land and a daughter or daughters of its ruling chief—still another version of the dynastic founding myth. In the same connection, the ruling nobility were renowned for their sexual and marital exploits. Manifest sign of the chief's reproductive powers, testimony in the human mode of a divine creativity, the number of "wives" of great kings ran to many score—difficult in fact to number because they included many secondary consorts (*vada*), whose status graded into simple domestics, as well as ceremonially married women of high rank (*marama*) (MMS Letters, Hunt:30 December 1839; Jackson 1967:421; cf. Thomson 1908:235). The chief's power to commandeer women was balanced by a certain noblesse oblige; he was ready to distribute the favors of the lesser wives, for example, in hospitality to visiting notables (Lyth, Remin:81; Daybook:1 July 1851; Hunt, Journal:19 February 1844). Illicit intercourse with the ruler's wife, however, was another matter. If the mother is the land, the father the chief, as the Lauan says, if the privileged right to woman is the sign of cosmic cum sovereign powers, then a liaison with the royal wife is lèse majesté. It is the negation of the king's rule and a claim to replace him, of which the early missionaries record more than one example (Lyth, Journal:18 October 1841; Hunt, Journal:11 January 1841, 8 February 1842, 8 April 1844). He who takes the king's wife is a political rival and potential assassin. In Fijian terms the outrage is literally an act of war: 'War!' (*Ai Valu!*) is the cry raised at its discovery. So it was understood by Namosimalua, ruler of Viwa:

About three hours after we had gone to bed last night, we were alarmed by the powerful voice of the chief crying, 'Hold fast, hold fast. A war, a war.' He then with a still louder voice called to some people of Bou [Bau] who were fishing near our shore [N.B., the Bau fishers are famous warriors, especially the Lasakau; and the Viwa chief was a close ally of Bau.] I soon ascertained that some man had been lying with one of the chief's wives, and this he considered as an indication that the party concerned were about to take his life, and that war would immediately ensue, hence he called the men who were fishing to assist him (Cross, Diary: 9 March 1840).

We can appreciate the force of the insult to the Bau war king Tanoa entailed in the distribution of his consorts, including his principal wife, by the brother of the latter, the Rewa king. Recall that it had been necessary to overcome Tanoa's own maternal relationship and longstanding loyalty to Rewa in order to rouse Bau to war. In this light, the Bau ruler's loss was doubly meaningful: the negation of the gift of the woman from Rewa, thus breaking off the marital reciprocities, as well as an attack on the aging Tanoa's sexual-sovereign powers. Not good timing on Rewa's part: "Old Snuff," as the whites called Tanoa, was always darkening his beard, calling for young girls, and otherwise worrying about his declining sexual powers (as if haunted by the footsteps of a rival stalking the sacred grove at Nemi).

The political metaphors draw their effect from the relationship between the uterine nephew (*vasu*) and his mother's people, which we encounter over and over again in this history. At this point we need to know more about it.

The quotidian ethnography of the *vasu* relation is perhaps well known already. The sister's son has a special claim on the movable wealth of his mother's brother: claim that may be exercised without leave, simply by appropriation, but more commonly takes the form of a request (*kerekere*) that can hardly be denied. These privileges of the *vasu* are socially generalized in proportion to his paternal rank and to the status of the family of his mother. A man of standing in Bau who is uterine nephew to the ruler of Cakaudrove (Tui Cakau) is a 'great *vasu*' (*vasu levu*) or a 'noble *vasu*' (*vasu tūraga*) in Cakaudrove as a whole; his powers extend throughout the domain of his royal mother's brother. We see why Fijians say that the internal *vasu* (*vasu i taukei*), maternally connected to an ancient ruling line of his own kingdom, is the greatest man of the realm (Hocart 1929:234; N.B. the analogy to the founding of the dynasty). The privileges of the foreign great *vasu* moreover are subject to another condition: the power of his own kingdom relative to that of his maternal kin. A Bauan noble *vasu* is a regular terror in Lau, but not vice versa.[28] The ruling chief of a lesser land whose mother is from Bauan nobility—such was the relation of the Suva paramount to Tanoa's family—is an honored man (*tūraga dokai*) in Bau, but he does not act there in a high-handed way. Whereas Ratu Qara of Rewa was *vasu* to the sacred king of Bau (Roko Tui Bau), hence insofar as Suva was connected to Bau, he could do what he wished in Suva. Seize the pig of a Suva chief, for example.

Hocart always insisted on the sacred force of the *vasu* rights. His field notes include Fijian texts that describe the system of cross-relations in terms such as 'gods' (*kalou*) and ritual taboos (FN 2575). "Much more

[is] involved in the cross-cousin system than the classification of relatives," he concluded; "there is a whole theology" (1970b:237). Accordingly, the *vasu*'s claims on the goods of ceremonial exchanges (*solevu*) are paradigmatic: he has the right to carry off the stuff formally presented to his mother's brother. Yet as all such prestations are offered to the god or gods of the recipient, the nephew's privilege is appropriately described as the right to seize the sacrifice. He replaces the god, the one who consumes the sacrifice. The *vasu* is the human, visible form of the god of his maternal relatives. Hence is the king, as *vasu* to the people, their human god (*kalou tamata*). Conversely, the great god (*kalou vu*) may be styled the *vasu* of the land (Hocart 1912:445). And insofar as all the things that come to the ruling town—cannibal victims, ceremonial valuables, first fruits of the crops—insofar as all are offered to the great god, they fall to the "child chief" who represents him in this world.

Fijians are also sensitive to the agonistic dimensions of their theory of sovereignty. Offspring in the paternal line of a dangerous foreigner, the chiefly sister's son forcibly seizes the offering and substitutes himself for the indigenous gods—he is a usurper. Hocart remarked the antagonism in the rituals of the *vasu* system: upon taking the sacrifice, the uterine nephew is beaten by his cross-cousins, the sons of his mother's brother—but they cannot take back the property (Hocart 1952:142, 205; 1923; FN:2777). Something similar is found in ordinary kinship practice. The normal patterns of relationship encode a little drama, unfolding over the generations, in which the denouement of the sacred respect for the sister's son is the prescribed exchange of humorous insults between cross-cousins—thus from deference to joking, which is also from the exchange of goods to "the exchange of bads" (Graeber MS). Mother's brother and sister's son are taboo to one another, their conduct marked by a reserve that is the sign of their mutual respect; but a man and his male cross-cousins are required to abuse each other, in sexual matters notably, banter that they are also bound to take in good spirit.

We need not be surprised, then, at the resentment attending the historic practice of *vasu* rights by ambitious chiefs. The hostile reaction evoked by Ratu Qara's seizure of the Suva chief's pig is one only of many such episodes (cf. Gordon-Cumming 1882:165; MMS Letters, Calvert:6 July 1861; Wilkes 1845, 3:77). In the early years of the Colony one of the members of the Council of Chiefs, complaining of the way whites were taking Fijian women and recruiting Fijian men, observed that "the evil caused by the white men, who despise us and our laws, is a great and increasing one. They are said to be 'Vasus to Heaven'" (Council of Chiefs 1875:14).

In like fashion, certain standing relations of rivalry between Fijian states were based on the *vasu* custom. Known as *veitabani* or relations of 'side-to-side', the rivalries came into effect between lands descended of a brother and sister respectively, hence of an exogamous marriage of the ancestors. Generalized cross-cousins, then, the states were hereditary rivals whose members were prepared to verbally flail each other on meeting and to come to blows at the slightest pretext. Bau stood in this side-to-side relation with both Verata and Rewa. As we have seen, the Bau kings were in origin *vasu* to these aristocratic lands, descended of an irregular union between the older sister of the Verata and Rewa ancestors and a local chieftain of no particular nobility (Figure 3). Bau's growing power and the fear this inspired in Rewa was encoded in the same terms as the particular incidents that ignited the showdown between them. The enmities at the personal level and the hostilities at the kingdom level were icons the one of the other.

Not all *vasu* relations between kingdoms, however, were so longstanding. Fijians also knew how to organize and reorganize current situations in these terms. Such were their marital politics. The marriages of noble women (*marama*), marriages that would give rise to sisters' sons in other clans and lands, amounted to a key arena of political practice.[29] In contrast to founding unions of royalty with indigenous women, these political alliances were more often with the ruling houses of outside places. Several tactics were employed, of which two are relevant to the events at issue here: the import of ranking women from foreign lands by the polygynous rulers of major states such as Bau; and the export of the daughters of these rulers to dependent lands such as Suva. In different ways, these alliances will then bring to bear the strategic position and powers of one state on the internal politics of another—that is, in the person of a sister's son of the one who is a

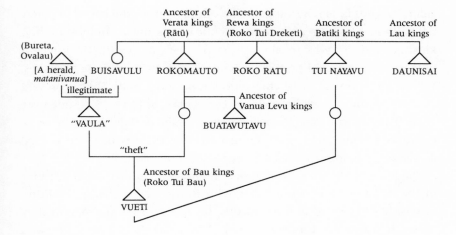

Fig. 3. Relations of Fijian sacred kingships.

prince and potential successor in the other. Here is another structural ground—coordinate to the Fijian system of hierarchy—of the social-historical individual.

The war king Tanoa, for example, had nine royal wives *(marama)*, all but two from lands outside Bau, including great states such as Rewa and Cakaudrove and dependencies such as the islands of Koro and Nairai. In the years just before the war, his Rewa wife (Adi Qereitoga) was evidently recognized as the official consort (Radini Levuka), though there is some evidence that earlier the Cakaudrove woman (Adi Talātoka) held the honor. No doubt there is a story hinging on political interest behind this change, as there would be for all Tanoa's marriages. Indeed the sequence of the Bau king's unions would make a shorthand chronicle of the recent geopolitical history of eastern Fiji. And the struggles for power and the succession that ensued in Bau among the sons of these wives, *vasu* to their respective maternal peoples, well and truly shaped the further political history of the region. The exogamous marriages of the king articulated the respective fates of whole lands with the careers of their sister's sons in powerful Bau—as reciprocally the success of the royal *vasu* in Bau might depend on pressures mounted by his mother's brother's land.[30] We can now understand why the fratricidal struggles in Fijian ruling families, notably the strife between paternal half-brothers, so readily transcend the bonds and sentiments of their kinship. And also why royal wives, respectively advancing the interests of their own sons and brothers, become key players in these tragedies. Yet the ambitions of these chiefs are not personal only. They represent in their persons an entire regional correlation of forces. The outcome of their heroic conspiracies and cruelties could change the fortunes of entire kingdoms. Here is a conjunction of structures that can indeed give synergetic impulse and effect to individual action.

The specific set of *vasu* relations among Bau princes was a factor in the declaration of all-out war with Rewa, at least as a condition of possibility. Fijians understood this, for among the information they passed to Reverend Hunt was a story of how Cakobau, alone of Tanoa's sons, answered his call to exact revenge for the loss of his wives to the Rewans (Journal:following 19 October 1845). As an account of Cakobau's ascension to the war king functions, the story is misleading since Cakobau had been so acting for years. The sense is otherwise: the disenfranchisement of the sons Tanoa sired by his Rewa and Cakaudrove wives, despite the titled status of these women as official consorts. But as we know, Cakobau was by contrast *vasu* of the people (*vasu i taukei*), his mother being the daughter of the ritual king (Roko Tui Bau). Unlike his half-brothers, Cakobau need have no loyalty to, nor dependence upon, the enemies of Bau. So when Tanoa responded to the appropriation of his women by the declaration of a war of extermination, he could safely entrust the war to Cakobau, who was at once the most gifted of all his sons and the most single-minded. Not long after the conflict began, Raivalita, Tanoa's son by Qereitoga, suspected of a conspiracy with the Rewan enemy, was assassinated on the orders of his father and his half-brother, Cakobau (Wallis 1983 [1851]:102 –5). In the same vein, when Cakobau successfully attacked Rewa and dispatched Kania the king, he is reputed to have said: "Treachery is your custom, you sisters' sons [*vasu*] of Bau everywhere. If another one of you incites a rebellion, you will be eaten by [my war club] Uvi ni Siga" (Toganivalu n.d.).

Finally, the *vasu* relation was in play in still another way. If Tanoa was already angered by Rewans for the attack on Suva, it should be remembered that the Suva ruler Ravulo was Tanoa's daughter's son—so a *vasu* to Bau (Figure 2). Bau did not itself produce many valuables (*i yau*) for exchange, but it did have a lot of noble women, or at least women of important clans—for this purpose one need not be very fussy —who could be accorded to ranking men of lesser lands. This was a major means of Bauan expansion, a classic kind of 'conspiracy à la Bau' (*vere vaka-Bau*). It functioned politically in a double way: the gift of the woman ensured the loyalty of the wife-taking chief, perhaps even canceling the latter's allegiance to another place such as Rewa; plus the Bauan wife could ennoble and empower the local chief, bringing to him the backing of her people—support from Bau, which could prove decisive in contests with his own rivals for rule of the land. The Bau kings were notorious for their ability to interfere this way in succession struggles of other places. They would decide the issue between contending brothers or houses by betrothing a woman to one of them, thus promising (in the person of her son) a local paramount who is sacred nephew to Bau. Fijian traditions commonly attribute the very constitution of government (*matanitū*) in lesser lands such as Suva to the acquisition of royal women from nearby greater kingdoms.[31] According to the Suva view of their history, they used to live in relatively unorganized (dispersed) fashion and marry with Rewa, until the ancient land people of Suva brought a noble woman from Bau, chose a man of the chiefly clan to marry her, and made him ruler of Suva. Thereupon the Suva polity was reorganized. The people were collected together under their chief and a new high god—from Bau. Here is Hocart's summary of Suva people's accounts:

They are now in the [colonial] province of Rewa; but they claim they were not subject to Rewa of old, but independent. When they became uterine nephew to Bau they turned to that state. This is how it happened. They used to live dispersed, in Vatuwaqa . . . in Nauluvatu . . . in Solia. At that time they intermarried with Rewa. Then the elders of Nadonumai, the clan of the Lord of the Green (Tui Rara) ['land people', *i taukei*] agreed to go to Bau to fetch a lady. They chose a man of the clan of Roko Tui Suva to marry her and be lord over them. Then they all lived in Solia to wait upon the lady of Bau. They gave up intermarrying with Rewa. The lady came with a god (*tevoro*) Cagawalu. Those who brought her, the envoys to Bau, are his priests.

That is how the nobles of Suva increased. . . . Bau and Suva have gods in common (Hocart HF:374b–374c; cf. Wall 1919).

These understandings of the *vasu* relations in hand, we are able to determine certain other historic structures evoked particularly by the incidents at Suva.

Traces

The incidents summon up historical relations—trace structures, they have been called (Sahlins 1985:66 n.)—which become dynamic factors in the situation. By the same token, these historical relations are put at stake in what is happening. A brief present thus becomes the resolution of a long past. But this present is not simply or necessarily the continuation of a given historical trajectory. Subject to the contingencies and other structures of the event, the old relations take a new turn.

Suva itself assumed a specific historic value in the relations of Bau and Rewa. Because of the shifting marital arrangements of Suva's ruling chiefs, the whole menacing rise of Bauan power surfaced in the local contretemps with Ratu Qara of Rewa. Ravulo, the Suva chief who battled Ratu Qara over the pig, was a *vasu* to Bau, as we know; whereas, his father and predecessor was *vasu* to Rewa (Figure 2). The pig incident thus comes as a sequitur to the shift in the marital alliances of the Suva ruling line from Rewa to Bau. To so change wife taking is to change political allegiances. Suva oral tradition is not so explicit. It maintains rather that Suva was independent before the marriage of Ravulo's father with Tanoa's daughter, which then made it Bauan land (*vanua vaka-Bau*). But this tradition was recorded when Suva was located in the colonial province of Rewa. Suvans would have a continuing interest in denying their ancient subordination to Lomanikoro—an interest that indeed continues the classic political maneuver they were engaged in during the early nineteenth century.[32]

The classic maneuver is reflected in the geopolitical situation of Suva as a Bauan land in the immediate vicinity of Rewa (Map 2). Thus have lesser Fijian states sought to escape domination by their larger neighbors, that is by placing themselves under the protection of the latter's powerful enemies. In this way the smaller land is able to avoid exploitation by the neighboring kingdom, while its distance from the kingdom to which it does submit precludes any systematic payments of tribute such as providing subsistence to the ruling town. The effect is the mosaic pattern of political affiliation that marks the landscape of eastern Fiji, testifying especially to the latter-day evolution of Bauan power. Nausori and the large land of Naitasiri are other Bauan outliers in the Rewa River drainage. In the northeast of Viti Levu are similar detached Bau lands that were once part of the Verata confederacy: the most famous defectors were great warrior peoples of the interior known as Waimarō; former fighting allies (*bati*) of Verata, they become a feared Bau army (Dri Tabua). So far as I am aware, Colman Wall was the first to recognize this distinctive Fijian geopolitics—precisely in regard to Suva and the origins of the Bau-Rewa war. In any fight between these two great kingdoms, Wall wrote,

Suva and Serua would side with Bau, while Namosi that lay between them would side with Rewa, for the simple reason that the smaller states preferred an alliance with a powerful but distant kingdom to one closer at hand, as while it could help them when needed, they ran little risk of being absorbed by it (Wall 1919).

The allegiances of these peripheral lands to great confederacies sometimes changed and were always uncertain. Subject to shifts in the regional balance of forces, the alliances were then recognized through tactical negotiations that left their traces notably in the history of the marriages of local rulers with noble women from powerful kingdoms. This must be why it was said that Tanoa of Bau had a special regard for his grandson Ravulo, the ruler of Suva, and why he was so vexed at the attacks on the town by Ratu Qara (cf. Jaggar, Letters:5 July 1845). By the same token the insult offered to Ratu Qara in Suva summarized Bau's encroachment upon Rewa and the danger thus posed to the established order in Fiji.

The Suva affair, moreover, elicited other structural traces that likewise exaggerated the historical consequences. For the trouble between Ratu Qara and the Suva paramount Ravulo was actually a confrontation between *two* sacred nephews of Bau, who were however *vasu* to the two opposed royal lines of the Roko Tui Bau (sacerdotal king) and the Vunivalu (war king). Ratu Qara's mother was a daughter of the house currently detaining the sacred kingship.[33] That house had taken the title, and the support of the numerous clans and villages appended to it, in the earlier nineteenth century after the war kings had killed the reigning Roko Tui Bau and deposed his lineage. In every subsequent civil dispute in Bau, however, the two kings continued to be on different sides. And while it was generally acknowledged that the war kings since Tanoa's father or grandfather had become supreme, reversing the traditional ranking in the diarchy, the sacerdotal king still received the first cup in kava ceremonies and otherwise continued to play the ritual part of the 'human god' (*kalou tamata*). Paradoxically, the war king needed the sacred king in order to confer legitimacy on the powers he had usurped. And wherever the Roko Tui Bau's writ ran, there Ratu Qara, as sacred nephew, could please himself with the people's property. Fijian sources, Bauan included, explicitly understand Ratu Qara's requisition of the pig in Suva as his *vasu* right (Anonymous 1891:8; Toganivalu n.d.). But, then, since Ravulo of Suva was *vasu* to Tanoa, his contention with Ratu Qara of Rewa was a displaced form of the ancient conflict within Bau between the ritual and warrior kings.

Here is another synergetic interaction in the event, a system of correlated antagonisms, making a kind of chiasmic structure, such that the outbreak of hostilities in one opposition would be magnified by the force of the other (Figure 4). It is a double "schismogenesis," with built-in dynamics of "deviation amplification." For on the principle that the enemies of one's enemies are one's friends—and the corollary that the friends of one's enemies are one's enemies—by stimulating any one rivalry in the system, the whole set of solidarities and hostilities will come into action. In the event, the showdown in Suva acquires a significance for Tanoa, again invisible in its characteristics as an empirical happening, that evokes a reaction proportionate to what has thus been put at issue—his own rule in Bau, as well as Bau's rule in Fiji.

Conclusions: Dimensions of the Event

In other studies I have in effect described the evenemential process as a "structure of the conjuncture," meaning the way the cultural catego-

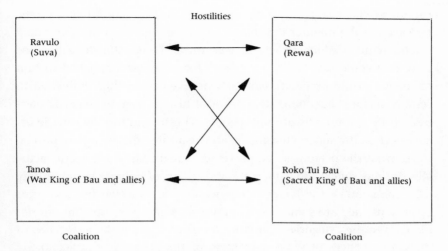

Fig. 4. Chiasmic structure of the conjuncture.

ries are actualized in a specific context through the interested action of the historic agents and the pragmatics of their interaction (Sahlins 1981; 1985:xiv, 125f., 152, etc.). The present essay is a development of the concept as it applies notably to internal events. From the concrete discussion of the origins of the Polynesian war, we can abstract some salient dimensions of the event-in-general.

The event unfolds as a conjunction of different structural planes respectively marked by phenomena of different order. It entails a dialogue between the larger relations and forces that constitute the historical object, such as the Fijian kingdoms whose history is at issue, and the local interactions through which this history runs its course. The synthesis requires complementary processes of mediation: the devolution of the global forces to the terms of the local action and conversely the expansion of local actions to global significance. It is thus half true that the event is a unique realization of a general structure. The other half is the realization of the unique event as a new general order.

Three moments may be distinguished in this dialectic of the event. First a moment of *instantiation* wherein the larger cultural categories of the history are represented by particular persons, objects, and acts, in the manner that Fijian lands are embodied in their ruling chiefs. With as much structural warrant as Louis XIV, the Fijian sacred king could say, "*l'état, c'est moi*," for whatever happened to him happened to the kingdom. Not only are collectives thus embodied in certain persons, but the course of social history may likewise be epitomized by certain acts of these people. The second moment is the *denouement* of the incarnated forces and relations, the incidents proper, being what the persons so empowered as main historical agents actually do and suffer. What they do and suffer, of course, is not simply the expression of the larger categories they are putting in play, since as persons they are subject to circumstances and interests that are not foreseen in the categories. The third moment, then, is the *totalization* of the consequences of what happened, or the return of the act to the system by the attribution of general meanings to particular incidents. The chief lost his wife to another—this was an attempt on the sovereignty; a pig was taken by a Rewa chief in Suva—this was defiance of the historic expansion of Bau. But it should be cautioned that in specifying these three "moments," one makes an analysis of the event that is not necessarily its sequence; the temporal relations are usually more complex.[34]

The dialectic of the event is symbolically constituted, the symbolism drawing on general structures of the cultural order, whence its intelligibility and efficacy. Instantiating a group in a person or a history in an episode, as also universalizing a chief's anger as an affair of state —these entail various kinds of metaphors and metonyms. Yet even when improvised, the play of tropes is never completely free. It is logically motivated in and engages existing cultural schemes, such as the Fijian cosmology of chiefship or theology of kinship.

I stress a point already noted: the three moments of the dialectic are also marked by structural discontinuities. Otherwise it would not be an event but the working out merely of the cultural order. What makes the event is a dynamics of the incident that alters the larger relations figuring there—that is, in the persons of the social-historical actors and their social-historical doings. And what makes the alteration of larger relations is the fact that in this lower-order incident, all kinds of considerations apart from the larger forces these actors instantiate, other forces of which they may be unaware, motivate them. Other beings and objects, with their own projects or causes and their own modes of action, affect them. Thus the famous "contingencies" of the event, with the effect of an "aleatory transition from one structure to another" (Le Roy Ladurie 1979:114). These other series, however, are not in themselves contingent. They are only so in relation to the object of historical study; in themselves, they may be quite systematic.[35] Here is a place, then, for psychohistory. For if by instantiation the totality devolves upon the person, and in the denouement the destiny of the first is submitted to the activity of the second, then society is decided by biography and—Durkheim and White forgive us —culture by psychology.

In the denouement the intersection of structures is itself structured. The global order enters into relations with diverse local orders. These are not just juxtapositions of, say, political forces and certain kinship connections. Since their intersection is through persons (thinking and feeling subjects), the different structures are in action put into definite relationships. *The structures interact in the medium of people's projects.* According to the nature and manner of the interaction, local structures can restrain, intensify, orient, and otherwise direct the development of larger historical forces. The main agent of a history of imperial expansion, the Bau war king Tanoa comes up against his royal maternal kin in the confrontation with Rewa. By virtue of the conduct appropriate to the uterine nephew (*vasu*), this link between kinship and kingdom established through Tanoa has an inhibiting effect on the military conduct of Bau. It took a series of untoward incidents to set off the destructive war with Rewa, culminating in the flight of Tanoa's Rewa wife to her homeland: a symbolic cancellation, this, of the kinship restraints on Bau's aggression. Whereas other structures of the conjuncture engaging Bau-Rewa relations in considerations of different orders had synergetic effects on the development of the conflict between them. One conflict is linked to another, the way Ratu Qara's quarrel with Suva and Bau was joined to his contention for power with his older brother, the Rewa king. So while his interest in the Rewa kingship would be served by exploits of violence against

Suva, the effect was to worsen the tenuous relations between Rewa and Bau—as it turned out, to the peril of the Rewa kingship. In the same general way the enmity of Rewa and Suva—by the *vasu* connections of their respective ruling chiefs—is displaced onto the frictions of the Bau dual kingship, which then allows Tanoa to strengthen his position in Bau by retaliating against Rewa.

These complex structures of the conjuncture are of different types, which would be well worth analyzing for their corresponding evenemential effects. But it would take another long paper.

Coda

Let me finish by referring to Georges Duby's great work *Le Dimanche de Bouvines* (1973), which has been a source of inspiration and instruction in the writing of this paper, though I have not much mentioned it. But as the present paper was written while Fiji was suffering the effects of a military coup, there is a passage in Duby's text about the difference between the medieval trials of sovereignty by battle and the methods of the modern-day tinhorn totalitarians that seems a fitting close to this reflection on the doings of Fijians chiefs of yore:

One sees why the last traces of the event disappear before our eyes. . . . Our times chase battles from memory. With reason. How would it be possible to remember an epoch when the chiefs of state sought to take each other's measure man-to-man, trusting their supremacy to the hand of God? In our day one scarcely sees the ruling power submitting itself to a test of arms or seeking its legitimacy in a victory. It is rather the reverse that happens. The renown, merited or not, of some dubious success, serves as a pretext for captains of greater or lesser stature to take power by force. When they hold it, they have no inclination to risk it. The war they wage is more shadowy, without overt battles. It employs other means, at once more insidious and more efficacious—means that truly destroy (Duby 1973:231).

Notes

1. The absence of reflection among historians on the nature of historical events has troubled more than one philosopher: "Curiously this question seems to have become of very little interest to historians, although what

is at stake is fundamental: what makes an event, an historical event?" (Molino 1986:265).

2. "The Annales school loathed the trio formed by political history, narrative history, and chronicle or episode (*événementielle*) history. All this, for them, was mere pseudo-history, history on the cheap, a superficial affair which preferred the shadow to the substance" (LeGoff 1972:340).

3. Hexter characterizes all this as Braudel's views on "the idiocy of the *événementielle*" (1979:100). On the antiquity of the oceanic metaphors, see Moretti (1986:187–88).

4. Not to neglect important studies of specific events that appeared about the same time, as Le Roy Ladurie's comments on the Chouan uprising (1972) and Georges Duby's great work on the battle of Bouvines (1973). In the same period (1972), Jacques LeGoff published the article "Is Politics Still the Backbone of History?"—the answer being a qualified *yes*.

5. "The great anthropologico-historical problem is to conceive history as a combination of auto-generative processes and hetero-generative processes (in which noise, event, accident contribute decisively to the evolution)" (Morin 1972a:13; cf. Morin 1972b).

6. Moretti observes that "one should not ignore the polemical exaggerations and the objections of *'politique culturelle'* present in most of the texts given to a [critical] 'discourse on the event'" (1986:190).

7. To an outsider it looks as if there are indeed structures of the long run, at least in historiography. One is reminded of Thucydides's dismissal of the marvelous reasons people gave for their actions in place of the deeper rationality he put into their mouths (in the famous speeches before the assembly). But as the Fijian said to the New Ethnographer, "That's enough talking about you; let's talk about me."

8. Lucien Febvre's original strictures on the evenemential historians' notions of elementary self-constituted "facts" had nothing to do with logical positivism—and still less with the positivism of Auguste Comte, of whom it can be said the Annales historians are modern heirs (Carbonell 1976:401 f.). The present sense of reproach in the term "positivism" comes from: (a) its common use to refer to the methods of the natural sciences; (b) the bad odor now atttached to the use of such methods in history and other human sciences (cf. Collingwood 1946).

9. I have in my possession a University of Chicago Libraries "Borrowers Card" (of a kind no longer used and now officially discarded) for the library's copy of Simiand's *Le salaire, l'évolution sociale et la monnaie*. It was borrowed on 18 July 1933 by "A. R.-Brown."

10. Although Lévi-Strauss has latterly taken to reconciling history and structure, for Saussure the opposition was a "radical antinomy": "One conse-

quence of the radical antinomy between the evolutionary and the static fact is that all notions associated with one or the other are to the same extent mutually irreducible. . . . The synchronic and diachronic 'phenomena', for example, have nothing in common. . . . One is a relation between simultaneous elements, the other the substitution of one element for another in time, an event" (Saussure 1966:91).

11. Moreover, the word *structure* is also an evident oversimplification. We shall see that what is characteristic of the event, or of the incident as event, is the connections it makes between different orders of structure (Sewell 1989)—alternatively, one could follow Sewell in speaking of different structures—in the culture of a given society.

12. I am aware of the looseness of the formulation of events as acts or incidents that change rather than simply implement structures. *Structure* here can mean anything from the state of relations between historic groups (as peace and war between nations) to institutional and categorical systems, depending on the choice of the historical object. There are also practical difficulties in distinguishing acts that reproduce an existing cultural order from those that alter it, insofar as every intelligible act is at once novel and continuous with the order (cf. Sahlins 1985). Cultural orders are event-systems, as they reproduce themselves by means of a world they do not themselves produce (Morin 1972a; 1972b). All this raises problems of the kinds and magnitudes of change necessary to qualify as "event." I deal with certain of these issues concretely only, in the following sections of the paper, leaving further consideration of the abstract problems to haunt me another time.

13. The Fijian name of the ruling town of Rewa is "Lomanikoro," although it has been called "Rewa" by Europeans since the early nineteenth century. I will continue the latter usage so long as the context makes the reference clear; otherwise I use "Lomanikoro." Notice of a few peculiarities of standard Fijian orthography will help in the pronunciation: *b* and *d* are prenasalized; *q* is near the "ng" sound in the English *finger*; *g* is the "ng" in *singer*; *c* is English "th."

14. I adopt the following conventions in translating Fijian political terms:

'State' or 'kingdom' for the Fijian *matanitū*, a term nowadays usually glossed as 'government'.

'Land' for *vanua*, the core of a state, a set of clans with a common history of migration and settlement, acknowledging a common ruler.

'Clan' for *mataqali*, a localized group, most of common patrilineal descent, having a status (*tutu*) and specialized office—such as priest, herald, carpenter—in the kingdom. A village usually has several such clans.

'Fighting allies' for *bati* and 'subject people' for *qali*: these are lands or states in their own right confederated with a given kingdom, the *bati* originally by negotiation and the *qali* traditionally by conquest. However, these lands, insofar as each is a 'land of itself' (*vanua vakai koya*), are apt to speak of themselves as independent, especially the *bati*.

What I call "confederacy" has no specific Fijian term, nor any determinate boundaries. It consists of a kingdom with its allied and subject lands, the latter being designated as lands of the dominant kingdom—e.g., Tokatoka (*a bati*) is a 'Rewan land' (*vanua vaka-Rewa*). However, the sense of the term *Rewan lands* or *Bauan lands* surpasses the actual political relations of the confederacy, for distant states traditionally connected to Rewa or Bau may be likewise so designated. For example, Nadrogā was of old a Rewan land, Lau a Bauan land, and so forth. Descriptions of the Bau and Rewa polities may be found in Waterhouse (1978[1866]), Toganivalu (1912), and Thomson (1908). Waterhouse gives some general account of the Bau-Rewa war, as do Williams and Calvert (1859, vol. 2), Wallis (1983 [1851]), Derrick (1946), Clunie (1977), Tippett (1973), Routledge (1985), and Sahlins (1987), among published sources. For a brief discussion of the unpublished sources see Sahlins 1987:326.

15. I hereafter translate Vunivalu as 'war king'. In the usual eastern Fijian hierarchy, this title is subordinate to the Roko Tui title, here glossed as 'sacerdotal king'—though not in Bau, where the rank of the two kings had been historically reversed (cf. Sahlins 1987). The title of the Rewa ruling king was Roko Tui Dreketi; here the Vunivalu was the second king. I do not want to make a big theoretical point by calling these rulers kings; it is mainly a convenient way of distinguishing the paramount from other *tūraga* or 'chiefs' (by the usual gloss).

16. "Ratu" is a Bauan honorific; the Rewan would be "Ro" or "Roko". However, Qaraniqio appears in contemporary missionary and later Fijian documents as "Ratu Qaraniqio" or "Ratu Qara," perhaps in testimony to his connection to the Roko Tui Bau through his mother (see below). His other names include Dakuwaqa and Lagivala (Longfellow). Kania was also known as Banuve and Bativudi.

17. As we shall see, Ratu Qara's liaison with his brother's wife was also the sign of his designs on the kingship. As a result of the quarrel with his brother that followed, Ratu Qara fled to Bau in late 1839 or early 1840. For what it is worth, one should note that contemporary European observers believed that an ensuing attempt of the Bau chief Cakobau to put things aright between the Rewa brothers by taking an atonement (*i soro*) to Kania on behalf of Ratu Qara contributed to the outbreak of the war. The offering

from Bau was refused; and when Ratu Qara soon after returned to Rewa and was reconciled with his brother without Bau help, Cakobau is supposed to have been miffed (Wallis 1983 [1851]:163). This never seemed an important incident to me, except as it may have contributed a bit to the erosion of the Tanoa-Kania solidarity, which was necessary for hostilities to begin but which was much more significantly affected by the flight of Tanoa's wife Qereitoga to Rewa (see below).

18. The Roko Tui Suva, Ravulo, is said to have single-handedly held off the Rewans at one of the town gates with a musket (Hocart FN:2508). It should be noted that the Suvans were well prepared, as the assault had been rumored for weeks in advance (Jaggar, Diaries:2 April 1842); according to the tradition, they were also forewarned by a Lami woman (Hocart FN:2508, 2564).

19. Even so, during a critical moment of the second assault, the Rewans were ready to back off until Ratu Qara rallied them. "You fly," the Suva tradition has him saying to the Rewan forces, "I shall go home to Rewa and die there; and you may get another chief" (Hocart FN:2565). See the remarks below on the identification of the people's cause with the chief's cause.

20. In two separate accounts collected by Hocart from Suva and Suvavou people, the well-known story of Bau's destruction of Rewa (in December 1845), when the Roko Tui Dreketi met his death, is connected as sequitur to Rewa's destruction of Suva (in April 1843; cf. Hocart, FN:2507f.; 2564f.).

21. Before Cakobau's visit, on 1 February 1843 a fleet left Lakeba carrying "property" to Bau, evidently a regular tribute. Included were: an "immense" new canoe, fifteen large packages of tapa cloth, some fifty tapa cloth mosquito screens, seven large bales of sinnet, ten whale teeth, and "the favorite daughter of the King" of Lau, the latter destined for Tanoa, who "is old enough to be her great-grandfather" (Williams 1931, 1:145 –46). When the Bau fleet arrived at Lakeba in May, it brought a relatively modest prestation for the Lau chief: two spears, more than thirty clubs, twenty whale teeth, one large kava root, and several hundred fathoms of Kadavu tapa cloth (ibid.:164). Apart from another large canoe and other things given Cakobau in May, the Bau party must have received an imcomparably greater return; we know not how much because Calvert and Williams left in August, before the departure of the Bauans, whose leaving would have been the occasion for substantial offerings of property by the Lau people.

22. The concourse of the famous Lasakau fisher-warriors of Bau was decisive in the restoration of Tanoa; they had been won over by Cakobau, among

other ways by the promise of a large number of canoes, which afterward were delivered through the Roko Tui Dreketi of Rewa, having been made by carpenters of Kadavu subject to Rewa (Cross, Diary:15 September 1838).

23. Bau and Rewa are "Kopaoo" and "Kolaiva" in Cook (1784, 1:368–69). I am indebted to Paul Geraghty for this information and the identifications of Cook's versions of Tongan pronunciations of Fijian names. Other early sources on the extent of Bau power include Lockerby 1925; Turpin, Diary; Dumont d'Urville 1832-34, 4:698ff.; Martin 1827.

24. Pierre Nora thus calls attention to the "nonevenemential" nature of the event, the large structural effects it carries. "The event is evidence less for what it translates than for what it reveals, less for what it is than for what it sets off" (1974:300–301).

25. Like Sartre's (1968) notion of "mediation," which was a stimulus to the present discussion, this process of instantiation is not a simple or direct reflection of larger groups such as social classes in individual acts. We shall see that the distinctiveness of the event develops from the imperfect reproduction of the larger system at the lower level, due to the intersection of other, local systems.

26. "The Roko Tui Bau was our 'human god.' He was the chief of the priests who attended the Vatanitawake [the principal temple of Bau]" (CSO–MP 5947/1917, testimony of Aisea Komaitai; cf. NLC/TR, Tailevu North). The same is said of the sacerdotal king of Cakaudrove: "In Thakaudrove only the chief (*turaga*) is believed in (*vakabau*); he is a human god (*e kalou tamata*)" (Hocart 1952:93; cf. 1970a:61; 1912:447; 1915). "The chiefs are the gods of Fiji" (Rakubu 1911:156; cf. Williams and Calvert 1859, 1: 183; Wallis 1983 [1851]:241; Waterhouse 1978 [1866]:338).

27. For some reason the Fijian is Bauan rather than the Cakaudrove dialect. The *vesa i sole mana* tied on the Tui Cakau's arm is 'the arm band of binding *mana*'. The last phrase of the text should be translated 'betroth the land to him'. The word for 'betroth' here, *musuka*, is notably used for the giving of chiefly women in marriage (Capell 1973:151).

28. The famous example is Ratu Mara Kapaiwai of Bau, first cousin of Cakobau, who was a great and feared *vasu* to Lau on the credentials of a woman of a former ruling line of Lau (Mataqali Cekena), who surrendered after battle to Ratu Mara's father's father (the Vunivalu, Banuve).

29. In major kingdoms the arrangement of betrothals of chiefly children—with an eye singular to the fortunes of the ruling house—was a primary function of the chief's herald, a chieftain of the land who generally acted as the ruler's man of affairs as well as ceremonial attendant. In the traditional

system this would be the 'inside-face-of-the-land' (*matanivanua e vale*), such as the Tunitoga of Bau, herald of the Vunivalu.

30. Shortly before the Bau-Rewa war a cousin of Tanoa, Komainaua, *vasu* to Cakaudrove, succeeded in stirring up the latter to military action against Bau, in all probability with a view toward an appropriation of power in Bau by Komainaua. In the same way, during the war, Tanoa rewarded his Rewa *vasu* Cokanauto, who defected to the Bau side, by installing him as ruler of Rewa, Roko Tui Dreketi.

31. Hocart cites a Fijian explanation of the term *matanitū* ('state' or 'government') that appeared in *Na Mata* in 1906: "In the old days, men used to seek their chiefs; they used to betroth ladies from various lands in which there was a noble line to marry into their own line so that her children might be noble and their land become a *matanitū* land thereafter" (HF:328; cf. Hocart 1970b:105–6).

32. The statement in Wilkes (1845, 3:206) to the effect that in 1840 the Suvans were "subjects of the king of Rewa" is an error. Wilkes indicates he was relaying information reported by a surveying party under the command of Lt. Emmons. But the relevant passage of Emmons's journal reads "subjects of the king of Bow," where Wilkes writes "subjects of the king of Rewa" (Emmons, Journal:19 May 1842). Wilkes always has to be watched.

33. This was the house of Nabaubau. In fact, the holder of the title Roko Tui Bau since the early nineteenth century descended from a member of the war king's clan (Tui Kaba) who was married into Nabaubau; he took the title in the absence of male heirs. No doubt the genealogical ambiguity was to the liking of the war kings. But the sacerdotal kingship itself would separate its holder from the war kings, since the title depended economically and politically on a different set of supporting clans and villages— who had not much use for the war king.

34. One can easily envision instances in other histories, instances of martyrdom, for example, in which the act as it were creates the instantiation and at the same time the totalization. But the same example would suggest the value of analytically separating the three moments of the event.

35. Compare Le Roy Ladurie's discussion of the Black Death, which was a catastrophic event in Europe and at the same time a systematic consequence of planetary history and epidemiology (Le Roy Ladurie 1979:112–13). But because the epidemic was systematic on a higher, planetary level, it was no less an event in France.

References Cited

Abbreviations

*	Unpublished material.
ML	Mitchell Library, Library of New South Wales, Sydney.
MOM	Methodist Overseas Mission.
PMB	Pacific Manuscripts Bureau, Australian National University Canberra, Microfilm Series.
SOAS	Library of the School of Oriental and African Studies, University of London.

Citations

Anonymous
1891   Ai tukutuku kei Ratu Radomodomo Ramatenikutu na Vunivalu mai Bau. Wase V, *Na Mata*, Mei:9–11.

Aron, Raymond
1981   *Introduction à la philosophie de l'histoire*. Paris: Gallimard.

Bastide, Roger
1980   Événement. *Encyclopaedia Universalis* 6:822–24.

Bloch, Marc
1953   *The Historian's Craft*. New York: Vintage Books.

Braudel, Fernand
1972   *The Mediterranean and the Mediterranean World in the Age of Philip II*. Tr. Sian Reynolds. 2 vols. New York: Harper & Row.

1980   *On History*. Tr. Sarah Matthews. Chicago: University of Chicago Press.

Burguière, Andre
1988   L'anthropologie historique. In *La nouvelle histoire*, ed. Jacques LeGoff. Paris: Éditions Complexe.

CSO–MP 5947/1917
*MP   Inquiry relating to chiefly privileges at Bau. Colonial Secretary's Office Minute Paper 5947, 11 July 1917. National Archives of Fiji.

Calvert, James
*Journals   James Calvert Papers, MMS Collection, SOAS (South Seas box 1).

Campbell, I. C.
1980   The Historiography of Charles Savage. *Journal of the Polynesian Society* 89:143–66.

Capell, A.
1973   *A New Fijian Dictionary.* 4th ed. Suva: Government Printer.
Carbonell, Charles-Olivier
1976   *Histoire et historiens: une mutation ideologique des historiens français 1865–1885.* Toulouse: Privat.
Cargill, David
1977   *The Diaries and Correspondence of David Cargill. 1832–1843.* Ed. Albert J. Schutz. Canberra: Australian National University Press.
Clunie, Fergus
1977   *Fijian Weapons and Warfare.* Bulletin of the Fiji Museum, no. 2. Suva: Fiji Museum.
Collingwood, R. G.
1946   *The Idea of History.* Oxford: Clarendon Press.
Cook, James, and James King
1784   *A Voyage to the Pacific Ocean . . . in His Majesty's Ships Resolution and Discovery.* 3 vols. Dublin: Chamberlaine et al.
Council of Chiefs
*1875   Unpublished printed proceedings of the Native Council, or Council of Chiefs, from 1875 to 1910. Suva: National Archives of Fiji.
Cross, Reverend William
*Extracts   Extracts from Letters and Diary, 1839–1842. ML (B686).
*Diary   Diary of Reverend William Cross, 28 December 1837 –1 October 1842 (ML/MOM 336).
*Journal   Extracts of the Journal of William Cross, sent to General Secretaries, Wesleyan Missionary Society Collection, SOAS (box 553).
Derrick, R.A.
1946   *A History of Fiji.* Suva: Government Press.
Duby, Georges
1973   *Le Dimanche de Bouvines.* Paris: Gallimard.
Dumont, Louis
1970   *Homo Hierarchicus.* Chicago: University of Chicago Press.
Dumont d'Urville, J. S. C.
1832–34   *Voyages de découvertes autour du monde et à la recherche de la Pérouse . . . sur la corvette L'Astrolabe pendent les années 1826 –1829.* Paris: Tastu.
Eagleston, John H.
*UD   Ups and Downs through Life. Manuscript autobiography of Captain John H. Eagleston. Salem: Peabody Museum.

Emmons, George Foster
   *Journal   Journals of George Foster Emmons on U.S. Exploring Expedition, 1838–42, in the Pacific. Beinecke Library, Yale University (Western Americana 166; microfilm copy).

Evans-Pritchard, E. E.
   1937   *Witchcraft, Oracles and Magic among the Azande.* Oxford: Clarendon Press.

France, Peter
   1969   *The Charter of the Land.* Melbourne: Oxford University Press.

Furet, François
   1982   *L'Atelier de l'histoire.* Paris: Flammarion.

Gallie, W. B.
   1968   *Philosophy and the Historical Understanding.* 2d ed. New York: Schocken Books.

Giddens, Anthony
   1976   *New Rules of Sociological Method.* London: Hutchinson.
   1982   *Profiles and Critiques in Social Theory.* Berkeley and Los Angeles: University of California Press.
   1984   *The Constitution of Society.* Berkeley and Los Angeles: University of California Press.

Gordon-Cumming, C. F.
   1882   *At Home in Fiji.* Edinburgh: William Blackwood and Sons.

Graeber, David
   *1987   The Generalization of Avoidance: Manners and Money in Early Modern Europe. M.A. dissertation, Department of Anthropology, University of Chicago.

Gruner, Rolf
   1969   *The Notion of an Historical Event.* Aristotelian Society Supplementary Volume 43:141–52.

Hexter, J. H.
   1979   *On Historians.* Cambridge, Mass.: Harvard University Press.

Hocart, A. M.
   1912   On the Meaning of Kalou and the Origin of Fijian Temples. *Journal of the Royal Anthropological Institute* 42:437–49.
   1915   Chieftainship and the Sister's Son in the Pacific. *American Anthropologist* 17:631–46.
   1923   The Uterine Nephew. *Man* 4:11–13.
   1929   *Lau Islands. Fiji.* Bernice P. Bishop Museum Bulletin no. 62. Honolulu: The Museum.
   1950   *Caste.* New York: Russell and Russell.

1952   *The Northern States of Fiji*. Royal Anthropological Institute of
              Great Britain and Ireland, Occasional Publication no. 11.
1969[1927]
              Kingship. Oxford: Oxford University Press (reissue).
1970a[1936]
              Kings and Councillors. Chicago: University of Chicago Press.
1970b   *The Life-Giving Myth and Other Essays*. London: Tavistock.
*HF   The Heart of Fiji. Turnbull Library, Wellington.
*FN   Fijian Field Notes. Turnbull Library, Wellington.
Hooper, Steven
*1982   A Study of Valuables in the Chiefdom of Lau, Fiji. Ph.D.
              dissertation, Department of Anthropology, Cambridge Uni-
              versity.
Hunt, John
*Journal   Fiji Journal of John Hunt, 2 vols., 1839–47. Methodist Mis-
              sionary Society Collection, SOAS (South Seas box 5B).
Jackson, John
1967[1853]
              Jackson's Narrative. In John E. Erskine, *Journal of a Cruise
              among the Islands of the Western Pacific*. Originally published
              in 1853. London: Dawsons of Pall Mall.
Jaggar, Thomas J.
*Diaries   Diaries of Thomas James Jaggar, 1837–43. National Ar-
              chives of Fiji.
*Letters   In-Letters, vol. 4, 1844–51, MMS Collection, SOAS.
Jayawardena, Chandra
1987   Analysis of a Social Situation in Aceh Basur: An Exploration
              in Micro-History. *Social Analysis* 22:30–41.
Johansen, J. Prytz
1954   *The Maori and His Religion*. Copenhagen: Munksgaard.
LeGoff, Jacques
1972   Is Politics Still the Backbone of History? In *Historical Studies
              Today*, ed. Felix Gilbert and Stephen R. Graubard. New York:
              Norton.
LeGoff, Jacques, ed.
1988   *La nouvelle histoire*. Paris: Éditions complexe.
LeGoff, Jacques, and Pierre Nora, eds.
1974   *Faire de l'histoire: I, Nouveaux problèmes*. Paris: Gallimard.

Le Roy Ladurie, Emmanuel
1972   Événement et longue durée dans l'histoire sociale: l'exemple chouan. *Communications* 18:72–84.
1979   *The Territory of the Historian.* Chicago: University of Chicago Press.

Lester, R. H.
1941–42   Kava-drinking in Viti Levu, Fiji. *Oceania* 12:97–121, 226–54.

Lévi-Strauss
1963   *Structural Antrhopology.* New York: Basic Books.
1966   *The Savage Mind.* Chicago: University of Chicago Press.

Lockerby, William
1825   *The Journal of William Lockerby Sandalwood Trader in the Fijian Islands during the Years 1808–1809.* Ed. Sir Everard Im Thurn. London: The Hakluyt Society.

Lyth, Richard B.
*Letters   Letters to and from Rev. Dr. R. B. Lyth, 1836–54. ML (A836).
*Daybook   Daybook and Journal, 11 August 1850–31 December 1851. ML (B539).
*Journal   Journal 1836–42, ML (B533); 1842–44, ML (B534); 1845–48, ML (B535); 1848–50, ML (B536); 1852, ML (B540); 1852–53, ML (B541); 1853–60, ML (B542).
*T/F   Tongan and Feejeean Reminiscences. 2 vols. ML (B549).
*Remin   Reminiscences 1851–53, ML (B548).

MMS
*Letters   In-letters of the Methodist Missionary Society. Methodist Missionary Society Collection, SOAS (box 533).

Martin, John
1827   *An Account of the Natives of These Tonga Islands . . . Compiled and Arranged from the Extensive Communication of Mr. William Mariner.* 2 vols., 3d ed. Edinburgh: Constable et al.

Moles, Abraham A.
1972   Notes pour une typologie des événements. *Communications* 18:90–96.

Molino, J.
1986   L'événement: de la logique à la semiologie. In *L'Événement (Actes du colloque organisé à Aix-en-Provence par le Centre Méridional d'Histoire Sociale . . . 1983).* Aix-en-Provence: Université de Provence.

Moretti, M.
1986   Fragments d'une analyse historiographique: origines et premiers developpements d'un 'discours sur l'événement' dans

l'experience des 'Annales'. In *L'Événement (Actes du colloque organisé à Aix-en-Provence par le Centre Méridional d'Histoire Sociale . . . 1983)*. Aix-en-Provence: Université de Provence.

Morin, Edgar
  1972a   Le retour de l'événement. *Communications* 18:6—20.
  1972b   L'événement-sphinx. *Communications* 18:173—92.

NLC/TR
  *Tailevu North
             Ai Tukutuku Raraba, Tailevu North: Tikina ko Bau, Yavusa Kubuna. Suva: Native Lands Commission.

Nora, Pierre
  1974   Le retour de l'événement. In *Faire de l'histoire: 1, Nouveaux problèmes*, ed. Jacques LeGoff and Pierre Nora. Paris: Gallimard.

Osborn, Joseph Warren
  *Journal   Journal of a Voyage in the Ship Emerald . . . during the Years 1832.4.5.6. PMB 223. (Original in Peabody Museum, Cambridge.)

Parry, John T.
  1977   *Ring-Ditch Fortifications of the Rewa Delta*. Bulletin of the Fiji Museum no. 3. Suva: Fiji Museum.

Pomian, Krzysztof
  1988   L'histoire des structures. In *La nouvelle histoire*, ed. Jacques LeGoff. Paris: Éditions Complexe.

Rabuku, Niko
  1911   Ai Sau ni Taro me Kilai. *Na Mata*: 154—58, 172—76.

Radcliffe-Brown, A. R.
  1952   *Structure and Function in Primitive Society*. London: Cohen and West.
  1957   *A Natural Science of Society*. Glencoe: The Free Press.

Ricoeur, Paul
  1965   *History and Truth*. Evanston: Northwestern University Press.
  1980   *The Contribution of French Historiography to the Theory of History*. Oxford: Clarendon Press.
  1984   *Time and Narrative*, vol. 1. Chicago: University of Chicago Press.

Routledge, David
  1985   *Matanitu: The Struggle for Power in Early Fiji*. Suva: University of the South Pacific.

Sahlins, Marshall
1981   *Historical Metaphors and Mythical Realities.* A.S.A.O. Special Publication no. 1. Ann Arbor: University of Michigan Press.
1983   Raw Women, Cooked Men, and Other "Great Things" of the Fiji Islands. In *The Ethnography of Cannibalism,* ed. Paula Brown and Donald Tuzin. Special Publication, Society for Psychological Anthropology. Washington, D.C.: The Society.
1985   *Islands of History.* Chicago: University of Chicago Press.
1987   War in the Fiji Islands: The Force of Custom, and the Custom of Force. In *International Ethics in the Nuclear Age,* ed. Robert J. Myers, Ethics and Foreign Policy Series, vol. 4. Lanham, Md.: University Press of America.
1988   Deserted Islands of History. *Critique of Anthropology* 8:41–51.
Sartre, Jean-Paul
1968   *Search for a Method.* Tr. Hazel E. Barnes. New York: Vintage Books.
Saussure, Ferdinand de
1966 [1915] *Course in General Linguistics.* New York: McGraw-Hill (First French edition, 1915.)
Sayes, Shelley Ann
*1982   Cakaudrove: Ideology and Reality in a Fijian Confederation. Ph.D. dissertation, Department of Public and Southeast Asian History, Research School of Pacific Studies, Australian National University.
Scarr, Deryck
1970   Cakobau and Ma'afu: Contenders for Pre-eminence in Fiji. In *Pacific Island Portraits,* ed. J. W. Davidson and Deryck Scarr. Wellington: A. H. & A. W. Reed.
Sewell, William
*1989   *Toward a Theory of Structure: Duality, Agency and Transformation.* Working Paper no. 392. Center for the Comparative Study of Social Transformations at the University of Michigan.
Simiand, François
1903   Méthode historique et science sociale: étude critique d'après les ouvrages récents de M. Lacombe et de M. Seignobos. *Revue de Synthèse Historique* 6:1–22, 129–57.
Stone, Lawrence
1981   *The Past and the Present.* Boston: Routledge & Kegan Paul.

Teggart, F. J.
1960   *Theory and Processes of History*. Berkeley and Los Angeles: University of California Press.
Thomson, Basil
1908   *The Fijians: A Study of the Decay of Custom*. London: William Heinemann.
Tippett, A. R.
1973   *Aspects of Pacific Ethnohistory*. Pasadena: William Carey Library.
Toganivalu, Ratu Deve
1912   The Customs of Bau before the Advent of Christianity. *Transactions of the Fijian Society for the Year 1911*.
*n.d.   Ai Tukutuku kei Bau. National Archives of Fiji (F62/247).
Turpin, Edwin J.
*Diary   Diary and Narratives of Edwin J. Turpin. National Archives of Fiji (MS 1).
Valeri, Valerio
1985   *Kingship and Sacrifice: Ritual and Society in Ancient Hawaii*. Chicago: University of Chicago Press.
VQ
*1947   Veitarogi ni Qoliqoli. Inquiry into Fishing Rights in Viti Levu, 1947. Suva: Native Lands Commission.
Veyne, Paul
1984   *Writing History*. Middletown, Conn.: Wesleyan University Press.
Vovelle, Michel
1988   L'histoire et la longue durée. In *La nouvelle histoire*, ed. Jacques LeGoff. Paris: Éditions Complexe.
Wall, Colman
1919   Sketches in Fijian History. *Transactions of the Fijian Society for the Year 1919*.
Wallis, Mary (A Lady)
1983[1851] *Life in Feejee . . . or . . . Five Years among the Cannibals. By a Lady*. Suva: Fiji Museum; facsimile of 1851 edition. Boston: William Heath.
Waterhouse, Joseph
1978[1866] *The King and People of Fiji*. AMS Press; facsimile of the original 1866 edition. London: Wesleyan Conference.
Wilkes, Charles
1844   *Atlas. Narrative of the United States Exploring Expedition during*

the Years *1838, 1839, 1840, 1841, 1842.* Philadelphia: C. Sherman.

1845   *Narrative of the United States Exploring Expedition during the Years 1838, 1839, 1840, and 1842,* vol. 3. Philadelphia: Lea and Blanchard.

Williams, Thomas

1931   *The Journal of Thomas Williams: Missionary in Fiji, 1840–1853.* 2 vols. Ed. G. C. Henderson. Sydney: Angus, Robertson.

Williams, Thomas, and James Calvert

1859   *Fiji and the Fijians.* 2 vols. New York: Appleton.

3. The Transformation of a Transformation

A Structural Essay on an Aspect of Hawaiian History (1809 to 1819)

Valerio Valeri

for Marshall Sahlins

Leur zèle dans la recherche est grand.

Maintes fois, à ce qu'on m'assure, des spectateurs de la race des ordonnateurs sont entrés dans la chambre aux transformations, où pourtant fréquemment des accidents graves ou la mort même atteignent l'adulte qui s'y expose, entré là dans l'espoir d'une rénovation.

Un obscurcissement de l'ancienne personnalité y est presque fatal. Mais ils s'y livrent sans regret, pour l'exaltant culte de la Métamorphose qui pétrit chairs et terre [. . .]

Vous avez vu Poddema sous un signe. Elle a vécu sous d'autres. Elle vivra sous d'autres encore. Métamorphose! Métamorphose, qui engloutit et refait des métamorphoses. Chez nous, un moment ouvre un océan de siècles.

—Henri Michaux, "Ici, Poddema," in *Ailleurs*

This essay, originally published in *Social Analysis* no. 10, May 1982, was written as a diachronic complement to my synchronic study of the Hawaiian political-ritual system in the second half of the eighteenth century (Valeri 1985a). Its main purpose is to bring to light and explain some hitherto unrecognized transformations of this system as reflected in the complex of temples attached to King Kamehameha's last residence in Kailua during the second decade of the nineteenth century.

On the one hand, the analysis of these transformations seems to vindicate the sincerity of Kamehameha's repeated claims of religious conservatism (for a statement made just before his death, see Kotzebue 1821:311). Indeed, as Sahlins (1981:46) points out, the very move to Kailua, away from the degrading commercialism of Honolulu, was motivated by the king's preoccupation with preserving the purity of the traditional ritual base of kingship.

But on the other hand my analysis also shows that the temple complex in Kailua translated in an outwardly traditional form certain changes that had occurred in Hawaiian society and that were undermining the traditional system of kingship. In this respect I hope to have furnished here another piece of the puzzle of the quick abolition of the traditional political-ritual system a few months after Kamehameha's death in 1819.

Since 1982, we have learned more about some of the points discussed here, particularly from Sahlins's *Islands of History* (1985). Nevertheless, I find little to change in my interpretation of the facts or in my general outlook on the relationship between structural analysis and historiography (cf. Valeri 1990). Therefore the essay is reprinted here unchanged, except for minimal stylistic and bibliographic adjustments.

0. Introduction

I begin my paper with a discussion of the available information on the royal temples of Honolulu and Kailua during the period 1809 to 1819. This discussion is necessary because of certain obscurities in the literature and because the systematic character of the relationships between and among the temples has so far remained unrecognized.

In order to follow this discussion it is necessary to keep in mind a few facts about the classification of the Hawaiian male gods. Many of them—not unlike Greek or Roman gods (cf. Gernet and Boulanger 1932:266–67)—have a binomial name, a feature that points to the fact that they are particularized forms of four major gods: Kū, Lono, Kāne, Kanaloa, in order of their importance. These "major gods" should be considered more as "categories of the divine" than as personal gods. It is their particularized forms that are the object of most cults, although it is possible to have recourse to the unmarked forms in an unmarked cultic situation or when the totality of the aspects of a major god is involved. The suffix added to the god category specifies which aspect of the god is being worshiped and it often indexes the worshiper as well. Thus Kūkā'ilimoku ('Kū-island-snatcher') is a violent warlike form of Kū, particularly associated with the ruling dynasty of the island of Hawai'i, to which Kamehameha belonged. The war gods of the other dynasties are also particularizations of Kū, but they have different names.

Among the suffixed forms of the four major gods, those that are suffixed by -nuiākea ('vast expanse') coincide with the god category. Consider, for instance, Kānenuiākea. Stokes, summarizing information obtained from Hawaiian sources, defines him as "a general name of a class of gods," that is, the class of the Kāne gods (Stokes n.d.:GR 2 box 2.2). Pukui and Elbert (1971:391), for their part, define Kūnuiākea as "the head of all the Kū gods," encompassing all the other forms, including Kūkā'ilimoku (cf. Beckwith 1940:26; Kauhane 1865).

Although the unmarked forms of the gods and those that are suffixed by -nuiākea are identical from the extensional point of view, the latter are more personalized than the former. The four god categories encompass, through their particularized forms, every aspect of reality (Handy 1972:23; Handy 1968). They are brought into relationship with society by the rituals connected with kingship.

Although there are four major gods, two of them, Kāne and Kanaloa, are hardly separable. As Beckwith (1940:60) remarks: "about Kanaloa as a god apart from Kāne there is very little information" (cf. Emerson 1892:16). As a matter of fact, these two gods are twins (Kumulipo v. 1714 in Beckwith 1951:230; cf. Bastian 1881:131–32; Liliuokalani 1897:23, 65; Marcuse 1894:97). Thus, underlying the quadripartition of the pantheon, we find a tripartition, with Kanaloa as an adjunct to Kāne. In fact, as we shall see, the major gods associated with the royal temples in Honolulu and Kailua are Kū, Lono, and Kāne. Kanaloa is never mentioned as having his own temple in the temple complexes associated with the royal residence in Honolulu and Kailua.

However, in the course of the paper, another divine triad will appear even more important. This triad is formed by Lono and the two most import forms of Kū: Kūnuiākea and Kūkā'ilimoku. Ultimately, it is the couple Kū/Lono that is crucial.

1. The Royal Temple Complex in Honolulu (1809 to 1812)

When he returned to O'ahu, in the fall of 1803 or in the winter of 1804 (Kuykendall 1938:47–49), Kamehameha took up residence in Waikīkī, the traditional seat of O'ahu royalty. We know that he stayed there at least until 1807 (Iselin n.d.:75; see also Patterson 1817:65–67) and that in 1809 he had already moved to Honolulu (Campbell 1967 [1822]:91).

Unfortunately, we do not have information on the structure of the royal residence in Waikīkī or on the temples attached to it. We only know that Kamehameha did not live far from Le'ahi, the site of the *luakini* temple of Papa'ena'ena, which was dedicated to Kū. The *luakini* were temples of human sacrifice in which the most important rituals controlled by the kings were performed.[1] These rituals concerned either war or the promotion of agriculture: in other words, either the conquest of the land or its fertilization by the king (Malo n.d., ch. 36 v. 78; ch. 37 v. 10).

From the time King Kahekili conquered O'ahu (traditional date: 1783; see Kamakau 1961:136; Fornander 1880, 2:222–27), Papa'ena'ena had been the most important temple of the island (Stewart 1830:298).[2] Since 1804 at least (Ii 1963:33–37), Liholiho—the sacred son of Kamehameha—had had the main role in its rituals. It is likely that this continued to be the case after the court moved to nearby Honolulu.

The temple complex constructed in association with the new royal residence is described by 'Ī'ī in these terms:

There was a beach there, and heiau ['temple'] houses, each one enclosed with a fence. Wooden female images stood outside of each enclosure, with *iholena* and *popo'ulu* bananas in front of them. There were *maoli* bananas before the male images at the *lele* altar inside the enclosure of lama wood. Back of the male images of wood was an *'anu'u* tower, about 8 yards (*iwilei*) high and 6 yards wide. It stood on the right side of the house, and was covered with strips of white *'oloa* tapa attached to the sticks resembling thatching sticks. The *opu* tower was just as tall and broad as the *'anu'u*, and was wrapped in an *'aeokahaloa* tapa that resembled a *moelola* tapa. The small lama branches at its top were like unruly hair, going every which way. The *opu* stood on the left side of the house, facing the images and the *'anu'u*. Between the two towers and extending from one to the other was a fine pavement of stones. In line with the middle of the pavement were the gate and the house which was called the Hale o Lono, where Liholiho was staying. It was thatched with dried ti leaves, just as Hale o Keawe in Honaunau, Hawaii, was thatched. Houses of this kind were all thatched with ti leaves, and all the posts and beams were of lama wood. The Hale o Lono was like a heiau. There were two others like it in the vicinity, one called the Hale Hui and the other, Hale o Kaili. The Hale Hui was the dwelling for miscellaneous gods and Hale o Kaili was for the god Kaili, or Kukailimoku (Ii 1963:56– 58; originally published in *Ka Nupepa Kuokoa*, 31 July 1869).

This text suggests that three houses or chapels—each "like a heiau" —were included in this temple complex:

(1) *Hale o Kā'ili* ('house of Kā'ili'): This was where Kamehameha's war god, Kū in his form Kūkā'ilimoku ('Kū-island-snatcher')—often abbreviated to Kā'ili —was kept (ibid.:58). Here Kamehameha himself worshiped.

(2) *Hale o Lono* ('house of Lono'): This temple, consecrated to the god Lono, was the ritual residence of Liholiho for the greater part of each month (ibid.:56 –58).

(3) *Hale hui* ('house for miscellaneous gods'): It is likely that this chapel was similar to the royal *hale hui 'ili mai'a* ('house for miscellaneous gods [but also: 'meeting house'] lined with banana fiber sheathing') at Kailua, which I shall discuss later (ibid.:123). This house contained Kamehameha's gods of political sorcery. Perhaps Honolulu's *hale hui* coincided with the *hale hui* that Ī'ī mentions in another context (ibid.:64) and that functioned as Kamehameha's *hale mua* or 'ritual eating house' (cf. Ross 1904:63).

Near the temple complex and, perhaps significantly, near the house of Kalanimoku, Kamehameha's "prime minister" (ibid.:91), were situated additional houses containing important sorcery gods (Kālaipāhoa, Kihawahine, etc.).[3] These too must have been *hale 'ili mai'a*, like the corresponding ones in Kailua (Kamakau 1964:135; 1961:179–80).

The description of "the King's morai ['temple']" given by Ross—who visited Honolulu in 1811—seems to confirm that, contrary to what Rockwood's map and reconstruction of the *hale o Lono* (in Ii 1963: 57, 65), in conjunction with the ambiguities of 'Ī'ī's text, may lead one to think, the *hale o Kā'ili*, *hale o Lono*, and *hale hui* were three different chapels in the same complex and not three separate temples.

It consisted of five low, gloomy and pestiferous houses, huddled close together; and alongside of the principal one stood an image made of wood, resembling a pillar, about 28 feet high, in the shape of the human figure, cut and covered with various devices; the head large, and the rude sculpture on it presenting the likeness of a human face, covered on the top with a black cowl. About thirty yards from the houses, all round about, was a clear spot called the "king's tabooed ground," surrounded by an enclosure. This sacred spot is often rigorously tabooed and set apart for penance (Ross 1904:65).

Two of the five "houses" mentioned by Ross could in fact be the "towers" mentioned by 'Ī'ī. A foreigner would not be able to tell the difference between a "tower" and a "house," since the former had proportions (8 yards high and 6 yards wide, according to 'Ī'ī) that would make differentiating it from a house difficult when it was seen at a distance. Three "real" houses are left: one could be identified with the *hale o Kā'ili*, another with the *hale o Lono*, and the third one with the *hale hui* "for the miscellaneous gods" (Ii 1963: 58). It seems likely that this last chapel was less important and noticeable than the other two, since Franchère, who was a companion of Ross, mentions only two "temples" that were attached to the "royal palace" (Franchère 1820:49).[4]

The material realization of each *hale* in fact matters little, since this term may refer both to a simple chapel and to a complex including several structures (see Valeri 1985a: 173–86).[5] For this reason I call "temple" any structure, whatever its complexity and scale, that houses a god (as well as other deities attached to him).

The material arrangement adopted in the royal residence at Honolulu, however, emphasizes that the different "temples" built there were conceived as part of one single system associated with kingship. This system is translated there into a visible whole. Hence its exemplary value for our attempt at analyzing the conceptual relationships between and among royal temples.

Before we proceed further, an important feature of the site chosen for building the royal chapels must be noted. It appears that it was identical with that of the temple of Pākākā, which, until 1783, had housed Kūhone'enu'u, the war god of the O'ahu dynasty (Kamakau 1865b; see also Westervelt 1915:27). In all probability, the image of that god was kept, along with that of Kūkā'ilimoku, in the *hale o Kā'ili*, thereby contributing to ensure Kamehameha's grip on the island (cf. Kamakau 1964:135).

The connection of Liholiho's and Kamehameha's chapels with the site of the old Pākākā temple is demonstrated by the fact that they were near the canoe landing of the same name, which was traditionally associated with the temple (see Rockwood 1957; Elbert n.d., 3:610; Pukui et al. 1974:175), and by a statement contained in a land case (Equity 200:9).[6] Apparently, Stokes even believed that 'Ī'ī's description of the temple houses quoted above referred to the traditional Pākākā temple (see Stokes n.d.:GR 2 box 2.4; GR 1 box 8.33). In support of this hypothesis, he gave an excerpt from Kamakau's 1865 article pertaining to the ancient temple and its god (1865b), with an excerpt from 'Ī'ī's text quoted above (whose authorship Stokes ignored; n.d.:GR 1 box 8.33). Some years later, the archeologist McAllister transformed Stokes's hypothesis into a "proven fact" by patching the two excerpts together and giving them as a single continuous text, which he attributed to S. M. Kamakau alone (McAllister 1933:81).[7] In fact, neither 'Ī'ī nor Kamakau explicitly indicate a connection between the temples built in 1809 and the old Pākākā temple. Nevertheless, this connection existed as we have seen. Indeed, it was usual for the conqueror to build his temple on the ruins of the temple of the conquered.

2. The Royal Temple Complex in Kailua (1813 to 1819)

Toward the end of 1812, Kamehameha and Liholiho returned to the island of Hawai'i. At the beginning of 1813, they settled in Kailua (Ii 1963:113; Barrère 1975:2). The royal temples conceptually associated with this new residence were the following:

(1) The *luakini* temple of Hikiau, situated at Kealakekua, at some

distance from Kailua. Being the highest ranking *luakini* temple of the district (Kona) in which the king resided (Ii 1963:115; cf. 160), Hikiau housed the highest ranking god: Kū in his all-encompassing form (cf. Pukui and Elbert 1971:391), called Kūnuiākea, 'Kū of the wide expanse' (King 1967:621, cf. 506, 516). This temple was connected with Liholiho, who, in 1801 or 1802 (Kamakau 1961:187–88) had become the head of the royal cults, thereby assuming the highest prerogatives of kingship. These involved a connection with the supreme form of Kū. Consequently, Liholiho regularly officiated in Hikiau at the beginning and end of each lunar month (Ii 1963: 123; cf. Laanui 1930 [1838]) and at any other important occasion.

(2) A second *luakini* temple was situated in Kailua proper. It was the temple named Keikipu'ipu'i, which, according to tradition, had originally been built by King Liloa, an ancestor of the dynasty to which Kamehameha and Liholiho belonged. It had been rebuilt or restored as a temple of the war god Kūkā'ilimoku (Fornander 1880, 2:52; cf. Stokes n.d.:GR 1 box 9.48, p. 16; Thrum 1908:70) in preparation for King Kalani'ōpu'u's war against Kahekili, king of Maui. Shortly before 1794 (Vancouver 1801, 5:100–103; Barrère 1975:4), Kamehameha had restored it again, as a preliminary to his expedition against Maui and O'ahu (which he conquered in 1795).

Since Keikipu'ipu'i had been a temple of Kūkā'ilimoku, one would expect it to correspond to Kamehameha's *hale o Kā'ili* in Honolulu. The fact is that in 1813 it was restored (Kamakau 1961:203; Marin 1973: 211) as a temple of Liholiho, *not* of Kamehameha, and no mention is made of a connection with Kūkā'ilimoku at that time. On the contrary, we know that this god continued to be associated with Kamehameha, and that its image was kept in the king's personal temple, 'Ahu'ena, together with sorcery gods (Ellis 1842, 4:427).

(3) Near Keikipu'ipu'i a *hale o Lono* was built and this became, as in Honolulu, the ordinary ritual residence of Liholiho (Ii 1963:110, 121).

(4) At some distance from the complex Keikipu'ipu'i *hale o Lono* were situated Kamehameha's residence (ibid.:119) and his personal temple, called 'Ahu'ena (ibid.:122–23). Like Keikipu'ipu'i, the original 'Ahu'ena had been built, according to tradition, by King Liloa, probably

as a war temple (Thrum 1907:43; Ellis 1842, 4:427). In all likelihood, it was renovated by several predecessors of Kamehameha (Barrère 1975:7). In 1813, Kamehameha rebuilt it as a *hale hui 'ili mai'a* (Ii 1963:123), a temple for sorcery gods (Kamakau 1961:179). It corresponded, therefore, to the *hale hui 'ili mai'a* of Honolulu.[8] However, as in Honolulu, the sorcery gods Kālaipāhoa, Kihawahine, and so forth, were housed in separate *hale 'ili mai'a* (Kamakau 1964:135; 1961:179 –80).[9]

Before addressing the question of the homologies and differences between the Kailua and the Honolulu systems, a few points must be discussed in order to add to our information or to assess parts of it. From 1813 to 1819, Liholiho, following the ritual calendar, alternately officiated in Hikiau, the main *luakini* temple of the island of Hawai'i', and in the *hale o Lono* at Kailua. This alternation manifested his role in connecting the two main forms of worship: the worship of Kū and the worship of Lono (Malo 1951:159). We have no direct proof that he had also officiated at both the *luakini* temple of Papa'ena'ena and the temple of Lono in Honolulu, when he lived there from 1809 to 1812; but this seems likely, since Papa'ena'ena was the main temple of the island O'ahu, as Hikiau was the main temple of the island of Hawai'i. It seems reasonable to infer that Liholiho, as "head of the worship" and therefore, as we shall see, principal king, had to maintain a regular relationship with Papa'ena'ena, as he did later with Hikiau. Moreover, it was precisely in Papa'ena'ena that Liholiho's position as "head of worship" was reconfirmed in 1804 (Ii 1963:33–37).

A further conclusion may be drawn from the structural equivalence of Hikiau and Papa'ena'ena. We know for sure that the main god in Hikiau was Kū in the form of Kūnuiākea (King 1967:621); we are not informed by our sources on the identity of the main god in Papa'ena'ena. However, he must have been Kūnuiākea because this god was usually associated with the principal temple of a kingdom.

We must, however, discuss a document that, at first sight, seems to prove that there existed—in 1804 at any rate—a connection between Papa'ena'ena and Kūkā'ilimoku. This is the prayer with which, in 1804, Liholiho consecrated three human sacrifices in that temple. The prayer begins in this way:

O Ku, Kukailimoku,
Ku of the bitter path,
Lononuiakea,
Kane and Kanaloa,
Here are all the offerings
Before you (Ii 1963:37).

In the first line, Kūkā'ilimoku is invoked after the unmarked Kū and there is no mention of Kūnuiākea in this prayer. Does this establish that the main god of Papa'ena'ena is Kūkā'ilimoku and not Kūnuiākea? Certainly not. In the first place, the prayer, as reported by Kamakau in an almost identical form and context, substitutes Kūnuiākea for Kūkā'ilimoku (Kamakau 1976:143). But even if we consider 'Ī'ī's version only, we must interpret it by taking into consideration the fact that Kūnuiākea and unmarked Kū are hardly distinguishable. From this point of view it is clear (and this is confirmed by the analysis of the temple ritual) that in the above-mentioned prayer Kū, who is mentioned first, is identical with Kūnuiākea, whereas Kūkā'ilimoku, who is mentioned second, is one of the encompassed forms of the god (cf. Pukui and Elbert 1971:391). One should remember that the use of the unmarked (instead of the marked) form of the name of the gods may be motivated by purely poetic constraints. Thus, in the third line of the prayer, Lono is mentioned in his extended form (Lononuiākea) because he has a whole line to himself, while Kāne and Kanaloa, crowded into one line, are given in their unmarked form. These differences have no demonstrable semantic content. At any rate, the occurrence of the name Kūkā'ilimoku in Liholiho's prayer is also explained by the fact that, as we shall see, Kūkā'ilimoku plays an important role in the temple of Kūnuiākea as well.

In conclusion, 'Ī'ī's text of Liholiho's prayer in 1804 does not establish that the main god worshiped in Papa'ena'ena was Kūkā'ilimoku instead of Kūnuiākea, any more than it establishes that this main god was Lono or Kāne or Kanaloa, who are also mentioned in the prayer and associated with the sacrifice to Kū. But, as we have noted, an invocation to Kūnuiākea also implies, in a sense, an invocation to Kūkā'ilimoku, since the latter is encompassed by the former. Moreover, in 1804, when Kamehameha and Liholiho had just arrived in O'ahu and their army was prostrated by an epidemic, there had certainly been no time to build a special temple for Kūkā'ilimoku. In fact, there is no proof that such a temple was built before 1809. Consequently, up to that time Kamehameha worshiped Kūkā'ilimoku in Papa'ena'ena and thus this god must have been more closely associated with Kūnuiākea. But by the same token, we must suppose that once a special temple was built for Kūkā'ilimoku in Honolulu after 1809, the Kūnuiākea aspect of Kū must have been given greater emphasis in Papa'ena'ena.

3. The Problems

Schematically, the Honolulu system consisted of a basic dichotomy: temples associated with Liholiho vs. temples associated with Kamehameha. Each term of the dichotomy was further dichotomized:

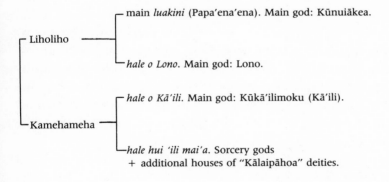

Liholiho
- main *luakini* (Papa'ena'ena). Main god: Kūnuiākea.
- *hale o Lono*. Main god: Lono.

Kamehameha
- *hale o Kā'ili*. Main god: Kūkā'ilimoku (Kā'ili).
- *hale hui 'ili mai'a*. Sorcery gods + additional houses of "Kālaipāhoa" deities.

The basic dichotomy was preserved in the Kailua system, but its content was partially modified:

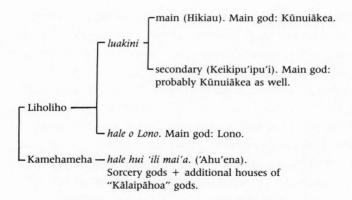

luakini —⌈ main (Hikiau). Main god: Kūnuiākea.

⌊ secondary (Keikipu'ipu'i). Main god:
probably Kūnuiākea as well.

Liholiho ——

hale o Lono. Main god: Lono.

Kamehameha — hale hui 'ili mai'a. ('Ahu'ena).
Sorcery gods + additional houses of
"Kālaipāhoa" gods.

The main modification was the neutralization of the *hale o Kā'ili* (Keikipu'ipu'i), which lost its connection with the war god and was moved into the Liholiho pole of the system. I shall attempt to explain this change in structural terms. But in order to be able to do so, it is first necessary to bring out the structure underlying the traditional system of royal temples, which was reflected in Honolulu (see Valeri 1985a:183–88).

This structure raises a number of problems. The principal one concerns the very signification of the diarchy Liholiho/Kamehameha and the connection of each ruler with different kinds of temples and gods. A second problem concerns the relationship between the two forms of Kū, the temples associated with them, and the rituals performed in them. A third problem refers to the special relationship that seems to have existed, via Liholiho, between Kūnuiākea and Lono. Finally, what is the relationship between the sorcery gods and Kūkā'ilimoku, a relationship indicated by the fact that they were both connected with Kamehameha?

4. The Diarchic Arrangement

A diarchic form of kingship recurs throughout Hawaiian history. Although this fact is of the utmost importance for the interpretation of several events and processes, it has not been fully understood.[10] Typically, the diarchy consists of an "active" ruler, who is of relatively inferior rank but who has a great deal of concrete power, and of a "passive" one, who has superior rank (cf. Hocart 1970). The active ruler tends to be involved in military activities, to be a "conquering king," whereas the passive one (who can even be female), is a "peaceful king" in whom are vested the supreme religious prerogatives of kingship. Of course, this scheme can be complicated. Also, it is by no means necessary that the two fundamental components of kingship (the "conquering" and the "peaceful," the "active" and the "passive," the "unstable" and the "stable," etc.) be identified with two different individuals. They can be associated with two different stages of a transformation that involves a single king. Moreover, this transformation can be realized at different levels and in different temporal units. It can, for instance, regulate the entire biography of a king, who will typically begin as a "wild conqueror" and end his reign as a "domesticated," peaceful ruler (cf. Valeri 1985b, in press).

In other words, the diarchic solution is only one possible manifestation of a more fundamental duality that concerns kingship itself and that, in Hawaiian thought, in fact characterizes every kind of power and "divine power" (*mana*) in particular (cf. Valeri 1985a:chs. 3, 5; Valeri 1985b). It is especially expressed and summarized by the opposition between the two main forms of Kū: Kūkā'ilimoku and Kūnuiākea. The former represents Kū (and more generally, the divine) in his conquering, active, violent aspect. Kūkā'ilimoku means 'Kū-island-snatcher': he is a war god and corresponds to the warlike activities of the king or to the warrior king, the active king. In contrast, Kūnuiākea represents Kū in his all-encompassing, stable, and restrained aspect. As I have noted, Kūnuiākea is identified with Kū as a class that encompasses all the Kū gods; he therefore encompasses Kūkā'ilimoku himself (cf. Kamakau 1964:7). In a sense, the two gods are complementary: Kūkā'ilimoku represents conquest, the movement toward encompassment; Kūnuiākea represents the achieved encompassment, the stabilized and restrained state of a divine power that is productively—as opposed to destructively—connected with the land.

A diarchy correlated with the two aspects of Kū is inscribed in the very origin myth of the dynasty to which Kamehameha and Liholiho belonged. According to this myth, King Liloa left the highest prerogative of kingship—the right to offer human sacrifices in the main *luakini* temples (and the supremacy over the land that went with that right; cf.

Ii 1963:4-6; Kamakau 1961:129, 120, 121; Fornander 1880, 2:308, 218)—to his sacred, genealogically legitimate son, Hākau. On the other hand, he left Kūkā'ilimoku to 'Umi, his illegitimate, "wild" son, who was conceived in the forest and in a polluting manner (Kamakau 1961: 3; Fornander 1916–20, 4:115).

This myth constitutes a charter for the kingship of the island of Hawai'i. It is not surprising, therefore, to see the diarchic arrangement inscribed in the myth repeated in later generations. For instance, the king who reigned at the time of Cook's visit, Kalani'ōpu'u, settled his succession according to the archetypal scheme: he left the supreme prerogatives to his sacred son Kīwala'ō and Kūkā'ilimoku to his nephew Kamehameha. It is well known that Kamehameha (like 'Umi before him) killed his co-ruler and usurped his rights. But the importance of the diarchic scheme is demonstrated by the fact that Kamehameha reapplied it when he gave the highest priestly prerogatives of kingship to his sacred son, Liholiho. This happened in 1801–2, on the eve of an expedition against Kaua'i, which was the immediate cause of Kamehameha's move from the island of Hawai'i to that of O'ahu (cf. Kuykendall 1938:48–49). The historian S. M. Kamakau narrates the cession in these terms:

When all the preparations for the expedition to Kauai were completed, Kamehameha called together his counsellors and hereditary kahunas ['priests'] [. . .]. And he appointed Liholiho, then in his fifth year, his heir to inherit the rule. This was proclaimed, and he was then for the first time given the tabu of the heiaus. Kamehameha made him the head of the worship of the gods, and he was carried by a *kahu* ['guardian'] to be proclaimed in the heiaus of Maui and Oahu (Kamakau 1961:187–88; cf. 221; cf. Thrum 1909:45).

Liholiho was thus officially appointed "heir to inherit the rule" of Kamehameha. But this entailed the immediate cession by Kamehameha to Liholiho of the highest prerogatives of kingship: the right to perform the main temple rituals and to consecrate human sacrifices to Kūnuiākea at least. Thus, the appointment of Liholiho as a successor was at the same time the creation of a diarchic arrangement —a crucial fact that has escaped the attention of students of Hawaiian history.

Kamehameha's decision to give the supreme prerogatives of kingship to Liholiho was equivalent to their reversion to Kīwala'ō's line, since Liholiho was the son of Kīwala'ō's only surviving issue, Keōpūolani (whom Kamehameha had captured and married) and therefore the legitimate heir to his maternal grandfather's prerogatives. Liholiho's rank was in fact superior to Kamehameha's, who treated him as his "god" (Kamakau 1961:208).

The attribution of those prerogatives to Liholiho was not only—if at all —due to Kamehameha's legitimism. It was also a clever political move. Maui and O'ahu were, through Kīwala'ō's mother (who was Kahekili's sister), Liholiho's inheritance. At a time when Kamehameha intended to conquer Kaua'i for good, he needed to be sure of the support of the people of Maui and O'ahu, who, in fact, welcomed Liholiho as their beloved ruler. This explains why Kamehameha spent one year in Maui, while Liholiho was busy making the circuit of the island, reconsecrating the main temples of each district and receiving the homage of the people (Kamakau 1961:188; Thrum 1909:44–47; cf. Thrum 1917:55). It also explains why in O'ahu Liholiho was solemnly reconfirmed in his role, as already mentioned. Moreover, it should be kept in mind that Liholiho was intentionally generated as the synthesis of the two dynasties—those of Hawai'i and Maui—that had competed for supremacy over the archipelago. He embodied, then, the unification of the islands Kamehameha had brought about as a conqueror but that he could not adequately personify himself. Only Liholiho could represent the peaceful and ordered culmination of Kamehameha's reign, a promised land that, apparently, Kamehameha could not reach, although he guided his people toward it. This explains why, as attested by Kamakau's text quoted above, the diarchic arrangement was also conceived as an arrangement for Kamehameha's succession or even as its partial anticipation. Thus, the synchronic complementarity of the two rulers expressed in fact a diachronic relationship, a direction impressed upon the entire political process of conquest on the eve of its completion with the conquest of Kaua'i.

5. The Ritual of Kū

We have now to understand the relationship between the diarchy and its ritual correlates. We shall begin by considering the basic plot of the ritual performed in the temples of Kū. I emphasize from the outset that this ritual seems to be identical for the temples of Kūkā'ilimoku and those of Kūnuiākea. This is demonstrated by the fact that all the descriptions of the ritual are in agreement, although two of them (Malo 1951:158–76 and Kelou Kamakau *in* Fornander 1916–20, 4:8–30) evidently refer to the rites performed in the temple of Hikiau,[11] which was consecrated to Kūnuiākea (King 1967:621), while another source (collected by Judd, in Wilkes 1845, 4:506, cf. 85) refers to the rites performed in the *hale o Kā'ili* in Kohala (cf. Stokes n.d.:GR 1 box 9.48).

In both types of temples the main image was in wood and is referred to generically in the texts by the name Haku 'ōhi'a, 'Lord *'ōhi'a'*. The name refers to the *'ōhi'a lehua* tree (*Metrosyderos macropus, M. collina*), from which the image was carved.

The ritual of Kū was extremely complex. I have analyzed it in detail elsewhere.[12] For present purposes it is sufficient to describe it in outline. Four main stages can be distinguished:

(1) The king, preceded by the feather images (the principal one represented the war god Kūkā'ilimoku), went to the zone in the mountains called *wao akua* ('the inland region of the gods') and there selected a tree from which to carve the main image for the temple. The tree was addressed as a god even before it was transformed into an image. It was the god Kū in one of its natural, wild 'bodies' (*kino*).

After a human sacrifice, the tree was felled. The direction in which it fell indicated, especially prior to a war, the land over which the king would rule (Wilkes 1845, 4:506).

After the image had been carved, the party, preceded by the feather gods, triumphantly returned to the inhabited land. Whoever was encountered on the path of the gods was put to death. Shouts and songs of victory accompanied the procession, which represented the violent conquest of the land by the god Kū. Following the arrival of the gods in front of the temple, the *kauila nui* rite was performed. In this rite, the idea was made even more explicit that Kū, in his violent form (represented by feather images), was conquering the land.

(2) The next series of rites took place inside the temple, where the Haku 'ōhi'a was symbolically born (his "navel cord" was cut), reached manhood (he was given a loincloth), and became an *akua maoli*, 'true,

real god'. Each of these stages in the development of the god was made possible by the rites that involved human sacrifices and thus neutralized his violent aspect by satisfying it.

(3) The next stage consisted of a ceremony in which the social hierarchy was reproduced during a collective meal. Hundreds of pigs were sacrificed and eaten by the congregation. The share received and the order in which it was received indexed the rank of each person. Significantly this rite was called *hono*, the Hawaiian equivalent of *fono* in Western Polynesia.[13]

(4) The final stage was represented by a rite in which the highest ranking chieftesses were brought into contact with the temple so as to be fertilized by the god.[14] The men, who had been separated from the women during the entire ritual period, were now reunited with them: thus the ritual fertilization of the women anticipated the empirical one.

In order to understand this ritual, it is necessary to remember that in Hawaii, as in other Polynesian cultures, the gods manifested themselves in natural species, in images, and in humans (Firth 1930–31; Gough 1973:195; Handy 1968). All these manifestations were related to one another in the temple ritual, which consisted of the transformation of a natural manifestation (*kino*, 'body') of the god Kū into an image (*ki'i*) of the same god. But the image of the god was in reality the idealized image of man. Moreover, it was considered the matrix of human life, the transcendental condition of its being. This is indicated by the fact that the fertilizing powers of the men that attended the ritual derived from the fertilizing powers of the god. The transformation of the god Kū also sustained the divinity of his main transformer, the king, who was considered, in one important dimension of his being, as a manifestation of Kū. Thus, the ritual had the effect of transforming a natural manifestation of the god into two interrelated cultural manifestations: the image and the king.

It would be futile even to attempt to summarize the amazing complexity of meaning of this ritual. Here, I mention a few points relevant to an understanding of the dual nature of Hawaiian kingship and of its religious correlates.

In his initial manifestation (the *'ōhi'a lehua* tree) the god had a wild form that, moreover, connoted the "inland region of the gods." That is, the tree was a metaphor of the divine in its totally transcendent, uncontrolled, and therefore dangerous aspect. In order to appropriate the divine powers and to control them, it was necessary to bring the wild god into society. By felling the tree in the forest, the king killed Kū in his natural form and opened the way for his rebirth in a controlled, humanized form.

However, this initial act was not sufficient to neutralize the wildness of the god, which manifested itself in the god's destroying every person encountered on his way from the forest to the temple.

The god became a positive and productive power only after having been "bound" in the "aha binding rites" inside the temple.

The king was associated with each state of the transformation of the god, which paralleled his own transformation. Like the god, the king was conceived as an initially uncontrolled and external power that penetrated the society and conquered it by violence. In fact, the first part of the ritual, the one that took place outside the temple, also constituted a threat from the king against both his enemies and his own people.

The ritual metaphorically posited force and conquest as its first and necessary moment. But it also set the stage for their transcendence, and so for the passage of the king from a state in which his power was not controlled by society to one in which it was identified with the society as a whole and therefore with its reproduction and its life.[15] This passage, encompassed by the passage of the god from an uncontrolled to a controlled state, legitimized the king every time the temple ritual was performed.[16]

The ritual of Kū, on both cosmological and political levels, manifested and mediated the duality of power. As I have noted, in its strongest form this duality was represented by the hierarchical opposition between Kūkā'ilimoku and Kūnuiākea. We have also seen that the latter was opposed to the former just as the final realization of a process is opposed to its initial condition. The hierarchical opposition of the two gods, therefore, was expressed by their different position in a temporal structure. Ultimately, Kūnuiākea was the *Aufhebung* of Kūkā'ilimoku, the latter a god who, as it were, was left behind as a stage in the process of the divine power. This tranformative relationship between the two gods was clearly represented by the temple ritual.

Outside the temple, the feather images of Kū, of which the image of Kūkā'ilimoku was the principal one, were foregrounded. In the procession from the mountain to the temple, they preceded the Haku 'ōhi'a. Moreover, this wooden image, destined to represent the domesticated form of Kū, was still covered with ferns and therefore invisible; it was also kept in a horizontal position, which contrasted with the erect position it would assume inside the temple. Even more striking is the fact that only the feather gods participated in the *kauila nui* rite, which explicitly represented the conquest of the land by Kū.

Inside the temple the wooden image predominated in all the rites and the feather gods receded into the background. As we shall see, it is not certain that the wooden image always represented Kūnuiākea (although Beckwith [1940:26], for example, takes this position); but insofar as it did, the ritual of Kū can be described as the transformation of a state indexed by Kūkā'ilimoku to a state indexed by Kūnuiākea.

Ultimately, at the political level the first state coincided with the violence and counterviolence that characterized the individualistic or factionalistic competition for power. At this stage, "wild," acquisitive power dominated.

As for the state indexed by Kūnuiākea, it represented the transformation of the king into the representative of the entire society. His stabilized power temporarily excluded struggle, violence, and competition; it even made them impossible.[17] Significantly, the passage from the outside of the temple, where Kūkā'ilimoku predominated, to the inside, where Kūnuiākea predominated, was connoted by the proscription of violence. Thus, the victims that were offered to the god *inside* the temple had to be slain *outside* it. Moreover, every trace of blood and any other sign of violence had to be eliminated before the corpse could be introduced into the sacred precincts (Valeri 1985a:337–38). The offerings that took place inside the temple, then, connoted the transcendence of violence by the denial of violence. In this way, the dead and disordered victims were transubstantiated into the living and ordered god.

6. From the Temple of Kūkā'ilimoku to the Temple of Kūnuiākea

The analysis of the ritual of Kū revealed an opposition between two forms of the god: the feather image and the wooden image, or Haku 'ōhi'a. We have also seen that the opposition between the two images was strongest when the former represented Kūkā'ilimoku and the latter Kūnuiākea. Evidently, this "strong" form of opposition could be realized in a temple—such as Hikiau—in which the Haku 'ōhi'a was identified with Kūnuiākea. But what about a temple consecrated to Kūkā'ilimoku? This problem is closely related to another: what differentiates a temple of Kūkā'ilimoku from a temple of Kūnuiākea? It is difficult to solve these problems satisfactorily given the evidence at our disposal.

As I have noted, Beckwith (1940:26) seems to believe that in all temples of Kū the Haku 'ōhi'a represented Kūnuiākea. Pukui and Elbert (1971:391) follow her in this opinion. They do not explain, however, why certain temples were specifically associated with Kūkā'ilimoku and what this implies. If we accept their hypothesis, we must admit that the name *hale o Kā'ili* was given to a temple simply because the feather image of Kū was stored in one of its houses, not because its main wooden image represented Kūkā'ilimoku.

There is a source, however, that identifies the main wooden image of a temple with Kūkā'ilimoku. This source is Ellis's journal and it concerns the temple of Pu'ukoholā on the island of Hawai'i.

Ellis reports having seen the holes

where wooden idols of varied size and shape formerly stood, casting their hideous stares in every direction. Tairi or Kukairimoku, a large wooden image, crowned with a helmet, and covered with red feathers, the favourite war-god of Kamehameha, was the principal. To him the heiau was dedicated, and for his occasional residence it was built. On the day in which he was brought within its precincts, vast offerings of fruit, hogs, and dogs were presented, and not less than eleven human victims were immolated on his altars (Ellis 1842, 4:98; 1828:83).

The reliability of Ellis's testimonial, however, must be doubted in view of two facts. First, he visited the temple after the abolition of the traditional religious system, when the images had already been removed. He did not himself see the wooden statue of Kūkā'ilimoku he describes. Second, his account betrays a certain confusion between Kūkā'ilimoku's feather image and the Haku 'ōhi'a. In fact, he writes that the wooden god was "covered with red feathers." Although a few feathers could be glued to a wooden statue as an offering (cf. Arago 1840, 2:61–62), it seems quite unlikely that a wooden image was covered with such precious feathers; they could not resist for a long time the attacks of rain and wind. Furthermore, Arago, who visited the temple in 1819, before the images were removed, did not observe any wooden god covered with feathers (Arago 1822, 2:161).[18] Ellis must have confused the feather image of Kūkā'ilimoku—whose foundation material is constituted by "split 'ie'ie aerial rootlets which are arranged into warps and wefts" (Hiroa 1957:505)—with the wooden Haku 'ōhi'a. His mention of the "occasional presence" of Kūkā'ilimoku's image in the temple confirms that his informant referred to the portable feather god.

Probably because he noticed the discrepancies in Ellis's account, Stokes took his description of the god to mean that Kā'ili was "a wooden idol crowned with a red-feathered helmet" (Stokes n.d.:GR 1 box 8.33). However, this is not quite what Ellis says.

Thus, the identity of the Haku 'ōhi'a in Pu'ukoholā temple seems difficult to establish with any degree of certainty. Perhaps we should take a clue from the very lack of a specific determination of the Haku 'ōhi'a in the texts that describe the temple rituals and entertain the possibility that this image was polyvalent. In other words, according to the contexts and occasions in which the temple ritual was performed, the Haku 'ōhi'a referred to variously named, more or less stabilized, forms of Kū.

This interpretation would make sense both of the reluctance of the texts, which describe a decontextualized ritual scenario, to identify more specifically the Haku 'ōhi'a, and of the fact that many temples could be used both for war and for peaceful or apotropaic purposes on different occasions (cf. Malo 1951:160–61; Ii 1963:33).

Nevertheless, I hesitate to identify the Haku 'ōhi'a erected in a *hale o Kā'ili* with Kūkā'ilimoku, because in the Hawaiian texts the name Kūkā'ilimoku seems to refer invariably to a feather image,[19] and in fact to one single image that had been handed down from the time of Liloa at least.

Since the transformation from the "wild" to the "domesticated" form of Kū took place in both the *hale o Kā'ili* and the temple of Kūnuiākea, the question of the articulation of these two apparently identical transformations arises.

I would maintain that the transformation that took place in a *hale o Kā'ili* was less complete in its results than the one that took place in a temple of Kūnuiākea. Therefore the *hale o Kā'ili* was more strongly associated with Kūkā'ilimoku, which in fact it housed, than with Kūnuiākea.

I would also argue that the transformation that took place in the supreme temple of the kingdom completed the one that took place in the *hale o Kā'ili* by repeating it at a higher level. The fact that the feather image of Kūkā'ilimoku was not permanently housed in such a temple indicates that in it Kūnuiākea was more strongly opposed to Kūkā'ilimoku.

Since the transformation that took place in the temple specifically associated with Kūnuiākea completed the one that was performed in the *hale o Kā'ili*, the former encompassed the latter. This encompassment, however, could take a synchronic form or a diachronic one. In the first case, the two performances were made at the same time by rulers of different rank, probably using different feather images. The relationship between the two performances was, then, only a special case of the relationship that obtained between the performances of the Kū ritual that were made in inferior temples all over the territory of the kingdom, and those that were made by the supreme ruler in the main temple. For instance, we know from the journals of the Vancouver expedition that in 1793, at the same time that Kamehameha was performing the Kū ritual in the main temple of Hikiau, one of his associates of relatively inferior rank, Ke'eaumoku, was performing it in the temple of Pu'ukoholā (Menzies n.d.:13 February 1793; Puget n.d.:13 February 1793; Bell 1929: October, 61–62; Manby 1929: July, 39; Vancouver 1801, 3:183, 187).

The most complex, but also the most revealing, articulation between a performance in a temple of Kūkā'ilimoku and a performance in a temple of Kūnuiākea was the diachronic one. This type of articulation is best understood when viewed in connection with war.

Let us briefly consider the facts. Each act of war was preceded by a performance of the temple ritual, in which divinatory and propitiatory rituals were also made (Ellis 1842, 4:150–51).

The ritual anticipated victory by representing it. Moreover, since enemies of the king, taken prisoner in previous wars, were often the victims of the human sacrifices, these vanquished enemies became icons of the enemies that the king hoped to vanquish.

As soon as the ritual was declared successful, the actual battle could take place. Divinations and propitiations were repeated on the battlefield (Ii 1963:14, Fornander 1916–20, 4:366); then the main war god (Kūkā'ilimoku in the island of Hawai'i) and the other feather gods were put in front of the army (Ellis 1842, 4:157–58). To these gods the first fallen enemies were offered (Kamakau 1961:73–74, 133, 136; Manby 1929:August, 43; Menzies 1920:93; Malo n.d.:ch. 38 v. 14). When the actual battle was won, a new performance of the temple ritual took place, during which the fallen enemies (together with some prisoners and/or transgressors) were again offered, this time to the Haku' ōhi'a, who represented, as we have seen, the stabilized state of the god Kū (cf. Kamakau 1976:142–43; cf. also Vancouver 1801, 3:254; Fornander 1916–20, 4:344–46; Byron 1826:8, 153).

I call the first performance anticipatory, the second confirmatory. As we know, they were formally identical in that they both represented the transformation of the uncontrolled form of Kū into the controlled one. But in the first performance this transformation was simply anticipated: by representing a passage from disorder to order it was hoped that it would be realized and therefore that the enemies would be defeated in the forthcoming battle. However, the ritual process was only a *symbol* of a real process, not its *substitute*.[20] Thus, after the performance of the anticipatory rites, the king had to go to battle in order to *realize* what had been simply represented. This shift to the battlefield also implied that in the anticipatory performance the passage from the wild to the domesticated form of Kū was not only imperfect, but also reversible. In fact, after the conclusion of the ritual, the emphasis had to be put again on Kūkā'ilimoku, who was brought to the battlefield to be efficacious there.

Only the confirmatory performance, the one that followed the real victory and destruction of the rebels or enemies, could represent a definitive and irreversible (for the time being) transformation of Kū.

I would maintain that, ideally, the anticipatory performance would take place in the temple that housed Kūkā'ilimoku, whereas the confirmatory one would take place in a temple of Kūnuiākea. It was also possible for the same temple to be the stage of both performances, but in this case, only the second would bring about a definitive transformation of that temple's Haku 'ōhi'a.

It should be noted that this is only a hypothesis, since most of the available descriptions of the temple rituals are totally decontextualized. However, a syntagmatic relationship of the type that I have indicated is not suggested by logic only; it is also suggested by certain historical events, for instance, by one that occurred toward the end of the reign of King Kalani'ōpu'u of the island of Hawai'i.

'Imakakoloa, the ruler of Puna, one of the six main districts of the island of Hawai'i, rebelled against Kalani'ōpu'u. The latter was at that time in the district of Waipi'o and prepared his army to crush the rebellion. Before departing, however, he built the temple of Moa'ula. Then he moved to Hilo, where he built a second temple. After these anticipatory and propitiatory rites, his army went to fight in Puna. 'Imakakoloa was eventually defeated and went into hiding. While waiting for his capture, Kalani'ōpu'u moved to the district of Ka'ū; and there he built the temple of Pākini, in which the rebel chief was finally sacrificed (Kamakau 1961:108–9; Fornander 1880, 2:202; Thrum 1908:55–56, 58; Pukui et al. 1974:153; Emerson n.d.:532).

Thrum (1908:55–56) writes that the temple of Moa'ula, in which the first set of anticipatory rites was performed, was consecrated to Kūkā'ilimoku. I infer from the following facts a connection between Kūnuiākea and the temple of Pākini, in which the confirmatory rites were made.

Before the war against 'Imakakoloa, Kalani'ōpu'u settled his succession by nominating his sacred son Kīwala'ō supreme ruler over the land. This implied that Kīwala'ō was connected with Kūnuiākea, the supreme form of Kū. To his nephew Kamehameha, who was inferior in rank, Kalani'ōpu'u left the war god Kūkā'ilimoku (Kamakau 1961: 107). The expedition against 'Imakakoloa was to be the first test of this diarchic arrangement. It is likely that Kamehameha, as keeper of Kūkā'ilimoku, was involved in the sacrifices that took place in Moa'ula, if, as Thrum claims, this temple was indeed consecrated to Kūkā'ilimoku. But it is certain that the plan was to let Kīwala'ō play the main role in Pākini, by offering the rebel in sacrifice. As it turned out, Kamehameha usurped Kīwala'ō's prerogative and offered the human sacrifice himself. This action was perceived as an intolerable attempt at a coup d'état, so much so that Kalani'ōpu'u asked Kamehameha to leave the court (Kamakau 1961:108–9). Fornander (1880, 2:202) marvels at this, because he believes that it was Kamehameha who had the right to offer human sacrifices, since he was the keeper of the god Kūkā'ilimoku. But Fornander, like other interpreters after him, fails to understand the opposition between the two forms of Kū and its correlation with the two aspects of kingship or even, as in this case, with two rulers. Kamehameha could perhaps be delegated to offer preliminary sacrifices to Kū in his form Kūkā'ilimoku, either in *hale o Kā'ili* or on the battlefield (cf. Ii 1963:9); but only Kīwala'ō, in his capacity of supreme ruler, could offer the concluding sacrifice to Kūnuiākea in the *luakini* temple. Therefore, the fact that the temple of Pākini was set up for Kīwala'ō to offer a human sacrifice indicates that it was dedicated to Kūnuiākea and not to Kūkā'ilimoku.[21] Kamehameha's planned exclusion from this sacrifice is obviously significant in this context. If my interpretation is correct, we have here a case in which the transition from the dominance of Kūkā'ilimoku to the dominance of Kūnuiākea is correlated with the transition from one category of temple to another and from one category of ruler to another.[22]

7. From Kūnuiākea to Lono

Having thus clarified, as much as is possible, the relationship between the two temples of Kū and between the rulers (or aspects of a single ruler) connected with them, we must now move on to a further problem: why is Liholiho, the ruler connected with Kūnuiākea, also connected with Lono and his temple?

It is well known that the cult of Lono was the second main cult associated with kingship (Malo 1951:159). Thus, it was quite natural for the main temple of Lono to be associated with a king. This, however, does not explain why it was associated with Liholiho, that is, with the ruler who was also associated with Kūnuiākea.

In order to explain this fact, we must consider the sequential relationship between the rituals of Kū and those of Lono. Every year, at the conclusion of the New Year's festival, during which the temples were closed, the king restored his main *luakini* or built a new one (Iselin n.d.:73; Malo n.d.:158; Ii 1963:122, Andrews 1865:155; Remy 1862: 74). The building of a *luakini*, doubtless because it was usually associated with war (cf. Malo n.d.:ch. 36 v. 78; ch. 37 v. 10), which brought about the destruction of the crops,[23] and because it distracted labor from the production of food, was said to cause a famine in the land (Malo 1951:189). Hence, after the ritual process that transformed Kū from his wild to his domesticated aspect had been completed, the king built a temple of Lono (of the *māpele* variety; ibid.) in order to "bring prosperity to the land" (ibid.).

Moreover, after the *luakini* and the *māpele* had been built,

the king went on a tour about the island, putting up *heiau* as he went. This circuit was called a *palaloa*. Next the king made an *uno o Lono* [another variety of temple of Lono], and each of the chiefs erected an *eweai* which was a *heiau* to bring rain [this temple was also connected with Lono] (ibid.:190).

When the chiefs had built their temples of Lono, the commoners could build theirs, so that "the land might live" (Kamakau 1976:129). And it did indeed come alive and produce. As Malo goes on to say:

If all these matters relating to the worship of the gods were attended to, then the king was highly commended as a righteous King. And when the people perceived this, they devoted themselves with diligence to their farms and their fishing, while the woman folk industriously beat out and printed their tapa. Thus it was that the king worked away in the worship of the gods year after year (Malo 1951:190).

It is clear, then, that the rites of Kū and the rites of Lono were part of a global process of transformation. This process began in wild nature, in which the divine power existed in its uncontrolled and destructive state. The god emphasized at this stage was Kūkā'ilimoku. The divine power was then appropriated and domesticated, and it was absorbed in part by the men who participated in the temple ritual, by eating the food consecrated to the god (Kamakau 1976:144). This second stage occurred under the aegis of Kūnuiākea. Finally, the men who had participated in the ritual applied to the women who had been excluded, and to the land, the divine fertilizing power that they had acquired in the temple. This last stage, during which the divine power was spread throughout the land and multiplied the crops and the people, was encompassed by Lono and his rites.

In this scheme, the gods are not considered as discrete entities, but as reified symbols of different states of the relationship between divine and human worlds, between nature and man. One god resulted from the transformation of another. As Kūnuiākea was, in a sense, the transformation of Kūkā'ilimoku, so Lono was the transformation of Kūnuiākea. The latter transition was already anticipated at the end of the temple ritual, when Kūnuiākea assumed, in relationship to the high-ranking women, the fertilizing role that Lono would assume in relationship to all women and to the land (impersonated by Papa, who was both the primordial ancestress and the flat surface of the land or the foundation of the latter).

Moreover, the ritual transformation of wild power into productive power brought about an empirical productivity that must be considered as part of the entire process.

As the passage by Malo quoted above suggests, the efficacy of the ritual ultimately derived from the fact that belief is self-fulfilling: by acting in agreement with the belief that ritual is successful and therefore by working under the leadership of a king, the people made the ritual really successful and therefore created the empirical conditions that confirmed their belief in its efficacy. But to be believable in the first place, the ritual must have represented a process whose outcome was desired and considered proper (cf. Mauss 1950:89–90, 118–19). This representation concerned both a process of the self and a process of the community. The two were in fact equated: the passage of the community from a state of disorder (war, conflict, etc.) to a state of order (peace, harmony, etc.) was represented as the ordering and growing of a person (the god), who appeared as the ideal, desired state of the subject. Thus the god and his closest reflection among humans, the king, represented not a static order, but order as the processual transcendence of disorder (cf. Valeri 1980).

In conclusion, if we consider the gods and their temples as stages in a process, Liholiho's connection with Lono follows from his connection with Kūnuiākea. Both gods represented the stable pole of kingship: one in its more transcendent, all-encompassing aspect; the other in its more immanent aspect, which was concretely connected with the land and with the people.[24]

Although the king conquered the land with Kūkā'ilimoku, he obtained authority over it with Kūnuiākea and Lono; no wonder, then, that when the diarchic solution was adopted, the supreme authority over the land was vested in the ruler associated with the transition from Kūnuiākea to Lono. By means of that transition, the king (represented by his gods) entered peacefully and productively into the land, instead of entering it in a violent and destructive fashion—as represented in the initial sections of the ritual.

8. Spatial and Temporal Realizations of the Transformation

The fundamental transformation from Kū to Lono, outlined above, was realized in different spatial and, especially, temporal forms. It seems, for instance, that a temple of Lono was often spatially connected with a temple of Kū. This was certainly the case in Kealakekua, where the *luakini* temple of Hikiau was associated with a *hale o Lono* (Samwell 1967:1162; Lisiansky 1814:105–6; cf. Manby 1929, July, 43; Bell 1929, October, 78). Also, from 1813 to 1819 the *luakini* temple of Keikipu'ipu'i was close to Liholiho's *hale o Lono* (Ii 1963:110, 121).

More important, and better documented, is the temporal aspect of the transformation from Kū to Lono. There was, as I have indicated, an initial transformation at the beginning of the eight-month period during which the temples were open and war was lawful; there were also transformations, of varying complexity, that took place in connection with acts of war. The timing of these performances was regulated by the calendar, which also determined the four regular monthly performances of shorter versions of the main rituals. Now it seems that the calendrical system inscribed the performances in a temporal framework that was itself organized by the transformation from Kū to Lono.

Let us consider the monthly cycle first. The first performance of the temple ritual, which began at the new moon, occurred during the *kapu* of Kū, the monthly period of time consecrated to Kū. The last performance occurred during the *kapu* period of Kāne. The third, during the *kapu* period of Kanaloa. It is tempting, therefore, to conclude that the second occurred during a period of time consecrated to Lono. However, the period in which the second monthly performance took place was called *kapu hua*, not *kapu Lono. Hua* refers to the full moon that occurred during the *kapu hua*. As for Lono, he gave his name to the last day of the *kapu Kāne*, a day that was also the last in which temple rituals were performed before the beginning of the new month.

Nevertheless a connection of the *kapu hua* with Lono can perhaps be established. In fact, the *kapu hua* coincided calendrically with the period during which the *ho'omahanahana* ('warming up') ritual was performed, following a full-blown (ten-day-long) temple ritual (Malo 1951:176). Since Malo declares that after the performance of the *luakini* temple ritual, the king performed rites of Lono in order to "bring prosperity to the land" (ibid.:189), it is likely that the *ho'omahanahana* ritual, which "warmed up"—most probably—the land to make it fertile, was connected with Lono.[25]

From the above evidence, it seems that the transformation from Kū to Lono was inscribed in the monthly calendar at two levels:

(1) When the performance that occurred during the *kapu Kū* continued for a full-blown ritual period (ten days: an *anahulu*), the "warming up" rite took place during the *kapu hua*, which then connoted Lono. As the moon was full, at the end of *kapu hua*, so was the process of transformation of the divine. In fact, the full moon was a principal metaphor of the divine: the day on which it occurred was called *akua*, 'divine' (ibid.:32).

(2) Since the first night of the ritual month was consecrated to Kū, and the last night of the month in which a ritual performance took place was consecrated to Lono, it seems that the regular monthly rituals were encompassed by a temporal structure that inscribed them in a global transformation from Kū to Lono. This transformation, then, coincided with the very direction of social time.

Turning now to the yearly cycle, we find that the same transformation from Kū to Lono occurred. In fact, the performance of the monthly form of the transformation for eight months brought about a yearly transformation. The period of eight months during which Kū was the dominant god was succeeded by a period of four months dominated by Lono. The latter period included the New Year's festival, from which Kū and the violence he represented were excluded.

The spatial context could combine with the temporal one. Although the two main stages of the transformation from Kū to Lono could take place in the same temple (the opposition, here, was exclusively chronological), it could also take place in different temples (in this case a spatial opposition was added).

We have examples of both cases. Thus, during the period 1813 to 1819, Liholiho performed both rites that opened the month and those that concluded it in the *luakini* temple of Hikiau, whose main god was Kūnuiākea (Ii 1963:123; cf. Laanui 1930 [1838]). He probably did the same in the temple of Papa'ena'ena from 1809 to 1812. But 'Ī'ī also mentions one case in which Liholiho, in the same years, performed the final rites of the month in a temple of Lono (Ii 1963:59–61). It is likely that the different meanings of the contexts in which each monthly transformation took place explain these variations. Thus, in the case reported by 'Ī'ī, Liholiho was probably emphasizing the healing consequences of the transformation by performing its last stage in a temple that had a medical connotation.

There was, then, an ideal and logical link between performances of the ritual at different times and in different temples. This link was specified by giving emphasis to different aspects of the ritual transformation connected with the different locations and times in which the performance occurred.

The king's presence at the different performances linked them in the most significant way. Rituals were regularly performed in each temple by the priests in charge. But a single performance and a fortiori groups of successive performances were given special relevance by the presence of the king or of some higher ranking noble in the role of principal sacrificer. (The performance of human sacrifices required, in any case, the presence of the king or of an *ali'i* ['noble'] specially delegated by him.) Thus, the king linked various performances in one "discourse" that continued throughout the month and the year. By his presence at selected temples at different moments, he could state his intentions (war, peace, etc.) and emphasize his connection with certain territories.

The king's linking of the temples also took place in a transannual temporality. His reign, as a whole, could oscillate between lengthy periods dominated by war (in which, therefore, the connection with the temples of Kūkā'ilimoku was preponderant) and periods dominated by peace (and therefore mainly connected with temples of Kūnuiākea and Lono). Moreover, it could also reflect an irreversible shift from one pole to another. Typically, a reign would begin with an emphasis on the Kūkā'ilimoku pole and terminate by being centered on the Kūnuiākea/Lono pole.

Thus, the transformation that in its normal form took place in the temple even characterized the life course of a king. This is illustrated by the biography of the paradigmatic king 'Umi. Moreover, 'Umi's biography actually correlates his shift from the Kūkā'ilimoku pole to the Kūnuiākea one with the analogous shift that took place during a crucial performance of the temple ritual in which he succeeded in taking Hākau's place as a supreme ruler! One could not demonstrate better the homology between the career of a king and the process that took place in the temple ritual (Kamakau 1961:14; Fornander 1916–20, 4: 198–205; Valeri 1985b).

Kamehameha's reign offers a striking example of the shift from the violent (Kūkā'ilimoku) to the peaceful (Kūnuiākea/Lono) pole. This shift is represented by the successive connections that Kamehameha established with various temples, either directly or indirectly through Liholiho. As we have seen, Kamehameha began his career being connected with Kūkā'ilimoku. He later usurped the prerogatives of Kīwala'ō, the supreme ruler. These prerogatives involved a special relationship with Kūnuiākea. However, it seems that during Kamehameha's period of conquest, his main connection continued to be, quite logically, with Kūkā'ilimoku and his temples. Kūkā'ilimoku reached the peak of his importance when Kamehameha built the temple Pu'ukoholā, which was said to have given him control of the entire island of Hawai'i. After he sacrificed Keoua, his last important rival, in 1792, Kamehameha gradually shifted toward the Kūnuiākea/Lono pole, as is testified by the fact that he resided near Hikiau, where Vancouver found him in 1793 (Vancouver 1801, 3:211). From 1793 to 1801, Kamehameha seems to have resided on and off near Hikiau (cf. Peron 1824, 2:159

−60; Townsend n.d.:7, 23)[26] with one major interruption. This was the time of the expedition of 1795–96 that secured the islands of Maui, Moloka'i, and O'ahu to his rule (Broughton 1804:32–34; 68–69). The beginning of a shift back to the Kūkā'ilimoku pole was already evident shortly before 1794, when Kamehameha restored the temple of Keikipu'ipu'i in Kailua (cf. Vancouver 1801, 5:100–103; Barrère 1975: 4), which, as we know from Fornander (1880, 2:151–52), was connected with Kūkā'ilimoku. The restoration of this temple clearly manifested his intention to wrest the leeward islands from the aging King Kahekili.

In fact, Keikipu'ipu'i evoked previous attempts to conquer those islands, since it had previously been rebuilt by Kalani'ōpu'u with that purpose in mind (Thrum 1908:70). The intervention of Vancouver, who attempted to bring about peace between Kahekili and Kamehameha, froze the situation. But shortly after Vancouver's definitive departure in 1794, Kahekili died in O'ahu (Kuykendall 1938:44). The events that followed his death gave Kamehameha the occasion to intervene and to secure O'ahu, Moloka'i, and Maui in 1795. Before his expedition, Kamehameha restored a *hale o Kā'ili* in Kohala (Wilkes 1845, 4:506; Stokes n.d.:1 box 9.48). He also attempted to conquer Kaua'i, the last island that escaped his control, but failed. Suddenly a rebellion broke out in 1796 in the island of Hawai'i and he had to return there to quell it (Kuykendall 1938:47–48).

During the next six years Kamehameha resumed his peaceful aspect and, significantly, lived near Hikiau again. But he also began building a great fleet in order to conquer Kaua'i. In 1801 the fleet was ready in Kawaihae (Andrews 1865:556) near the temple of Pu'ukoholā, where, undoubtedly, the rituals for war were performed, thereby emphasizing once again the Kūkā'ilimoku pole. At the same time, however, Kamehameha marked the fact that his reign was globally shifting toward the peaceful pole. He did this by establishing a diarchy in which Liholiho maintained a permanent connection with Kūnuiākea and Lono. By virtue of this connection, Liholiho represented and anticipated the all-encompassing, peaceful, and stabilized outcome of the entire political process initiated by Kamehameha: once Kaua'i could be taken, the conquering and violent aspects of Hawaiian kingship would be definitively overcome.

Thus, the Honolulu temple system must be seen both as a reflection of a traditional structural scheme and as a statement in context. As the latter, it connected past and future, it gave meaning to Kamehameha's career, and it pointed to Liholiho as his inevitable successor, not so much once Kamehameha had died but once the task of active reunification by conquest had been completed.

9. The Transformation as Realized in 1779

The hypothesis of a transformative relationship between Kū and Lono clarifies certain aspects of the historical events of which Captain Cook was protagonist in 1779. In their turn, these events contribute to lending validity to the hypothesis. It is therefore appropriate to discuss them at this point.

Let us first consider the temple of Hikiau, in which some of those events took place. It was divided into two parts by "a ruinous old building of wood" (Cook and King 1784, 3:6)—namely, the *hale pahu* or 'drum house' (cf. Ii 1963:33–35; Malo 1951:162). The part on the land side contained the main altar (*lele*) and the so-called oracle-tower, at the foot of which were situated twelve images. The middle one represented Kūnuiākea, the main god of Hikiau (King 1967:506).

The part of the temple situated on the sea side contained two houses facing each other. In front of one of these, at the entrance of the temple and probably guarding it (cf. Ii 1963:34–35), were two images. Inside, in the area between the two houses, two other images were found. These certainly represented Lono, since, as we shall see in a moment, a rite connected with this god was performed at their base.

It appears, then, that the higher, land-side part of Hikiau was connected with Kūnuiākea, while the lower, sea-side part was connected with Lono. This underscores the close relationship between the two gods, which is further illustrated, as we have seen, by the connection of Hikiau as a whole with the adjacent *hale o Lono*.

Now the "adoration that was paid to Captain Cook," as King describes it (Cook and King 1784, 3:6), manifested in transformative terms the hierarchical relationship existing between both these gods and the sacred spaces connected with them.

Cook arrived in Hawai'i during the season when the god Lono was believed to return to the archipelago in order to preside over the New Year's festival (Makahiki). Hence, he was identified with that god. When he landed on 17 January 1779, Cook was brought to Hikiau. He was first presented to the images at the entrance of the temple, then introduced into it. But the crucial point is that he was not immediately connected with the images of Lono, neither those in the lower part of Hikiau nor those in front of the adjacent *hale o Lono*. Instead, he was brought to the upper part of the temple and consecrated there to Kūnuiākea. From King's description it appears that the priest acted as Cook's sacrificer. First he reconsecrated a hog already laid on the altar in front of Kūnuiākea's image, by praying and, characteristically, letting the hog fall on the ground (cf. Malo n.d.:169–70, 173); then he led Cook to the tower, a means of communication with the god (cf. Ellis 1842, 4:97). At this point he wrapped Cook in red bark cloth and sacrificed a live pig by smashing it to the ground, again as in the *luakini* temple ritual. Finally, the officiating priest introduced Cook to the twelve images and asked him to kiss that of Kūnuiākea, which was wrapped in red bark cloth, like Cook himself.

This rite was very similar or identical to the one performed for the king when he sacrificed to Kūnuiākea. As I have demonstrated elsewhere (see Valeri 1985a), its purpose was to identify the king with the god. This identification was made possible by the victim, which substituted for the sacrifier and was integrated into the god by being "eaten" by him, and by the use of other symbolic devices, such as the wrapping of both the god and the king in red cloth or red feather cloaks.

After this rite was completed, Cook was brought into the Lono side of the temple and seated between the two images that were situated there. In that position he went through a rite identical to the *hānaipū* rite, in which the image of Lono as god of the Makahiki festival was consecrated by the feeding of his bearer (cf. Ii 1963:75; K. Kamakau in Fornander 1916–20, 4:40–43; Sahlins 1981:21).

Two things are clear. First, Cook was considered divine, just as a king was considered divine: he was a human manifestation of the god;

he was both king and god. Second, Cook could not simply *be* Lono; he had to *become* Lono by first being connected with Kūnuiākea. Apparently, only this transformation could fully establish his identity as the god of the Makahiki—that is, establish it in a ritually controlled way, not as an unmediated and uncontrolled fact, as was the case before Cook's arrival at Kealakekua bay, when he was still circling the island.

Only after this rite had taken place was Cook worshiped as a manifestation of Lono-of-the-Makahiki, first in the principal *hale o Lono*, then in several other similar temples of lesser importance (Cook and King 1784, 3:13–14). This again seems to correspond to the prescribed sequence, as reconstructed above.

This historical event, then, confirms the existence of a transformative relationship between Kūnuiākea and Lono. But it also shows that by connecting Cook only with the second part of the ritual transformation (from Kūnuiākea to Lono), the priests of Hikiau implicitly presented him as the end of a process of which at that time the reigning king Kalani'ōpu'u represented only the initial stage. Since 1776, Kalani'ōpu'u, being at war with King Kahekili of Maui, had been emphasizing his connection with the war god Kūkā'ilimoku at the expense of his connection with Kūnuiākea and Lono. There are several indications of this fact. We know that, shortly before going to war, the king had refurbished the temple of Keikipu'ipu'i, which housed Kūkā'ilimoku and which had been placed in the care of the priest Holoa'e (Fornander 1880, 2:151–52; Stokes n.d.:GR 1 box 948, p. 16; Thrum 1908:70, 43).

In contrast, Hikiau, the temple of Kūnuiākea that was controlled by the highest priest in the island, Ka'ō'ō (Samwell 1967:1169; cf. King 1967:620),[27] and which was closely associated with Lono as well, was in a state of disrepair (King 1967:507; Samwell 1967:1177), an evident sign of the fact that it had not been renovated by the king for several years. Moreover, it is significant that at the time of the festival of Lono as New Year god (Lonomakua), Kalani'ōpu'u was not present at Hikiau, where the image of the god was apparently kept (cf. Ii 1963:115; Malo 1951:150), but was still waging war on Maui, perhaps even during the period in which warfare was tabooed by the New Year god (cf. Kuykendall 1938:16).

This situation probably explains why in 1779 the priests of Hikiau were eager to oppose Cook to Kalani'ōpu'u.[28] The former could be seen to represent the final stage—sanctioned in this case by the god Lono himself—of a transformation from violence to peace that Kalani'ōpu'u seemed incapable of effecting. As long as Kalani'ōpu'u remained identified with the violent pole of kingship, indexed by Kūkā'ilimoku, he was unable to restore Hikiau and fully move into the pole of kingship indexed by Kūnuiākea/Lono.

However, Cook's status remained ambiguous since it was possible to interpret it in two different ways: he could either follow the ritual schedule of the Makahiki festival and leave the island at the time when Lono annually returned to Kahiki, the land of the gods, or he could stay permanently, thereby becoming the realization of a permanent transformation of kingship.

In point of fact, as Sahlins has demonstrated (Sahlins 1981), Cook did leave "on schedule." Once he left, the ambiguity seemed to have been dispelled: Cook/Lono did not permanently take Kalani'ōpu'u's place, thereby frustrating, one suspects, the secret hopes of at least some of the priests of Hikiau.

An accident, however, suddenly reversed this interpretation of Cook's status. The foremast of the *Resolution*, one of Cook's ships, was damaged, thereby necessitating a return to Kealakekua for repairs. Cook/Lono was at this point violating the annual ritual schedule. It seemed as if he wished to take permanently the place of Kalani'ōpu'u. Though, understandably, the priests of Hikiau (or some of them) remained on friendly terms with Cook, Kalani'ōpu'u and his party displayed an increasing hostility. The crisis was precipitated when Cook attempted to take Kalani'ōpu'u prisoner, an act that was probably interpreted as the consummation of the king's deposition. As a consequence, Cook was slain. However, his bones were incorporated as regalia by Kalani'ōpu'u (cf. Sahlins 1979, 1981).

Following Cook's murder, the "passage to the Lono pole" remained purely "symbolic" and, apparently, the normal order of things was restored. In reality, the appropriation of Cook was eventually to bring about the irreversible transformation that it had attempted to avoid.

In point of fact, the king's relationship with Cook became an index of his relationship with the foreigners, which created the conditions that made possible an enduring reunification of the archipelago and thereby the transcendence of war (cf. Golovnin 1979:195). Thus, with the progress of the reunification and the development of trade, the Cook aspect became more and more prominent in Lono. At the same time that Liholiho's connection with Lonomakua was emphasized (cf. Campbell 1967 [1822]:130), the bones of Cook were brought in procession during the Makahiki festival (Ellis 1842, 4:136; Martin 1817, 2:66–67; Mathison 1825:431–32; Sahlins 1979:335).

The growing importance of this transformed cult of Lono connected with Liholiho, which has been documented by Sahlins (1979, 1981), parallels the growing importance of sorcery, at the expense of war, in the Kamehameha pole of kingship. It is precisely this phenomenon that explains the modifications interposed in the system of royal temples in 1813. But in order to address this problem, it is first necessary to explain the relationship between war gods and sorcery gods in the traditional system.

10. The Sorcery Gods

The political function of Kamehameha's sorcery gods, particularly the so-called Kālaipāhoa gods (Kamakau 1964:135–36), is quite apparent. They were called *mau akua 'imi aupuni* ('gods who sought kingdoms'). Kamakau, who reports this information, also writes: "they were all gods in tree form who helped their worshippers to attain kingdoms" (ibid.:129). Their function was thus quite similar to that of the war gods (cf. Kamakau 1961:166). Both destroyed the enemies of order: rivals of the king or transgressors. But the connection between the war gods and their effect was visible to everybody. In contrast, the role of the sorcery gods in the misfortunes or the death of the king's enemies was not patent and was discoverable only by interpretation. Nevertheless, the victims of sorcery were considered equivalent to the sacrificial victims proper, as a glance at the text of the sorcery spells used to kill enemies will demonstrate.

Consider, for instance, these lines taken from a spell:

> Seize the victim, O Kama!
> The maggots crawl in your head, o victim! (Kamakau
> 1964:123)

Not only is the spell directed against a man who is called "victim" but the maggots mentioned in the second line parallel the maggots in which Kū materializes in order to devour the sacrifices offered to him (hence the appellation of Kūwahailo: 'Kū-maggot-mouth').[29]

Consider also this spell:

> For a life, a death,
> a great *ka'upu* bird is calling
> sounding nearby, calling out.
> What is the food it is calling for?
> A man is the food it is calling for. (Ibid.:125)

Here again, there is a parallel with sacrifice proper, since the bird of prey (*ka'upu*, in this case) is one of the forms the god took to devour the victim,[30] and also because the idea of substitution (a death for life), so typical of sacrifice, is exploited.

Of course, the connection between sorcery and human sacrifice, invisible and visible violence, was based on the fact that in both practices the gods were considered as the main agents and the main beneficiaries: they fed on the victims. Hawaiian sorcery consistently relied on the operations of special gods and not only on the power of the spell (moreover, sorcery often implied the performance of sacrifices). Actually, it was precisely in sorcery that the role of the gods was paramount (everything happened invisibly), while in war and in sacrifice human action played a fundamental role.

The connection between sorcery gods and war gods is confirmed by the fact that the war gods could also be used in sorcery. Indeed, Beckwith goes so far as to write that "all images of war gods named under the Kū group are in fact sorcery gods" (Beckwith 1940:110). In the context of sorcery, the modus operandi of Kūkā'ilimoku was similar to that of the sorcery gods and in particular of the Kālaipāhoa gods: they took the form of a light that moved very quickly and struck the intended victims; they could also appear as a shooting star or as lightning (Ellis 1842, 4:119; Kamakau 1964:137; Westervelt 1915:114). Like certain sorcery gods (such as Kāneikōleamoku), Kūkā'ilimoku could take the form of a bird and move around in this way (cf. Kamakau 1961:211).

Sorcery gods and war gods had another important feature in common: they were less distinguished from their material embodiment than, for instance, Kūnuiākea. Actually, the sorcery gods (and the Kālaipāhoa gods in particular) were essentially fetishes. As Kamakau writes, "Kalaipahoa *ma* were not images of gods, *akua ki'i*— they were themselves the gods, *he akua*" (Kamakau 1964:136). To some extent, the war gods had the nature of fetishes as well. For instance, the war gods of Maui and O'ahu inhered in the wood from which part of their image was made (Westervelt 1915:23–27). Their image, then, was not simply a representation that could be carved again from another piece of wood. Of course, Hawaiian writers, conditioned by the special horror that their Calvinist teachers felt for "idolatry," exaggerated the opposition between sorcery gods and the "great gods." They claimed that the images of the latter, contrary to those of the former, were "only images" and not the gods themselves. This rigid opposition was hardly justified. As we have seen, even the image of Kūnuiākea was carved into a tree that was supposed to be a natural manifestation of the god; moreover, the image was not just a representation, since at one point of the temple ritual it was referred to as *akua maoli*, 'real (or true) god'. Nevertheless, the god did not coincide with the image, although he was controlled through it and contained in it. From this point of view, the opposition established by the Hawaiian authors was justified. Moreover, we find that this opposition corresponded to the opposition between two successive states of the Haku 'ōhi'a in the temple ritual. In its first state the Haku 'ōhi'a was essentially a fetish god[31] associated with other fetish gods, such as Kūkā'ilimoku. In its final stage, however, the Haku 'ōhi'a was partially defetishized. This process of partial defetishization was also a process of deindividualization of both the god and his worshipers. When the gods have no existence separate from their empirical embodiment, they are then purely individual and can only be controlled by those who own them. They can therefore be put to purely individual ends. When, on the contrary, the gods have a transcendent existence separate from their representations or material embodiments, they do not belong exclusively to any individual (insofar as different individuals or communities can make a representation of the god, they can all establish a relationship with him) and they cannot, therefore, be identified with individualistic or particularistic ends.[32]

Two facts emerge from this discussion:

(1) The sorcery gods were a milder equivalent of the war gods and in fact sorcery and war could be two fields in which the same gods manifested their power.

(2) The sorcery gods occupied the extreme pole in a continuum in which one pole was associated with individualistic action, which employed completely fetishized gods, and the other was associated with forms of action that represented the global society and its values, and which employed relatively defetishized gods. The temple ritual transcended the former in order to establish the latter.

11. From Human Sacrifice to Sorcery

The preceding discussion of sorcery makes it possible for us to consider the temples connected with Kamehameha and Liholiho during their residence in Kailua (island of Hawai'i) from 1813 to 1819 (the year of Kamehameha's death).

As we have seen, the Kailua system was similar in structure to the one in Honolulu. Both systems were centered on the main *luakini* temple of the island; in both, there was a basic opposition between the personal temples of Liholiho and those of Kamehameha, and Liholiho was connected with a *hale o Lono* and with the main *luakini* temple.

However, the Kailua system differed from the one in Honolulu in two important respects:

(1) The temple of Keikipu'ipu'i, which used to house Kūkā'ilimoku, was restored as a temple of Liholiho and lost its connection with the war god (Freycinet 1839, in Freycinet 1824–39:524, 552–53, 598; Arago 1822, 2:114–15).

(2) Kamehameha's personal temple was not a *hale o Kā'ili* but a *hale*

hui 'ili mai'a (Ii 1963:123, cf. Kamakau 1961:179)—that is, a temple for the sorcery gods (cf. Barrère 1975:8).

In order to understand these innovations, a brief glance at the political context is necessary.

We have seen that, in 1802, Kamehameha left the island of Hawai'i in order to conquer the last stronghold of resistance, Kaua'i, which was then ruled by King Kaumuali'i. After a sojourn in Maui, Kamehameha's fleet reached O'ahu in 1803 (cf. Cleveland 1843, 2: 228, 230; Turnbull 1813:204). There, an epidemic decimated the army and the expedition against Kaua'i had to be postponed. Finally, by threats and diplomacy, Kaumuali'i was persuaded to come to Honolulu to recognize Kamehameha's supremacy (1810). Having peacefully completed the conquest of the entire archipelago, Kamehameha could return to the island of Hawai'i at the end of 1812. Significantly, both he and Liholiho attended to the rites of the Makahiki (the New Year's festival presided over by Lono) near Hikiau, the temple that represented the peaceful and stable pole of kingship (Ii 1963:115). At the beginning of 1813 the two rulers moved to Kailua.

The building or restoration of temples in that locality provided an occasion to express the definitive transcendence of war that had been achieved by the peaceful settlement of the Kaua'i affair. Both the decision to neutralize Keikipu'ipu'i's connection with war by associating it with Liholiho and the building of a sorcery temple as the personal temple of Kamehameha were related to this transcendence. At the same time, the association of Keikipu'ipu'i with the memory of the wars waged by Kalani'ōpu'u and Kamehameha against the leeward islands must have been still too fresh not to warrant the impression that its restoration also contained an implicit threat against those islands, which the court had just left. Peace reigned, but if the people of O'ahu or Maui wanted to rebel, Kamehameha was quite prepared to move Keikipu'ipu'i back into the Kūkā'ilimoku pole and to replicate the expeditions of 1795 and 1802. In sum, Keikipu'ipu'i contained, after 1813, two opposite statements: one explicit, the other tacitly present in everybody's mind.

The neutralization of the war temple also meant that the only temple left for Kamehameha to claim as his own was a temple for the sorcery gods, who represented the milder form of the active, violent pole of kingship. We have already noted that 'Ahu'ena, Kamehameha's personal temple, housed his sorcery gods. Let us now demonstrate this statement in full.

'Ī'ī (1963:123) describes 'Ahu'ena in these terms:

Ahuena house, which was a heiau, was enclosed with a fence of lama wood and within this fence, toward the front on the west and facing inland, there was an *anu'u* tower. A row of images stood along its front, as befitted a Hale o Lono. Images stood at the northwest corner of the house, with a stone pavement in front of them that extended as far as the western gate and as far as the fence east of the house. On the west side of the outer entrance was a large image named Koleamoku, on whose helmet perched the figure of a plover.

In the center of the house was a fireplace for cooking bananas. Opposite the door at the back wall of the house, in line with the fireplace and the entrance, was a Kane image. This image was of the nature of an *ololupe* god, a god who led spirits; and that part of the house was his place. All the bananas cooked there were laid before his *kuahu* altar, where those who took part in the ceremonies prayed.

This is one of the prayers:

> Ololupe ke alaka'i uhane,
> Pau ai kamahele,
> He kanaka he 'kua e kane.
> Ololupe, guide of spirits,
> Destroying traveler,
> [Destroy] the man [and] the spirit, O Kane.

There were many more prayers of that nature. Prayers of today are much better than those of yesterday. Indeed, the old religion even condoned killing.

A secret council met there to discuss matters pertaining to the government and to loyalty and rebellion. This was a continuation of the practice on Oahu. The council said that the *ololupe* god would perhaps be charged to bring hither the spirits of the rebellious to be destroyed.

It should be noted from the outset that the appellation *hale o Lono*, which 'Ī'ī gives en passant to 'Ahu'ena, refers to the architectural type to which this temple belongs, not to the fact that it was consecrated to the god Lono. The only *hale o Lono* proper belonged to Liholiho; moreover, all the gods mentioned in connection with 'Ahu'ena were unrelated to Lono. In reality 'Ī'ī's text clearly establishes that 'Ahu'ena was the equivalent of the *hale hui* in Honolulu. In addition to this main sorcery temple, special houses for the Kālaipāhoa gods were built in Kailua, as they had been in Honolulu.

The offering of bananas to all these sorcery gods (Kamakau 1964: 135; Ii 1963:123) and the banana fiber sheathing of their houses (*hale 'ili mai'a*) immediately indicate that these gods were forms of the god Kāne. According to Hawaiian theory, the species offered to a given god had to be the ones in which he materialized, his *kino lau* ('innumerable bodies'). Now bananas were usually offered to the twin gods Kāne and Kanaloa. And among the numerous forms of these "major gods," we find, precisely, some of the most important gods worshiped in the various *hale 'ili mai'a* of Honolulu and of Kailua. That the so-called Kālaipāhoa gods were connected with Kāne is confirmed by their origin myth. The main god that "entered" the trees in which the Kālaipāhoa gods were later carved was Kāneikaulana'ula, one of the forms of Kāne (Kamakau 1964:129; Ellis 1842, 4:93). As for Ololupe, 'Ī'ī refers to him as a "Kane image" (Ii 1963:123). He is addressed as the god Kāne in the prayer quoted by 'Ī'ī (ibid.; cf. also Malo 1951:113). The other god connected with 'Ahu'ena, Kōleamoku, whose large image stood in front of the temple house, was also a form of Kāne, as his full name (Kāneikōleamoku)—given by 'Ī'ī in another context (1963:45)—testifies. This god was connected with medical sorcery (Malo 1951:109).

Interestingly, in Honolulu Kāneikōleamoku was not worshiped in Kamehameha's *hale hui 'ili mai'a*, but in a special house that, together with that of Lonopuhā (another healing god), was kept by a medical priest (Ii 1963:45–46). It is possible that these houses had a connection with Liholiho, since they were adjacent to his "profane" residence, Ho'okuku (Ibid.:59). Moreover, we know that Liholiho performed various medical rites in a house (*hale lau*) dedicated to Lonomakua, which was some distance from Ho'okuku (Ibid.:60). Since all three houses for the healing gods were near Liholiho's profane residence, it is possible that they were part of the same complex to which Liholiho was connected through the house of Lonomakua. At any rate, we have seen that there was a conceptual connection between Liholiho and the healing cults. In Kailua, however, Kamehameha was directly connected with Kāneikōleamoku. This fact is related to a global shift of Kamehameha toward the "domesticated" pole of kingship, a shift testified by his decision not to build a *hale o Kā'ili* but to replace it with its "milder" equivalent, the temple of the sorcery gods. Since sorcery (*'anā'anā*) can be used for both negative and positive purposes, the sorcery gods could function both as destroyers and as healers in 'Ahu'ena (cf. Pukui et al. 1972–79, 2:122).

Our previous discussion of the relationship between war cults and sorcery makes the signification of 'Ahu'ena clear: it was a temple dedicated to a political use of sorcery, which perpetuated the violent aspect of kingship in its purely invisible, interpretive form. Death and sickness were not visibly and directly inflicted by the warrior-king but were imputed to the invisible and indirect practices of the sorcerer-king. However, as we have seen, both practices were conceptually related and considered equivalent: Kūkā'ilimoku himself seems to have been housed in 'Ahu'ena (Ellis 1842, 4:427) but evidently was downgraded to his sorcery dimension. Thus, when Kamakau writes that Kamehameha established 'Ahu'ena "for the sacrifice of human beings to his blood-thirsty gods" (1961:180), we should not take his words literally, but interpret them in the light of 'Ī'ī's statement to the effect that "the *ololupe* god would perhaps be charged to bring hither the spirits of the rebellious to be destroyed" (Ii 1963:123).

With Kamehameha's shift, however, the opposition and complementarity between himself and Liholiho became less intense. In fact, a certain return toward the indifferentiation of kingship seems to have begun. This is already indicated by the fact that Kamehameha took over some of the healing gods apparently connected with Liholiho and therefore assumed some aspects of the beneficial and peaceful ruler. Again, Kamehameha increasingly occupied himself with the promotion of productive work (fishing and agriculture) among his people. The warrior-king appears to have become a fisherman-king and a farmer-king (see Kamakau 1961:174, 177–78, 190, 192; Pogue 1858:51). Production and fertility were thus seen less as the consequence of Liholiho's symbolic transformation of violence into stability and peace than as the consequence of an absence of war that was directly attributed to Kamehameha.

At the ritual level, the loss of importance of Liholiho's functions must have been dramatically apparent because of the decrease in the number of human sacrifices.[33] Moreover, the few victims sacrificed during this period were transgressors; the principal victims, the enemy warriors, were completely lacking (Golovnin 1979:207; Laanui 1930 [1838]).

Thus, the *real* transcendence of war by Kamehameha undermined its symbolic transcendence by Liholiho. This must have been apparent already in Honolulu, since there, too, human sacrifices were few and limited to transgressors. But, at least until 1810, war was a real possibility and was explicitly planned by Kamehameha. The complementarity of the warrior-king and of the priestly king could therefore be sustained at the symbolic level. However, when it became superfluous even to plan war, the entire system was implicitly threatened, emptied as it was of its main purpose.

The building of 'Ahu'ena was in a sense the recognition that something irreversible and new had happened and that the kingly power was assuming a new and less transcendent basis. S. M. Kamakau shows himself conscious of the profound transformation implied by the choice of sorcery as a generalized language for expressing relationships of power.

In the old days, and down through Kahekili's time, there were no conspicuous god-houses built for Kalaipahoa ma. The gods were kept restricted lest the people imitate them and get out of control, and worship these gods in order to take the lives of other people or to menace the lives of the chiefs. But some of the chiefs acquired *kalaipahoa (kumuhaka)* gods, and their *kahu* ['keepers'] kept them hidden away inside the house [. . .]. But when they [the people] saw that Kamehameha I openly built houses for his Kalaipahoa and Pua gods, then these evil ways of killing men grew (Kamakau 1964:137).

Sorcery, then, implied a generalized competition for power in which, in essence, the king was bound to be increasingly conceived as an individual among other individuals, only much more powerful than his competitors.[34] The choice of sorcery as the dominant form of expression of political relations, then, exactly translated the new realities of power that had been taking shape in Hawaii since, at least, Vancouver's time. Kamehameha's victories were, to a large extent, due to his ability to accumulate the new economic and symbolic power that came from trade with the Europeans;[35] and in the early part of the nineteenth century, the development of the sandalwood trade increased the importance of the new economic power (Bradley 1942:53–120). It is not by chance that the settlement of the Kaua'i question by diplomacy coincided with the development of the sandalwood trade; in fact, European traders had an important role in bringing about the settlement (Kuykendall 1938:50).

Kamehameha's downgrading of his war gods and the emphasis he gave to sorcery, then, translated the new situation at the ritual level. Sorcery perfectly expressed, in traditional Hawaiian idiom, the two features that characterized this new reality: the transcendence of war and the individualistic, competitive nature of the accumulation and use of commercial wealth.[36] Moreover, sorcery harmonized with this incipient individualism because it tended to "internalize" the conceptualization of social processes and consequently to devalue their objectified ritual expression.[37]

The increasing importance of sorcery as a substitute for war, and therefore of the Ololupe and Kālaipāhoa worship by Kamehameha, paralleled the increasing importance of the transformed cult of Lono, which I have mentioned above. In this cult the "Cook" aspect of Liholiho was heightened at the expense of his Kūnuiākea aspect. A consideration of this parallel shift concerning Liholiho adds, perhaps, another dimension to the decision, taken in 1813, to neutralize the traditional opposition between Keikipu'ipu'i and Hikiau. That opposition had been a factor in Cook's death; but his death had been the beginning of a process that ultimately brought about the transcendence of that opposition by transcending war and human sacrifice once and for all. Thus, retrospectively, Cook's death must have appeared as the sacrifice that eventually put an end to all sacrifices. Hawaii was then ready for Christianity, before it knew it. Christ would soon take the place that Cook had occupied in his stead. No wonder, then, that the English discoverer would become the bête noire of the missionaries for his impious usurpation of a god's place.

But to return to the shores of Kailua. As a result of the transformations outlined above, the traditional ritual and ideological basis of kingship was crumbling when Kamehameha died in 1819. Significantly, Liholiho could become Kamehameha's actual successor only by making official the de facto desacralization of the king and abolishing the entire ritual system connected with kingship. He, the sacred king, had to become the unhappy and powerless figurehead of an oligarchy of merchant-chiefs. And his cousin Kekuaokalani, to whom Kamehameha had, somewhat perversely, left the care of the god Kūkā'ilimoku (and therefore his own role as warrior-king vis-à-vis Liholiho), bitterly discovered on the battlefield that the old order that he had attempted to uphold against the European-backed army of Liholiho had become as empty and powerless as Kūkā'ilimoku himself. Thus—as in a more famous story—the twilight of the gods was brought about by the power of gold. But as long as Kamehameha was alive, the gods in the royal temples continued to reconcile the past and the present and to conjure the dark future. Although his enterprises brought Hawaii to the threshold of the "modern world," one can say of Kamehameha, as Henry James said of the "last of the Valerii," "he never was, if you will, a completely modern man."

12. Conclusion: Structure and Historical Process

We may pause, in conclusion, to consider some of the implications of this study and to formulate its substantive conclusions in a larger context. In this essay I have tried to illuminate a historical process by reference to a structure and, reciprocally, to illuminate a structure by reference to a historical process. In the latter, the structure displays itself; in the former, the process can be perceived as orderly. The structure is therefore a condition of intelligibility of the process as much as the process is a condition of intelligibility of the structure. Neither is intelligible per se, without reference to the other. The paradoxical result of this fact is that the structure becomes fully intelligible only in the process of change and the process is intelligible only when it displays a certain changelessness.

This complementarity of structure and process is particularly relevant in the Hawaiian case, where the structure itself was conceived as the scheme of a process. In fact, we have seen that the royal ritual attempted to organize the political process by orienting it in a particular direction, by transforming war and conquest into peace and stability. But this implied a contradictory relationship between ritual and social praxis. On the one hand, ritual was a model for reality. Because of its molding effect and because it created consensus around a ruler who impersonated the model, ritual had a *direct* relationship with social reality. But on the other hand, the reproduction of ritual, and therefore its very existence, was an index of the fact that what it symbolized was never really translated into practice, could never be.

In other words, a ritual that described the transcendence of war could survive in a meaningful way only because it coexisted with a social reality in which war could not really be transcended, except provisionally. The whole paradox of the historical process that I have described is that the fulfillment of the promise contained in ritual undermined the existence of ritual, since only its nonfulfillment could reproduce it. Thus it is not a matter, here, of viewing ritual as a "reflection" of a praxis in its own right, which enabled the lag between the ultimate ideological justification of political action and its actual realization to be provisionally obliterated. To put it differently: the fact that ritual had to be abandoned once what it represented could acquire a sustained existence of its own was the secret implication of ritual itself. No wonder, then, that in 1819 the process of translating representation into sustained existence was brought to a conclusion by rejecting the ritual that had anticipated it at the symbolic level.

If my analysis of the royal ritual is correct, then, this ritual was the symptom and the expression of a lack of fit between ideology and practice. A few words will give an idea of the reasons for this.

In order to control or to conquer a territory, a king needed to attract a large number of followers. He could do so by means of gifts and promises of land grants, which were fulfilled once a certain district was conquered with his allies' help. Thus the political system promoted conquest and expansion, until they encountered their limits. These were constituted by the inability of the king to retain his control over an increasing number of subordinate allies, each of whom attempted to emulate him, and by the resistance of his potential victims, at whose expense he attracted new followers or maintained the old ones. Moreover, once all the conquerable lands had been obtained, the king had little to offer his subordinates. On the contrary, he required prestations from them. He became burdensome and revolts broke out. The political system was thus generated by war and inevitably generated war. Accordingly, the permanence of peace and stability was structurally impossible. The process of transcendence of conflict and war, the "rebinding" of society, guided by the ritual that represented them, had to be repeated endlessly.

The real transcendence of war was only made possible by an exogenous factor: European technology and European trade. The process of pacification and unification of the archipelago correlated with a transformation of the traditional political system brought about by Kamehameha (cf. Kuykendall 1938:51–54). This transformation affected ritual partly through conscious manipulation (as testified by the building of different varieties of temples), partly because of "mechanical" effects. As we have seen, the lack of war devalued the role of Kūkā'ilimoku; it made it impossible to represent in its full and due form the passage from Kūkā'ilimoku to Kūnuiākea and from the latter to Lono. To this "mechanical" effect of the political process on the ritual one, Kamehameha reacted by establishing the ritual diarchy upon an increasingly new basis. He himself developed the sorcery aspect of kingship. Liholiho had to develop the Cook/Lono aspect, although he continued to perform the old ritual in the form in which it could be performed in the absence of war. During the Kailua period, the old and the new structures uneasily coexisted. But the new structure in formation was more successful in undermining the old system than in establishing a new one. For one thing, sorcery could not procure enemies as victims to be sacrificed in the temple of Kūnuiākea; it simply "killed" people. It was more like police work than like sacrifice, and it could not dynamically connect the two rulers in the same ritual process.

It is clear that, in Kamehameha's mind, sorcery had to take care of the internal political relationships, whereas Liholiho's connection with Hikiau, in addition to being a relic from the traditional past, was meant to establish the legitimacy of the new system by reference to an encompassing exterior that was increasingly associated with the new gods revealed by Cook, who had initially appeared as an old one in that temple: the Europeans (the British in particular) and their wealth (see Sahlins 1979). But beyond a certain point, the basis of power could as well become this wealth pure and simple. Indeed, real trade definitely did displace ritual trade. I do not know, then, if the abolition of the ritual system in 1819 is more impressive for the spirit of innovation that it shows or for the historical respect for the past it displays. The past had indeed become past: it could not be meddled with by going too far on the road of ritual manipulation. Consciousness intervened in the unconscious or semiconscious process. As usual in such cases, a turning point, a "revolution," was the result.

Notes

Acknowledgments. The research on which this essay is based was funded in part by the Lichtstern Fund of the Department of Anthropology of the University of Chicago and by the Social Sciences Division of the same university. To both I wish to express my deepest appreciation.

I also extend my thanks to the Bishop Museum of Honolulu, in whose library much of my research was done. In particular, I am grateful to its staff, and to Cynthia Tymberlake above all, for their generous help. An equally warm thank-you goes to the staff of the Hamilton Library of the University of Hawaii, especially to Renée Heyum.

I also gratefully acknowledge the crucial help received from Dorothy and F. Waldron Barrère, Kajorn Howard, and Barbara Sahlins. As usual, I am in great debt to Marshall Sahlins for all I have learned during many stimulating conversations on Hawaiian subjects.

A first draft of this paper was read in October 1980 at the Twenty-eighth Annual Meeting of the American Society for Ethnohistory in San Francisco. I am grateful to my audience for its patience and its comments.

Much of the present version was read in May 1981 at the Monday seminar of the Department of Anthropology, University of Chicago. I am thankful to this notoriously patient audience as well. Finally, I wish to express my gratitude to Dorothy Barrère, Jane Bestor, Judith Huntsman, Susan McKinnon, and Marshall Sahlins for their invaluable comments and corrections.

1. The definition of the word *luakini* quoted by Andrews in his dictionary (Andrews 1865:351): "o ka *luakini*, oia ka heiau a ke alii nui e noi aku

ai i na 'kua ona" ('the *luakini* is the king's temple in which he makes requests to his god').

2. The sources of Papa'ena'ena are the following: Whitman 1979:68, Sandwich Islands. Journal of the Mission, *Missionary Herald* 20 (September 1824):282; Mathison 1825:377; Stewart 1830:298–300; Tyerman and Bennet 1831, 1:423; Gough (ed.) 1973:134; Meyen 1834–35, 2:149; Jarves 1843:59–60; Bates 1854:94; Ii 1963:33; Johnstone 1908:162; Thrum 1926; McAllister 1933:71–74.

3. A close reading of the evidence demonstrates that these houses were indeed near the royal temple complex. 'Ī'ī mentions the existence of a trail passing between "the houses of the gods and the heiaus" (1963:91). Moreover, it appears that Kalanimoku's residence (and therefore the houses of the sorcery gods that were near it) was close to the royal temples, since it was situated to the west or northwest of chieftess Kekauonohi's place (cf. ibid.:100, referring to Mokuaikaua, one of Kalanimoku's houses), and not the east, as erroneously shown on Rockwood's map of Honolulu in 1810 (included in Ii 1963:65, 90). According to Dorothy Barrère (letter to the author, 5 August 1981), the location near the royal temples is confirmed by Gorham Gilman's description of Honolulu in 1840 (Gilman 1904:76; cf. Ii 1963:100).

4. Note that Franchère mistakes Honolulu for Waikīkī. His description of Kamehameha's compound, however, especially when compared with that given by his traveling companion Alexander Ross, who does not make the same mistake, establishes beyond doubt that he is speaking of Honolulu instead of Waikīkī. To complicate matters even further, 'Ī'ī writes in another passage: "Papalima was the keeper of the god Kaili in the coconut grove of Honuakaha" (Ii:1963:101). Honuakaha was quite distant from Kamehameha's residence and from Liholiho's *hale o Lono* (ibid.:90). But it is likely that this statement does not imply that the *hale o Kā'ili* was situated in that grove; rather, it implies that the keeper of Kūkā'ilimoku performed there certain rituals pertaining to the god such as, it seems, scooping out the eyes of the transgressors (ibid.:101).

   On the so-called "King's morai [temple]" of Honolulu, see also Whitman 1979:24–25 and the rather different description by Kotzebue (1821, 1: 60) and von Chamisso (1864, 4:139–40), who saw the complex after it had been reconstructed in the absence of Kamehameha, following its destruction by fire in 1816 (cf. Choris 1822:124; Kotzebue 1821, 1:303–5, 333–35; Corney 1965:157–58).

5. Particularly in the case of the *hale o Kā'ili*, a separate complex of different structures was the more usual arrangement (see, for instance, Wilkes 1845, 4:506; Stokes n.d.:GR 1 box 9.48, pp. 24, 83; Ellis 1842, 4:98, 119).

6. Marshall Sahlins has kindly provided me with a copy of this important document. The temple complex of Pākākā is, unfortunately, not mentioned in the standard work on the sites of O'ahu (Sterling and Summers 1962).

7. Moreover, he claims to have found this "text" in Thrum's collection of papers, preserved in the Bishop Museum Library in Honolulu. I have been unable to find such a text in Thrum's papers. It is more probable that McAllister's source was Stokes, whom he misunderstood, at any rate.

8. Kamehameha's renovation was completed in June 1813 (Marin 1973:211). The literary and iconographic documentation on 'Ahu'ena is excellently discussed by Barrère (1975:7–9 and passim).

9. It seems that two Kālaipāhoa images had a closer connection with 'Ahu'ena. This can be deduced from a comparison of Choris's sketch of 'Ahu'ena with a passage by Ellis. According to the latter, Kālaipāhoa "was a middling-sized wooden image, curiously carved; the arms were extended, the fingers spread out, the head was ornamented with human hair, and the widely extended mouth was armed with rows of shark's teeth" (Ellis 1842, 4:91). Now, Choris represented two images with extended arms and fingers spread out on 'Ahu'ena's stone platform, just behind the tower, but on the outside of the fence encompassing the temple (see a reproduction of Choris's sketch in Barrère 1975:7). One similar image survives and is preserved at the British Museum. From a photograph published by Cox and Davenport (1974:28), it appears that it has at least one shark tooth.

10. See my studies of this fact, published after the present essay was written (Valeri 1985b, 1990, in press). Diarchic tendencies are common to many systems of kingship (cf. Valeri 1980). So far, there has been no complete study of the Hawaiian political system. See, among others, Levin 1968; Valeri 1972, 1976; Earle 1978; Sahlins 1981.

11. Cf. Valeri 1985a: xxiv, xxvi, 198, 255. Note also that Malo's description of the *luakini* temple closely parallels that of Hikiau in the journals of Cook's expedition (cf. Valeri 1985a:242).

12. See Valeri (1985a:ch. 8) for both this complete analysis and the sources on which the following summary is based. For the present purpose it is sufficient to describe it in outline.

13. The *fono* is usually an assembled body of ranked titleholders, with various social functions (cf. Goldman 1970:271–75, 335, 373).

14. This is the so-called *ka'i'oloa* rite. The contact is established through the goddesses worshiped in an annex (*hale o Papa*) of the *luakini* (Malo n.d.:178 –79; Kelou Kamakau in Fornander 1916–20, 4:29). See the discussion in Valeri 1985a:327–32.

15. As the prayers uttered during the ritual demonstrate, its aim was, ultimately, to promote the life of the entire society. The Hawaiian temple ritual certainly conformed to Hocart's idea that ritual is a "technique of life-giving" (Hocart 1970:33) or, even better, an "organization for life" that depends on the "co-ordination of actions" (Ibid.:37). See, for instance, Kamakau's reflection: "Hawaiians were people who prayed much for the life of the body" (1865c).

16. The necessity of constantly repeating the ritual indicates that the contradiction between the two aspects of kingship is never definitively transcended. This correlates with the absence of a coronation or installation ritual proper in Hawaii. The installation ritual was traditionally the temple ritual itself, and it had to be constantly repeated.

Interestingly enough, the early stage of Indian kingship, as described by Heesterman (1957 and 1978), was similar to the Hawaiian in this respect. In both societies, the king was periodically relegitimated by establishing a connection between the "wild" outside and the "cultivated" inside. According to Heesterman, this reflects the following paradox: "the king has to belong to the community, but at the same time he must be foreign to it so as to guarantee his authority" (Heesterman 1978:9). In the Hawaiian case, however, the "foreign" character of the king was rather a metaphor of the dimension of force and constraint, which was the precondition of authority. Authority itself was obtained by the transformation of force inside society, by harnessing it to the values of the society. As I have noted elsewhere, Heesterman's interpretation is too mechanistic and it underestimates the transformative and dialectical aspects of the ritual legitimation of the king (see Valeri 1980:751–53).

17. Thus, Kū manifested himself in two opposite, but complementary, aspects, which corresponded to analogous aspects of the king. Like the god, the king was conceived as all-powerful and therefore as dangerous in his "free," "wild" state. He had therefore to be transformed into a totally constrained being. The temple ritual, of course, brought about this transformation, but its effects were maintained by the everyday ritual prescriptions and taboos that surrounded the king and made him, at times, totally dependent, materially speaking, on his subordinates. The paradoxical relationship between the "total freedom" of the king's power and the "total ritual constraint" whereby that power is sublimated and preserved was by no means confined to the Hawaiian kings. Norbert Elias has effectively shown that these "zwei Seiten der gleichen Erscheinung" (Elias 1968:211) also characterized modern European kingship.

18. It is not mentioned by previous visitors either (see Menzies 1920:57). On Pu'ukoholā, see also Patterson 1817:71; Iselin n.d.:71; A.B.F.M. Missionaries 1821:113–21, 115–16.

19. See, for instance, the first chapter of "Ka Mooolelo o Hawaii nei" by S. M. Kamakau (1865a), where Kūkā'ilimoku is referred to as *he akua hulu*, 'a feather god'.

20. On the distinction symbol/substitute, see Gombrich 1978:1–6; Skorupski 1976:141–44; Lewis 1980:111, 193.

Of course, since ritual was believed to lend efficacy to the real war actions, its symbols must have been considered as more than mere symbols. They provided no substitute for real action, however. Also, they proved to be more than mere symbols only retrospectively, when the symbolized had been *made real* on the battlefield. The confirmatory ritual confirmed, precisely, that such a realization was ultimately due to the performance of ritual, to which the extraritual event was now brought back. Thus, belief was fixed and reproduced through a complex dialectics of ritual and extraritual events.

Naturally, the whole question of the relationship between symbol and symbolized is infinitely complex. For the present purpose, I have drastically simplified my position (sketched in Valeri 1981b), which is equally distant from that of Lienhardt (1961:283) and from that of Skorupski (1976:141 –44).

21. This is further confirmed by a tradition reported by Emerson. According to his informant, the sacrifice that Kīwala'ō was due to consecrate in the temple of Pākini belonged to the category named *puku* (Emerson n.d.:525, 532). This word is glossed 'final offering; to end' by Pukui and Elbert (1971:325). Thus Kīwala'ō's sacrifice was indeed concluding, confirmatory: it was supposed to mark the end of the process opened with war.

22. The temple of Pākini was considered at the times of Handy's research (1935, 1954, 1959) as a *heiau ho'oulu'ai* ('temple for the increase of food') and was said to be dedicated to Kāne'apua, "Kane of the clouds" (Handy 1972:580–82, cf. 387). Although the appellation *ho'oulu'ai* is not incom-

patible with a *luakini* (Malo 1951:152), for reasons that will appear later, Pākini's ancient connection with the royal rites of human sacrifice, and therefore with Kū, is still testified today by the fact that it is also called a *heiau po'okanaka* (Pukui et al. 1974:175). This name means 'temple of the human head', and it refers to the custom of putting the skulls of the human victims on the temple railings. According to Stoller, however, the name should be translated 'temple of the leader of the people' (ibid.:GR 1 box 8.33). He explains that "in this class would be conducted all the services affecting the head of the government and the people as a whole" (ibid.:GR 1 box 9.48, p. 5). At any rate, this confirms that the temple of Pākini was originally conceived of as the temple of the supreme, all-encompassing ruler and therefore of his god Kūnuiākea.

23. As Menzies writes, the destruction of the plantations "is their principal mode of carrying war, for we understand that their battles, though frequent, were not of any long continuance or very bloody" (Menzies 1920: 115, cf. 117:cf. Beaglehole 1967:578; Shaler 1808).

24. It was in this sense that Lono was a "god of the people," a "popular god," as he is often called.

25. The connection between the *kapu hua* and Lono, god of fertility, seems to be confirmed by two interrelated facts. *Hua* means 'fruitful', and because of that nuptials took place the night before the beginning of the *kapu hua* (see Pukui and Elbert 1971:24, the entry for *ho'ao*).

26. He had occasionally resided there even before (cf. Mortimer 1791:52; Quimper 1937:2).

27. A confusion created by Fornander (1880, 2:183 n. 1) and reproduced by Beaglehole in his edition of the journals of Cook's expedition (Beaglehole 1967:510 n.2 and passim) must be dispelled at this point. Fornander believes that Ka'ō'ō (spelled "Kao" or "Cahoo" by the British) and Holoa'e were probably two names given to the same person—namely, the "high priest." Fornander's hypothesis is motivated by the fact that whereas the English accounts mention Ka'ō'ō as the high priest, the Hawaiian tradition claims that Holoa'e was the priest of Kūkā'ilimoku at that time. Since Fornander, as we have seen, fails to recognize the difference between Kūkā'ilimoku and Kūnuiākea, he cannot understand why two different priests should be mentioned. In my opinion, the Hawaiian tradition and the British accounts must refer to two different priests, since the former points to Holoa'e's connection with Keikipu'ipu'i, while the latter indicate that Ka'ō'ō was connected with Hikiau. This connection is demonstrated by the fact that all the gifts that the English received from the priests of Hikiau were made in the name of Ka'ō'ō (King 1967:509, 510), and by the fact that his grandson "Kaireekeea" presided in his absence over the rites performed for Cook (Cook and King 1784, 3:159; King 1967:509, cf. 514–15).

To my thesis that Holoa'e and Ka'ō'ō were two different priests, it could be objected that Holoa'e is never mentioned by the British; but this objection is easily repelled. It is likely that, as a priest of Kūkā'ilimoku, Holoa'e was excluded from the festival of Lono and, a fortiori, from approaching Cook, who was identified with Lono.

28. An obvious index of this adoption of Cook by the priests of Hikiau is given by the fact that they provided most of the gifts received by the British.

29. Moreover, Kuwahailo was both the introducer of human sacrifice and a sorcery god (Pukui and Elbert 1971:391).
30. This explains why it is called "an unclean bird" by Kepelino (1858:1133).
31. As a matter of fact, the tree was initially a purely individual materialization of the god.
32. My analysis, here, obviously owes much to the writings of Robertson Smith (1889) and Evans-Pritchard (1937, 1956). For a wider background, see Valeri 1979.
33. The decrease accelerated in Liholiho's time but had already begun with Kamehameha's reunification of the island of Hawai'i (cf. Bell 1929 –30, 2 [1] December:90; Lisiansky 1814:120; Shaler 1808:167; Corney 1965: 198; Hussey 1958:36; Golovnin 1979:207).
34. The diffusion of sorcery from the king to his subjects was openly acknowledged at the death of Kamehameha, when his Kālaipāhoa gods were divided into as many pieces as there were principal chiefs and distributed to them (Ellis 1842, 4:91–92).

    The spreading of sorcery in Hawaii, as a correlate of the increased individualism and of the weakening of the kingly authority, is paralleled by the spreading of sorcery and witchcraft in Africa for similar reasons. See, for instance, Turner 1968:128–29.
35. "A Mr. Butler of Lahaina claimed that Kamehameha won his wars entirely by the help he received from white men" (Webb n.d.).

    On Kamehameha's fondness for trade and European wealth, cf. A.B.F.M. Missionaries 1820:334.
36. Naturally, Kamehameha reduced the competitive aspect by controlling trade; but his successor was unable to retain this control.
37. Choris, who visited the islands in 1816, wrote that at the time "les insulaires semblaient ne pas avoir beaucoup de respect pour ces images des dieux; ils en faisaient des objets de plaisanterie" (Choris 1822:123; see also von Chamisso 1864:139–40; A.B.F.M. Missionaries 1820:335.) Cf. Kamehameha's attitude in Gough (1973:135). This treatment of images and gods was traditional in certain contexts, however (see Valeri 1981b); it was only intensified and generalized at the end of Kamehameha's reign.

References Cited

A.B.F.M. Missionaries
    1820   Journal of the Missionaries. *Missionary Herald* 16 (July).
    1821   Journal of the Missionaries. *Missionary Herald* 17 (April).
    1824   Journal of the Missionaries. *Missionary Herald* 20 (September).
Andrews, Lorrin
    1865   *A Dictionary of the Hawaiian Language*. Honolulu: H. M. Whitney.
Arago, Jacques
    1822   *Promenade autour du monde*. 2 vols. Paris: Leblanc.

1840   *Souvenirs d'un aveugle: Voyage autour du monde.* 2 vols. Paris:
                Lebrun.

Barrère, Dorothy
1975   *Kamehameha in Kona: Two Documentary Studies.* Pacific An-
                thropological Records no. 23. Honolulu: Bernice Pauahi
                Bishop Museum.

Bastian, Adolf
1881   *Die heilige Sage der Polynesier: Kosmogonie und Theogonie.*
                Leipzig: Brockhaus.

Bates, G. W. (Haole)
1854   *Sandwich Islands Notes.* New York: Harper & Row.

Beaglehole, John C., ed.
1967   *The Journals of Captain James Cook on His Voyages of Discov-
                ery. Vol. 3: The Voyage of the Resolution and Discovery
                1776–1780.* Pts. 1 and 2. Cambridge: Cambridge University
                Press.

Beckwith, Martha W.
1940   *Hawaiian Mythology.* New Haven: Yale University Press.
1951   *The Kumulipo: A Hawaiian Creation Chant.* Chicago: Univer-
                sity of Chicago Press.

Bell, Edward
1929–30   Log of the Chatham. *Hawaiian Mercury.* 1(4) September:7–
                26; (5) October:55–69; (6) November:76–96; 2(1) Decem-
                ber:80–91; (2) January 1930:119–29.

Boelen, Jacobus
1835–36   *Reize naar de Oost- en Westkust van Zuid-America, en van
                daar, Naar de Sandwichs- en Philippijinsche Eilanden.* 3 vols.
                Amsterdam: Ten Brink & De Vries.

Bradley, Harold W.
1942   *The American Frontier in Hawaii.* Stanford: Stanford Univer-
                sity Press.

Broughton, William R.
1804   *A Voyage of Discovery to the North Pacific Ocean.* London:
                Cadell-Davies.

Byron, George A.
1826   *Voyage of H.M.S. Blonde to the Sandwich Islands, in the Years
                1824–25.* London: Murray.

Campbell, Archibald
1967[1822]
                A Voyage Round the World, from 1806 to 1812. Facsimile re-

production of the 3d American edition, 1822. Honolulu: University of Hawaii Press.

Chamisso de Boncourt, L. K. Adelbert von
1864   *Chamissos Werke*, 4: *Reise um die Welt*, 1. Berlin: Deutsches Verlagshaus Bong & Co.

Choris, Louis (Ludovik)
1822   *Voyage pittoresque autour du monde*. Paris: Firmin Didot.

Cleveland, Richard J.
1843   *A Narrative of Voyages and Commercial Enterprises*. 2d ed. 2 vols. Cambridge, Mass.: John Owen.

Cook, James, and James King
1784   *A Voyage to the Pacific Ocean*. 3 vols. London: Nicol and Cadell.

Corney, Peter
1965   *Early Voyages in the North Pacific, 1813–1818*. Fairfield, Wash.: Galleon Press.

Cox, J. Halley, and William H. Davenport
1974   *Hawaiian Sculpture*. Honolulu: University Press of Hawaii.

Earle, Timothy
1978   *Economic and Social Organization of a Complex Chiefdom: The Halelea District, Kaua'i, Hawaii*. Anthropological Papers no. 63. Ann Arbor: University of Michigan, Museum of Anthropology.

Elbert, Samuel H.
1956–57   The Chief in Hawaiian Mythology. *Journal of American Folklore* 59:99–113, 341–55; 60:264–76, 306–22.
n.d.   *Place Names of Hawaii*. 3 vols. Typescript in the Bishop Museum Library, Honolulu.

Elias, Norbert
1968   *Die höfische Gesellschaft: Eine Untersuchung zur Soziologie des Konigtums und des Adels*. Neuwied/Berlin: Luchterhand.

Ellis, William
1828   *Narrative of a Tour through Hawaii*. 4th ed. London: Fisher & Jackson.
1842   *Polynesian Researches*. 4 vols. London: Fisher & Jackson.

Emerson, Joseph S.
1892   Lesser Hawaiian Gods. *Papers of the Hawaiian Historical Society* 2:1–24.
n.d.   Pule ha'i [*sic*] kanaka. Prayer when offering a human sacrifice. Emerson's Collection in Hawaiian Ethnographical Notes, 1:525–33. Unpublished ms.

Equity 200
Ms.   Land Case (4 February 1862). Archives of Hawaii.

Evans-Pritchard, E. E.

1937   *Witchcraft, Oracles and Magic among the Azande.* London: Oxford University Press.

1956   *Nuer Religion.* London: Oxford University Press.

Firth, Raymond

1930–31   Totemism in Polynesia. *Oceania* 1:291–321, 377-98.

Fornander, Abraham

1880   *An Account of the Polynesian Race, Its Origin and Migrations and the Ancient History of the Hawaiian People to the Times of Kamehameha I.* 3 vols. London: Trübner.

1916–20   Fornander Collection of Hawaiian Antiquities and Folk-Lore. Memoirs of the Bernice Pauahi Bishop Museum nos. 4–6. Honolulu: Bishop Museum Press.

Franchère, Gabriel, fils

1820   *Relation d'un voyage à la côte du nord-ouest de l'Amérique Septentrionale, dans les années 1810, 11, 12, 13, et 14.* Montréal: Pasteur.

Freycinet, Louis Claude Desoulses de

1824–39   *Voyage autour du monde [. . .] pendant les années 1817, 1818, 1819, et 1820.* Paris: Pillet.

1839   *Historique,* vol. 2, pt. 2.

Gernet, Louis, and A. Boulanger

1932   *Le Génie grec dans la religion.* Paris: La Renaissance du Livre.

Gilman, G. D.

1904   Streets of Honolulu in the Early Forties. *Hawaiian Almanac and Annual.*

Goldman, Irving

1970   *Ancient Polynesian Society.* Chicago: University of Chicago Press.

Golovnin, V. M.

1979   *Around the World on the Kamchatka, 1817–1819.* Honolulu: University Press of Hawaii.

Gombrich, Ernest H.

1978   *Meditations on a Hobby Horse.* London: Phaidon.

Gough, Barry M., ed.

1973   *To the Pacific and Arctic with Beechey: The Journal of the Lieutenant George Peard of H.M.S. "Blossom," 1825–1828.* Cambridge: Cambridge University Press.

Handy, Edward S. C.

1968   Traces of Totemism in Polynesia. *Journal of the Polynesian Society* 77:43–56.

1972   *Native Planters in Old Hawaii: Their Life, Lore and Environment*. Bernice Pauahi Bishop Museum Bulletin no. 233. Honolulu: Bishop Museum Press.

Heesterman, Johannes C.

1957   *The Ancient Indian Royal Consecration*. The Hague: Mouton.

1978   The Conundrum of the King's Authority. In *Kingship and Authority in South Asia*, ed. J. F. Richards. Madison: University of Wisconsin Press.

Hiroa, Te Rangi [Sir Peter H. Buck]

1957   *Arts and Crafts of Hawaii*. Bernice Pauahi Bishop Museum Special Publication no. 45. Honolulu: Bishop Museum Press.

Hocart, Arthur M.

1970   *Kings and Councillors*. Chicago: University of Chicago Press.

Hussey, John Adam, ed.

1958   *The Voyage of the Raccoon [. . .], 1813–1814*. San Francisco: Book Club of California.

Ii, John Papa

1963   *Fragments of Hawaiian History*. Ed. D. Barrère, 2d ed. Honolulu: Bishop Museum Press.

Iselin, Isaak

n.d.   *Journal of a Trading Voyage around the World, 1805–1808*. New York: McIlory & Emmet.

Jarves, James Jackson

1843   *History of Hawaiian or Sandwich Islands*. Boston: Tappan & Bennet.

Johnstone, A.

1908   Storied Nuuanuu. *Hawaiian Annual*, 160–67.

Judd, Walter F.

1975   *Palaces and Forts of the Hawaiian Kingdom: From Thatch to American Florentine*. Palo Alto: Pacific Books.

Kamakau, Samuel M.

1865a   Ka Mooolelo o Hawaii nei. *Ka Nupepa Kuokoa*, 15 June.

1865b   Ka Mooolelo o Hawaii nei. *Ka Nupepa Kuokoa*, 22 June.

1865c   Ka Mooolelo o Hawaii nei. *Ka Nupepa Kuokoa*, 12 August.

1961   *The Ruling Chiefs of Hawaii*. Honolulu: Kamehameha Schools Press.

1964   *Ka Po'e Kahiko*. (The People of Old). Bernice Pauahi Bishop Museum Special Publication no. 51. Honolulu: Bishop Museum Press.

1976   *Na Hana a ka Po'e Kahiko* (The Works of the People of

Old). Bernice Pauahi Bishop Museum Special Publication no. 61. Honolulu: Bishop Museum Press.

Kauhane
1865   The Story of Ku, His Character and His Works. *Ka Nupepa Kuokoa*, 26 January, by T. G. Thrum. Bishop Museum Library, Thrum Collection.

Kepelino, K.
1858   Hooliili Hawaii. Tr. M. K. Pukui. In *Hawaiian Ethnographical Notes* 1:1127–55. Honolulu: Bishop Museum Library.

King, James
1967   Log and Proceedings of James King from 22 August 1779. In *The Voyage of the Resolution and Discovery 1776 –1780*, ed. J. C. Beaglehole. Cambridge: Cambridge University Press.

Kotzebue, Otto von
1821   *A Voyage of Discovery to the South Seas [. . .] in the Years 1815 –1818*. 3 vols. London: Longman & Co.

Kuykendall, Ralph S.
1938   *The Hawaiian Kingdom*. Vol 1: *Foundation and Transformation (1778–1854)*. Honolulu: University of Hawaii Press.

Laanui, Gideon
1930[1838]
      Reminiscences of Gideon Laanui, Reared in the Train of Kamehameha I, 1800–1819. Tr. from "Kumu Hawaii," March –April 1838. *Hawaiian Annual*:86–93.

Levin, Stephanie Seto
1968   The Overthrow of the Kapu System in Hawaii. *Journal of the Polynesian Society* 77:402–30.

Lewis, G.
1980   *Days of Shining Red: An Essay on Understanding Ritual*. Cambridge: Cambridge University Press.

Lienhardt, Godfrey
1961   *Divinity and Experience: The Religion of the Dinka*. Oxford: Clarendon Press.

Liliuokalani, Queen
1897   *An Account of the Creation of the World According to Hawaiian Tradition*. Boston: Lee and Shepard.

Lisiansky, Urey
1814   *A Voyage Round the World in the Years 1803, 4, 5 & 6*. London: Booth & Longman.

Malo, David
n.d.   Ka Mooolelo Hawaii. Unpublished manuscript. Honolulu: Bishop Museum Library.

| 1951 | *Hawaiian Antiquities.* Bernice Pauahi Bishop Museum Special Publication no. 2. Honolulu: Bishop Museum Press. |

Manby, Thomas
| 1929 | Journal of Vancouver's Voyage to the Pacific Ocean, 1791 –1793. Honolulu Mercury 1(1) June: 11–25, (2) July: 33 –45, (3) August: 39–55. |

Marcuse, Adolph
| 1894 | *Die hawaiischen Inseln.* Berlin: Friedlander. |

Marin, Francisco
| 1973 | Journal. In *Don Francisco de Paula Marin,* ed. R. H. Gass and A. Conrad. Honolulu: University Press of Hawaii. |

Martin, John
| 1817 | *An Account of the Natives of the Tonga Islands [. . .] Arranged from the Extensive Communications of Mr. William Mariner.* 2 vols. London: John Murray. |

Mathison, Gilbert F.
| 1825 | *Narrative of a Visit to Brazil, Chile, Peru, and the Sandwich Islands, 1821–1822.* London: Knight. |

Mauss, Marcel
| 1950 | *Sociologie et Anthropologie.* Paris: Presses Universitaires de France. |

McAllister, J. G.
| 1933 | *Archaeology of Oahu.* Bernice Pauahi Bishop Museum Bulletin no. 104. Honolulu: Bishop Museum Press. |

Menzies, Archibald
| n.d. | Journal. British Museum Addit. Ms. 32641. |
| 1920 | *Hawaii nei 128 Years Ago.* Honolulu: New Freedom Press. |

Meyen, F. J. F.
| 1834–35 | *Reise um die Erde, Ausgefuhrt auf dem Schiffe Prinzess Louise den Jahren 1830, 1831 und 1832.* 2 vols. Berlin: Sander'schen Buchhandlung. |

Mortimer, George
| 1791 | *Observations and Remarks Made during a Voyage to the [. . .] Sandwich Islands.* London: Cadell. |

Patterson, Samuel
| 1817 | *Narrative of the Adventures and Sufferings of Samuel Patterson Experienced in the Pacific Ocean, and Many Other Parts of the World, with an Account of the Feegee and Sandwich Islands.* Palmer, Mass.: from the Press in Palmer. |

Péron, François
| 1824 | *Mémoires du Capitaine Péron sur ses voyages.* 2 vols. Paris: Brissot-Thivars & Bossange. |

Pogue, John F.
1858   *Ka Mooolelo Hawaii*. Honolulu: Hale Paipalapala Aupuni.
Puget, Lt.
n.d.   A Log of the Proceedings of His Majesty's Armed Tender
            Chatham. London: Public Records Office Adm. 55/17.
Pukui, Mary K., and Samuel Elbert
1971   *Hawaiian Dictionary*. Honolulu: University of Hawaii Press.
Pukui, Mary K., Samuel Elbert, and E. T. Mookini
1974   *Place Names of Hawaii*. Honolulu: University Press of Hawaii.
Pukui, Mary K., E. W. Haertig, and C. A. Lee
1972–79   *Nānā i ke kumu* ('Look to the Source'). 2 vols. Honolulu:
            Hui Hanai (Queen Liliuokalani Children's Center Publica-
            tion).
Quimper, Manuel B. del Pino
1937[1822]
            The Sandwich Islands. Tr. from the original Spanish (1822)
            by Clark Lee. Honolulu: Bishop Museum Library.
Remy, Jules, ed.
1862   *Ka Mooolelo Hawaii: Historie de l'archipel hawaiien*. Text and
            translation. Paris and Leipzig: Franck.
Rockwood, P.
1957   Map of Honolulu in 1810. Honolulu: Bishop Museum Press.
Ross, Alexander
1904   *Adventures of the First Settlers on the Oregon or Columbia Riv-
            ers*. Reprinted as vol. 7 of *Early Western Travels, 1748 –1846*.
            Ed. R. G. Thwaites. Cleveland: Clark.
Sahlins, M.
1979   L'apothéose du capitaine Cook. In *La Fonction symbolique*,
            ed. M. Izard and P. Smith. Paris: Gallimard.
1981   *Historical Metaphors and Mythical Realities*. A.S.A.O. Special
            Publication no. 1. Ann Arbor: University of Michigan Press.
1985   *Islands of History*. Chicago: University of Chicago Press.
Samwell, David
1967   Journal. In *The Voyage of the Resolution and Discovery 1776–
            1780*, ed. J. C. Beaglehole. Cambridge: Cambridge Univer-
            sity Press.
Shaler, William
1808   Journal of a Voyage between China and the Northwestern
            Coast of America. *American Register* 3:137–75.

Skorupski, J.
1976 *Symbol and Theory: A Philosophical Study of Theories of Religion in Social Anthropology.* Cambridge: Cambridge University Press.

Smith, William Robertson
1889 *Lectures on the Religion of the Semites.* Edinburgh: Black.

Sterling, Elspeth P., and Catherine C. Summers
1962 *The Sites of Oahu.* Honolulu: Bishop Museum Press.

Stewart, Charles S.
1830[1828]
  Journal of a Residence in the Sandwich Islands, 1823, 1824, 1825. (Reprint of 1828 ed.) London: Fisher.

Stokes, John F. G.
n.d. Notes on Hawaiian Temples. Unpublished manuscript. Honolulu: Bishop Museum Library.

Thrum, Thomas G.
1907 Heiaus and Heiau Sites throughout the Hawaiian Islands (pt. 1). *Hawaiian Annual* 33:36–48.

1908 Tales from the Temples 2. *Hawaiian Annual* 34:48–78.

1909 Tales from the Temples 3. *Hawaiian Annual* 35:44–54.

1917 Maui's Heiau and Sites Revised. *Hawaiian Annual* 43:52–61.

1926 Leahi Heiau (Temple): Papa-ena-ena. *Hawaiian Annual* 52:109–14.

Townsend, Ebenezer
n.d. *Extract from the Diary of Ebenezer Townsend, Jr.* Hawaiian Historical Society Reprint no. 4. Honolulu: Hawaiian Historical Society.

Turnbull, John
1813 *A Voyage around the World, in the Years 1800, 1801, 1802, 1803, and 1804.* 2d ed. London: Maxwell.

Turner, Victor W.
1968 *The Drums of Affliction.* Oxford: Clarendon Press.

Tyerman, Daniel, and George Bennet
1839 *Journals of Voyages and Travels.* 3 vols. Boston: Crocker & Brewster; New York: Leavitt.

Valeri, Valerio
1972 Le fonctionnement du système des rangs à Hawaii. *L'Homme* 12:29–66.

1976 Le brûlé et le cuit: mythologie et organisation de la chefferie dans la société hawaiienne ancienne. Thèse de doctorat de 3ème cycle (Ethnologie). École Pratique des Hautes Études, Paris.

1979   Feticcio. *Enciclopedia* 6:100–115. Turin: Einaudi.

1980   Regalità. *Enciclopedia* 11:742–71. Turin: Einaudi.

1981a   Rito. *Enciclopedia* 12:210–43. Turin: Einaudi.

1981b   Pouvoir des dieux, rire des hommes: divertissement théorique sur un fait hawaiien. *Anthropologie et Sociétés* 5:11–34.

1985a   *Kingship and Sacrifice: Ritual and Society in Ancient Hawaii.* Chicago: University of Chicago Press.

1985b   The Conqueror Becomes King: A Political Analysis of the Hawaiian Legend of 'Umi. In *Transformations of Polynesian Culture*, ed. Antony Hooper and Judith Huntsman. Memoir no. 45. Auckland: The Polynesian Society.

1990   Constitutive History: Genealogy and Narrative in the Legitimation of Hawaiian Kingship. In *Culture through Time*, ed. E. Ohnuki-Tierney. Stanford: Stanford University Press.

In press   Diarchy and History in Hawaii and Tonga. In *Culture and History in the Pacific*, ed. J. Siikala. Transactions of the Finnish Anthropological Society. Helsinki: The Society.

Vancouver, George

1801   *A Voyage of Discovery to the North Pacific Ocean, and around the World [. . .] Performed in the Years 1790, 1791, 1792, 1793, 1794, and 1795.* 6 vols. London: Stockdale.

Webb, L.

n.d.   Death of Keawe. *Hawaiian Ethnographical Notes* 1: 2744. Unpublished manuscript in the Bishop Museum Library, Honolulu.

Westervelt, W. D.

1915   *Legends of Old Honolulu.* Boston: Ellis; London: Constable.

Whitman, John B.

1979   *An Account of the Sandwich Islands.* Ed. J. Dominis Holt. Honolulu: Topgallant Publishing Co., Salem: Peabody Museum.

Wilkes, Charles

1845   *Narrative of the United States Exploring Expedition during the Years 1838, 1839, 1840, 1841, and 1842.* 5 vols. Philadelphia: Lea and Blanchard.

4. Inside, Outside

A Hawaiian Community in the World-System

Jocelyn Linnekin

I n works of Braudelian erudition and scope, Immanuel Wallerstein (1974, 1979, 1980) has described the global expansion of capitalism. Wallerstein's model at once raises issues of cultural transformation and the "historical efficacy" (Sahlins 1977:22) of events in the encounter between Western and non-Western economies, particularly for those societies that in his scheme constitute the periphery of the world-system (see Wallerstein 1974:301 –2).[1] One can acknowledge the existence and overwhelming influence of global capitalism without concluding that it wholly determines the form of subordinate economies. Local modes of exchange and distribution may yet retain their own unique characteristics. As Sidney Mintz (1977:253) has noted, the sweeping character of Wallerstein's model invites response from area specialists, and it is fitting that anthropologists such as Mintz, Andrew Strathern (1982), Michael Taussig (1980), and Katherine Verdery (1983) have offered caveats and qualifications to his thesis.

In like spirit, this essay examines a Hawaiian community's internal and external exchange relationships in the present and in the past. My startling premise is that the global economy is not the whole story; prior categorical schemes and precapitalist modes of exchange are not eradicated by events. In economies formerly based on exchange-in-kind and gift giving, the involvement with the external market is not all-encompassing. Moreover, indigenous cultural factors affect how local economies are integrated into the world-system. This essay is therefore a foray into the "local-response" variant of dependency theory (very capably explicated in Verdery 1983:9–13; see also Mintz 1977).

The concept of dependency was formulated as a critique of development theory, which defines most of the societies studied by anthropologists as "underdeveloped" and sees indigenous cultural factors as potential obstacles to development (see, for example, Bauer and Yamey 1957: 64–71; Hodder 1968:48–53, 171; Hoselitz 1952:46–47; Mountjoy 1963:9–15).[2] As articulated by Verdery (1983:11), the essence of the local-response objection is that the world-system model "gives too much weight to exogenous determination of local forms." Similarly, Marshall Sahlins (1985:viii) states that world-system theory rules out the possibility of an "autonomous cultural-logic" operating in the contact situation. The latter charge is perhaps too harsh, however. If applied without sensitivity to local variations, dependency theory—like development theory—does seem fatally one-sided to an anthropologist. The local-response writers attempt to correct this flaw; their work is intended to temper, rather than refute, world-system theory.

Both development theory and the world-system model give priority to the vantage point of the global economy; both perspectives are outside local culture, looking in. Even for Eric Wolf (1982), the history of the people without history is made by introduced capitalism. In contrast, this essay works from a culturalist position—the vantage point of the local community, looking out. At issue here is what constitutes history in the encounter between the world-system and indigenous societies. Although I find world-system theory persuasive and powerful for explaining a local economy's relationship to the global system, I am primarily concerned in this chapter with the nature of the local response, and particularly with how people on the periphery construe their own economic history. I will suggest an indigenous model of the global economy (cf. Taussig 1980) that is also a local conception of Hawaiian economic history.

Conventional structuralist methodology focuses similarly on indigenous categories but aims to demonstrate that structures reproduce themselves in spite of all manner of catastrophic events. Lévi-Strauss (1966: 67–73) conceptualizes history as events external to the system: change is precipitated from outside, although conscious human actors play a role in making structural adjustments to "the contingencies of history" (ibid.:73). He relates, for example, how a group of native Australians, decimated and relocated, adopted a scheme of classification that recreated the prior section system (ibid.:157). Though emphasizing the self-determination of indigenous exchange systems, I am not suggesting a simple duplication of precontact forms. Rather, I will argue for structural change in the encounter, moving in contrapuntal fashion between the perspectives of the local community and the world-system. The issue is not cultural reproduction *or* transformation but how both occur in what Sahlins (1981a, 1985:xiii–xvii) calls "the structure of the conjuncture." This essay explores the meeting of two cultural orders by detailing a Hawaiian community's historic and present-day participation in the capitalist economy.

In Ke'anea,[3] a rural community on the windward coast of Maui, Hawaiians participate simultaneously in two qualitatively different forms of exchange. They work as wage laborers and grow taro for the market, thus participating in the capitalist economy, but they also engage in exchange-in-kind with their relatives, friends, and neighbors—a form of gift giving strikingly similar to the "archaic" modes of reciprocity described by Mauss (1967). Exchange-in-kind is not a trivial aspect of social life in Ke'anae. Relationships on the local level hinge upon the maintenance of equivalent reciprocities. The community has survived by means of links to the external economy and is inextricably dependent upon its ties to the market system.[4] But the egalitarian, in-kind ethic that dominates local-level social relations cannot be explained by reference to the introduced capitalist economy alone. Moreover, indigenous values and local perceptions of exchange impact supply and demand schedules, thus affecting how the community interacts with the market economy.

Taussig (1980) has described how the devil beliefs of proletarianized South American peasants embody a perception of capitalism as fundamentally inhuman and unnatural. As will be shown, the Hawaiian categorical opposition "inside/outside" is in part an indigenous model of capitalism, but one that is descended from a prior cultural opposition. In this sense the model is overdetermined: an explanation in terms of the political and economic history of Hawaii—the introduced market, Hawaiian land alienation, and proletarianization—does not exhaust its meanings. The point here is not to deny transformation, nor to minimize the effects of capitalism. Rather, my intent is to show that there are significant continuities within the discontinuities introduced by the colonial relationship, and that these continuities pertain to the ways that rural Hawaiians perceive and experience their relationship to the external economy. Symbolic schemes too have histories.

A Transactional Contrast

Famed as a taro-producing area since ancient times, Ke'anae is perceived by islanders and tourists alike as a traditional Hawaiian place. Village residents identify themselves as people engaged in farming and fishing, descendants of the Hawaiian commoners, the *maka'āinana*. Villagers still grow taro, but today the Polynesian staple is grown primarily for the market. Most of Ke'anae's taro is destined for Honolulu supermarkets in the form of factory-ground poi, the starchy paste that once formed the bulk of the Hawaiian diet. No one in Ke'anae subsists solely by farming and fishing. Taro marketing, wage labor, pensions, and social security link the community to the outside economy. Several men commute daily to work in construction or road labor while their wives and children maintain the taro patches. Except for retired residents, all but one of the adult males in the village held salaried jobs at the time of fieldwork; only one householder was a full-time taro grower.

Ke'anae Hawaiians use the terms *inside* and *outside* to distinguish the windward countryside from town society, where Orientals and haoles ('whites') are politically and economically dominant. The opposition has both social and geographical referents. The contrast is country/city, Hawaiian/foreign, east—toward Hāna, an old Hawaiian settlement at the far end of Maui—as opposed to west, toward the town of Kahului in the urbanized center of the island. The contrast is also ecological: the country is wet and lushly forested, whereas the outside is hot, dry, and given over to sugarcane plantations, cattle pastures, and tourist hotels. More important are the cultural and transactional dimensions of the dichotomy.

Inside/outside encodes an ostensibly ethnic distinction that can only partly be explained by reference to national origin. Given the historically high frequency of marriage between Hawaiians and foreigners, the vast majority of those who identify themselves as Hawaiian today are of part-Hawaiian descent. In Ke'anae, only one family is reputed to be pure Hawaiian. Most villagers are Chinese-Hawaiian, the descendants of Chinese men, former plantation workers, who settled in Ke'anae in the late nineteenth century and married Hawaiian women. In 1957, the community was designated "most Hawaiian in the islands" —officially because it had the largest percentage of residents of Hawaiian ancestry in the state (Lueras 1975:A3). The designation reveals more about Ke'anae's cultural identity than about its demographics: to residents and outsiders alike, Ke'anae is *culturally* a Hawaiian village. In Ke'anae, almost anyone with part-Hawaiian ancestry may be called Hawaiian if he or she acts Hawaiian. And acting Hawaiian is primarily a measure of participation in symmetrical, in-kind exchanges.

The inside/outside dichotomy opposes the market economy to exchanges of foodstuffs, services, and favors between Hawaiians. Ties between Ke'anae and the outside society take the form of impersonal monetary transactions and are perceived to be mutually exploitative. Most Ke'anae men are employed as laborers by the state, the county, or the local irrigation company, which is a subsidiary of one of Hawaii's "Big Five" corporations. Retired residents subsist on pensions and social security payments and go to town to shop and pay bills. *Inside* and *outside* thus denote, on one level, different media of exchange: a distinction between cash and in-kind transactions (cf. Finney 1973a:98–100).

Inside, and between relatives and peers, exchange-in-kind is the stated rule. As an informant explained to me, "In Ke'anae, you *give*, don't sell." A taro farmer always tries to muster unpaid labor from within the family to harvest for the weekly market order. Growers who successfully manipulate family ties may even prevail upon younger relatives to drive in from outside for the occasion, rather than pay nonrelatives.

Although the categorical opposition suggests a dualism, the inside/outside dichotomy describes a gradient of social distance and forms of exchange and thus approximates Sahlins's (1965:145–49) scheme of generalized, balanced, and negative reciprocity. Between relatives, whether demonstrable, stipulated, or fictive kin, generalized reciprocity pertains. Open-ended exchange is also the norm between persons in different generations, who may call one another aunty, uncle, niece, and nephew. Hawaiians recognize an obligation on the part of the young to assist the old, whether related or not. Between such persons, "the expectation of reciprocity is indefinite" (ibid:147). There is no reckoning of accounts, and a one-way flow may go on for some time.

Between unrelated persons of the same generation—neighbors and friends—exchanges are expected to balance out over time: balanced reciprocity (ibid.:147–48). Ke'anae villagers are attuned to the weighty implications of giving and receiving and are sensitive to the status differences that may result from asymmetrical exchanges. Thus neighborly relationships at times take on an agonistic, competitive character. One party may strive to indebt the other, prompting an anxious overcompensation by the unwilling recipient. Outside the sphere of kinship, relationships tend to cycle between amity and avoidance in response to perceived inequities in exchange. The terms of exchange inside are goods and work: primarily foodstuffs, but also transportation, hospitality, taro shoots for planting, and various other small services and favors (see Linnekin 1985). The grammar of exchange is based on a value hierarchy of the items, which are ranked according to a long-established Hawaiian—and more widely, Polynesian—valuation of their intrinsic qualities. Some goods are higher than others in their compensatory value and in their power to obligate the recipient to make a return gift.

There are of course other dimensions to the protocol: grammars of situation and social category. Normally, the most valued gifts pass between relatives rather than nonrelatives. Between nonkin, the choice of a gift depends upon the occasion and the prior balance of reciprocities between the parties. Accepting hospitality for a night is more portentous than dropping in to "talk story" for an afternoon. Certain commodities are appropriate to particular situations, but the rules may be manipulated to create indebtedness and to impel a more valuable return gift. Accepting poi—symbolically the staff of life—from anyone but a close relative would be shameful. For fear of incurring indebtedness, elderly people and those with no patches open are confronted with the irony of living in a community known as "the taro place" and having to buy poi at the supermarket in town.

Pork is the highest food gift. The main course at a luau, the Hawaiian feast, is always *kālua* pig, cooked in an underground oven; in the Hawaiian religion, this was a ritual offering made to gods and chiefs. Other dishes on the modern luau menu, such as *laulaus*, bundles of steamed meat and taro leaves, and *kūlolo*, a taro-coconut pudding, are demonstrably descended from the ceremonial offerings of the indigenous religion, which was overthrown in 1819. At a luau, the guests are expected to consume much and to carry away the balance when they leave. The luau foods then become the stuff of many future in-kind exchanges. Elderly women with small appetites vie to assist in preparations for a luau because the workers are rewarded afterward with extra allotments of highly prized foods.

For similar reasons, residents stand a vigil at the wharf when a fishing crew is at work offshore. When I lived in Ke'anae, a group of Japanese and Filipino fishers periodically came inside to look for schools of *akule* (mackerel). By Hawaiian custom, anyone who helps the fishers will receive a share of the catch. Those who covet the fish most eagerly seem to be single older villagers. One resident who was reared in an upland locality on the dry side of Maui admitted that she did not care much for fish. Yet she spent a day waiting at the wharf for the catch to be brought in, and another day cleaning and salting the fish she received. Exchange-in-kind is the reason why a deep freezer is standard equipment in Hawaiian households in Ke'anae. A freezer full of *laulau*s and *akule* is a bank for future transactions.

In spite of the stated in-kind ethic, money does change hands within the village. Taro farmers do occasionally hire other villagers as day laborers. A resident who specializes in the healing arts may agree to prepare herbal medicine for a neighbor and may be paid in cash for the store-bought ingredients; one such tonic is made from honey, whiskey, and watercress. Yet these instances do not negate the in-kind ethic. Paid day laborers recruited from within the village tend to be social anomalies or people of little consequence: typically low-status individuals with no family in the village and no land of their own. And to pay a neighbor for whiskey as a medicinal ingredient is simply a transaction with the outside, once removed. Preparing the remedy is no less a service, one in a cycle of in-kind transactions between neighbors and friends, and is neither equated to nor compensated by the cash payment.

The inside/outside contrast has another significant referent: a difference in the relative status of the parties in exchange. The distinction opposes symmetry to asymmetry in exchange, equivalence to hierarchy. Although Hawaiians have recently won a greater voice with the establishment of the Office of Hawaiian Affairs, they have historically occupied the political and economic bottom of island society. Most Ke'anae Hawaiians see themselves as essentially poor although, as I will show, not all households bear out this perception. As stated above, neighborly relationships in Ke'anae are ideally egalitarian. Superficially, the material circumstances of life are much the same for all Ke'anae households as the result of a more-or-less conscious effort not to appear more prosperous than one's neighbor. Violating the egalitarian ethic usually leads to a breach of communication, mutual avoidance, "talk stink" (censorious gossip), and accusations of social climbing—"acting high." Acting high can mean entertaining haoles in one's home, having a shingle roof when everyone else's is corrugated iron, or trying to create indebtedness by giving too much in exchange. The inside/outside opposition thus encodes both a scale of social distance and a hierarchy. People who are high are outside the social sphere of Hawaiians; they are by definition strangers. Acting high—the creation of hierarchy —is antithetical to Hawaiian ideals of behavior.

The inside/outside opposition has a history of transformation, in both senses of the word: a history of change but also of permutation. Ke'anae Hawaiians conceptually oppose the solidarity and egalitarianism of social relations inside to the impersonality and hierarchy of the society outside. These dimensions of the inside/outside opposition draw on prior categorical distinctions and might serve equally well as a model of early nineteenth-century Hawaiian society from the commoners' perspective. Hawaiian commoners were differentiated from the chiefs as an indigenous people subordinated to high foreigners (see Kamakau 1961:376; Malo 1951:6; Sahlins 1981a:29–30).

Moreover, the exchange relationship was asymmetrical, the people feeding the chiefs through the mechanisms of tribute and through increasingly expropriative taxation after the formation of the state. A Ke'anae informant articulated the unequal exchange relationship between chiefs and people in these terms: "The chiefs made all the money from the land and the people got nothing." Sahlins (1981a:30) has pointed out "the Hawaiian symbolic proportion—the chiefs are to the people as the Europeans were to Hawaiians in general." The modern version of the Hawaiian symbolic equation can be expressed as follows:

Inside : Outside ::
Native : Foreign ::
Low : High ::
Symmetrical : Asymmetrical exchange ::
Gift giving : Buying and selling ::
Exchange-in-kind : The cash economy.

The above constitutes an indigenous model of Hawaii's colonial history—a view from the inside, looking out. I suggest that this conceptual scheme is part of Ke'anae people's world view, categorical system, or, if you will, semiotic code. Moreover, this model is a product of the encounter between capitalist and in-kind modes of exchange and continues to shape the way that Ke'anae is integrated into the wider society. The issue for dependency theory is whether such schemes have any effect on the outcome of the colonial encounter. The remainder of this essay will pursue the anthropological objection: that, as Sahlins (1981a, 1985) has shown, indigenous peoples have their own interpretations of events, and these constructions do in fact shape the outcome of those events. History is not solely the global history of capitalism but is made in the conjuncture or, to use Dening's (1980) imagery, on the "beaches" where different cultural orders meet.

The Market Economy in Hawaii

In an essay such as this, one can only offer a brief sketch of the intrusion of the market economy in Hawaii (see Bradley 1968 [1942]; Mathison 1825:458–67; Morgan 1948; Sahlins 1981a:26–28, 43–44). For comparative insights into Ke'anae's economic history, particularly regarding the impact of capitalism, I will refer to accounts describing rural cultivators' encounter with the Western economy. Taussig (1980:91–92) relates the participation of Colombian peasants in wage labor to the whittling away of their landholding by large-scale capitalist farmers, to the point where the size of peasant plots was "less than that required for subsistence." As a result, the peasants were "obliged to become wage laborers—semiproletarians—who provided part of their subsistence from their peasant farming and, in some cases, used their wages as remittances to sustain the peasant farm" (ibid.:92; cf. Geertz 1963a:89 –90). Taussig sees semiproletarianization following from the loss of economic self-sufficiency: colonized people participate in the capitalist economy when their previous subsistence mode is rendered nonviable.

Hawaii's nineteenth-century economic history is of course crucial for understanding Ke'anae's transformation from a village of subsistence agriculturalists and fishers to a community of salaried workers and taro marketers. When and to what extent were Ke'anae Hawaiians "obliged to become wage laborers"? To answer this question, I will outline some of the contingencies that impacted rural Hawaiians in general during the nineteenth century and then consider how these factors pertain to Ke'anae's economic history as far as it can be reconstructed from tax rolls, property conveyances, and archival materials.

From the time of Cook's arrival, Hawaiians supplied foreign ships with produce and meat in exchange for imported goods. But until the midnineteenth century this trade, like participation in wage labor, engaged primarily those living near Honolulu and Lahaina and consisted largely of in-kind transactions rather than buying and selling for cash. Through the 1840s, little currency was in circulation among commoners except in the port towns (Morgan 1948:104–5), and even in Honolulu payments—including wages—were generally in kind (ibid.:106–7; Wyllie 1844:7, 63). Missionaries paid for native labor with knives, fishhooks, and cloth (S. Whitney, Station Report of 1823, HMCS)[5] and Hawaiian contributions to the missions were correspondingly in the form of cloth, mats, salt, timber, produce, and livestock (L. Lyons, Station Report of 1840, HMCS).

Through the first half of the nineteenth century, a steady stream of Hawaiians left the rural areas for Honolulu and Lahaina. Commoners living on the land were subjected to increasingly exploitative tax demands on their labor and produce (see, for example, Kamakau 1961: 231–32; L. Lyons, Station Report of 1837, HMCS). But as long as they could meet these demands with locally available resources (see Kamakau 1961:177–78), Hawaiians in remote areas might remain insulated from the money economy. Changes in the medium of tax payments radically altered this situation. The 1841 tax law (Thurston 1904: 55–56) recommended payment in money but still listed monetary equivalents for such products as arrowroot, kukui nuts, pigs, turmeric, and fish. Nevertheless, in some districts local chiefs independently required remittance in cash. In 1850 payment in currency became mandatory. Missionary letters and station reports attest that this had the effect of driving rural Hawaiians from the land and into the market economy.

A class of landless workers had arisen in Honolulu by the 1840s. Significantly, "since they held no lands they were excused from the land and labor taxes" (Morgan 1948:114). Concurrently, Hawaiian emigration from the land had become recognized as a social problem. Missionaries and foreign advisers to the government pressed for the establishment of private property as an incentive for commoners to remain on the land as farmers. The Great Māhele, the land division of 1846 –55, was supposed to ensure the rights of commoner Hawaiians to the lands that they cultivated and lived upon. Ironically, the Māhele's overall effect was to enable Hawaiians to alienate their lands permanently

—precisely at a time when political and economic conditions were encouraging them do so.[6] Eric Wolf (1982:317) points out that with the spread of capitalism "peasants became farmers," growing cash crops on small holdings. His explanation for this transition in nineteenth-century Europe is also applicable to the Māhele's effect in Hawaii: "this was accomplished . . . by freeing the peasantry economically and politically from tributary obligations to a class of overlords, enabling the peasants to employ their land and labor as market factors of production."

In many rural localities in Hawaii, subsistence agriculture became nonviable in the latter half of the nineteenth century, but in contrast to Taussig's Colombian case, it was not the absolute size of Hawaiian landholdings that was problematic. Taro is extremely productive; missionaries estimated that twenty to twenty-five people could be sustained by an acre of irrigated taro land (Wyllie 1855:82). The Māhele had a major impact on the self-sufficiency of rural areas through the alienation of the *kula*, the uplands or open country where Hawaiians gathered wild plants and cultivated scattered plots of secondary cultigens (see Linnekin 1987). Before the Māhele, commoners had access to these upland tracts and forests as an expression of the ruling chief's aloha (love, affection) for them. Taro, grown in the irrigated bottom lands, was the staple, but the products of the *kula*—firewood, house thatch, fiber for fishnets, trees for canoes—made for local self-sufficiency. In the Māhele, claimants were entitled only to the lands that they "actually cultivated for a living" (Chinen 1958:30). In practice, this usually meant only irrigated taro lands, plus houselots; lands lying fallow were rarely awarded, and the scattered stands cultivated in the uplands hardly conformed to the Western definition of real property.

In the Māhele, open and upland tracts were for the most part awarded to chiefs or retained by the king or the government. At the insistence of Kamehameha III, legal protection for the people's gathering and access rights was incorporated into the 1850 Kuleana Act, which authorized the granting of awards to the commoners. Prominent chiefs and foreign landowners were adamantly opposed to any such residual rights, however, and the clause appears to have been largely ignored in the aftermath of the Māhele (see Linnekin 1987). After the Māhele, crown and government lands became available for purchase. Foreigners took this opportunity to acquire vast tracts and aggressively sought to buy up or assimilate contiguous Hawaiian holdings. The fate of Hawaiian lands during this period parallels the situation in Java, where in 1870 the Dutch similarly adopted the principle that uncultivated "waste" land reverted to the state and became available for lease to plantations, to the great benefit of sugar interests (Geertz 1963a:83–84).

The Hawaiian commoners were particularly vulnerable to pressure from large landowners because, in many cases, the awards made to commoners lay adjacent to or surrounded by foreign-owned ranches and plantations. The haole successors to the chiefs, the former owners of the *kula*, also made no effort to prevent their livestock from wandering over the commoners' holdings and destroying crops. There is ample evidence documenting the depredations of cattle on Oʻahu, and Kuykendall (1938:318) writes that in the 1840s, cattle roamed freely over Maui's central plain, causing extensive damage to cultivated fields. The cattle were replaced by sugar plantations in Maui's isthmus in the 1860s. In 1863 the local missionary noted with approval that these "waste" lands were being prepared for sugar planting and would at last become productive—and profitable (W. P. Alexander. Report of Wailuku Station for 1863. HMCS). Another factor encouraging Hawaiians to turn from agriculture to wage labor after the Māhele was the eventual collapse of the market for ships' provisions (see Morgan 1948: 81–85, 150–54). The demand for produce and meat peaked in the mid-nineteenth century and fell off rapidly after 1859 with the demise of the whaling trade: "With cattle and staple products comparatively worthless, a large part of agriculture was in an uncertain state of transition. . . . [W]ith the passing of whaling went the last effective impulse toward general farming" (ibid:153).

It has often been noted that when non-Western societies are drawn into the economic sphere of colonial powers, indigenous peoples take up cash cropping to the detriment of local subsistence agriculture (see, for example, Finney 1973a). For rural Hawaiians in some areas, cash cropping was one solution to the problem of money after the Māhele. Marion Kelly (1980:13–15) cites sources from the early 1860s describing the importance of *pulu* fern as a cash crop in Kaʻū, a remote district of the island of Hawai'i. *Pulu* fiber, used as mattress filler and a dressing for wounds, enjoyed a brief heyday as an export in the latter half of the nineteenth century, with peak volume occurring in 1862. In Ka'ū, Kelly's sources describe it as a source of wealth (used primarily to purchase fancy goods at the foreigner's store), but leading to the neglect or abandonment of taro. The *pulu* industry ended when a better filler was found (Neal 1965:10).

The history of *pulu* in Hawaii exemplifies the hazard of cash cropping: one's livelihood is inexorably tied to an outside market, and when the cash crop loses value in the world-system, people are often unable to fall back on traditional subsistence means. Yet cash cropping, for all the justifiable criticisms that have been leveled at it, at least has the potential for allowing people to remain on the land as peasants, with some control over the organization and the products of their labor (Taussig 1980:18); the alternative way to participate in the market economy—as landless wage laborers— certainly permits less autonomy and seems more exploitative in human terms. In Hawaii cash cropping by Hawaiians was a short-term, localized response that could not sustain the rural community's economic viability over the long term. Ke'anae is no exception to this statement because, as will be shown, villagers have never relied totally on a single market crop for their livelihood. After the 1875 Reciprocity Treaty with the United States made Hawaiian sugar enormously profitable, local cash cropping was rapidly eclipsed by plantation agriculture controlled by haoles. In the face of a multitude of factors acting to drive them from the land, the ultimate fate of most Hawaiians was proletarianization.

Ke'anae and the Market Economy

It is important to note that the chronology of proletarianization in Ke'anae differs significantly from the port towns of Hawai'i and even from rural areas on other islands, where many Hawaiians abandoned their landholdings during the latter half of the nineteenth century. Wage labor and the cash economy intruded relatively late in Ke'anae. Here Hawaiians were not driven into the market economy by dispossession. That Ke'anae historically escaped land alienation is in large part due to its remote location and rugged terrain: these lands have never been desirable for large-scale agriculture or ranching. Unlike the South American peasantry described by Taussig (1980:88–89), Ke'anae villagers are not directly threatened by expanding agribusiness. Several plantation and ranching ventures were tried in the Hāna region in the nineteenth and early twentieth centuries, but nearly all failed. Attempts to produce sugar in Hāna in the 1850s and 1860s were hindered by wet weather, labor problems, and the difficulty of finding dry fuel for the mill (D. T. Conde. Station Report of 1853, HMCS; Sereno Bishop to A. Bishop, 16 February 1863 and 11 May 1863, HMCS). A sugar plantation survived at Hāna until the end of World War II, but its profitability consistently suffered from labor problems and the community's isolation (Wenkam 1970:69–72).

The persistence of Hawaiian landholding in Ke'anae must also be traced to the fate of the local *kula*. In this, Ke'anae differs markedly from the rural areas of O'ahu. The primary taro lands in Ke'anae lie in two contiguous areas, Lower Ke'anae Peninsula and neighboring Wailua Valley, and are separated from the uplands by steep cliffs. After the Māhele, cooperatives (*hui*) of Hawaiians purchased large upland tracts as royal patent grants, thereby preventing foreigners from gaining control of these lands. To this day, the hopelessly tangled titles to the *hui* lands have effectively thwarted their appropriation by outsiders, although they have made it equally difficult for the Hawaiian owners to activate their shares.

After 1850, Ke'anae villagers, like other rural Hawaiians, must have faced the necessity of procuring cash for their tax payments. The Ke'anae church reports (S. K. Kamakahiki, 1867–88, HMCS) indicate that the years following the Māhele were a difficult time for the community. In his report for 1867, Reverend Kamakahiki stated that few of his parishioners could afford to support the church, "for the majority are in poverty" (ibid.). Offerings that year included "two bundles of *olonā*"[7] valued at five dollars. The church statistics show a steady decline in membership between 1867 and 1878. One cannot say that the decline is solely due to emigration, for undoubtedly there were church-leavers who remained in the village. But as an indication of emigration, in 1873, although 205 members are listed "in regular standing," 132 are described as "living at other places without dismission." The numbers in the latter category increased steadily in the years immediately following the Māhele.

Yet the community survived. With few local opportunities for wage labor, how did Ke'anae people procure money? The evidence indicates that the community participated in the external market after the Māhele, if not before, by selling agricultural products—taro, possibly beef—to the outside. Elderly informants attest that, at least by the early twentieth century, prime taro-growing areas such as Ke'anae served as regional poi bowls, selling taro for cash to other Hawaiian communities (cf. Boggs 1977). Significantly, Ke'anae's pastor noted in 1867 that "money is obtained by taro growing and the people who have money have good houses." In the early 1870s a ship regularly stopped at Ke'anae en route to Hāna (S. K. Kamakahiki, letters of 2 August 1870 and 7 July 1873. HMCS). By the time of the Māhele, commoner Hawaiians kept livestock—cows, horses, mules—of their own. Hawaii had exported hides and salt beef since the late 1830s, and beef was in demand for the shipping trade (see Kuykendall 1938: 317–19). Tax records indicate that by 1887, many Ke'anae residents possessed a few head of cattle and a horse or mule and that the *hui* lands were used for pasturage (Real Property Tax Books. AH).

In 1868, Kamakahiki reported, "I'm going to the mountains tomorrow for most of the people are there for *olonā*." I have no conclusive evidence proving that Ke'anae people sold *olonā* to outsiders during this period, but Neal (1965:319–20) writes that "early traders bought olona cordage for their ship rigging. Olona fiber is said to be stronger than hemp." *Oloñā* fiber was an acceptable medium of tax payment in Kamehameha's time (Kamakau 1961:177). Kamakau (1976:44; see also Stokes 1906) describes *olonā* as highly prized: "It was very valuable for trading, and planters raised it extensively. It was the main item in obtaining fish, for out of it were made nets, long fishing lines, ropes, every kind of binding cord."

In 1850, Foreign Minister R. C. Wyllie wrote that *olonā* was still used extensively for fishing nets and sold "at a price upwards of $2. per lb." (Wyllie to John Smith, 11 November 1850, Foreign Office Book 11–a, 497. AH). In a letter dated 30 March 1861 (HMCS), Reverend

Kamakahiki explained that he was sending several bundles of *olonā* to a Hawaiian missionary stationed in Micronesia. *Olonā* thrives only in moist windward settings such as Ke'anae. In their claims to the Māhele Land Commission, Ke'anae Hawaiians consistently asked for their "clumps of *olonā*" in the uplands. Although none of these was subsequently awarded, the damp uplands were included in some of the *hui* lands later acquired by groups of Hawaiians. That large numbers of villagers were gathering *olonā* in 1868 suggests that it was not solely for local use and distribution.

In the late nineteenth century, Ke'anae Hawaiians also obtained money from the sale of rice to the outside—albeit indirectly. From the 1880s on, many Ke'anae landowners leased their lands for cash to Chinese rice planters, former sugar workers who settled in the village after their labor contracts expired. Wolf (1982:314) points out that plantation agriculture requires simultaneous production of a basic staple to feed the labor force. In Hawaii as in Asia, "the expansion of plantation agriculture . . . went hand in hand with the expanding production of rice" (cf. also Geertz 1963a:56–57, 79–80). Property conveyances involving Chinese in Ke'anae abound between 1884 and 1894. The Chinese married Hawaiian women and their children were reared and identified as Hawaiian (Lorden 1935:455–56). The Chinese therefore also had Hawaiian affines and, presumably, reciprocal obligations to them; modern Ke'anae informants assert that Chinese boys make good husbands and sons-in-law because they are "good providers." The 1890 tax rolls (Real Property Tax Books. AH) show that about half the Chinese rice planters also had holdings in taro, and more than half the total acreage of irrigated land is still listed as planted in taro.

Although Ke'anae Hawaiians benefited from the rice industry, rice planting was dominated by and identified with the Chinese. An elderly informant said that when all the Chinese died, Ke'anae Hawaiians again took up planting taro because "they would rather eat poi." The Hawaiian rice industry peaked in the early years of this century and declined rapidly thereafter (see Coulter and Chun 1937; Krauss 1937). The Chinese Exclusion Act of 1898 put a stop to further immigration and contributed to the diminishing local demand for Chinese-style rice. In Ke'anae, property conveyances reveal that land was leased to a Chinese for rice planting as late as 1926, but the lease also mentions taro growing on the land.

Indications of how Ke'anae residents have made their living in the past hundred years can be found in the commercial directories of the late nineteenth and early twentieth centuries. The equivalent of today's telephone directories, these list local residents with their occupations, and they indicate that through the 1920s the primary occupation of Ke'anae Hawaiians was taro farming. Chinese rice planters are most numerous in the 1890s. The 1888 commercial directory describes Ke'anae as a remote "fishing station with only native and Chinese inhabitants." The village had a general store and a post office, however. Today the nearest store and postal station are in Hāna, about an hour's drive from Ke'anae along the narrow, winding Hāna highway. The 1890 directory lists twenty-eight taro planters, two teachers, a storekeeper, a carpenter, and a policeman, as well as two Chinese rice companies.

The 1920 commerical directory lists several storekeepers and rice planters with Chinese surnames and four Hawaiian laborers. This is the first time that some local men gave their primary occupation as wage labor, although in the 1910 directory several Ke'anae residents are listed with no occupation and may indeed have hired out to others. In 1920, one laborer and one foreman are listed in the employ of the East Maui Irrigation Company. A subsidiary of a major sugar company, "E.M.I." still employs Ke'anae men to maintain the Ko'olau Ditch, the upland aqueduct that feeds central Maui's sugar plantations. But Ke'anae people entered into this employment relatively late. Construction of Maui's windward irrigation network began in 1878, shortly after the Reciprocity Treaty was signed and Claus Spreckels secured the water right to the Hāna coast (see Kuykendall 1967:64–66). In 1881, a letter to the minister of the interior protested that should Spreckels's upland "reservoir" be completed, "the residents of Ke'anae, in Hana, would be deprived of water" (Interior Dept., 10 September 1881. AH).

Between 1920 and 1930 the occupations of Ke'anae residents undergo a dramatic shift, coinciding with the demise of the rice industry and the opening of the Hāna highway in 1927. The road maintenance department and a prison camp built at Ke'anae—later a Civilian Conservation Corps camp—provided new opportunities for Ke'anae men to engage in salaried employment. The 1930 directory lists thirteen laborers and truck drivers, several guards for the Ke'anae Prison Camp, and only eight taro planters. The late 1920s probably saw the appearance of Ke'anae's current occupational pattern—of male residents engaging in full-time wage labor and part-time taro growing, with women doing much of the day-to-day taro-patch work. Although many Ke'anae Hawaiians took up wage labor during the 1920s and 1930s, this does not mean that they abandoned taro farming. If the present is any indication, the salaried workers of 1930 also grew taro for the market as well as for household use. Ke'anae is renowned for the quality of its poi; local Hawaiians call it "the taro place." Elderly informants recalled that in their childhood—approximately the 1920s—Ke'anae supplied rice and poi to Kīpahulu, which lies beyond Hāna, and to Kaupō, on the dry side of Maui. One resident who had married into Ke'anae from Kaupō described how as a girl she was charged with taking a mule train to Kīpahulu to pick up the poi ordered from Ke'anae. Significantly, these were monetary transactions, with payments in cash: the poi was purchased in one-dollar, five-dollar, and ten-dollar bags.

The commercial directory for 1930–31 lists, for the first time, a poi seller; two are listed in the 1940–41 directory. The Ke'anae poi shops sold directly to other Maui communities, at least on the windward side. Informants attest that local growers also sold raw taro to the poi factories in Honolulu. Ke'anae informants who were children during the 1940s describe working in the poi shops, washing and grinding taro, "for aloha" and for the fun of it. An informant reported that by the late 1940s, only one poi shop remained and "most people sold outside," as Ke'anae taro farmers do today. I do not know when the last poi shop in Ke'anae closed, but I would guess the early 1950s, concomitant with the attrition of windward Maui's population and the shrinking local market for poi.

Throughout this century the economic, if not social, importance of infra-island exchange—Hawaiians with Hawaiians—has diminished, but local trade may have made the difference for the survival of remote rural communities such as Ke'anae into the twentieth century. I hypothesize that Ke'anae Hawaiians may have sold or traded their *olonā* to other Hawaiians, who sold to foreigners. Historic and secondary sources (see Lind 1949:70–75; Powers et al. 1932) describing the Kona coast of the island of Hawai'i in the early twentieth century suggest a similar economic pattern: a combination of infra-island trade, cash cropping, selling produce, and leasing land to foreigners (Japanese coffee growers). Over the long term, however, very few rural Hawaiian communities survived. The demise of local trade went hand-in-hand with rural depopulation. Ke'anae's population has steadily declined during this century, but the community has survived by combining wage labor with taro marketing.[8]

Production, Consumption, and Exchange

I have said that what distinguishes Ke'anae residents from most other Hawaiians is their identification with the land: the fact that here Hawaiians were not dispossessed after the Māhele and have largely retained ownership of the awards and grants established during the last century. As factors in the persistence of local Hawaiian ownership, I pointed to such factors as Ke'anae's isolation, the rough terrain, the acquisition of the uplands by groups of Hawaiians after the Māhele, and the selling of agricultural commodities to outside markets as a source of cash. Ke'anae Hawaiians are not peasants, because the primary source of income for most households is wage labor or a pension from previous wage labor. But because of their local control of the land, neither are they simply proletarians.

Could Ke'anae Hawaiians subsist on their landholdings today without engaging in wage labor? Without some qualification the question is meaningless, since subsistence requirements are never a matter of objectively defined minima but always reflect culturally defined needs and priorities (Sahlins 1972)—needs that change with foreign contact. It would be ludicrous to suggest that today's rural Hawaiians could "live off the land" by beating bark to make tapa cloth and processing *olonā* to make fishnets. The intrusion of capitalism into a subsistence economy always involves coercion, but sometimes the form of the coercion is not as obvious as outright land appropriation or mandating tax payments in currency. A market economy also generates a local demand for consumption goods (cf. Kelly 1980:14–15). People participate in a market economy not merely to survive, but also to obtain a variety of imported items that only cash can buy.

In Wallerstein's formulation, the periphery of the world-system is not only a producer of commodities but a consumer of goods imported from the core states. In fact, turning the periphery into a consumer as well as a producer of commodities is absolutely necessary if the core state is to harness the local labor force. The problem, as stated quite explicitly in an undergraduate text on tropical development, is one of stimulating wants in the indigenous population:

All the evidence seems to suggest that changes in the attitudes of tropical peasants to work can only be effected by making the peasant want to work harder. . . . This is very much a problem of changing his attitudes toward cash incentives. . . . In primitive societies, extra income . . . may not be enjoyed as much as in more advanced societies because of the limited ranges of possible uses. . . . The tropical peasant is continually acquiring new wants, and is showing himself increasingly willing to work to satisfy them without compulsion (Hodder 1968:50–51).

The resultant exchange between core and periphery is unequal, because the periphery exchanges its "low-wage . . . low-profit" products for the "high-profit, high-capital intensive" goods produced in the core (Wallerstein 1974:351). As Wolf notes (1982:258), the sandalwood trade in early nineteenth-century Hawaii exemplifies this relationship: sandalwood, harvested by forced labor through the mechanism of chiefly tribute, was exchanged for foreign luxury items such as guns, cloth, iron, and even yachts (see Sahlins 1981a:27–31, 43–44). But the periphery also consumes commodities produced within the periphery—sugar, tobacco, coffee, rice, meat, tea (see Wolf 1982:318–53). In any situation of Western contact, tobacco, coffee, and sugar have been among the first commodities to be introduced and have rapidly become viewed as necessities by indigenous peoples. This reliance on imported commodities is the other side of the periphery's dependency. Observers have often noted that many Pacific islanders with free access to the sea nevertheless consume more canned fish than fresh. A *kama'āina* (old-timer) of Moloka'i described selling taro in the early twentieth century and purchasing supplies with the proceeds: coffee, salt, sugar, flour, and kerosene (Boggs 1977). A city-dwelling Hawaiian informant listed rice, sugar, salmon, sardines, tuna, Spam, corned beef, and soap as basic purchases (ibid.). Parts of the periphery thus consume commodities produced in other parts of the periphery, with the core-state acting as intermediary and receiving the profits from the transactions.

Many Ke'anae Hawaiians enjoy access to fresh local foods that are essentially free: taro, bananas, avocados, sweet potatoes, guavas, breadfruit, fish. In this they are more fortunate than urban Hawaiians. But except for taro, the items regarded as staples by most Ke'anae residents are purchased outside at supermarkets, as are most other groceries. No Ke'anae family literally lives off the land. Even in taro-growing households, rice is at least as much a staple food as poi, and some residents with no patches open eat taro infrequently unless they receive it from a relative. Rice, bread, coffee, sugar, canned soft drinks and syrup for "juice," butter, canned corned beef, sardines, Vienna sausages, Spam, powdered coffee creamer, and packaged cereals are frequently purchased, as well as some fresh meat, cigarettes, and beer. The store-bought rice, bread, and sugar are usually the white, refined varieties. Locally grown produce, except for taro, is more important for exchange-in-kind than for subsistence. Watercress, bananas, avocados, sweet potatoes, and fish have become the treats of the inside, to be given to relatives and friends in town and eventually compensated for by the treats of the outside, such as store-bought Chinese dumplings (*manapua*), *char siu* (Chinese roast) pork, liquor, cigarettes, and bakery sweets.

The diet of Ke'anae Hawaiians is probably better than that of urban Hawaiians but still seems inferior to that of precapitalist "fish-and-poi" Hawaii. Why do even these rural Hawaiians purchase most of their food when, theoretically, one might become nearly self-sufficient with a little work and a lot of exchanging? That the answer seems self-evident reveals the interconnectedness of the world economy: we take for granted the absolutely necessary character of commodities that we cannot produce ourselves. Participation in the market economy, whether through wage labor or production of a cash crop, siphons labor from subsistence agriculture. As Tahitians gave up growing food in favor of cash crops, fresh vegetables simply became too expensive (Finney 1973a:73). Starchy foods are cheaper, and imported sweets, although relatively expensive, give more of a lift, albeit a temporary one—a sugar-induced feeling of well-being. Finney (ibid.:71) reports that for breakfast and the evening meal, Tahitian peasants eat bread and coffee or tea laced with a "staggering" amount of sugar. One is reminded of Wolf's (1982:318–53) discussion of the importance of stimulants as commodities.

To rephrase the initial question: can Ke'anae residents satisfy their daily needs and wants with the income gained through taro marketing alone? The fact that at the time of fieldwork only one householder did so suggests that it is possible but difficult, or at least, that taro marketing alone will not adequately sustain the kind of life-style that Ke'anae Hawaiians want. There is firstly the problem of managing resources and planting activities. To ensure a steady, year-round income from taro marketing, a grower in Ke'anae aims for a continuous harvest. But in practice this goal is difficult to attain. The farmer must be a skilled manager of land and labor, clearing and planting even while harvesting, and able to muster enough labor at the end of every week to fill the market order (see Linnekin 1985).

But I suggest that the primary reason that Ke'anae Hawaiians cannot rely solely on taro marketing for their income is the limited market for taro, with concomitant price fluctuations that the average grower has no way to predict. Taro in Hawaii is an unusual cash crop in that it only supplies the local market. The demand, historically rather stable, has increased steadily in recent years, making taro farming more profitable. A University of Hawaii study (1965:32) noted that price fluctuations in the Honolulu produce market "are frequent and violent." Since 1879, there have been attempts to generate new markets for taro with products such as taro flour and taro macaroni, but none has proved commercially successful (Allen and Allen 1933:9; University of Hawaii 1967:5). The principal commercial use for taro remains poi, which at present is only marketable in Hawaii. There has been a limited effort to sell poi in jars as a baby food, and taro chips are sold as a snack food, but these products seem viable only in the islands. In 1965 a University of Hawaii study (1965–67:80) noted that even in Hawaii poi was "a relatively expensive food item" and that the demand was declining. Currently, local production cannot meet the demand, and taro is imported from Samoa. Even in 1975, Ke'anae informants who did not have a source for home-ground poi complained about the high price of the store-bought product.

The unpredictable market is a major problem for taro growers (cf. Taussig 1980:92). When the price escalates, people put more land into production; absentee landowners bring their Ke'anae lands under cultivation and come inside to work the patches on weekends. Younger people take a sudden interest in the fallow lands of their elderly relatives and take up part-time taro farming to supplement their salaried jobs. Price rises were largely responsible for the rejuvenation and repopulation of Ke'anae that I have observed since the late 1970s. In 1975, I found the predominance of elderly householders worrisome for the community's future. Although residents are still concerned about the exodus of local youth, taro's current profitability has forestalled depopulation for the time being. But increased taro production inevitably brings about a fall in the external demand. For Ke'anae taro farmers, it is not the size of their holdings but the arbitrariness of the market—impersonal and outside them—that necessitates their participation in wage labor.

Economic Priorities and Local Response

In general, Ke'anae Hawaiians fit Taussig's definition of semiproletarians: they derive part of their subsistence from farming, but their participation in wage labor makes their farming activities possible. Their mode of production resembles that of peasants in that they still enjoy a measure of autonomy, of local control over resources: "the direct producers control means of production and organize work themselves" (Taussig 1980:18). They could not live in the United States without procuring cash, but they are not capitalist farmers because their expenditures are geared to "the satisfaction of an array of qualitatively defined needs" (ibid.:25), not to future capital gains (cf. Wolf 1955:

1). And these needs are not wholly dictated by the society outside. Alan Howard (1974:25) has said that modern Hawaiians "emphasize affiliative values and deemphasize individual competitive achievement." Only by examining indigenous values can one understand the "indifference to wage incentives" often found among peoples undergoing proletarianization (Taussig 1980:19–22). Employers often complain that Hawaiian wage laborers do not seem to strive to be promoted. Yet Ke'anae Hawaiians are exceedingly industrious when preparing a luau feast or undertaking entrepreneurial activities in a familial context. Earlier studies of Hawaiians noted that obligations to relatives and friends took precedence over financial considerations (Beaglehole 1937:29; Yamamura 1941:72). In Ke'anae, when a beloved relative returns from the Mainland for a visit, the celebration may include parties, luxury car rentals, and lavish gift giving—all conducted with little regard to cost.

Describing the survival of precapitalist economic orientations, Taussig writes of "the creative resistance of use-value orientations" (1980:20) and "the enduring quality of traditional domestic production based on the production of use-values" (ibid.:21). Nineteenth-century missionaries and plantation overseers called Hawaiians lazy. In twentieth-century ethnographic studies, Yamamura (1941:24) and Beaglehole (1937:30) noted that Hawaiians simply demand more time free from wage labor and prefer sporadic work to sustained drudgery. One must point here to a crucial difference in economic goals and priorities. Two hundred years after Western contact, many rural Hawaiians still have not been induced to strive for wealth and personal advancement along the lines of the capitalist model, although they will work with tremendous dedication when the payoff is measured in terms of social relations (cf. Gallimore and Howard 1968:10).

Not all Ke'anae residents are poor, however. There are wide income disparities within the community. At the time of fieldwork, one elderly widow subsisted on $185 monthly from social security. Another household, with three salaried adults, had an annual income of at least $30,000. Nevertheless, the residence of the latter was not markedly different in style or appearance from others in the community. In order to be esteemed by one's neighbors in Ke'anae, one must outwardly deny any special status. Paradoxically, being a person of influence in

Ke'anae hinges upon one's ability to maintain ostensibly egalitarian social relationships—to deny that one is materially higher than one's neighbors and peers (see Linnekin 1985). Drawing an analogy to Melanesian leaders who achieve personal status in an egalitarian context, I have referred to the influential people in the community as "big men."

When I did fieldwork in Ke'anae, I was particularly impressed with this striving for egalitarianism in interpersonal relationships, sometimes expressed as a concern for balance in everyday social exchanges. But with Ke'anae's increased prosperity in recent years has come a wave of new entrepreneurial activities and more open competition between local people. The market economy long ago made it possible for stratification to develop at the local level, but social sanctions kept a well-to-do peasantry from emerging. In the mid-1970s there were no explicitly acknowledged patron-client relationships. No one in Ke'anae dared to lord it over others outside the family, at least not overtly. "Acting high" was a term of condemnation and resulted in ostracism. This threat constituted a powerful check on overt individual aggrandizement.

I must confess that, in speaking of recent changes in Ke'anae's social ethos, I am speculating on the basis of very limited data. Nevertheless, the fact remains that some local residents are today engaging in the sorts of public, service-oriented ventures that were roundly criticized a decade ago. When families began to provide services to passing tourists, commercial activity quickly progressed from vending machines to fruit stands to lunch counters. As a result, a more overt economic competition has developed between people who are viewed and view themselves as traditionalists and guardians of cultural knowledge. Whether entrepreneurial ventures characteristic of modern tourist-oriented Hawaii tend to contradict Ke'anae's rural Hawaiian identity is a matter of some local discussion.

Viewed in the context of the present, inside/outside thus appears as a social model, a symbolism of economic relationships, and an ideology of opposition. This model continues to evolve in interaction with history. The politics of the past decade must be invoked in this regard; as a result of the Hawaiian cultural renaissance and the rise of nationalism, the Hawaiian/haole opposition is ever more salient. But as a transactional contrast, inside/outside expresses a dichotomy that has been diminishing for more than a hundred years—a contrast that has mitigated significantly even in the recent past. Capitalism is certainly alive and well in Ke'anae today, but a review of the community's economic history shows that local capitalism is nothing new. What is different about the present is the sense of internal contradiction in a social model that once neatly clarified issues of identity and cultural integrity.

Conclusion: Inside and Outside Models of Exchange

The contrasting pair inside/outside, an apt metaphor for the perceived differences between Ke'anae and town society, also describes two analytic perspectives that have been engaged in dialogue in this essay. Dependency theory sees the village in the context of the world economic system, from the outside looking in. The local-response objection, here raised by means of a historical analysis of local-level exchange in Hawaii, looks to indigenous cultural forms that condition the response to capitalism. The analysis of non-Western exchange systems has frequently been the purview of structuralism in anthropology, whereas dependency theory is associated with historical materialism. An oft-noted deficiency of structuralism is the assumption of reproduction, with a concomitant inability to account for structural change. But dependency theory, if applied without qualifications, is also one-sided in its focus on complete transformation—the wholesale imposition of capitalism on the local economy. The conclusion of this essay will continue the dialogue between the two perspectives in contrapuntal fashion, inside and outside, structuralist and world-system, reproduction and transformation, in an effort ultimately to arrive at a synthetic resting place.

In many respects Ke'anae resembles a closed corporate peasant community as described by Eric Wolf (1957; see also Wolf 1955, 1966). Such communities are characterized by, among other attributes, pressures on members "to redistribute or to destroy any pool of accumulated wealth" and by "the maintenance of strong defenses against the threatening outsider" (1957:12–13). Wolf explains the emergence of the closed corporate peasant community historically and functionally, as a response to colonization and "the dualization of society into a dominant entrepreneurial sector and a dominated sector of native peasants" (ibid.:8). Foreshadowing the thesis of dependency theory, he relates the structure of such communities to "the characteristics of the larger societies which gave rise to them" (ibid.:7).

A comprehensive discussion of Ke'anae vis-à-vis the peasant literature is outside the scope of this essay. Suffice to say that there are many ways in which Ke'anae differs from the ideal type of Wolf's closed corporate peasant community. Most Ke'anae men are full-time wage laborers as well as taro farmers. In Taussig's terminology, they are semi-proletarians rather than peasants. More importantly, however, my focus differs from that of the peasant literature, which at least in its earlier manifestations was primarily concerned with developing typologies and formulating cross-cultural regularities. In contrast to the line of argument pursued here, for example, Wolf emphasizes the contemporary functions of leveling mechanisms and egalitarianism for peasants living within "a dualized capitalist society" (ibid.:13). Asymmetrical exchange is similarly a feature of Wallerstein's model: "high-profit, high-capital intensive" goods produced in the core states are exchanged for "low-wage . . . low-profit, low-capital intensive goods" produced in the periphery (1974:351). Undeniably, exchange-in-kind and egalitarianism may be quite functional for the economic survival of Ke'anae today, but I would add that such practices have indigenous cultural precedents in Hawaii. They did not appear de novo after the introduction of capitalism.

Wolf implies a cultural tabula rasa for post-Hispanic peasant communities in Mesoamerica. In contrast, I have emphasized indigenous exchange modes and cultural models. The justification for this focus is historical and ethnographic as well as theoretical. Unlike the Mesoamerican corporate peasant community, which Wolf calls "a creature of the Spanish Conquest" (1957:7), and unlike most other rural Hawaiian communities, Ke'anae did not suffer major discontinuities in its resident population. Many villagers are demonstrably descended from the Land Commission awardees of the Great Māhele. There is also ethnohistorical evidence to support the thesis that local-level egalitarianism is not new —it characterized social relations among commoners living on the land at least in the early contact period.

The corporate peasant community type is similar to the world-system model in that it adopts the vantage point of the larger economic structure and emphasizes transformation rather than indigenous cultural factors. The local-response objection can be raised here too. In his study of South American peasants and wage laborers, Taussig points out that involvement in the wider economy does not erase the boundaries between the local community and the world-system:

A peasant . . . community can be involved in commodity production, but this need not constitute it as a reified culture. A community can in many ways be affected and controlled by the wider capitalist world, but this in itself does not necessarily make such a community a replica of the larger society and the global economy (1980:139).

To call rural Hawaiians semiproletarians is to point out ways in which they resemble other colonized peoples who live in a condition of economic dependency. Terms such as *peasant, semiproletarian,* and *world-system* are formulated and used by outsiders. They are useful for describing Ke'anae's relationship to the external economy, but they can never fully explain modes of exchange such as the reciprocity of goods and services that pertain inside. In internal social relations, Ke'anae Hawaiians observe ethics and priorities that reflect precapitalist values and categories. "Transactional continuity" (Strathern 1976 and this volume) such as this makes for a unique local response to the intrusion of the market economy that is nonetheless comparable to that of many other non-Western societies. Cultural precedents shape not only the way in which colonized peoples perceive capitalism, but also the ways in which they respond to it. The details of this response cannot be predicted in advance. Precapitalist values and ideologies are not irrelevant to the world-system, however powerful that system may be, for they materially affect how the local community articulates with the wider economy.

The above constitutes an anthropological caveat to Wallerstein's thesis —an ethnographic objection in that it derives from the inside, looking out. How well, from the perspective of the outside looking in, does Wallerstein's model of core, semiperiphery, and periphery describe Ke'anae's current relationship to the external economy? In the case of modern Hawaii, the boundaries between these sectors seem not so easily drawn. Wallerstein states that historically, European expansion depended on harnessing *"cheap* labor *far away"* (1974:86; emphasis in original). Accordingly he defines the periphery of the world-system as

that geographical sector of it wherein production is primarily of lower-ranking goods (that is, goods whose labor is less well rewarded) but which is an integral part of the overall system . . . because the commodities involved are essential for daily use (ibid.:301–2).

By Wallerstein's criteria, Hawaii qualifies as belonging to the periphery of the world-system: it is a former colony (cf. ibid.:349), geographically distant from the core-state, and its colonial status was imposed primarily because it was a source of an important agricultural commodity, sugar. But Wallerstein's typology seems more appropriate for the nineteenth century; Hawaii's modern economy presents inescapable problems of fit. Today Hawaii's most important product is service rather than crucial commodities. The Hawaiian sugar industry has fallen upon hard times because of competition from cheaper Mainland beet sugar and corn sweeteners, and pineapple is still not an essential food in most American households. Other local products, such as Kona coffee and macadamia nuts, are relatively expensive and are marketed as souvenirs and gourmet items. Hawaii's "Big Five" corporations, which long dominated the Hawaiian scene on the basis of agricultural commodity production, all suffer from diminishing profitability and are falling prey to corporate takeovers. Federal spending and tourism are the bulwarks of the state economy.

Ke'anae Hawaiians likewise are not directly involved in production for the world market. They are engaged in providing services—road work, manual labor, some skilled construction crafts—and in producing a cash crop for a limited local demand. Today Hawaii is less a supplier of raw materials and commodities to the core-states (see Wallerstein 1974:219) than it is a provider of services and a consumer of imported goods—a transition presaged even in Hawaii's early contact history by the sandalwood trade (see Sahlins 1981a:27–31, 43–44). One can argue that when Hawaii finally became one of the United States, its strategic military importance far outweighed its economic contributions to the core-state. My point is that Wallerstein's model illuminates the period of European expansion, but the modern situation is more complex. Many nations of the peripheral sector—territories and former colonies—have undergone a further economic transformation. Hawaii is not unique in the diminishing value of its commodities within the world-system, nor even in its dependence on tourism. These developments were all prefigured in the original core/periphery relationship. The ascendency of tourism and the eclipse of commodity production in Hawaii seem to have foreshadowed the future of many Third World nations that are seeking economic revitalization by becoming tourist havens for the core-states (see Clay 1982; Finney and Watson 1974; Smith 1977). In these respects, Hawaii represents the mature development of the periphery (cf. Kent 1983).

In counterpoint to the above discussion, I return once again to the perspective of the inside. The categorical distinction between Hawaiians and outsiders is at one level a contrast between different ethics and media of exchange, one identified as indigenous and appropriate to social relations inside, the other perceived as foreign and appropriate to the society outside. By means of this opposition, Ke'anae Hawaiians identify themselves with cultural continuity and distance themselves from cultural transformation—even though it is apparent that Hawaiian culture as represented in Ke'anae today is neither unchanging nor pristine, and that the local economy is continually adjusting to external conditions. Ke'anae residents are still subordinated to the outside, producing partly to support themselves and partly to pay their tithe to high foreigners. In this sense their dependency—at least their subordination—is not new, and the inside/outside equation remains an apt model of island society from the villagers' perspective. But commoner Hawaiians, low vis-à-vis the chiefs, are not the same as modern Hawaiians, economically and culturally disenfranchised vis-à-vis haoles. The latter is a class relationship within the global economy. To assert that rural Hawaiians conceptually put capitalism in its place is not to deny the largely negative effects that this economic structure has had upon them. The inside/outside model is both the enabler and the outcome of exchange relations, and is continually being revised in Sahlins's "structures of the conjuncture" (1981a, 1985). The symbolic equation is not static.

The commodities of the outside—using Wolf's (1982:310) definition of *commodities* as "goods and services produced for a market"—have been incorporated into local exchange-in-kind. Inside, these things become gifts. But does this mean that they have lost their essential nature as commodities? The high goods of the outside recall Wolf's list of the products of the periphery (1982:318–53). In Ke'anae, store-bought goods—prepared, imported items—seem to be valued more highly in exchange than the raw produce of the country. In part this reflects a preexisting symbolic scheme in which labor invests items with higher value: things that are prepared and altered in some way, as by cooking or drying, are more highly valued than raw, unaltered items. But Hawaii's contact history suggests that the goods of the outside are valued precisely because of their association with high foreigners. It is also possible that such items are valued because they were purchased with money—because they are commodities.

Sahlins has commented that indigenous ideological schemes are "the true organization of historical practice" (1981b:110). This does not mean, however, that such schemes replicate themselves without alteration. One cannot claim that Hawaiian exchange-in-kind has stayed the same: that it has successfully assimilated foreign goods without internal revision, without revaluation. This point follows from Sahlins's argument that cultural categories are "revised in practice" (1981a:54 passim). Arguing for a culturalist perspective on the colonial encounter, Sahlins writes that "from the vantage of the so-called dominated people, European wealth is harnessed to the reproduction and even the creative transformation of their own cultural order" (1985: viii).

The highest goods of the Hawaiian countryside—those given to one's closest relatives and best friends—are flesh foods prepared for a luau feast: *kālua* pig, *laulau*s, lomilomi salmon. But there is a competing set of high goods associated with the outside, produced as commodities and, incidentally, nutritionally inferior, and these must be bought.

Today exchange-in-kind relies fundamentally on the market economy. And it is at least a possibility that the status anxiety I observed in Ke'anae—the concern for paying back gifts, for not becoming indebted to another in exchange—has been exacerbated by an economic system that places a dollar value on everything. The weightiness of accepting taro, for example, may at least partly be based on the fact that today one knows precisely the dollar value of poi.

The world-system model assumes transformation—the global economy imposed on the local level; Lévi-Straussian structuralism privileges reproduction—the structure manages to replicate itself in spite of historical contingencies. Neither paradigm addresses the historical encounter between indigenous and introduced systems. Again, the crucial issue is not whether reproduction *or* transformation takes place, but whether we can develop theories that allow for both by addressing the interaction of inside and outside structures. History is made in the conjuncture of capitalist and precapitalist modes. Like gift giving and the market economy, the inside and outside perspectives—structuralism and dependency theory—are not irreconcilable. They meet in the present.

Notes

Acknowledgments Fieldwork in Hawaii from 1974 to 1975 was supported by a grant (GS–39667) from the National Science Foundation and a predoctoral training fellowship from the National Institute of Mental Health. For the thrust of the argument presented here, I am indebted to Aletta Biersack, who as usual offered invaluable critical comments and kept spurring me to produce a better paper.

1. For a recent application of dependency theory to industrial development in Third World countries, see Gereffi (1983). Thomas's review (1984) is a critique by an ideological opponent, but it serves to explicate some of the issues in the debate.
2. See Finney 1973b and Geertz 1963b for anthropological consideration of indigenous exchange modes and entrepreneurship in economic development.
3. Diacritics for place names are used in accordance with Pukui et al. (1974), but I use "Hawaii" to refer to the archipelago and "Hawai'i" to refer to

the island of that name. Hawaiian words are spelled as in Pukui and Elbert (1971). Direct quotations of Hawaiian texts appear as in the original, however.

4. Although "Ke'anae" properly refers to the ancient *ahupua'a* land section including upper Ke'anae Valley and Ke'anae Peninsula, I use the term here to include also neighboring Wailua Valley and the inhabited uplands between them. Today this area is effectively a single community.

5. Citations for unpublished archival materials will be given in the text, using the following abbreviations for sources: AH, Public Archives, State of Hawaii, Honolulu; HMCS, Hawaiian Mission Children's Society Library, Honolulu.

6. See Linnekin 1987 for a more detailed discussion of Hawaiian land alienation.

7. The bark of the *olonā* (*Touchardia latifolia*) shrub was cultivated for its fiber, which was resistant to sea water and highly durable. See Kamakau 1976: 44–45 for a detailed description of its cultivation and processing.

8. In 1930 the secretary of the territory estimated Ke'anae's population at 527, with 2,210 in Hāna District (Clare and Morrow 1930:14). The 1970 census gave 510 as the population of Hāna District, which encompasses the eastern half of East Maui (State of Hawaii 1974:17, table 9). By my field census, the resident population of Ke'anae in 1975 was 148.

References Cited

Allen, O. N., and Ethel K. Allen
    1933   The Manufacture of Poi from Taro in Hawaii. Hawaii Agricultural Experiment Station Bulletin no. 70.

Bauer, P. T., and B. S. Yamey
    1957   *The Economics of Underdeveloped Countries*. Chicago: University of Chicago Press.

Beaglehole, Ernest
    1937   *Some Modern Hawaiians*. Honolulu: University of Hawaii Research Publication no. 19.

Boggs, Stephen T.
    1977   The Meaning of *'Āina* in Hawaiian Tradition. Ms., files of the author.

Bradley, Harold Whitman
    1968[1942]
           The American Frontier in Hawaii. Gloucester, Mass.: Peter Smith.

Chinen, Jon
1958   The Great Mahele. Honolulu: University of Hawaii Press.
Clare, Alice, and Jack Morrow
1930   Maui: A Few Facts About the Valley Isle. Ms., Maui Public
            Library, Wailuku.
Clay, Jason, ed.
1982   The Tourist Trap: Who's Getting Caught? Cultural Survival
            Quarterly 6:3.
Coulter, John Wesley, and Chee Kwon Chun
1937   Chinese Rice Farmers in Hawaii. University of Hawaii Bulle-
            tin 16:5.
Dening, Greg
1980   Islands and Beaches: Discourse on a Silent Land, Marquesas
            1774–1870. Honolulu: University Press of Hawaii.
Finney, Ben R.
1973a   Polynesian Peasants and Proletarians. Cambridge: Schenkman.
1973b   Big-Men and Business. Honolulu: University Press of Hawaii.
Finney, Ben R., and Karen Ann Watson
1974   A New Kind of Sugar: Tourism in the Pacific. Honolulu: East-
            West Center.
Gallimore, Ronald, and Alan Howard, eds.
1968   Introduction. Studies in a Hawaiian Community. Pacific An-
            thropological Records no. 1. Honolulu: Bernice P. Bishop
            Museum.
Geertz, Clifford
1963a   Agricultural Involution. Berkeley and Los Angeles: University
            of California Press.
1963b   Peddlers and Princes. Chicago: University of Chicago Press.
Gereffi, Gary
1983   The Pharmaceutical Industry and Dependency in the Third
            World. Princeton: Princeton University Press.
Hodder, B. W.
1968   Economic Development in the Tropics. London: Methuen.
Hoselitz, Bert F., ed.
1952   The Progress of Underdeveloped Areas. Chicago: University of
            Chicago Press.
Howard, Alan
1974   Ain't No Big Thing. Honolulu: University Press of Hawaii.
Kamakau, Samuel M.
1961   The Ruling Chiefs of Hawaii. Honolulu: Kamehameha
            Schools Press.
1976   The Works of the People of Old. Tr. Mary Kawena Pukui. Ed.

Dorothy B. Barrère. Bernice Pauahi Bishop Museum Special Publication no. 61. Honolulu: Bishop Museum Press.

Kelly, Marion

1980   *Majestic Ka'u: Mo'olelo of Nine Ahupua'a*. Honolulu: Bernice Pauahi Bishop Museum. Department of Anthropology Report 80–2.

Kent, Noel J.

1983   *Hawaii: Islands Under the Influence*. New York: Monthly Review Press.

Krauss, F. G.

1937   Starting Changes in the Rice Industry Since Year 1900. *Honolulu Advertiser*, 8 August 1937.

Kuykendall, Ralph S.

1938   *The Hawaiian Kingdom, 1778–1854: Foundation and Transformation*. Honolulu: University of Hawaii Press.

1953   *The Hawaiian Kingdom, 1854–1874: Twenty Critical Years*. Honolulu: University Press of Hawaii.

Lévi-Strauss, Claude

1966   *The Savage Mind*. Chicago: University of Chicago Press.

Lind, Andrew W.

1949   Kona—Haven of Peoples. *Social Process in Hawaii* 13:66–79.

Linnekin, Jocelyn

1985   *Children of the Land: Exchange and Status in a Hawaiian Community*. New Brunswick, N.J.: Rutgers University Press.

1987   Statistical Analysis of the Great Māhele: Some Preliminary Findings. *Journal of Pacific History* 22:15–33.

Lorden, Doris

1935   The Chinese-Hawaiian Family. *American Journal of Sociology* 40:453–63.

Lueras, Leonard

1975   Keanae: The Hawaii That Used To Be. *Honolulu Advertiser*, 18 December 1975:A1.

Malo, David

1951   *Hawaiian Antiquities*. Bernice Pauahi Bishop Museum Special Publication no. 2. Honolulu: Bishop Museum Press.

Mathison, Gilbert F.

1825   *Narrative of a Visit to Brazil, Chile, Peru, and the Sandwich Islands*. London: Charles Knight.

Mauss, Marcel

1967   *The Gift*. Tr. Ian Cunnison. New York: W. W. Norton.

Mintz, Sidney W.
1977   The So-called World System: Local Initiative and Local Response. *Dialectical Anthropology* 2:253–70.
Morgan, Theodore
1948   *Hawaii: A Century of Economic Change*. Cambridge, Mass.: Harvard University Press.
Mountjoy, Alan
1963   *Developing the Underdeveloped Countries*. New York: John Wiley and Sons.
Neal, Marie C.
1965   *In Gardens of Hawaii*. Honolulu: Bishop Museum Press.
Powers, H. A., J. C. Riperton, and Y. B. Goto
1932   *Survey of the Physical Features That Affect the Agriculture of the Kona District of Hawaii*. Hawaii Agricultural Experiment Station Bulletin no. 66.
Pukui, Mary Kawena, and Samuel H. Elbert
1971   *Hawaiian Dictionary: Hawaiian-English, English-Hawaiian*. 3d ed. Honolulu: University Press of Hawaii.
Pukui, Mary Kawena, Samuel H. Elbert, and Esther T. Mookini
1974   *Place Names of Hawaii*. Honolulu: University of Hawaii Press.
Sahlins, Marshall
1965   On the Sociology of Primitive Exchange. In *The Relevance of Models for Social Anthropology*, ed. Michael Banton. London: Tavistock.
1972   *Stone Age Economics*. Chicago: Aldine-Atherton.
1977   The State of the Art in Social/Cultural Anthropology: Search for an Object. In *Perspectives on Anthropology 1976*, ed. A. F. C. Wallace. American Anthropological Association Special Publication no. 10. Washington, D.C.: American Anthropological Association.
1981a   *Historical Metaphors and Mythical Realities: Structure in the Early History of the Sandwich Islands Kingdom*. A.S.A.O. Special Publication no. 1. Ann Arbor: University of Michigan Press.
1981b   The Stranger-King: Dumézil among the Fijians. *Journal of Pacific History* 16:107–32.
1985   *Islands of History*. Chicago: University of Chicago Press.
Smith, Valene L., ed.
1977   *Hosts and Guests*. Philadelphia: University of Pennsylvania Press.

State of Hawaii
1974   *The State of Hawaii Date Book.* Honolulu: Department of
              Planning and Economic Development.
Stokes, John F. G.
1906   *Hawaiian Nets and Netting.* Memoirs of the Bernice Pauahi
              Bishop Museum 2(1):105–62. Honolulu.
Strathern, Andrew
1976   Transactional Continuity in Mount Hagen. In *Transaction
              and Meaning,* ed. Bruce Kapferer. Philadelphia: Institute for
              the Study of Human Issues.
1982   Tribesmen or Peasants? In *Inequality in New Guinea High-
              land Societies,* ed. Andrew Strathern. Cambridge: Cambridge
              University Press.
Taussig, Michael T.
1980   *The Devil and Commodity Fetishism in South America.* Chapel
              Hill: University of North Carolina Press.
Thomas, Lacy Glenn
1984   Underdevelopment: Test of a Theory. *Science* 224:711 –13.
Thurston, Lorrin A., ed.
1904   *The Fundamental Law of Hawaii.* Honolulu.
University of Hawaii
1965–67   *An Economic Study of the County of Maui.* Honolulu: Univer-
              sity of Hawaii Economic Research Center.
Verdery, Katherine
1983   *Transylvanian Villagers.* Berkeley and Los Angeles: Univer-
              sity of California Press.
Wallerstein, Immanuel
1974   *The Modern World-System.* New York: Academic Press.
1979   *The Capitalist World-Economy.* Cambridge: Cambridge Uni-
              versity Press.
1980   *The Modern World-System II.* New York: Academic Press.
Wenkam, Robert
1970   *Maui: The Last Hawaiian Place.* San Francisco: Friends of the
              Earth.
Wolf, Eric
1955   Types of Latin American Peasantry: A Preliminary Discus-
              sion. *American Anthropologist* 57:452–71.
1957   Closed Corporate Peasant Communities in Mesoamerica
              and Central Java. *Southwestern Journal of Anthropology* 13:1
              –18.
1966   *Peasants.* Englewood Cliffs, N.J.: Prentice-Hall.

1982   *Europe and the People Without History.* Berkeley and Los An-
            geles: University of California Press.
Wyllie, Robert C.
1844   Notes on the Shipping Trade. *The Friend* 2:9.
1855   Answers to Questions. In *Annual Report of the Minister of
            Foreign Relations.* 1849:49–95. Honolulu: Polynesian Press.
Yamamura, D. S.
1941   A Study of the Factors in the Education of the Child of Ha-
            waiian Ancestry in Hana, Maui. Master's thesis, University
            of Hawaii.

5. Struggles for Meaning

Andrew J. Strathern

During the massive break-up of the ice fields that followed the end of the Radcliffe-Brownian era in British social anthropology, several leading practitioners in the 1960s and 1970s turned their hands to the vexing problem of the relationship between anthropology and history—as though these conceptual entities could somehow be given separate existences and then compared. The arrangement of categories in this debate revealed partial views of what both disciplines were about—for example, as to whether the aims of social anthropology were idiographic or nomothetic (as per the old master himself). In practical terms the question then was as posed by Isaac Schapera: should anthropologists be historians? There is scarcely anyone now who would answer "no" to such a question. But much less certain is the answer to the question: "What sort of history are anthropologists best equipped to write?" By predilection and training we should be inclined to write "ethnographic history," attempting to give running synchronic accounts of societies and converting these into diachrony by means of theories of "social change." We are also inclined to stress the participants' own views and understandings, insofar as these can be recovered by historical scholarship, and to subject these to interpretation in the way that Marshall Sahlins has done so elegantly for Captain Cook and the Hawaiians whom Cook encountered. Hidden "voices" may thus be discovered, and the role of meaning in history is simultaneously amplified.

The melting of the ice fields that I mentioned above was followed by a strong flood of Marxist theory, which aimed to engulf entities such as "anthropology" and "history" in its own all-pervading system of ideas. Marxism was seen as the answer to all problems. However, as time has passed, Marxist anthropologists have come to terms with at least some of the categories of conventional anthropology and history, agreeing that they may not be entirely the products of bourgeois or tribal false consciousness. ("Segmentary lineage" is one concept that seems to have been rehabilitated in this way.) The "crude" or "unrefined" Marxist phase has left us with a valuable legacy of ideas, prominent among which is the stress on the role of conflict in producing change within systems and the debate on the place of economic factors in determining sequences of change. In the "refined" Marxist versions, "meaning" is allowed in at almost all levels and hence the models of causation tend to be dialectical rather than linear. In this paper, I follow that trend, in particular arguing that meaning is central rather than incidental to what we call history and that people's attempts to construct their history, both contemporaneously and in retrospect, are attempts to construct sets of meanings for the course of events in which they are involved.[1]

In one sense this argument might be thought jejune, since we would hardly expect people to operate without some sense of meaning in their lives, and we do not need an elaborate argument to make the point. Interest lies at the level of discussing precisely what sets of meanings people construct and what factors constrain them in so doing.

Pervasive and perdurable schemata, in terms of which people interpret the world around them and their own place in it, are found both in Western societies and in the small-scale societies of Papua New Guinea. These schemata in turn may become means of understanding or projecting history. Aletta Biersack (this volume) has shown clearly how a set of classifications has greatly influenced the Paiela view of what their history is and how it should develop in the future. A similar situation holds for the Melpa. At the same time, problems arise when the basic schemes of interpretation of the world are challenged or contradicted by untoward events. It is then that struggles for meaning occur.

The meaning of the *moka* exchanges in Mount Hagen is a topic that has occupied me since I first worked in the area in the 1960s. From the outset it appeared clear that *moka* was a major preoccupation of the people, that it took up a great deal of their time and energy, and that the current state of exchanges between groups constituted the basic framework of Melpa local-level politics. This was so despite, or in conjunction with, the fact that massive changes were also occurring in the area, with the introduction of cash cropping, plantations, missions, local government councils, parliamentary democracy, capitalist business, health services, vehicular transport, and the like. In the 1960s *moka* prestations were constructed, as it were, "on the back of" compensation payments for deaths, as transactions subsequent to them. In this sense, they belonged to intergroup politics. As pointed out in extenso also (Strathern 1971), they provided a vehicle whereby big men could compete to demonstrate their ability to give away large numbers of pigs and valuables, their influence over supporters, their command over labor, and their virtuosity in decorating, dancing, and orating. In addition dozens of other individuals of middling status and renown used these venues to pursue their own partnerships, strengthen their marriages, pay back debts, ensure the health of their children, and so forth. The absurd discussion that sometimes marked debate about Melpa exchanges, as to whether either an individual or a group focus of analysis is to be preferred, entirely ignores the multifunctionality and multivocality of these events. Layers of meaning inhere in people's actions from the group level down to that of the individual, and the same act possesses significance by virtue of inclusion in widening spheres of action. A man may have received pigs in advance; still, he brings them, or replacement ones, back to the stakes at the ceremonial ground to be given away again formally, on the concerted occasion of the *moka*.

There is a summation of individual activity molded into a group event, which is the final *moka* dance itself.

Furthermore, just as a *moka* expresses values, meanings, and purposes at different social levels simultaneously, so also does the act of giving itself carry sets of meanings, which may even be in contradiction with one another. The basic contradiction has to do with the relative status of the partners in a given *moka* transaction. To give generously means that one is honoring the recipient, but it may also be that one is putting him to shame by giving him more than he can comfortably repay. Honoring implies that the recipient is temporarily placed above the giver, but this placement is signaled by the giver himself. Shaming implies the reverse. In any instance of gift giving, the resolution or steadying out of these two contradictory meanings tends toward an impression of roughly equal status between the partners. Equality is thus not static but dynamic, continuously threatened, continually recreated. The fact of making a *moka* partner is also a statement of independent decision-making powers, a demonstration that one is on one's own ground and can do these things as one's forefathers did. The friendship that is expressed toward partners is voluntary in the same sense. It has its background in past action, precedent, debts, constraints, yet it is also a new creation each time a *moka* takes place. At the individual level the partners are often affines, and payments for wives and children merge into the blueprint of *moka* activity. In *moka* the imbalance between wife-givers and wife-takers is rebalanced by their mutual engagement in the *moka* exchanges themselves.

All of these values are contingent on successful performances over time. Every *moka* represents an arrested point in time when the ongoing flow of wealth is given direction and shape. At the same time the speakers refer back to the past and forward to the future, making it clear that this is only one event in a series that links people together over time and between places.

Nothing in *moka* is automatic. People give well or badly. A good performance in one *moka* does not guarantee that the next one will go well. Recipients know a lot about what they are going to get, but at the same time they are kept ignorant, right up to the gift giving itself, of the full spectrum. Not to know may mean that they are going to be surprised with some extra items or, per contra, that the donors will renege on some of their debts. This uncertainty, and the constant probing and challenging, combined with the conventional politeness that goes with it all, are what gives *moka* much of its excitement and also much of its temporal flexibility and adaptability. Delays in giving are "normal," in the sense that they almost always occur, and indeed must occur, if people are to live up to what they say they will do. Interdependency of prestations (the "rope of *moka*" itself) across several group boundaries means that the relevant arena for politics is constantly widened and at the same time the task of getting any one event actually to happen becomes correspondingly harder.

The history of a group, then, is decisively bound up with the history of its *moka* transactions, and each *moka* is both an expression and a redirection of that history. The very stability and strength of the group is marked by the size, age, upkeep, and history of usage of its ceremonial ground. There is a dynamic element as well in that big men often lay out new grounds for a *moka* in which they plan to be prominent. Transience is also marked out: I have seen the grounds of Tipuka Eltimbo men, used in the 1964–65 sequence of *moka* in the Möka Valley, subsequently carved up into gardens and house sites; and this process reflected the scattering and relocation of this fragile group in another territory close to the Gumant River in the Wahgi Valley to the southeast.

A major preoccupation or focal institution of this sort does not fade away easily. Predictions of its demise, from outside and inside, have been made at least since 1964. Yet twenty years later it is still very strong; and among the groups with which I have identified, at any rate, it shows no signs of petering out. I discussed this issue more than ten years ago (Strathern 1976), and after a further decade I can simply report that *moka* remains as important today as it was in 1964. In the late 1970s, experiencing the strain of living under the relentless enthusiasm of an established big man (Ndamba), younger men of the Kawelka Kundmbo clan at Golke did begin to mutter that they should drop *moka* and concentrate on "business" instead. In their case, it is true, the opportunities for business were, and are, limited, and as a result not much came of their stirrings. The situation is quite different with the current majority of the group, who live in a fertile area close to town. Yet here, too, the *moka* is still vigorously practiced, concurrently with cash-making activities. In this area, however, it has also taken on a new context of meanings, associated with the movements of people from place to place. Indeed it is one of the capacities of *moka* that its performers can blend into it their current concerns while still preserving the basic form of *moka* prestation itself. In 1964 most of the expansion of exchange was associated with pacification and the "good times" brought by the white men. Twenty years later the colonial power had gone, massive commercial developments had taken place all around the group, and land claims were not an issue of concern. It is my argument that although these problems were perceived clearly enough by the actors, their approach to solving them employed the same social logic they applied to exchange relations in general and that this approach still rested on premises of equality and friendship rather than on ideas of dominance and subordination or politico-legal dependency.

Before continuing the discussion, it may be helpful if I stress again the extent to which the Melpa people as a whole are tied in with the introduced system of economic change and development. Mount Hagen town is the commercial and political capital of the Western Highlands Province, where the Melpa live. It has banks, supermarkets, garages, light manufacturing industries, government offices, a large police barracks, and hotels. Many educated Melpa of both sexes now work in Hagen town or in other urban centers in Papua New Guinea. Others are employed as wage laborers in factories or in government departments. A few are prominent or rising business people in their own right. In the rural areas everyone grows the cash crop coffee, there are numerous owners of passenger motor vehicles and trade stores, and women regularly sell vegetables for pin money. Earning, spending, and perhaps especially *counting* money are favorite activities and topics of conversation. An undeniable and unmistakable commoditization of services has taken place; for example, people pay money to get fencing or roofing materials, which in the early 1960s they could obtain on a basis of reciprocal help from kin and friends. The overall encroachment of the new monetary system is great and obvious indeed. People spend regularly on clothes, trinkets, and food supplies from town, and they save up large sums to buy vehicles. So why do they bother with the *moka* at all?

The answer is simple. These new activities do not in themselves constitute relationships between persons in the Melpa social system. They are all activities oriented toward others: other people, other structures. By preserving *moka* and certain associated key institutions, notably bridewealth payments, the Melpa have retained a sphere for their own continuous history, which acts as a filter in respect of the outside. It lets in enough to "color" the *moka* actions and enable the *moka* itself to play a role in contemporary adjustments, but not so much that the outside world would swamp or sweep away the internal world of meanings the Melpa themselves continue to construct.

Putting the matter in this way may suggest that the actors make completely conscious choices about maintenance of the *moka* in the face of pressures to abandon it. This indeed has been so from time to time. In the 1950s adherents of the Lutheran mission in Dei Council were told to give up *moka* because it caused bad feelings between people (the opposite, of course, of its express purpose!). Agricultural officers who introduced cash crops in the 1960s sometimes saw *moka* as standing in the way of economic development (or what we might now rather call "peasantization") and for that reason discouraged it. In 1984, I observed an unusual compensation ceremony at Nunga ceremonial ground in the territory of the Tipuka people. It was made by and on behalf of the Tipuka Oklembo clan to relatives of a young Minembi Yelipi clansman who had been knifed and left for dead after a drinking party. The victim had not yet died, but to forestall trouble the Tipuka gathered a huge payment and had both their member of parliament and the deputy premier of the Western Highlands provincial government present, inter alios. The latter, swinging a bunch of keys at his waist, rather grimly announced that he felt all this money going for a compensation—and it might as well have been *moka* to which he was referring, for he has inherited his sentiment from officers in colonial times—was a waste and a hindrance to proper development. When faced with disapproving noises of this sort, it is clear that people *do* choose to persist in what they do. But this is not always so. For the most part the Melpa continue to make their plans and their own history without direct interference from others. Indirectly, however, the sphere in which they can freely do so is contracting.

It should also be made clear that the Melpa who engage in *moka* do not "resist" business or cash cropping. Far from it. These activities are linked together. People earn money and use it to hire or buy dance plumes, pay for pigs, hire cars, contribute direct amounts of money —all toward *moka*. It is therefore incorrect to see Melpa history as a matter of resisting the inroads of capitalism in any simplistic sense. One might rather argue that Melpa embrace the capitalist world enthusiastically. Everyone is keen to do business and get money. The point is, however, what they do with their money once they have it. For the majority, including those who adopt the role of local-level leaders, much of their money goes back into their network of social ties. This is shown *in micro* in the endless round-robins of card games that take place. Spare amounts of cash are quickly thrown into such games, which absorb people's attention for hours on end; and there is disapproval for winners who try to take all their money out and put it in a bank or spend it in town. What happens *in micro* during the card games mirrors the larger event-spans of *moka* between groups over time. We arrive, therefore, at a paradoxical point in my argument: the Melpa are both keen and not keen on capitalism. The paradox is resolved when we put it another way. The Melpa are keen to use the new economic system in order to make money, but they still want to spend a good proportion of that money on *moka*; and this spending pattern diverts them away from a wholesale switch to capitalistic relationships in their everyday lives.

I return now to my more detailed description of the activities, and thus the history, of the Melpa group with which I am best acquainted. I have been studying the activities of one group in Hagen, the Kawelka, since 1964. This group currently numbers some sixteen hundred people, now mostly concentrated at Kuk, around a government agricultural research station of the same name that was established on land that traditionally belonged to the Kawelka themselves and was purchased from them in the year I first came to Hagen. I have spent some time with the Kawelka during every year (up to 1987) since 1964, except for 1966 when I was writing my doctoral dissertation in Cambridge.

In 1964 the bulk of the Kawelka lived at Mbukl, a hilly and high-altitude territory on the Sepik-Wahgi Divide north of Hagen town. They had migrated there during the early part of this century as a result of warfare with the Mokei people, who lived nearby. After colonial peace was imposed, from the early 1950s onward the Kawelka began to move back to the more favorable and fertile land at Kuk, specifically at first with the aim of raising large pigherds and subsequently for the purpose of cash cropping (mostly coffee). The cold weather, high altitude, and less-rich soils at Mbukl make both coffee growing and pig rearing slower affairs than at Kuk. Furthermore, it is much easier to travel into Hagen town from Kuk and thus to gain access to shops, government officials, and health services. The attractions of Kuk are obvious and manifold. But there is one snag. Far too much land was alienated in the 1960s to the government research station and to the company Manton Bros., which established a tea plantation immediately to the east of the station itself. The result is that today, although a small proportion of the Kawelka have regular or temporary employment at Kuk station or at Tibi plantation as tea pluckers, the bulk of the population is now short of land even for subsistence purposes. This is a situation of which the Kawelka themselves are well aware, and it has been compounded by their generous invitation to immigrants from the Tambul region to come in and share their land with them.

This vital issue of land claims has been dealt with by discussions couched in terms of exchange relations between groups. Herein lies the core of my argument. Is this "conversion" of issues into exchange simply an example of ideological mystification? If we regard it as mystification, whose interests does this serve? I argue against such a simple explanation of the phenomenon. The discussion of issues to do with land in terms of exchange is not, in fact, a device to ensure the dominance of any one social category. To the contrary, it actually reduces the potentials for such dominance, as though the participants were concerned rather to preserve a degree of equality between themselves instead of emphasizing inequality. This process is in stark contrast with other processes of land acquisition for business purposes by companies, individuals, and development corporations throughout the Western Highlands Province. The activities of these corporations (including those owned by Hageners themselves) cannot be converted back into local exchanges, and so they represent the irreversible movement of the capitalist mode of production into the Hagen countryside. Eventually, perhaps, one can foresee a time when the *sphere of exchange*, as I am using the term here, is reduced to the point where it is scarcely viable. At this point indigenous schemes of meaning would finally collapse. On coming to live at Kuk, where the people are surrounded by development and its effects, I had expected, from 1983 onward, to find this process of narrowing the sphere of exchange more advanced there than at Mbukl. At Mbukl, I had observed the "domestication" of money through its incorporation into *moka* exchange, replacing pearl shells, especially during the 1970s. But at Kuk, as I have noted already, the town is closer, there is more wage labor, there is a greater ethnic and linguistic "mix" of people, and the stage seems set for a rapid social change. However, events have not borne out this expectation. Rather, at Kuk the Kawelka have struggled to reconstitute themselves in a network of exchanges, and it is a set of younger men, now in their thirties, who are prominent in doing so, not the established set of older big men who already had high status at the time when most people were still living at Mbukl. These facts gradually became apparent to me as I was involved in, and studied, the ramifications of a performance, completed in mid-1984, of the *Amb Kor* ('Female Spirit') cult sponsored by one of the younger leaders, Ru-Kundil. Ru's increasing engagement with this cult and with exchanges scheduled to occur both before and after it led me to realize the extent to which the Kawelka (Figure 5) at Kuk are creating meaning for themselves in their regained but diminished territory. Objective shortages of land may help to explain, as background factors, why people like Ru act as they do; but they by no means define the mental universe he and others are attempting to create for themselves and their posterity.

An important aspect of activities in Hagen is the scheduling of events. Individuals and groups not only renew and recreate relationships over

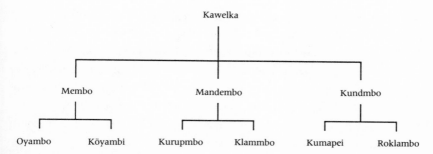

Fig. 5. Kawelka subdivisions.*

time, but they do so in sequences, and these sequences are themselves objects of discussion, struggle, comment, and evaluation. From the struggle, in effect, certain meanings are extracted. The first part of this interpretation was already apparent to me in 1971, when I published *The Rope of Moka* and included a chapter on "disputes and struggles precipitated by *moka* occasions." My point there was that the timing of *moka* events is frequently made an occasion for competition between big men. Those who are ready try to advance the date; those who are not, to delay it. Often, again, the result is a split between factions. The same holds for other events, including *Amb Kor* itself. In 1973, for example, the Kawelka Kundmbo clan split into two sections, which performed the cult simultaneously but separately. A senior leader, Ndamba, was trying to assert his preeminence in the whole group through the cult. But what emerged instead was a widening of the existing division between his supporters and a congeries of younger men who had established a different cult site on land belonging to the other main section of the Kundmbo clan at Golke. Only for the final dance did the two sections at last combine. (On the *Amb Kor* in general see Strathern 1970 and 1979).

In the case of the cult performance sponsored by Ru in 1983–84, no such serious split emerged within the group itself, even though there

---

*The Kundmbo who live at Kuk are all known as Kumapei, since their fathers did not go down to Mbukl but scattered elsewhere and returned later. Rather confusingly, two of the subclans of Kundmbo living near to Mbukl are *also* categorized as Kumapei. Kurupmbo and Klammbo act as substantially separate, though linked, entities.

were moments of opposition accompanied by bad omens during parts of the cult rituals. Instead, Ru had two different sorts of problems. One was to get men in other sections of the Kawelka to contribute pigs in *moka* to his own group and thus help them to kill a sufficiently large number of pigs for the cult. This is reminiscent of Rappaport's discussion of the Maring *kaiko* pig-killing festival.[2] As this process dragged on, Ru's second difficulty became greater: to persuade his own clansmen to contribute their pigs and money in time for each successive stage of the cult festival itself. There was little doubt that the setbacks he experienced were in general a result of "social change." People's minds are diverted by so many activities and pastimes these days, it is hard to get them to concentrate on such a taxing and arduous sequence as the *Amb Kor* involves.

Ru was well aware of this, but he rationalized or rephrased the problems in two ways. One was to criticize the surrounding groups for not playing their parts according to the proper sequence, and the other was to impute misfortunes to the displeasure of the *Amb Kor* herself. Because people were not providing the necessary pigs quickly enough, it was said that the goddess would become angry and cause misfortune, sickness, and death in the would-be celebrant group. As time went on, the setbacks that occurred were regarded either as reasons why the goddess was likely to become angry or as signs of her already awakened displeasure. School buildings were burned down; car engines blew up; wives left their husbands, causing lengthy court disputes; people became involved in court charges for offenses they had not committed. All these events delayed preparations; they were also said to be the result of the goddess's anger at the delays. A positive feedback loop of interpretations wound itself around people's minds. At the same time, leaders like Ru used the same series of events as springboards for haranguing their clansmen. If they wished to avoid even worse disasters, they *must* fight against the odds and finish the cult. To do so would "switch off" the disasters and, they hoped, "switch on" the benefits the cult was designed ritually to secure, most notably the birth of male children to the wives of the cult members.

There were two main potential sets of donors of pigs for the *Kor*. These were:

(1) Tipuka Oklembo clansmen, clustering round a single old big man, Kele, who is the father of Ru's third wife, Mande. The Oklembo live by the Möka River in the Dei Council area proper, and Ru's own family used to live with them until the early 1970s, when he transferred to Kuk after having had numerous disputes with his hosts. Following the break in coresidence, relationships were reconstituted in terms of exchanges and Kele was now due to give pigs for Ru's *Kor*.

(2) Poika (elsewhere I have spelled this "Poyaka") tribesmen who have migrated in from the Tambul region to join the Kawelka were due to give prestations of pigs to Kundmbo clansmen (their hosts) and the Kundmbo to hand these on to the Kurupmbo, Ru's group, in time for the *Kor* to take place. Though individual men of the Poika fulfilled obligations in time to their Kundmbo/Kurupmbo partners, one leading big man appeared endlessly to drag his feet. This was Pipur, who had constructed his own ceremonial ground on territory previously occupied and owned by the Kurupmbo themselves and whose gardens and pig pastures were mostly on land belonging to the Kundmbo big man at Kuk, Minembi-Ken.

Early in 1984 a "bet" had taken place between Pipur and Kele as to which of them would be the first to make their *moka* and so set things in motion for the *Kor*. Kele, not noted in Dei Council for his speed in giving *moka*, nevertheless managed to beat Pipur to it in this case, and the reception of Kele's pigs at Kuk was celebrated in triumphant songs by women of Ru's group, much to Pipur's discomfiture. The chief reason for Pipur's delay was that his *moka* debts were tied in to the Enga *tee* system, stretching over to the Minyamp Valley and the well-known big man there, Yuponda Kepa. The Enga system is notoriously slow in moving and is probably worse now, since the Enga area as a whole has been disrupted for many years by persistant tribal fighting. Whatever the specifics of the situation, Pipur was held up by his dependency on partners linked to the *tee*. In addition, of course, he now lived apart from some of his clan, and the distance between the two places was such as to inhibit regular and easy movement between them.

Later in 1984, as pressure began to build to get the *Kor* completed and Pipur still would not release his pigs, Ru and a number of others of Kurupmbo purchased a quantity of beer and drank all night. At dawn they burst out in a dance formation and advanced down Pipur's ceremonial ground to the front of his dwelling house, where they proceeded to hold a "demonstration" against his delays. They threatened, in fact, to go ahead and hold the *Kor* without bothering to wait for Pipur and his pigs. Could he not see that they had already brought home the special pigs purchased with cash from commercial establishments all the way up to Hagen from Lae on the coast? If he couldn't, he must wash his eyes with soap to enable himself to see better! These pigs were supposed to indicate that the Kurupmbo were all set to hold the final stage of their cult; and this was the message then, with drunken license delivered to Pipur. Pipur listened impassively and set yet another false date for his *moka*. The Kurupmbo went off, elated with the impression they thought that they had made.

Minembi commented that the Kurupmbo claims were probably hollow, because they would still have to depend on him for pigs and he in turn on Pipur. The Kurupmbo men's point, however, was rather different. Pipur was supposed to be making *moka* partly to justify his occupation of Kawelka land, including some of the Kurupmbo's own claims. Their "reliance" on him for pigs to use in the *Kor* was an expression of the ties of friendship between them; and, as I began by noting, this stress on friendship is also a means of dealing with the issue of land occupation. In saying that perhaps they would not "rely" on him after all, they were also obliquely saying that they might bring up questions of land claims in a direct way. This was a threat that was never carried out, even though Pipur did not, in fact, make his *moka* in time. Delivering the message while drunk left the Kurupmbo free either to follow it up or to forget it later as words spoken while under the influence of liquor. The threat of inequality was thus made less immediate. At the same time, their impatience with Pipur was made very clear, as was their latent claim to superiority in land rights.[3]

The implications of what the Kurupmbo were saying, spoken while drunk or otherwise, to Pipur must be considered carefully. Pipur was an immigrant, invited in not by the Kurupmbo but by Minembi, a Kundmbo big man who himself had migrated to Kuk from the Ronye area in 1970. Minembi's claims were not challenged by the Kurupmbo, except in respect of pieces of land that they cultivated before he did. These, however, included the ceremonial ground where Pipur and his extensive family and dependents all lived and on which he was due to stage his *moka*. In marching onto this area to make their announcements, the Kurupmbo were reminding him of that fact. Verbally they did not even mention the matter of land claims. My knowledge of their feelings is based on separate conversations with them before and after this event, since my own field house was built on a piece of land just next to Pipur's settlement.

The underlying idea is this: guests are invited into an area on a basis of friendship, but there is still a rule of priority with respect to land claims. This rule generates a certain inequality of standing between hosts and guests with respect to the rule itself. *Moka* gifts are a means of redressing that inequality by setting up flows of reciprocal exchanges. The same holds with regard to bridewealth payments: the implied imbalance in these is "corrected" through conversion into *moka*. The nexus of arrangements converging on Ru's *Kor* performance at Kuk was a piece of local social engineering designed to link together the *Kor* and the *moka* sequences (see Figure 6). Thus, the Poika were supposed first to give to their immediate hosts of the Kundmbo and these in turn to give to the Kurupmbo, who would "convert" these gifts into sacrifices to the goddess and attempt by this means to ensure for themselves

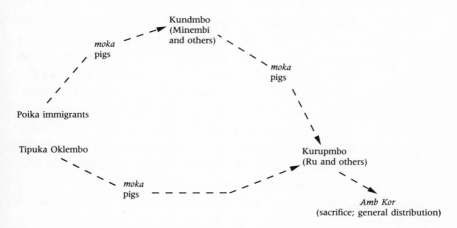

Fig. 6. Links between Kor *and* moka *sequences.*

patrifilial continuity on their land as well as increased fertility and health for their crops and pigs. The Kurupmbo also had to put large numbers of their own pigs and amounts of money into the *Kor* in order to pay for the services of outside experts who came to do the rituals necessary to the cult. The final effect of this conversion sequence was thus a transformation of human labor into social prestations, these into sacred gifts, and these in turn into a dance display and wide distribution of foodstuffs to all the groups around Kuk. Integration between groups of people and between one pivotal group and the realm of the sacred was thus achieved. The meaning of the total sequence is about as far removed from the capitalist mode of production as it can be.

The potential benefit of the cult was referred to twice by ritual experts who came to officiate at the major stages of pig killing for the goddess. On both occasions they were handing over the main *tamb mel* or sacred plants and substances to Ru and another man, Oklom, respective leaders of the "men's house" and "women's house" sections of the celebrant group (Strathern 1979). "This cult is not about anything else, it is about these things only, and we use them because they help us to bear sons." After the items were handed over, two men, one from each section, took tinder and firethongs and used the thongs by friction to create a spark and light the fire for heating the cooking stones. At the final stage the fire was lit also in a special, secluded house where only certain of the men were allowed to go, and in this were housed the actual cult stones decorated in white and red. It is a bad omen if fire cannot be produced from the thong, and in this case the operator was a man who had lately been in opposition to Ru as cult leader. His action was taken as an omen that the cult might not be completed and that the goddess was displeased at the development of disunity within the group. Implied also was the threat that she might not grant her blessings to the group after all if they did not pull together. Ru took the omen quietly and did not allow himself to be too discouraged. Eventually his patience succeeded, because the cult was held and at the final performance there were no more untoward omens.

At a personal level, for Ru, the aim of having many sons was important. He had four wives, but the fertile one kept producing daughters; and he had only one son still alive, whom he decorated and inducted into the cult along with himself. Two of his wives, after having children, conceived no more (presumably because of pelvic infections, which are common enough in Hagen). His plans, mooted from time to time, of taking another wife for a last try, were opposed vigorously by the existing wives, who declared that in such a case they would either all get baptized into various mission sects or would simply leave him. (Six months after the cult was actually over and the youngest of his wives had in fact left him and gone back to Enga, where she came from, Ru was set free to remarry a youngish woman after all. But at the time of the *Kor*, his wives put pressure on him not to remarry, or they would withdraw pigs from the cult itself as well as getting baptized and becoming sexually inaccessible to him. The missions do not allow baptized women to cohabit with a polygamous husband.) At the time of the cult, then, Ru's hopes for male successors were placed in the goddess and her powers; while, objectively, the demands of the cult placed a heavy strain on his relationships with his actual wives.

One aspect of the cult's "meaning" was obviously that through their display of decorations and their gifts of pork, the Kurupmbo impressed on the groups around them their existence and strength. In this regard the *Kor* functions in the same way as the *moka*. But there are added elements in the *Kor* that give it a peculiarly dramatic quality. The final dance is performed only once, and the celebrants decorate secretly inside the cult enclosure before bursting through a high fence to do it. And the gifts of pork they make are handed out in small pieces to a very wide assortment of recipients in a way quite different from *moka*. There is a feeling almost of "largesse" in the occasion as well as great enthusiasm and enjoyment on the part of the crowd, who come thrusting spears at the noses of the celebrants, begging for pieces of meat to be skewered onto their weapons. These are the *external*, manifest meanings. *Internally*, the meaning is one of fertility, of production and reproduction, and patrifiliation. This internal meaning is worthy of further comment.

The aim of producing more sons corresponds to Hagen male ideology in general and also fits with the Kurupmbo's desire to assert themselves as a major force among the Kawelka at Kuk. They have not taken in many immigrants from other groups. Still, their aim might be thought irrational, in view of the impending problems of land shortage at Kuk following the earlier alienation of land to the government. However, the cult promises general fertility as well— that is, that crops and livestock will do well—so in a sense it can be seen as an attempt to stimulate the productivity of the Kurupmbo men's gardens, and this is certainly a rational aim.

My remarks above are intended to help explain why it was the Kurupmbo who sponsored the *Kor* performance at Kuk in 1983–84. I do not mean that the *Kor* has always to do with land shortage. Not at all. It is a circulating cult, widely diffused among the Hagen groups. Its rituals remain largely the same regardless of which group is currently performing it. I only suggest that for the Kawelka, hemmed in as they are by other groups and by tracts of their own ancestral land that they have alienated to the capitalist world, the choice to put on a *Kor* does require some further discussion. No group accepted Ru's offer at the end of the distribution to send the *Kor* on to them; and this indicates clearly that the cult is under threat, both from the competing claims of secular activities and from the aggressive evangelizing of the new Pentecostal churches in the area. Just as the *moka* was condemned in the 1950s by the Lutheran mission and others, so in the 1980s the remaining manifestations of indigenous religion are roundly attacked by the fundamentalist churches. Interestingly, the Roman Catholic church has taken a rather quieter view of these matters, based on its own historical symbiosis with variations such as Mariolatry and veneration of the saints. It is clear, at any rate, that here is another sphere where a struggle for meaning is taking place.

The stress on exchange was not exhausted with the completion of Ru's cult itself. After it, Ru planned to hold another round of exchanges, starting with gifts of live pigs to his mother's people. Earlier he had tried to work this in before the cult but had failed, so he simply staged it afterward instead. And once more the question of dependence on the Poika came up. Some of the Poika were to give pigs, which they had not handed over for the cult itself. Looked at from an economic perspective, Ru's constantly devised festivals were a means of extracting pigs from the Poika as immigrants on Kawelka land. But two further factors must immediately be considered here if we make such an "interpretation" or "representation" of the events. The first is that the Kurupmbo are *not* the major sponsors of these immigrants. The major sponsors are the few Kundmbo men who live at Kuk, among whom Minembi is by far the most prominent. And the second is that a proportion of the pork actually went *back* to the Poika donors. A "profit" motive should not, therefore, be imputed. However, it is true that the Poika were supposed mainly to give first to the Kundmbo and these to pass the gifts on to the Kurupmbo, thus creating a chain of the form immigrants-hosts-equal exchange partners with the meaning of the prestations changing at each of the two links in the chain. In practice, Poika men *also* made partnerships directly with Kurupmbo.

The position of the Kundmbo is interesting. They are original landholders at Kuk because one man of their clan, called Kundi, stayed near Kuk itself after the exodus of most of the Kawelka to Mbukl, and he was on the spot to encourage others to return after the area was pacified and administered by the colonial regime. Makla, one of his sons, lives at the head of the central ceremonial ground at Kuk, and Makla also makes special claims himself in relation to all the ground the Kundmbo and others occupy. There is a kind of underlying disagreement between the Kurupmbo and Kundmbo on this point. Minembi, the most prominent of the Kundmbo men, nevertheless does not have quite such a priority in land matters because he was brought up among the Ronye (Rone) people at Wurup (his father's mother's mother's people) and was accepted there as a Ronye leader before deciding in 1970 to return to his original clan land. Yet in exchange terms he is strongest as a polygamist and a big man, and he tends to overshadow Makla in this respect. The Kundmbo are, then, in a paradoxical position: they are important landholders at Kuk, but their claims are not entirely recognized by the Kurupmbo. They are sponsors of the Poika, yet the Poika are also independently linked with other Kawelka. And their most prominent leader is not the one who has most the powerful "ancestral" claims to land. As may be predicted, the tensions set up by these factors are released by the practice of ostensibly "equal" exchanges among

Kundmbo, Poika, and Kurupmbo. Yet the jockeying for priority is evident enough, even in day-to-day disputes such as occur from time to time about the internal division of gardens.[4]

The general point remains the same here. What actually determines the standing of persons in relation to one another and to the land on which they live is the current state of exchange relationships, not any rule of registration of ownership or any form of land purchase conducted under the terms of capitalist assumptions and procedures. If the *moka* were taken away or abandoned, this mode of handling disputes and tensions would no longer be available. Those who adhere to the *moka* are quite clearly, then, struggling to maintain this set of meanings in relation to their land (Gregory 1982:116, 192).

Evidence of the "new" ways to handle questions of ownership is easy to find for the Kawelka since they are surrounded by land that they themselves sold to the administration and to tea companies. If they work on this land, they do so as laborers and other employees, working for a set wage and with no further claims on those who are now the owners. During 1985 the tea company replaced many manual tea pickers with a single machine, so the bulk of the Kawelka no longer even have pin-money jobs with the company. They seem to have accepted this situation with some regret but with no struggle. It is outside of their sphere of effective control, and at least the situation is stable. Their ambitions extend also to the possibility of taking over plantations, such as the one next to them, with the aid of government schemes and bank loans. But as of 1984 this was a remote possibility only for the Kawelka. Other groups, it should be noted, have actually done this. The biggest of these is the Pipilka, composed of a congeries of clans linked vaguely by common myths of ancestry. These were shaped into the nucleus of a business corporation by a young university graduate, Michael Mel, in the 1970s; and the corporation has now advanced to the point of taking over the biggest coffee plantation in the Western Highlands, Gumanch Plantation. The Pipilka are therefore quite clearly a part of the new capitalist structure of relationships, and the power of "ownership" in this structure is shown by the rate of growth of the corporation and its business assets. From this perspective the Kawelka have quite definitely been "left behind" in the process of development.

It remains of interest to see how groups such as the Kawelka handle their own transactions over land in the customary sphere. In this sphere, land has not become commoditized. Its status as a "good" is still defined in terms of a nexus of exchanges and kinship identities that go to make up the group history.

My final example of this theme takes us back to the latter part of 1983; and the focus of affairs shifts from the Kurupmbo-Kundmbo axis to that of the Kawelka.

When the Kawelka came back to Kuk from the late 1950s onward, they settled in rather different parts of the whole area. The Membo, and to a lesser extent the Klammbo, occupied parts near the Ndika Kelambe clan. The Kurupmbo moved to a remote but fertile place to the east of Kuk known as Kuning Tip. The Kundmbo and some of the Kurupmbo later moved into places near Kuk proper where there is an ancient stele or megalith supposedly set up by a big man named Koi; and it is in this locality that their chief ceremonial grounds, *Kor* site, and also now the Kuk community school are to be found. Membo Goimba, a senior big man, originally built a new Kawelka ceremonial ground at Kenta, inside land claimed by the Ndika; and it was not long after this that land disputes broke out. The Membo were forced out of Kenta by the Ndika and regrouped themselves closer to the station, beginning then to realize the problems with selling their safe land claims to the government.

Membo borders with Ndika and Keme groups are still subject to un-certainty. During 1983 there was talk of making a *moka* to the Ndika. It was not a death compensation or a war payment. One might have supposed that the Membo would have been the leaders in this move, since they were certainly in the forefront of the land disputes and they have by far the greatest population of all the Kawelka clans. But they were not. Indeed, in ceremonial affairs in general, it is hard to avoid the conclusion that the Membo have been dilatory, at least since 1980 in the Kuk area.

It was the Klammbo who took up the problem, and the *moka* to the Ndika was eventually held on their ceremonial ground at Wayake. Membo young men decorated elaborately for the *mörl* dance along with the Klammbo, but they did not make their promised money contribution; and after much uncertainty and recrimination, the money part was postponed and only pigs were given. Klammbo leaders asked Membo, Kurumbo, and Kundmbo spokesmen to make speeches at crucial points in the debates. The Kundmbo were not really involved, for their claims are far from those of the Kelambe and are secure. The Membo were vociferous in defending themselves, but still failed to produce the goods. The Kurupmbo had a secure "alibi" as they were preparing for their *Kor* and their resources were understandably committed. The goddess is a jealous deity, also, and forbids her celebrants to dance in full regalia for any other occasion until they have finished all the stages of devotion to her. So the Kurupmbo appeared in "second best" dress for the *mörli* round dances and not for the stately *mörl* itself. The economic burden accordingly fell on the Klammbo; and they responded as best they could with major contributions from their leaders, including Ongka. Yap, Pakl, and Ongka were also the major speechmakers.

Yet it was left to Ru, of Kurupmbo, to bring out in an explicit way the background issues that lay behind the *moka*. The Ndika speakers were implying that the gift was in a sense a payment for land. Ru, while agreeing that land was the reason for the *moka*, said that the gift was really to thank the Ndika for the planting materials and food supplies they had given the Kawelka when they first came back from Mbukl and had no existing gardens of their own. In this way he refused any definition of the issue in terms of "ownership" and insisted that it was a matter of reciprocity and friendship. He cast the Ndika as friendly sponsors rather than rivals and thus turned the edge of their claims to superiority and set up the Kawelka as their equals. Ru's shrewd, diplomatic speech, in other words, placed a persuasive "meaning" on the event, in opposition to those who were seeing it as a payment for land itself; and he constructed this meaning in the context of the whole position of the Kawelka at Kuk, consciously aware of the issues on his Kurupmbo-Kundmbo side of the territory and applying his insight to the Ndika-Membo-Klammbo front.

As on other occasions, Ru's interpretive genius defined the event in the right way for Kawelka history. (The second leg of this presentation, a large gift of money, took place in December 1985 and was accompa-

nied by a huge dance display in which all the Kawelka clans participated.) These examples—which, incidentally, are all internally linked
chronologically, spatially, structurally, and in the perceptions of the actors—must suffice to show how the Kawelka construe their own performances and thus construct their history.

It remains to comment on what sort of "history" emerges here. It
is "history" imbued with Kawelka values, and there is a sense in which
it is "history" that denies the encroachment of history in the wider
sphere. It is "anticapitalist" history, stressing the paramountcy of exchange as against the significance of units of production and the creation of inequality through differential access to these. The Kurupmbo's
involvement and investment in their *Kor* say the same thing—that the
old cultural values are still to be pursued—except that there is also
an incidental "fit" with land shortage through the idea of increasing
the land's fertility. It should also be remembered that all of the Kawelka
are enmeshed in the cash economy as such and the ramifications of
the new economy have "folded themselves" into the context of ceremonies. But the ceremonies still exert a real transforming pressure on the
economy itself. When the Kawelka come to make their history, it is
in terms of the exchanges they hold and the meanings they attach to
them rather than simply in terms of bank balances, numbers of trucks,
or trade stores. They want and seek these new things, too; but the
ultimate conversion still has to be into exchanges. It is in this sense
that the Kawelka can be said to have a very general orientation. It
is their wish that competition be balanced by friendship. The limitations
on expression of this ideology are certainly material. If land shortage
grows worse, it will probably break down in practice. In the last instance, however, it would appear incorrect to argue that conditions
for the emergence of such an ideology are either exclusively "material"
or "mental," since all human action is a product of the interaction between the human brain and its environment, and since the formula
of competition/friendship that dominates social life in Hagen emerged
in the complex and concrete historical context of clan groups "coming
to terms" with one another in the manner identified long ago by Marcel
Mauss.

Notes

1. These paragraphs were written before I had seen John Comaroff's 1984 review article in the *American Ethnologist*. I can only say that my views check well with those of Comaroff and also, as he indicates, that a growing number of scholars are aware of the complexities involved in seeking historical explanations for the development of structures and ideologies over time.

2. See, for example, Rappaport 1984:153ff. The problem is one of indeterminacy beyond a minimal level. At the other end of the continuum, there are constraints in terms of carrying capacity. In between there is room for much individual decision making. As Rappaport says, "It is certainly the case that he gains prestige if he makes large presentations, but there is in most cases no specific amount required to meet a man's obligations" (ibid.).

3. Another event that took place about a month after the dawn chorus to Pipur shows how the delay of the *Kor* was by this time preying on people's minds. About the time of darkness, a few of the Kurupmbo men were standing around outside their houses when two children were said to have walked past, through the ceremonial ground and out onto the road, where they disappeared. These were a girl and a boy, the girl walking ahead. One of the Kurupmbo met them and said, "Where are you two going?" They replied, *"Met okla moklp wi mana mbil onombukl"* ("We have come from above there and are on our way down here"). This was obscure. If they had been local children, they would have specified whose house they had been to. But the Kurupmbo did not recognize them. As soon as they had gone, the men began to speculate. Ru was convinced that the pair were actually the goddess herself and that she was leaving the cult site in anger because the pigs were not being sacrificed to her in good time. He used this interpretation, which was widely accepted, to renew his exhortations to his clansmen and others to help him get the cult done; otherwise, the goddess would surely send more misfortunes. As a strange "second act" to this event, a few days later Ru's Enga wife took a young boy who was her relative on a bus ride and lost him, whereupon his kinsfolk came and demanded a high compensation from Ru, saying he was responsible. This would indeed have held up the cult, and Ru was first bemused and then almost panic stricken as his searches for the boy failed. After four days the boy was actually found staying with some Hagen people, who claimed a reward, but this was still much less than the compensation would have been. This "disappearing boy" thus presaged the real disappearance of a boy, but in the end matters were put right. Ru himself made this interpretation of the two events. The *Amb Kor* was issuing warnings

to him that either he must hold the cult for her or else he must face the loss of male members of his family rather than gaining more male children as a result of the goddess's influence.

4. The story of Minembi and his family's residence and affiliation shifts is complicated and interesting in its own right. Though Minembi did not actually have very explicit titles to land at the place he then occupied, Klupöng, he was welcomed by the other Kundmbo as a big man who was a leader in exchanges; and he subsequently invited some Poika men to come and share the land he was using, thus converting them into quasi-dependents or clients. By the *moka* process they were not asserting themselves as "true" local group members of equal status with their hosts, but this claim caused considerable tension.

On the paternal side of his family, Minembi is a "straight" Kawelka Kundmbo. Figure 7 depicts his genealogical connection with the Ryone. The Ryone woman Gerengen married a Lköika man but brought her children back to her own place with the Ryone. From there her daughter

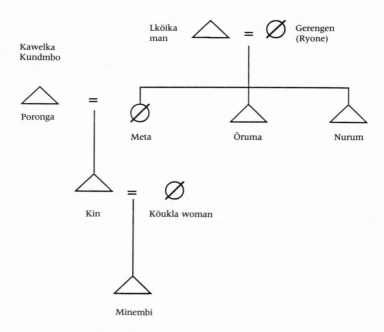

Fig. 7. *Minembi's connection with the Ryone.*

was married to Poronga. When the Kawelka were involved in heavy fighting at Kuk, Poronga sent his wife and young son away to her place at Kintu. The Kawelka fled to Mbakla, and Meta and her sons stayed permanently at Kintu. Ther Kin, Minembi's father, grew up to be a Ryone leader, marrying a Köukla wife and fathering Minembi, who subsequently returned to his father's father's place, having been brought up in what was strictly speaking the land of his father's mother's mother. For a version of the Kawelka origin story, see A. J. Strathern 1972:36–39; and for further data on the Kawelka, see P. Gorecki 1979. Gorecki dates the Kawelka's flight from Kuk to about 1900 (Ibid.:98). If this is correct, and Kin was about five years old at this time, as Minembi estimates, and further if Minembi was born when Kin was twenty-five years old, this would make Minembi about seventy today.

References Cited

Comaroff, John
1984   The Closed Society and Its Critics: Historical Transformations in African Ethnography. A Review Article. *American Ethnologist* 11:571–83.

Gorecki, P.
1979   Population Growth and Abandonment of Swamplands: A New Guinea Highlands Example. *Journal de la Société des Océanistes* 35:97–108.

Gregory, Christopher
1982   *Gifts and Commodities*. London: Academic Press.

Rappaport, Roy
1984   *Pigs for the Ancestors*. 2d rev. ed. New Haven: Yale University Press.

Strathern, Andrew J.
1970   The Female and Male Spirit Cults in Mount Hagen. *Man* (N.S.) 5:571–85.

1971   *The Rope of Moka*. Cambridge: Cambridge University Press.

1972   *One Father, One Blood*. Canberra: Australian National University Press.

1976   Transactional Continuity in Mount Hagen. In *Transaction and Meaning*, ed. Andrew Strathern. Cambridge: Cambridge University Press.

1979   Men's House, Women's House: The Efficacy of Opposition, Reversal and Pairing in the Melpa *Amb Kor* Cult. *Journal of the Polynesian Society* 88:37–54.

6. Prisoners of Time

Millenarian Praxis in a Melanesian Valley

Aletta Biersack

The valleys of the Papua New Guinea highlands are remote outposts of the world-system. Yet they are also worlds unto themselves. No doubt out of ethnic pride, but also by way of placing themselves cosmically and historically, the Paiela people of the Enga Province designate themselves as "we who live at the center." One may know them quickly from without, by observing their dress, their current ritual practices, their food, their implements, and their household goods, all of which bear the imprint of the European's presence. To know them from within is not so easy. In and of themselves, appearances offer no clue, save to the world the white person has always known. Shifting beyond a self-evident and familiar horizon requires careful listening and a retraining of the imagination.

It also requires some paradigm shifting. The world of the people who live at the center is as fully open, as fully appropriative, as the world-system now impinging upon it. Moreover, within this world, transformation rather than reproduction (which is viewed negatively, as an undesirable restoration of the status quo ante) is the norm. Not the ethnographic present, not the past of ancestral tradition, but the future is at the heart of the Paiela cultural vision. The future belongs to the center and the center people; and in designating themselves "we who live at the center," Paiela claim the future for themselves.

Though structural analysis is ipso facto inappropriate, we can retain from it its interest in internal, organizing principles, although these operate in this valley with respect to action and history rather than structure. Properly understood, the dualisms that abound encode axes of praxis and the dialectics thereof. Moreover, local texts inscribe values and meanings that attach to communally espoused real-world goals —to history, that is. In this culture *of* practical reason, the pragmatic and the semantic are one (Biersack 1990). To know the world of the Paiela from within is to demonstrate how all dimensions of human existence that are suppressed in increasingly obsolete frameworks— consciousness, reflexivity, agency, the event, history—may be elevated to the level of the collective and placed at the heart of both cultural analysis and comparative inquiry.

Signaling this elevation, the first three subdivisions of this essay focus on the principal agents of this society: the big man, the creator, and nowadays the white man.[1] In the first section, the field of action within which events are generated and regulated, along with the ordering principles of this field, are elucidated. The second section anchors this field of action in a cosmic sky-earth axis and the dialectics thereof, to reveal the millenarian significance of the dynamics discussed in the first section. The third section centers on the white man. Today Paiela divide all history into two eras: "before the white man came" and "now that the white man has come." The arrival of the white man is surely history in the making, but what history and of whose making? The third section argues that the open world of the center people absorbed the white man and appropriated him for its millenarian purposes. World-system theory, structural and geopolitical in its language, cannot provide this insight. Within this framework, the white man is irredeemably an outsider "impinging upon" indigenes and transforming their culture according to his own agendas of change. If this framework is set aside and another, indigenous discourse valorized, it becomes possible to see that the momentous and exogenously motivated event of contact is situated *locally*, within a history monitored by the center people, as the climax of that history. History is not outside Paiela culture; it is within, instigated by a dialectic and a dynamic the center people, as millenarian agents, themselves organize.

To a considerable degree, this analysis aligns, at least implicitly, with a substantial and theoretically diverse literature on cargo cults in the region (Burridge 1960, 1980; Jarvie 1964; Lawrence 1964; Worsley 1968). Here I argue that cargo-cultic activity is a circumstanced improvisation upon a local theme—though exogenously triggered, endogenously inspired. The *rot bilong kako* is an *axis mundi*. Today the principal messianic figure of Paiela chiliasm is the white man; but the white man acquires ascendancy *as* big man, *as* millenarian agent. The Paiela political system rests upon a charismatic tradition. Every age knows its prophet and his "coming."

Not to deny that these improvisations were *circumstanced*. The coming of the white man was unprecedented to just that degree that his wealth was *not* cargo but rather market-generated commodity. At the close of the essay I locate any friction between white and black worlds and the historicity characteristic of each in the realm of agenda, procedure, agency, and instrumentality—construing, then, Ortner's "anthropology of practice" (Ortner 1984) as Sahlins's "anthropology of history" (Sahlins 1985a)—to argue for a new relativism based on variations of praxis rather than structure or meaning. What a community of speakers *makes* is as diacritical as what it says, and it, too, will vary from one island or valley to another. The "real time" of culture contact is a deeply situated time, one that unfolds in the interpolations and mediations of the beach (Dening 1980) or Sahlins's "islands of history" (Sahlins 1985b). As such it is driven as much by conflict and contradiction as by the agent's desires (cf. Comaroff 1985); it reflects the limits no less than the power of intentionality.

The Big Man

Mana and Action

Though *mana* has long perplexed anthropologists, among Paiela the concept is simple and familiar, even to a Westerner. *Mana* means knowledge, knowledge of the preferable course of action. "Good *mana*" is the exemplary choice, "bad *mana*" the mistaken choice, between alternative means and ends. Much of *mana* is trivial. It is "good *mana*" to pick an axe up by its handle, for example, "bad *mana*" to pick it up by its head. But the most highly prized *mana* is moral in character: the understanding that it is better to live in peace than at war and the skill (at once practical and moral) to live pacifically. Though *mana* reflects cultural standards of right and wrong, in its implementation it is also responsive to the specific circumstances of decision making. If *mana* is choice, there is no *mana* without a choice maker (a *mana*-"carrier") and a set of circumstances. The locus of *mana* is the human voice as that voice is historically raised. *Mana* is an attribute of the historical subject.

Mana is "carried" in the only human faculty Paiela recognize, the *nembo*. *Nembo* may be translated as 'will', 'spirit', 'judgment', or 'conscience'; but to anchor it the more firmly in the rationalistic ethos informing the concept, *nembo* will herein be referred to as 'mind' (cf. A. Strathern 1981). *Nembo* or 'mind' is a discriminating faculty. It chooses and desires, "sorting" the "good" from the "bad," selecting between alternative courses of action and their projected outcomes. In the absence of rational (and in the most important cases moral) decision making, behavior and its effects become 'random' (*ambe pene*), a word that suggests mixed outcomes (willy-nilly good-and-bad), the presence of a contaminant. In some contexts *random* simply means "bad," undesirable. The rational decisionmaker is "he or she who has mind," "he or she whose mind lies good," "he or she whose mind is straight"; and his or her impact upon the course of events is "sorted," "straight," "good." Some "have no mind" or their mind "lies bad," however; and the events for which they are responsible are "random," "crooked," "unsorted," "bad." Passion of any kind (lust or other "craving," especially anger) robs the human subject of his or her rationality, morality, and humanity.

Since *mana* is knowledge, it is taught and learned. The "father's *mana*" is a body of moral law "said dropping" from father to child in the name of the social ideal of "kinship amity" (Fortes 1969). Independently of judicious choice making, however, there is no *mana*; and the child is free to reject his or her father's *mana*. The autonomy of the student places all Paiela tutorials at risk. Children many not "hear" the father's *mana* ("hearing" suggests obedience, or, as I would prefer, learning); they may 'ignore' (*tuyape*) the father, willfully persisting in error. At best, the father can only 'try' (*mandeke pii*) to impart his values so that his child might "take his place," as the child ideally does. At stake is the completion of the project the father, along with his kinspeople, has initiated, as will be shown, not the perpetuation of tradition.

Paiela divide the human organism into two parts, outer and inner. The outer part in turn divides at the neck between the head or *kawane* and the torso or *angini*. Organs of seeing and hearing are mounted on the head; and the head is associated with speaking and the source of speech, the mind, lodged "inside" in the 'heart-lungs' or *yamapane*. Seeing, hearing, and speaking form a single operational complex centering on *mana* and its power. The verb 'to see' is also the verb 'to know' (*anda*) —judgment and the "carrying" of *mana* are contingent, rooted in concrete circumstance and the decisions arising therefrom—and speaking and hearing have as their most important function the transmission of *mana*. Over against the head and the operational complex it participates in, the torso—blind, deaf, and dumb—is nonetheless essential for any kind of doing. The upper torso or "arms" "make," "hold," "take," and "give." The lower torso or "legs" "come and go" and in intercourse "make genital," activities having their own distinctive purposes.

The neck—anatomical marker of the distinction between "mind work" and "hand work"—divides purposing and intending, the "carrying" of *mana*, from implementation, *mana*'s "holding." These dualisms pertain to a diachronic rather than a synchronic logic. Action as process is unified. "First the mind, then the body": first the selection of a goal, then implementation and actualization. Decision making is closely allied with the speech that gives it voice. All "good *mana*" is anchored in a *saying*—a "saying, 'Let it be good'," let the outcome be desirable. Conversely, all "bad *mana*" is anchored in a "saying, 'Let it be bad'," let the outcome be undesirable. The movement from "mind work" to "hand work" joins word to deed and makes action purposive. *Mana* is never disinterested, abstract, theoretical, knowledge for its own sake.

It is through and through pragmatic, though we have yet to discover its principal consequences. The unity of mind and body, head and torso, word and deed, anchors agency-governed events in the mind as the 'root', 'source', or 'cause' of, the 'reason' (*tene*) for, actual events. If power is the ability to control events, then this ability as it is locally construed is intensely personal (Biersack n.d.).

Never citing a rule to explain behavior, Paiela simply observe that a person does what he or she does 'with his or her mind' (*balana nembo mane*). My efforts to elicit behavioral predictions in search of a rule were consistently met with incredulity. Puzzled by my social scientism and its ideology, informants would disclaim in exasperation: "How should I know? Did I see?" Did I see, did I know, what the person was thinking when the decision was made? (Unlike the body, the mind is invisible, cloaked by an outer shell.) Were the human mind perfect, behavior would be predictable, for only correct decisions would be made. Reluctance to predict behavior follows from the perception that human decision making is fallible. Behavior surprises, discloses to its witness the quality of the mind underlying it, be it "good" or "bad," "straight" or "crooked" (cf. Kirkpatrick 1985:234).

A locally recognized principle insists that behavior is intrinsically unpredictable, choice or *mana* governed rather than rule governed, ethical and not mechanical. Behavior occurs in real time, in a present that reveals a hidden past (the decision, the intention), and is oriented toward a real future. Moreover, social action becomes a dramatization of the forces of good and evil. Paiela "animism" extrapolates these principles beyond their range of competence to account for natural phenomena such as thunder and landslides in terms of decision making, its power and its morality—in terms of saints and villains.

Social Formations and Millenarian Time

Paiela are grouped in exogamous units called *yame*s. Marriage is ideally concentrated between *yame*s through 'woman exchange' (*wanda lawa lawa*). By a cognatic rule, the children born to woman exchangers "take" the ancestral names both their parents "took" and ipso facto are "blood" kin having "one mother and one father."[2] The purpose of woman exchange is to "make *yame*" ("We do it saying, 'Let's make *yame'"*)—that is, to produce a kind of super-*yame*, one that combines the membership of the two intergamous *yame*s of the previous generation. Since the generation produced through woman exchange "takes" the ancestral names of its matri- and patrikin, the boundary (*tombo*) between the two prior intergamous groups is dissolved; and the affinal ties that had been established across a social breach are transformed into bonds of consanguinity as two *yame*s are made one. Every existing *yame* is the result of this process. Every existing *yame* has a history that is rooted in the *saying* of woman exchangers.

However different descent and alliance regimes may be, they are nevertheless similar in their essential function: to perpetuate prevailing social arrangements, to reproduce some structure. In its commitment to self-transformation, Paiela society exemplifies neither. Though ancestors figure in the way consanguinity is reckoned (those who share ancestral names ipso facto share blood), and though woman exchange is instrumental in "making *yame*," the prevailing ideology centers on consanguinity rather than descent or alliance. The unrelated should become related; those who "say brother-in-law" to each other in exchanging women should father the brothers of the next generation. This above all is the father's *mana*, for the father was first husband, first speaker of the *mana* "Let's make *yame*." Descent and alliance are means to that end. Hence the cognatic rule, which positions the 'carried people' (*mandi yene*, the 'sexually reproduced'³) of every generation 'in-between', 'at the center', or 'at the boundary' (*tombo ene ga*) of parental *yame*s. Transformation, not reproduction, is the manifest function of woman exchange, which organizes sexual reproduction in such a way that woman-exchanging groups are fused.

In the main, the distinction between center and periphery so commonly drawn contrasts friendly and unfriendly territorial zones and groups. Those who locate each other "at the center" are consanguineally and/or affinally linked. Those who locate each other "to the side" have no ties and can expect the worst from each other. Fearing attack, Paiela hesitate to venture into the periphery, doing so (in long distance trade, for example) only with trepidation. Ordinary activities are restricted to "where kinspeople are."

The transformation of two *yame*s into one *yame* pacifies by shifting boundaries to higher levels of inclusiveness and rendering enemies friends. The Paiela Valley is reticulated by major and minor watercourses and criss-crossed by bush paths. Waterways segregate settlements ('grounds' [*yuu*], the "census points" of Australian colonial records), whereas bush paths ("roads") join them. The "owners" of the "bone" or interior of each "ground" are the descendants of the ancestor associated with it. Those who "own" the "skin" or exterior of each "ground"—the houses and gardens resting upon a foundation of "bone" —may or may not be descendants; as likely as not, they are the spouses and affines of "ground bone" owners who have extended usufructuary privileges to them. Marriage is always between rather than within settlements, so that bush paths, if used, articulate affinally related areas. Marriage opens up a "road" between wife giver and wife taker. "Road" literally refers to the bush path itself. Over this road, husband and wife, sister and brother, "come and go," visiting one another. They may even sojourn on one another's "ground skin," cultivating gardens and building houses. The residential composition of any one "ground" reflects the processes of territorial expansion underway.

But the idiom of "road" has a metaphoric value as well. The bridewealth transaction inaugurates affinal exchange partnerships, and the flow of valuables, more than the facilitating road, places woman exchangers at a common social and transactional juncture. Though not identical, affinal exchange partnerships are similar to consanguineal exchange partnerships. Affines as well as consanguines pool wealth to make major prestations (particularly homicide compensation and bridewealth); and affines as well as consanguines distribute to one another from the receipts of such prestations. Affinal exchange anticipates consanguineal exchange as a provisional "bridge" erected across the historical chasm dividing woman-exchanging groups. This "bridge" ceases to be provisional if the sons of the fathers who had exchanged women "take their fathers' places," transacting with one another as consanguines. Only if the "road" between former enemy groups is perpetuated do the groups in fact fuse. "Hearing" the father's *mana* is requisite to group formation.

Extrapolating this process over time produces the longitudinal trajec-

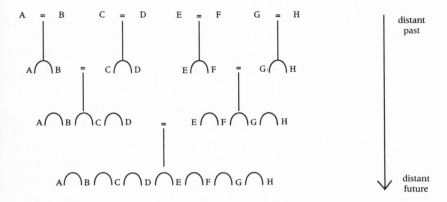

Fig. 8. The father's mana: *serial filiation* qua *serial transformation in Paiela millenarianism.*

tory of Figure 8, in which serial filiation is portrayed as serial transformation. The figure models an informant's statement.

Long before *yame*s married, then they continued to marry, and now, if they marry yet again, all the *yame*s will be mixed up and undifferentiated [that is, *yame* boundaries will disappear]. All will have become one *yame*; all will have become one talk. Those who lived before married and then they married again, then again, continuing to bear children, until there are no distinctions.

Territorially this process amalgamates centers progressively as it erodes peripheral no-man's-lands. Within each emerging center, mobility is unfettered and valuables flow along ever-lengthening chains of exchange.

Were these processes rule governed, Figure 8 would be an adequate representation of them. But they are governed by *mana* rather than rule—governed by the choices of the participants. For Figure 8 to be an adequate representation of the dynamics of Paiela history, two conditions would have to be met. First, every historical male would have to "say [in his own time], 'Let's make *yame*'" and exchange women. Second, every historical male would have to "take his father's place," perpetuating the exchange partnerships his father had initiated. Each of these conditions will be considered in turn.

The exchange of women is an act like any other act, rooted in the actor's *nembo*, the subject's decisions. Any male of age has a choice: he may or may not marry a woman who is related to the spouses of his own kinspeople. The first option ("carrying straight") is the preferred option; the second ("carrying randomly") is strategically inferior. Those who "carry straight" ("sexually reproduce straight") marry in such a way that their children will be situated "at the boundary" of two intergamous *yames*. Exchanging women, they bear children who belong to an emergent center within the valley. Those who "carry randomly" marry women who are unrelated to the spouses of their kin, and their children are positioned willy-nilly in social space, beyond the unfolding process of Figure 8. The only sanction against "carrying randomly" is the difficulties it poses. Those who "carry randomly" will not have the support they need to assemble a substantial bridewealth and other prestations. But some do indeed carry randomly. The exceptions only prove the rule: that there is no behavior-determining rule, there is only *mana* as choice making. In mounting an effort to exchange women, it is necessary to produce a *we* who *say*, "Let's make *yame*." In Paiela political philosophy, no anterior general will governs and dehistoricizes collective behavior. Historical choices are generalized and historical action is collectivized in situ.

The generation positioned "in between" the woman exchangers of the previous generation share certain ancestral patri- and matrilateral names. By cognatic rule they are "one blood." But they are not yet "true" brothers. A person who fails to support his genealogical kin, contributing to their prestations and distributing to them from exchange receipts, is declared a "false" brother, and the genealogical tie is renounced or "forgotten." Such a person has failed to "take his father's place." Transmission of the father's *mana* is never automatic. The father who intends to "make *yame*," "carrying straight," faces the possibility that his son will abort his project. Patrifiliation links a father who does "mind work"—purposes, establishes a goal—and a son who does the "hand work" of exchange through which the father's intentions are realized. The division of labor in the patrifilial bond is the division of labor underwriting the unity of action. But here a second decision—the son's decision, reflecting his own *mana*—intervenes. Those who exchange women "merely try"; they cannot do.

Never an isolated incident, the renunciation of kinship occurs against the backdrop of factionalism arising within the emerging center. If exacerbated, conflict may result in fission, a two-*yame* rather than a one-*yame* result. Fission restores the status quo ante. But the reaffirmation of boundary merely sets the stage for further intergamy as a necessary, though not sufficient, condition of the merging of the two groups. Fission may even be triggered by endogamous elopement. With an exchange of bridewealth between men genealogically "in between" but in fact supporting competing factions, intra-*yame* rift is fully acknowledged, but only by way of preserving the forward motion of Paiela history.

The motion of Figure 8 is sometimes, though never predictably, interrupted by setbacks. In the event, reintergamy transforms a regression into a recursion, thus guaranteeing, in the long run if not the short, the teleology of the process (see Figure 9) and, incidentally, the efficacy of the father's *mana* (serial filiation qua serial transformation). At the end of the process, all men will be brothers. "We will no longer discriminate between kin and nonkin"; then "we will marry our sisters." The project envisions a millennium in which peace is universalized and the processes of Paiela society and their principal source, the organization of reproduction ("carrying") through woman exchange, are suspended.

Figure 9 acknowledges the possibility of error that *mana*- rather than rule-governed behavior creates. The temporal index to the right of Figures 8 and 9 follows indigenous categories: distant past (*wamba*, 'long ago'), present (*andipa*), and distant future (*awe*). The categories deceptively suggest temporal succession, the unbroken linear time of Braudel's *l'histoire événementielle* (see Sahlins, this volume). T y refer instead to millenarian time, to progress *as it is culturally defined*. When a *yame* splinters, each resulting group refers to the other as 'woman ancestress' (*wanda auwanene*) and as 'the women-men of long before' (*wanda-akali wambane*); when two *yames* fuse, the members speak of one another as "those who live now" and also as "brothers." Temporal markers position formations within a millenarian course. Time *is* mille-

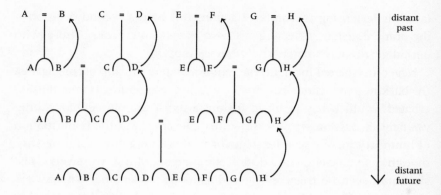

Fig. 9. Recursivity in Paiela millenarianism.

narian motion. When this motion ceases, time—the time of serial filiation qua serial transformation—ceases. When all men are brothers, "we will marry our sisters."

Millenarianism and the Big Man

As elsewhere in the highlands, Paiela traditional leaders are called 'big men' (*akali andane*). In a very real sense, their bigness consists in the size of the audience they command. He who "comes and goes" over a "long road," whose face is "seen" by many people, and whose words are heard by crowds of constituents, is "big." His "name" or renown is "big." The big man is identified with "mind work" and "talk work," the public speaking that gains him renown.

(Paraphrase[4]) The big man works with his mouth. He says good talk and we give him good food to eat to recompense him. He does not use his hands. Fighters use their hands; they don't talk. When the big man is in his house, he works. But on cleared ground [*ama*; the public plaza where big-man leadership is exercised] he should not. He should only talk with his mouth. When we do hand work, we do not speak. When we speak, we do no hand work.[5]

The big man's "good talk" is grounded in the law of kinship amity, and his leadership consists in his "dropping" *mana* to those who are ignorant. He is the 'fight talk man' (*wai pii akali*), celebrating peace and decrying war.

The most commonplace arena of big-man peacemaking is mediation.[6] A felt breach of reciprocity has set disputants against each other. Their "anger" with each other makes them hostile and uncompromising. By participating in a trialogue, the big man intervenes to assist the two disputants in negotiating a contract each will consider just. The court does not "die" until restitution has been made. But such "hand work" is sequitur to the "mind work" of mediation itself. In this trialogue, the big man "sorts" the "good talk" from the "bad talk," judging some claims reasonable, others not, as he urges the disputants to restore harmony in the name of their bond (affinal and/or consanguineal) and the center with respect to which this bond functions. He "drops *mana*"; and if he succeeds in teaching, he "inverts" or "straightens" the minds of the disputants, "takes and makes their minds lie good," rehabilitating the wayward. Mediation is a "finding of the road," a negotiating of the terms under which the relationship will be repaired and contractually perpetuated. This "road" is always sought in the name of peace (cf. Goldman 1983:ch. 2; M. Strathern 1972:ch. 1).

In helping the disputants "find the road," in "taking and making their minds meet," the mediator exercises no coercive power; neither does he have the authority to adjudicate the case. His power is a personal rather than an institutional effect, a product of the voice of reason he raises. Like the father, he can only "try" to persuade.

This power is reflected in a complex representation of dispute mediation. To make this representation, a person holds his or her arms out from either side of the body at shoulder height. Then he or she points the forefingers in toward each other. The two fingers represent the disputants, their estrangement and contention. Justice lies somewhere between the two disputants' positions, in an as-yet-unformulated compromise. The two fingers are then brought toward each other until they meet. The terms under which equity and reciprocity will be restored have been negotiated, and the dispute will "die" when the "hand work" of transaction honors these terms. The fingers are coordinated under the surveillance of the eyes, which represent the mediator and his *mana*, judgment, righteousness, and wisdom. By envisioning a midpoint, a bilateral center, the mediator is able to ascertain the margin of error in each disputant's opening position. The eyes "look ahead," not "to the side," targeting a center as *telos*, envisioning a possible compromise. If at the close of the process the disputants are purged of their anger and once again "happy" with each other, it is because of the reforming presence of the big man. As represented, nothing in this process is preordained. The dispute could not have been foreseen. Nor can the exact compromise point be predicted. It must be "found," through the exploratory work of mediation. The image suggests an open-ended but also teleological process, one that is governed, without being determined, by the trialogue itself.

Figure 9 represents the same process, a process that is entirely dependent upon the presence of the big man, his "mind work," his words.

Instead of a prescriptive rule and an elementary structure, Paiela have a far sparer system, one that rests upon a simple categorical distinction between the marriageable and unmarriageable (stranger and relative). Marriage between units can never be "mechanical," then. It depends, instead, upon leadership, the initiative and example of public speakers. In marrying, the big man acquires affines who can supply sisters to his own kin and who are potential husbands for his own sisters. Promoting marriages between his consanguines and affines, the big man is a center man, "in between" wife givers and wife receivers; and he and all his followers will father the constituents of a center he himself has instigated. Men say "Let's make *yame*" only because the big man first said so.

To "make *yame* is to shift from a disjunctive two-*yame* state to a conjunctive one-*yame* state.[7] In form and purpose, woman exchange and its ideal aftermath are the same as the contractual process of dispute mediation. Nor can *yame* unification proceed independently of dispute mediation. Genealogical connection is a necessary but not sufficient condition for center formation. Among Paiela, kinship amity must be contractually achieved, however much the blood bond itself is ascribed.[8] Those who are "one blood" must acknowledge the felt friendship their blood bond merely betokens if the center is to hold. At stake in any dispute is such acknowledgment. Disputants are enmeshed in a network of consanguineal and affinal ties that *is* the emergent center, and disputes threaten to polarize this network if not resolved. Dispute mediation is thus integral to group formation. The representation of dispute mediation evokes and affirms the fusion project and is an icon of that process.

If dispute mediation is integral to group formation, then the big man himself is integral to group formation. Unlike systems in which leaders assume titled positions over autonomous, self-forming entities, in the Paiela system groups and leaders are conditions of each other. Big men require their audience to be big, and their audience requires a leader to have convened at all. Paiela groups have no "objective" existence. *Yame*s form and function *historically*, as units of action rather than structure (Biersack 1990). Independently of big-man initiated projects and the leader-follower relation, the group has no existence (cf. Kracke 1978). Corporate life is event dependent.

Dialectics and Hierarchy

Should a dispute escalate and the community of in-between men be polarized by it, fission and possibly violence will occur. The instigators of war (the "root, cause, source of war") represent the two resulting *yame*s. The purpose of Paiela warfare is to "end the anger," thus paving the way for new peace initiatives. During the war, the big man becomes passive. The time for mediation has passed. But once the war has ended, he intercedes again, encouraging the principals to assemble massive homicide compensations. "Dropping *mana*," he tells the two *yame*s that they should exchange women; he himself inaugurates the process by marrying a woman from the group to which he is no longer related; and subsequently he fosters matches between his consanguines and his new affines.

The big man thus intervenes at the opening and the closing of a process, and he is the essential facilitator throughout. Moreover, he reinaugurates the process once fusion is an accomplished fact. How to capture the rhythm of his intervention? How to reconcile its circularity with the temporality of the trajectories of Figures 8 and 9?

Between the big man and his followers there is a strict division of labor. He does "mind work"; his followers do "hand work"—in particular, the "hand work" of exchange. The big man is himself a major transactor, of course, but only by way of setting an example. His most important pedagogical tool, however, is his rhetoric. He is 'head' (*kawane*). His followers, instead, are 'body women-men' (*wanda-akali angini*), an idiom suggestive of their physical labor. If the forward motion of the figures is preserved through the intervention of the big man, then its underlying rhythm is the rhythm of all action: "First the mind, then the body"; first mind work, then hand work; first the head, then the torso. In Figure 9 this rhythm becomes circular. If the "hand work" of exchange engenders unresolvable disputes, possibly the violent "hand work" of war, fission reestablishes the condition of intergamy, and the big man intercedes to encourage intermarriage between the two resulting groups. Hand work gives way to mind work, doing to saying (Figure 10).

But a moment's reflection tells us that this reversal is general. A man may not marry a consanguine. Thus, fusion always establishes a new frontier of millenarian activity. However, though centers may swell, the plurality of centers and the friction this plurality betokens remain. Outcomes, whether they involve fusion or fission, will always be wrong ("bad," "crooked") until they are absolutely right.

If intergamy is to occur across novel social gulfs, the big man must "say, 'Let's make *yame*'" and initiate intergamy by himself taking a wife from beyond the border. (Big men are polygamous.) In the subsequent generation, the big man's sons and the sons of his followers will do either the "hand work" of exchange or the "hand work" of war, either/or. All that has been established through the *mana* the big man has "dropped" and his own example is the potential for conflict resolution; and whatever the eventuality, new men will arise to "drop" further *mana* and to set further examples. Saying establishes the possibility of a certain kind of doing, but all doing also establishes the further possibility of a certain kind of saying. Saying and doing condition and trigger each other. It follows that all rhythm and circularity are inscribed within a full-fledged dialectic (Figure 11). This dialectic is suspended with the final boundary shift, which breaks the internal link between doing and saying by universalizing kinship. Like Figures 8–10, Figure

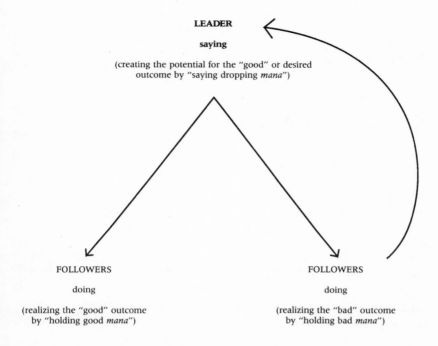

LEADER

saying

(creating the potential for the "good" or desired
outcome by "saying dropping *mana*")

FOLLOWERS	FOLLOWERS
doing	doing
(realizing the "good" outcome by "holding good *mana*")	(realizing the "bad" outcome by "holding bad *mana*")

Fig. 10. Filiation and transformation recast as action and its rhythm.

11 and its dialectic is governed by the presence of the big man. Cognation is not kinship, exogamy is not intergamy, and all marrying out is not marrying straight. His presence guarantees that whatever the actual event, history will remain directional and millenarian. The motion of all the figures is *logos* dependent (Biersack n.d.).

However impressive in scale, moral midgets are "merely large in the flesh." They do not, like the big man, 'have mind' (*nembo yene*), by far the more common epithet for the big man; they do not "carry *mana*." The axes of Figures 10 and 11 join an exemplary speaker with the reprobate. In Figure 10 the big man exercises his power as exemplary speaker with respect to a single merger. Two *yame*s attempt to become one by intermarrying. Though necessary, consanguinity is not sufficient for fusion. By definition the big man's constituency contains lesser (smaller) people, those who "carry *mana*" only if they "hear" the big

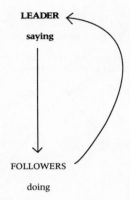

Fig. 11. The dialectic of action.

man's words. Independently of the audience-speaker relation, they are prone to 'selfishness' (*popatsia*), divisive gossip, and violence.[9] The audience-speaker, leader-follower axis engenders the *possibility* of virtuous behavior, but it does not guarantee it. The possibility of error is a constant.

Figure 12a generalizes the moral axis upon which the leader-follower relation rests. Whether responsible for initial intergamy, reintergamy, or again initial intergamy in the event of fusion, the big man is the standard-bearer of *mana* in the presence of countervailing forces. The

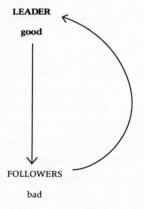

Fig. 12a. Moral hierarchy and millenarian process.

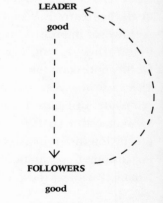

Fig. 12b. The telos.

population from which he draws his followers is corrupt. In the absence of his chastening word, his followers would "carry randomly," fail to "take their father's places," dispute, wage war, "hold bad *mana*." The big man's ascendancy is a *moral* ascendancy; the political hierarchy is an *ethical* hierarchy grounded in an ethical duality. Paiela sometimes refer to themselves as "we, the good and the bad." *Because* Paiela are both good and bad, *because* there are followers as well as leaders, Paiela are engaged in a millenarian process organized by the leader-follower relation (Figure 12a). The *telos* of this process is universal kinship as a state of *moral* purity. This is the *absolutely* right outcome, the ultimate expurgation of error. The "work" of the political axis—pacification —is thus terminated, the political system dismantled (Figure 12b).

Ama and Yuu

Ama—a cleared place kept perfectly flat and free of weeds and rubbish, impurities of any kind—is the place where big-man leadership is exercised. Here crowds gather to hear the big man speak, to observe and participate in dispute mediation, and to assemble and receive major prestations. Chief among these are homicide compensation and bridewealth, prestations associated with distinctive phases of the pacification process. Those who congregate on *ama* arrive there from their separate homes, the "gardens and houses" of the various 'grounds' (*yuu*) or residential districts surrounding *ama*. Each "ground" is associated with a single ancestor, and it is the "bone" of the "ground" that descendants "own." The residents of the "grounds" convening on any one *ama*—participating in the millenarian process—are linked through a combination of affinal and consanguineal ties, however. On the "ground skin," they have lived and gardened together with one another, and they have exchanged women.

No matter what the actual spatial relationship, one always goes "up" to *ama*, "down" to home. This hierarchical axis is moral. Residential districts contain all the impurities *ama* is free of: elevations and depressions, rubbish, in particular human rubbish, "bad" people. *Ama* is dominated by an exemplary speaker, he who makes minds that "lie bad" "meet," he who produces centers "at the boundary" of competing interests, he who transforms competition into cooperation through the projects he launches and oversees.

People assemble on *ama* 'at midday' (*otonga*), a period lasting from about 10:00 A.M. to 3:00 P.M. Early in the morning, late in the afternoon, and at night, people are at home in their "gardens and houses." Only at midday do millennium-promoting exchanges occur and the groups that foster them form. Figure 13 is both a temporal and spatial representation of the leader-follower relationship. While "on the ground" (rather than *ama*) and also during the darker periods of the day, Paiela are "forgetful" of the *mana* they last heard "dropped" on *ama* and resentments fester. At midday and on *ama*, the teaching relationship between leader and follower is reengaged and the possibility of collective moral action is recreated. Only at midday and on *ama*

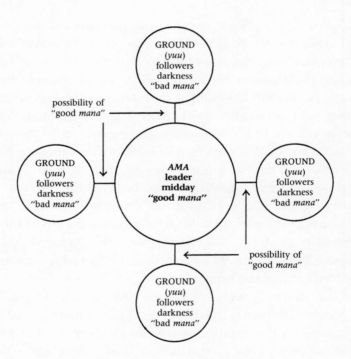

Fig. 13. The leader-follower relationship viewed territorially.

are the "women-men" of Paiela "*real* women-men," moral beings. The figure contrasts center/periphery and also light/dark in moral, social, political, and processual terms.

For the duration of the process, there are many *ama*s and many big men. Figure 13 therefore requires an outside. Beyond the various "grounds" and the *ama* upon which their residents convene lies a no-man's-land, impassable and uncivilized. Beyond *ama* and the various "roads" of social intercourse and transaction the *ama* represents lies the 'forest' or 'bush' (*tsiapu*)—unknown, hostile, savage, "where we do not go," "outside." In the forest no big man's voice is raised, no

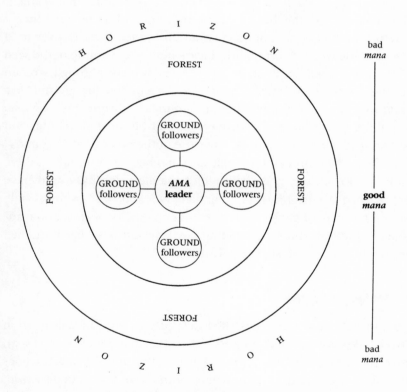

Fig. 14. The world and its moral gradient from the point of view of any one yame *and its affines.*

audience assembles to hear (Figure 14). The bush eludes the "work" of the moral axis of Figures 11 and 12 (see Biersack n.d.). But it does so only for a time, until the dialectic unfolds further to reclaim it through woman exchange. The reclamations of any one center are progressive. If by time we mean the time of Figures 8 and 9, then over time the number of "grounds" participating in the activities of any one *ama* increases as "roads" are extended and articulated (Figures 8 and 9) and the metaphoric forest recedes.

In giving bridewealth, donors are said to "plant" bridewealth in return for the woman's fertility and the access to affinal "roads" of exchange she creates. Women are the "pig seed," a metaphor that is today rendered as 'shell house', 'cargo house', 'tradestore' (*pindu anda*). When Paiela say of the forest that "there is no work to be done there" (to return to the question of pragmatics), they refer ultimately, I would submit, to the work of metaphorical gardening: the planting of the seed of *social* transformation in an act of *social* reclamation through woman exchange. Since such transformations are serial, "on the ground" we would expect to find the number of "grounds" utilizing any one *ama* expanding, the number of effective *ama* and big men shrinking, and the "virginal" forest receding. At the close of the process, all "grounds" would be unified through the single *ama* and big man they share, there would be no outside, and civilization's manifest destiny would have been reached (Figure 15). But, then, there would be no "ground," only *ama*, for the state of perfection that knows no duality of *mana*, no leadership and followership, no good and evil, would have been attained and the dialectic suspended (Figure 12b).

The Maker of Light

As in other Pacific cosmologies, the Paiela cosmos turns on a distinction between sky and ground. Sky is 'above the mountains' (*ati kenga*), above the horizon. Ground (*yuu*) is below the horizon and includes all features of the earth's surface, along with a clandestine underworld. The cosmic status accorded ground suggests a linkage between the concerns of the previous section and those of this section. The language

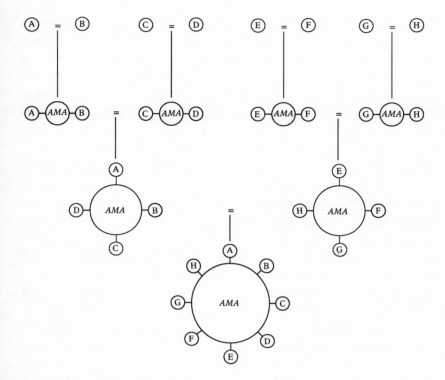

Fig. 15. The process of Figure 8 viewed territorially.

here will in part be new. Novel categories of actors will preoccupy us —in particular, *yama*, the generic term for invisible, incorporeal beings, and also the solar deity. But we have already met these, albeit under different names and guises. Among Paiela there is never anything new under the sun, only a single process of serial transformation and the various modes of its expression. What remains to be brought into view is the religious significance of this process.

Ground and the Presence of Boundary

Ground is split along horizontal and vertical axes. Viewed concentrically, residential areas—a combination of "gardens and houses," the "ground" of Figures 13 and 14—oppose the forest, as 'inside' (or 'at the house' [*andaka*]) contrasts with 'outside' (*kakita*) and as 'near' (*mandaka*) contrasts with 'far' (*tepandia*). The referents of near/far (as well as the other contrasts) are social, not geographical. "Proximate" people are recognized to be kin and affines; "distant" people are recognized to be neither. Geography is a metaphor for recognized social distance. The matter of kinship rests as much upon transactional commitment as upon genealogy. People who live "far away" from each other either exchange minimally or they do not exchange at all and are reckoned "strangers and enemies," beings of the forest. So much is already familiar. But forest is cosmic as well as social space; and as cosmic space it houses another category of being, *yama*, the generic term for disembodied spirits. Those living in the clearing, on the other hand, are called "real women-men." Their corporeality makes them "real," but so does their morality as followers of big men.

Vertically transected, the ground divides between "ground skin" and "ground bone," terms mentioned in another context. This division may also be expressed as a division between "outer" and "inner ground," "ground above" and "ground below." The metaphors are biological: human skin is an outer shell cloaking a hidden interior. These metaphors multiply. The inner ground, reservoir of rainwater, is, like mud, associated with the "juice" or "grease" of the ground, a word that also means 'body fat', *ipane*. The outer skin is dry and solid, like human skin.

There are many "ground skins" and "ground bones," as many as there are territorial blocks, the "grounds" of the previous section. Domiciled within the "ground bone" are the dead (*omene*) or the spirits of the dead (*talepa*), members of the *yama* category. Death is a permanent rupture of the mind/body relation, in which the mind goes to the 'house of the spirits of the dead' (*talepa anda*, a synonym for 'ground bone'). This rupture ("death") becomes final and irreversible once the corpse has putrified. The principal symbol of death is then bone, residue of the past. All the dead who inhabit any one "ground bone" are either descendants of the apical ancestor identified with the "ground bone" or the apical ancestor. On the "outer ground" dwell a category of beings varyingly called "women-men," "women-men with shining, seeing eyes," "real women-men," and "body women-men." These are the living descendants of the ancestor, their spouses, and their affines, those who have "come" to sojourn for a longer or shorter period on the "ground skin."

Among Paiela, social intercourse is always transactional, and the body is the primary transactional instrument. The dead—disembodied spirits —"exist hiding"; they "are not seen." (The living are "patent" instead, accessible for exchanges of every kind.) With one qualification: the dead may "return to see" the living. But they never do so out of friendship. Transacting with the dead is risky business. A dying person pledges to "keep a distance" rather than "return to see." Like all pledges, this pledge carries no guarantee. A change of heart (an "inversion" of "mind") may cause the spirit to break his or her promise. Like the living, spirits occasionally "crave" pork; but unlike the living, they domesticate no pigs. Craving pork, they become parasites upon the living, "shooting," "striking," "eating," or "killing" them, extracting a prestation in return for neutrality. In the best of all possible worlds, the living are shielded from the dead by the 'ground boundary' (*yuu tombo*), the curtain of skin/bone drawn between the living and the dead at the moment of interment. The grave is a secret passageway leading to mysterious and unknown realms that insulates the living from the dead and protects them from danger. "On what road did the deceased travel? We don't know, and so we stay separate." "When we have finished mourning, we forget the dead and go to live elsewhere, breaking off with them." "The spirits of the dead should stay far away. Between the living and the dead, there should be a boundary" (cf. Gibbs 1977: 7–8). Through various strategies, the "road" of the grave is in effect reopened in sacrifice, but only to meet the transactional condition the spirit has placed upon his or her renewed neutrality. Sacrifice terminates with a "blocking of the road" thus opened up and an exhortation to the spirit to "go."

The language of sacrifice is reminiscent of the language of homicide compensation (*yamba, maku, akali kulini* ['man bone'], or *kulini* ['bone']). Those compensated are on the enemy side, and they threaten retaliation if their "craving" for pork is not satisfied. In its most extended meaning, 'craving' or *yiya* signifies unreasoned passion, a "mind" that is "bad," "crooked," "lost," "nonexistent." Big men are present at the distribution of the pork to make sure that everyone who has lost kin in the recent war will receive "enough" to be placated. When everyone has eaten to capacity, the big man bids the recipients return to their own "ground" and "stay away," "stay hidden," in effect returning a pledge of neutrality for the pork they have received.

We gain a clearer understanding of the personality of the dead by exploring the character of *yama*, that category of being to which the dead belong (see Biersack n.d., Gibbs 1977:7–9). Of *yama*s it is said, "Whatever real people like, *yama*s do not like; whatever *yama*s like, real people do not like." *Yama*s "stand" in the night, for example; "real people" "stand" in the day. *Yama*s like pork fat (the "juice" of the pig); and though "real people" like pork fat as well, they prefer pork flesh, the "body" or carcass of the pig. *Yama* "roads" are waterways; the "roads" of "real people" are solid "bridges" crossing waterways. *Yama*s prefer bone to skin, forest to clearing. (The great fear Paiela have of walking in the bush follows in part from their belief that the forest is *yama* infested.) The upside-down, inside-out world *yama*s inhabit (cf. Babcock 1978) is a product of their preferences, their *mana*. The reality of "real" (also "body," corporeal) people lies in their morality, their capacity to cooperate with and act benevolently toward others of their kind. Parents will tell misbehaving children to be "real," to "hear" their own adult *mana*. The source of "real" people's morality is the big man who leads them. *Yama*s are associated with the forest—which lies beyond the pale of moral regeneration—not the clearing. The will of the *yama* is perverse. In everyday conversation, the terms "*mana* of the *yama*" and "bad *mana*" are synonymous. *Yama*s are corrupters of the human will, cause of the evil they symbolize.

Warfare itself, the greatest evil of all, is *yama*-like and *yama* instigated. "When we war, we imitate the *yama*s. We chop down houses with our axes and burn them. We rape women. We eat/kill our fellow humans." And: "enemies imitate the *yama*s." Enemies may simply be called *yama*s. "Enemies and *yama*s frighten us. Both should stay far away [in the forest]. When the spirits come, they eat us. When enemies come, they kill us." Ancestors have the notorious reputation of the superordinate category. "The spirits of the dead are bad. The carried people [the living descendants] are good." Whenever Paiela go to war, they sacrifice to the ancestors and are accompanied into battle by them as helpmates. "Our ancestors kill and give us men." Embroiling Paiela in spiraling episodes of payback, the revenge motive itself is attributed to the "return" of the spirit of the deceased, who, in influencing the mind of the living kinsmen, cause kinsmen to 'crave a man' (*akali yiya*) and seek revenge.

Ground is if anything material. It can be seen, touched, smelled, even tasted. Matter has duration and extension, like skin and bone. The temporality of the ground, its duration, will shortly claim our attention. Focusing for the moment on extension, it is immediately apparent that the ground is a highly fractured space. Whether we examine it on its surface or vertically, across the skin/bone divide, the ground is a conglomerate of localities segregated by the very boundaries the dead and other *yama*s employ as "roads." As cosmic element, as *significant* element, the ground symbolizes a divided, conflict-ridden society, heterogeneous in its moral, social, and political makeup (Figures 16a and 16b).

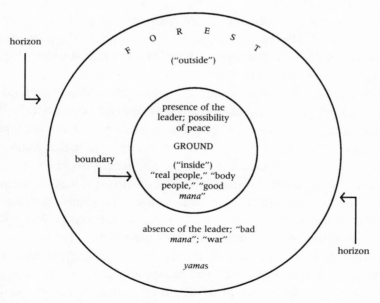

Fig. 16a. "Ground" viewed along its horizontal axis.

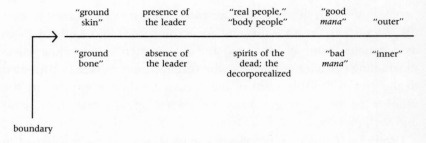

	"ground skin"	presence of the leader	"real people," "body people"	"good *mana*"	"outer"
	"ground bone"	absence of the leader	spirits of the dead; the decorporealized	"bad *mana*"	"inner"

boundary

Fig. 16b. "Ground" viewed along its vertical axis.

Sky

Ground is cosmically contextualized by sky—that immaterial, indivisible mystery "above." ("Above the mountains there is no forest.") This contextualization stigmatizes the ground as profane.

The sky is dominated by a being who created the ground in "dropping" rocks, trees, animals, and human beings, the ancestors. Though this being is referred to throughout as the Sun, this being is not the sun but the being the sun symbolizes. (Anthropologist: "What of the Sun do you see?" Informant: "I see nothing. I only say his name.") The solar orb is the eye of this being, not his body. What, then, do the names of the Sun (Nai, Ewa, Yakane, and in magical spells Aluni[10]) and the sun-as-eye symbol signify?

Seeing entities are sentient, and the Sun is obviously some kind of subject. An extraordinary subject, Paiela are quick to point out. Unlike human beings—who see near but not far, the clearing but not the forest, outer but not inner—the Sun "sees everything." He is the 'Maker of Light' (*Waa Piyane ko*). The verb 'to see' also means 'to know' (*anda*), and in being all-seeing the Sun is also all-knowing. His *mana* or knowledge is perfect and unchanging. Just as the expressions "bad *mana*" and the "*mana* of the *yamas*" are synonymous, the expressions "good *mana*" and the "*mana* of the Sun" are synonymous. The Sun's *mana* is specifically moral: the law of kinship, which is additionally a law of exchange. The sun-as-eye and all his names signify universal peace. "He is above in the middle of us all": transcendent in his affirmation of a global center, transcendent in his perfect lawfulness.

The symbol of sun-as-eye is richly exploited in delineations of the sacred. Incorporeal, the deity's vision is liberated from the constraints of time and space. He "sees far as well as near," "below as well as above" (he "sees everything"; cf. Gibbs 1977:9–10). The "road" he travels is "very long"—indeed, global. At dawn he "comes outside," brightening the outer ground; but at dusk he "goes inside," journeying to the underworld and bringing daylight to the dead. "He sees those who died very long ago, those who died very recently, those who are still living. . . . He sees both the people of before and the people who live now." In contrast to the anthropocentric order, the theocentric order is boundaryless: sans here and there, sans past and present, sans (by implication) enemy and friend. Symbolizing an eventless, warless eternity, he is 'immortal' (oma na pene), beyond all genesis and expiration. "He was not born and he will never die."

Unlike the ever-wakeful, ever-living deity, the "women-men" "on the ground" beneath him ("he looks down and we look up") live in time and space, differentiating near from far, forest from clearing, below from above, past from present, enemy from friend. Human (as opposed to divine) life oscillates between wakefulness and sleep and moves between the poles of life and death. Awake and alive, the person dwells in a daytime world, the "outer ground." But when the Sun "goes inside" at night, the eyes of the living "wrinkle shut," and the mind of the sleeper leaves the body and journeys to the "house of the spirits of the dead" (also called the "ground bone"), where it dream-encounters the dead and fellow somnambulists. At dawn the mind returns to join the body and consciousness and wakefulness are restored. The blindness of the sleep state as well as the very temporality of the cycle reflect the alienation of human life from its divine source. "At night we go with the yamas. During the day we are among women-men." "At night we hold bad mana; during the day we hold good mana."

Except for its irreversibility, the death state is the same as the sleep state. In death as in sleep, the "eyes wrinkle shut" and the mind departs the body to travel to the land of the dead. Death is permanent blindness, permanent moral blindness. "The spirits of the dead are bad; living women-men are good." All the axes of the spatiotemporal "ground" reduce to a single set: seeing and not seeing, knowing and not knowing, being seen and not being seen, being known and not being known.

(Parapharase and quotation): The Sun has a large eye. It sees everything and is seen by everyone. [The Sun is a millennial being, like those who will exist "in the distant future" at the endpoint of the process of Figure 15.] But women-men have small eyes. We see a little and we are seen by only a few. [We are premillennial beings living in the epoch of Figure 14.]

Or: "We are one-eyed; the Sun is two-eyed." This adage summarizes the cosmos in all its complexity. It sets off sky from ground, sacred from profane, extraspatial from spatial, extratemporal from temporal, immortal from mortal, exemplary from corrupt, divided from undivided. It indicates ground's dependency upon sky—the dependency of day—but also ground's alienation from sky—the alienation of night. Moreover, it suggests motion: the rhythm of diurnal variation.

Sky and Ground, Cosmogony and Eschatology

The verb translated here as "to create" means "to make light"; and in designating the Sun as "Maker of Light," Paiela designate him the creator. In an important sense, to say that the Sun's *mana* is perfect is to say too little. *Mana* is not man-made; it is Sun-made. As perfect subject and perfect knower, he is the only possible source of *mana*, for *mana* is a moral absolute that exists only insofar as it is thought and spoken by a morally perfect being. Law is not prior to the subject; it is "author-ized" into existence.[11] In designating the Sun as the creator, Paiela divinize the law as word (cf. Biersack n.d.). This word—as it is spoken, heard, and obeyed—*is* his creation. The creator creates in replicating himself as subject through the power of divine revelation. He communicates—educates—the creature into existence.

The creator has no body (only an eye) and does not himself speak. He thinks, knows, and "gives" his *mana* through his own incarnation, the big man as spokesman. That the big man does "mind work" but no "hand work," that he talks rather than acts, signifies his spirituality. In a very real sense, Sun and big man complete each other as "head" (Ibid.). The Sun speaks through the big man, sees through the big man. All *mana* originates with the deity. The eyes in the local representation of dispute mediation symbolize the divinity of the big man as the enlightened one. "The Sun looks with his eyes. The big man speaks his thoughts."

As in other religions, the word ("good talk," "straight talk," "fight talk") is spoken in a sacred place and at a sacred time. Sacred time is midday, the brightest part of the day; and sacred space is the open plaza called *ama*, the big man's forum, cleared so as to reflect solar radiation perfectly. Outside this context, the Sun remains 'hidden' (*oo wa*), a term more appropriately translated in some settings as 'keeping a secret', 'remaining silent', 'failing to disclose'. In essence, at midday and on *ama*, the big man and the Sun are one, one subject. Historical big men, each the deity incarnate, are so many instances of the creator's immanence in the temporal affairs of the "ground" (Figures 13–15), an immanence the sun-as-eye preeminently symbolizes. A common epithet for the Sun is "big man"; and when Paiela speak of "*That* Big Man," they speak of the Sun.

If historical big men are so many instances of "*That* Big Man's" immanence, then the dynamic of Figures 8–12 and 15 is the dynamic of the relationship between sky and ground, and we would expect to discover both a cosmogony and an eschatology that are symbolically consistent with the trajectory of Figure 8.

The most telling feature of the local cosmogony is that it accounts for the origin of the ground. 'When the ground originated' (*yuu ungi lea angi*), the Sun "dropped" an order that was 'random' (*ambe pene*).[12] The word *random* implies the presence of undesirable elements or impurities. In colloquial usuage it may simply mean "bad" (as opposed to "good," "straight," or "sorted," idioms suggestive of purity). The ground originates as an unreformed order.

Though Paiela recognize tangible impurities (blemishes on the skin, garbage), they also recognize spiritual and moral impurities. "When the ground originated," the Sun "dropped" the evil person as well as the good person, the enemy as well as the friend. (He dropped, in short, the ancestors, who—in their multiplicity and "ground bone" associations—belong to a divided social landscape.) To his creature he said, "Stand randomly. Hold good *mana*. Hold bad *mana*. Hold both kinds of *mana*." "The Sun made the bad and the good—only the Sun. He fashioned *yama*s and real people. The Sun created them—he." This act mandated a profane, morally corrupt subject, a human subject, the subject of which Paiela speak in speaking of themselves as "we who live on the ground" and "we, the good and the bad." It mandated terrestrial space (Figures 14, 16).

But the injunction also mandated terrestrial time: the relationship between historical big men and their equally historical followers and the process of reform inscribed therein—inscribed, that is, within the relationship between sky and ground (see Biersack, n.d.). This process unfolds as a dialectic of good and evil, the reprobate act and the chastening word, through progressive divine revelation. "In the beginning" the Sun revealed very little *mana*. He was "far away" and "kept a secret." Now, "we see [or know] some of the Sun's *mana*, but some is still kept secret from us." "We have not taken his mind entirely. In part we make wrong decisions." The person describing the incompleteness of human knowledge—and by implication the presence of moral contaminants within the human order—improvised a simile to illustrate his meaning. "Taking the Sun's mind" is like reading a book, he said. (Paraphrasing) "Now we only see above"; we have only begun to read the book. "But some day all will be revealed to us."

Now the creator is keeping a secret. He is not expressing his thought to us. Later, creating, he will reveal his thought to us, speaking to us. He is not speaking to us now. He is silent, keeping a secret. Later, when he has finished creating, he will speak to us, disclosing his thought.

The informant's metaphor suggests the progressive purification of *mana* through the incremental revelation of the divine word over time (Figure 17).[13]

In "dropping" the creator 'merely tried' (*mee mandeke pii*), an idiom explicated earlier. The educator "merely tries" to teach; but he cannot do so under his own power, for the student must also learn. To "merely try" implies a partial, conditional, and contingent agency. A goal is embraced but not actually attained. A man "merely tries" when he participates in woman exchange; a housebuilder "merely tries" when he sketches the dimensions of the house he intends to build on the

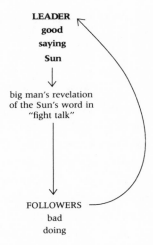

Fig. 17. Taking the Sun's mind is like reading a book: the progressive revelation of the Sun's mana.

ground. To "merely try" is to merely plan, to anticipate a future that, as future, remains unattained.

Merely trying, merely planning, the Sun did not complete. The ground originates as an incomplete order, a zone of becoming, the where of a when, a historical zone. Hence the stratigraphy of the ground. Originally there was no distinction between "ground skin" and "ground bone." When the first ancestors descended from an exalted and transcendent plane, all was "skin." These ancestors, all male, lived in autonomous, disjointed territories, the "ground bone" of the present day. At first they did not exchange women, but eventually they did. Today, in the "now" of a partially reformed order, the bones of the ancestors are located "far below at the end of all being," in the nether-most reaches of the underworld. Those who died later in other genera-tions live "in-between." Just below the surface lie the bones of the recently dead, and just above a threshold we know to be moral dwell the living on the "ground skin." The ground, in short, is a stratified graveyard of material remains. The relationship between this stratigra-phy and the process of Figures 8–9 is transparent. The difference between contiguous generations (and adjacent cosmic strata) is mille-narian. Children (the 'carried people' [*mandi yene*]) are placed "in be-tween" the ancestors of *both* parents. Interment and the succession of strata it creates all carry the burden of representing a succession of social transformations. The conventional genealogical form—A "car-ried" B, B "carried" C, C "carried" D, and so forth, "and so we the carried people are now"—refers to this process and not to descent. The verb 'to carry' (*mandi*) can mean—and in this context definitely does mean—to sexually reproduce. As Paiela are acutely aware, it takes two people, a male and a female, to produce offspring. The genealogical form reflects the undeniable fact that serial filiation, mediated as it is by woman exchange, is serial transformation. The verp *pai pii* means 'to change', 'to switch around', 'to invert'; and it is this verb that appears in what are easily mistaken for accounts of lineal continuity. "Those who lived before [*wamba*] did not stay as they were. . . . They died and the carried people [*mandi yene*] were transformed [*pai pii*]. These died and the carried people were transformed. And so we are now." When the dead are denounced as "bad," the "carried people" extolled as "good," Paiela recast genealogy as millenarian history.[14]

Cosmogony combines with an eschatology that envisions for the 'dis-tant future' (*awe*) an "end" to the ground (cf. Lincoln 1989:ch.3). Ground cannot end without all of its axes—sky/ground, inner/outer, the living /the dead, good/evil, friend/enemy, day/night, and leader/fol-lower—being dissolved; and it is this dissolution that is emphasized in all the accounts of ground's end I recorded. The most obvious exam-ple is the prophecy of a solar eclipse. In the present, unreformed cosmos, Sun and moon are separated in both time and space. He governs day and sky; she governs night and ground (Biersack 1987). Between them they divide the cosmos. "When the ground ends," however, Sun and moon will be "fused" with the sky, or the Sun and moon will "spin around each other" (becoming one). Also obvious is the prophecy that the dead will come "above in the middle," that they will return to speak to us when the ground ends. Another vision of ground's end is inspired by the significance of the *ama*/ground dichotomy. Ordinarily the ground is stationary. Earth tremors occur extraordinarily, but then always as sign. When the Sun causes the earth to move, when he flips it over, rendering all *ama*, then the ground will end. *Ama*/ground represents the principal political and moral axis, the leader-follower relationship qua the sky-ground axis. (The big man's *mana* originates with the Sun.) Through this relationship, the millenarian process is inaugurated and sustained (Figures 10–15) as a process of progressive divine revelation (Figure 17). The loss of this axis reflects the loss of its condition, the presence of evil, and the restoration of the precosmogonic order of sky (compare Figures 12 and 18).

Since ground symbolizes a social reality—the presence of conflict within the human community—the idioms through which ground's end is conceptualized are sometimes social rather than cosmic. Paiela intermarry with their neighbors to the east, the Enga. But they do not, at least not on my side of the valley, intermarry with peoples living in the Lake Kopiago region to the southwest. From the vantage of those surrounding me, the Enga are affinal insiders whereas the Duna of Lake Kopiago are outsiders, in the enemy camp. "If an Enga man goes to

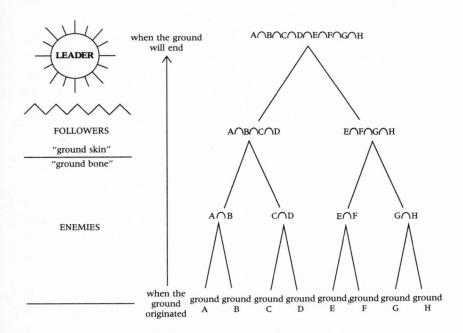

Fig. 18. Cosmology as millenarian discourse.

Lake Kopiago and a Lake Kopiago man goes to Enga-land, [the distinction between friend and enemy will be overridden and] the ground will end." Of a man who had traveled to Port Moresby, the nation's capital, and married a woman there, it was predicted that the ground would end in the lifetime of his children. For a people whose knowledge of geography has until recently been limited, this vision of world's end shifts the project of universal brotherhood to a "global" plane, between and among known ethnicities. Nowadays, with the recent explosion of knowledge contact has brought, Europeans must be assimilated too. Thus: if the "dark-colored people" and the "light-colored people" (Europeans) go to the sky after they have died, the ground will end.

The ground is a temporal and spatial—that is, a material—field; and the key symbol of its temporality, spatiality, and materiality is the human body (Biersack 1987). The ground itself is a kind of body, all skin and bone. Encased in the body, the human spirit knows night as well as day, sleep as well as wakefulness, death as well as life, contingency and conditionality, and the profanity of alienation. In the millennium this spirit will be liberated from the body. It will not be delivered, as in sleep and death, unto night, which is contingent, however. Rather, it will be delivered unto panchronic day, the timelessness of the creator. When the ground ends, the "road" to the Sun will no longer be "covered"; we will see his face. The Sun will no longer conceal his thought; all will be revealed. "Our bodies will be finished and our thoughts will be above where the Sun is. Our thoughts will be new and different." All will be changed utterly.[15]

And so the millennium: "All men will be brothers and we will marry our sisters." When "sky and ground" are once again "flush," the end of the dialectic. The suspension of the incest taboo signals the dissolution of the principal moral axes—good and evil, friend and enemy, relative and stranger, leader and follower—expressed, as they are, in the millenarian imagery of ground's end. To return to the antecedent of the millennium, the sky/ground cosmos, it may be argued that in its spatiotemporal partitions, it calibrates progress as it is locally defined. The underworld, with its strata of deceased, traces the social history of the past; the outer ground represents the present as a further unfolding of the process; and the sky—that originless, unconditioned condition of all beginnings and all endings—represents the *telos* of universal kinship and peace and the perfection of human *mana* (Figure 18). The being the sun-as-eye symbolizes is source of the spatiotemporal order but is not himself of this order, like the architect, source of motion and becoming but not himself transformed through it, immanent "at midday," when all assemble to hear his word on *ama*, but transcendent, eternal, and absolute—in and of himself having no midday, no *ama*, only panchronic, panspatial sky, the unmade maker, fatherless father (Biersack n.d.).

The White Man

The white man moved into the highlands from the east. Lying far west of major centers of impact such as Goroka and Hagen, the Paiela region was among the last to be contacted. Initial contact was made in the 1930s, probably when Taylor and Black passed through the valley on their famous marathon Hagen–Sepik patrol. Many years would pass before Europeans would arrive in the valley with any regularity. In the intervening years, Paiela participated in a millenarian cult introduced into the valley by four Enga men, soon to be described. In 1961 the Australian colonial government opened a patrol post in the valley just east, Porgera, and from that time Paiela was patrolled periodically as an outlying district.

Missionaries also arrived. Seventh-day Adventists, Lutherans, Apostolics, and the fathers of the Catholic Society of the Divine Word (SVD) competed for converts. Of these, Lutherans and Catholics obtained the largest following. Pastors and fathers patrolled the valley regularly to administer the sacraments and preach, and they opened up stations manned by their own trainees to serve as a base of operations during patrols and to preserve the mission's presence in their absence. On these stations churches (*pii anda*, 'talk houses'), trade stores (which subsidize the work of the missions), and eventually an elementary school were erected. Two Lutheran missionary families resided successively in the valley, and in 1968 an airstrip was cleared to provide ease of access to missionaries and government patrol officers living in nearby valleys. At the time of my arrival, all Paiela in the airstrip area, where

I based myself, affiliated with the mission, if only to attend church services. (Baptism was by no means universal.) Mission and government stations flanked the airstrip, and these were run on a daily basis by mission- and government-trained personnel (pastors, catechists, interpreters, storekeepers, and schoolteachers).

When I arrived in the valley in 1974, interest in the 'light-colored women-men' (*one wanda-akali*) was keen. Any and all Europeans were welcome, even the anthropologist. This interest survived Papua New Guinea's acquisition of independence in 1975 and it did so explicitly in resistance to and in protest against the postcolonial nationalism raging elsewhere. How to place this interest? How to account for the rather facile success European enclaves have enjoyed in the valley? Here I argue that the "coming of the white man" served as millenarian sign and that the event-as-sign fell subject to a local hermeneutic informed by ancient ideologies and practices persisting to this very day. The would-be cultural expropriator was himself culturally appropriated. To make this point, it is only necessary to examine the discourse surrounding the contact scene. However pidginized, neologisms replicate the indigenous meaning of an older discourse. The account begins at the beginning, with a prophecy of the "coming" of the white man, which triggered certain ritual innovations.

Prelude: Guta

For a time, Paiela called the Sun "Guta," a name given currency by four Enga men who entered the valley in the mid-1940s and initiated what Meggitt (1973) has called the Cult of Ain. The cult began among the Taro Enga living to the east of the Ipili speakers of the Porgera and Paiela valleys. It then spread westward and southward, encompassing much of the region that engulfs Paiela along with Paiela itself (Gibbs 1977). It also spread eastward into the Tombena area of Enga speakers (Feil 1983).

The cult was initiated at a time when an epidemic was threatening the lives of the Taro Enga and their pig herds. Enga people acknowledge the sun and the moon to be "'the father and the mother of us all'" (Meggitt 1965:197; 1973:21); and the four Enga men, at the behest of their father's ghost, urged Enga to suspend sacrifices to the dead and to sacrifice to the sun instead. A platform was built so that the four men could be closer to the sun, and they stared at the sun along the shaft of a spear and shook. The participants understood the shaking to be a "concomitant of entering into contact with the sun" (Meggitt 1973:22, n. 21). Followers were urged to "'break their spears'" and give up warfare (ibid.:23). They should also set aside their fear of female pollution and abandon their bachelor puberty rites (ibid.). The goals of the ritual, in short, centered on personal health and the health and fertility of pig herds.

Among the Ipili speakers of the Porgera and Paiela valleys, the cult acquired novel millenarian dimensions. The same four men promised not only these benefits but immortality and an ascension to the sky if the people of the area turned to "'our father' the sun" for help (ibid.:27). Again, a platform was built and the four brothers stared at the sun along spears, shaking. They also stood in the fire and handled embers "to demonstrate the invulnerablility their new knowledge had conferred on them" (ibid.). A time of darkness was forecast.

> Within a few months massive discharges of lightning would signal the coming of a great darkness that would cover the land for days or weeks, during which time the local people must shelter within the cult house and intone the spells that would invoke the help of the sun to disperse the cloud of darkness. . . . Then enormous . . . pythons would hang suspended from the sky, and all the people and their pigs would make their way into the sky-world along the 'paths' formed by the bodies of the snakes (ibid.:28).

According to Meggitt, the intention of the ritual was to help the sun destroy the darkness, presumably with his light. The prophets addressed the people as follows:

> We have driven the sickness out of you to be carried away by the water, just as we drive away the ghosts of the dead. Give up fighting, observe the food taboos we have laid down, do not copulate for a month, then, when the time of darkness comes, you will all follow 'a good path'. There will be no more sickness or death among you and hence no more ghosts or any need for rituals to propitiate them (ibid.:30).

The report Gibbs offers us for the Porgera and Paiela valleys is substantially the same. It was prophesied that the earth would end and that people would ascend to the sky, where they would never sicken or die (1977:12ff.). Gibbs translates the term *tawetoko* as 'sky'. Literally it means 'sky-bridge' or 'sky-platform', however; and the sense of the prophecy appears to have been that people would ascend to the sky over a bridge, road, or path, the term appearing in Meggitt's account. As among the Enga, there was a wholesale abandonment of sacrifices to the dead and other *yamas*. Giving bridewealth was suspended, and people awaited a time of darkness (see Blong 1982) in a single round house where special taboos, but not the taboo on intersexual congregation, were observed. Sacrifices were made to the sun. Gibbs even suggests that incest occurred (1977:19).

Gibbs focuses on the Ipili speakers of Porgera, and Meggitt makes scant use of Paiela informants. Here I supplement their accounts with material garnered from two Paiela informants, the one a man on the threshold of old age but still "strong," or so he claimed, the other an elderly woman who has since died. Both had witnessed and participated in the cult. According to them, the four men entered the valley on the pretext of having been sent by the white man "to cut a road" and prepare the way for his coming. To Paiela, the four men promised access to a new teaching, the white man's knowledge or *mana*, and Guta, the Sun, was the source of this knowledge.

In the Paiela valley the ritual introduced was essentially the same as the ritual reported by Meggitt and Gibbs. The men stood on rooftops and raised pigs' carcasses aloft, addressing the Sun and sacrificing to Guta. Additionally, at midday and on *ama*,[16] men "looked up" at the sun along the shaft of a spear and became *kee*, a term that means 'impassioned', 'intoxicated', 'confused', or 'crazy'. Like the *yiya* state, the *kee* state is a state in which a person loses the power of discernment and does "bad things." The mind of *kee* people has been "taken and inverted" or "taken and carried away" by *yamas*; it has been "lost." A *kee* person may attack his spouse, children, and/or brothers. He does not "hold good *mana*."[17]

During the trance, these men spoke words that were thought to express the Sun's and also the white man's *mana*. But the words were gibberish. Some assumed they were the white man's own language.

Then, after the participants had stopped shaking, they "dropped good talk," the intelligible words of the vernacular, revealing the Sun's *mana*. The ritual is best interpreted from the audience's point of view. As long as the shaker remained *kee*, the audience remained unenlightened. Released from trance, communication between the shaker and his audience became possible and the word of the Sun was revealed. The express purpose of the ritual was to transform a "mind that lay bad" —an ignorant, unenlightened mind—into a "mind that lay good"; and the process the shaker himself underwent, from trance and *kee* to rationality, reflects the process his audience underwent. The ritual, in short, transmitted divine knowledge; it *performed* revelation and creation— on *ama* and at midday.

These performing shakers were "fight talk men," and the teaching they imparted as the Sun's *mana* was the teaching they customarily impart. "Stop fighting, live in peace, don't commit adultery, don't steal, don't kill your relatives, don't gossip." The message contextualizes the ritual's symbolism. It is along the shaft of a spear that the divine messenger looked. Once he had entered the trance state, he not only shook but walked about brandishing his spear, raising it in mock attack, then lowering it menacingly, frightening onlookers. These antics abated once he was released from trance, and it was only then that his message was intelligibly imparted. If revelation was performed, so was pacification.

As elsewhere, ground's end was said to be imminent. Nighttime would become "little," the light would "return," and "we would not die." Anticipating ground's end and upon the encouragement of the four Enga men, Paiela threw all caution to the wind. Classificatory siblings mated, and the taboos ordinarily observed to protect men from the polluting power of women were abandoned. For the duration of the cult and in flagrant violation of protocols of sexual segregation, man and woman sat together, the woman cupping her husband's hand in the palm of hers (as it was described to me); and the incest taboo was abrogated. *Paluni*, heritable wealth, was thrown into the river. Once the ground ended, people would no longer become sick and die —such was the prophecy. During my stav in the valley some thirty years later, Paiela were still experimenting with a relaxation of intersexual taboos and attendant practices, inspired in part by the white man's seeming immunity to pollution even though he himself observed no taboos, in part (and relatedly) by millenarian expectations.

One feature of the Paiela variant of the Cult of Ain Meggitt and Gibbs fail to mention is this: though only men looked at the sun and shook, women as well as men ate pork kidneys cooked over an open flame, and some of these also achieved the trance state. The woman I talked to was among these. While in a trance, she took a journey that had unmistakable millenarian overtones. She wandered along rivers and saw that they had dried up. Rivers are the primary boundary markers of the Paiela social order, and they are the arteries of spirit travel. The woman interpreted what she saw as a sign that the ground would end, that the dead would soon be reunited with the living. Today the expectation that the dead will be resurrected has no doubt been intensified by Christianity, yet oral history confirms the presence of this expectation in the valley almost twenty years before the missionaries arrived.

Toward a Universal Center

Whether missionary or patrol officer, the white men who eventually did "come" have all approached the valley with a message of peace. The initial effort of the Australian colonial government upon penetrating a new territory was to "control" it. Warfare was curtailed, dispute mediation was intensified, and penal institutions were developed. Missionaries have no less strenuously advocated pacification, employing coincidentally an idiom very close to the local idiom of peace, not kinship but brotherhood. Church sermons, more often than not delivered by local and national catechists and pastors, typically emphasize brotherhood and the broader kinship in the name of peace. At the time of my research, the white man was identified especially with this message, the epitome, so far as Paiela were concerned, of the "white man's *mana*." "The white man has a little anger; we have a lot." Rumor has it that the white world is warless, this despite the fact that the original confrontation with Europeans was violent. Even in the 1970s, Paiela still recalled that several of them had died at the hands of the white man and his gun.

Though incidents of violence still occur, in local perception these incidents are few and far between compared with the dark ages "before the light-colored man came." To arrest the vicious circle of payback that has plagued the valley (and in all truth continues to plague it), Paiela readily resort to the substitute for payback the white man has provided, jail. Those incarcerated reportedly suffer humiliation and privations, going hungry and "shoveling their own shit" and becoming defiled. Jail is dubbed the "white man's war": punitive but nonviolent. Pacification necessarily eliminates social boundaries, consolidates and centralizes the social order; and it is these processes that are emphasized in local pronouncements upon the benefits of contact:

We used to be afraid of our enemies. But now that the white man has come, we've forgotten. We live in peace. Everyone is our brother. . . . Before there was no center place. There were only the divisions that made watercourses. We talked about "over on that side of the river" and "over on this side of the river." Before we didn't go to a place far away because that was enemy territory [Figure 14]. Now we travel distances because we've forgotten our enemies and everyone is our brother [the *telos* of Figure 15].

The centerplace of which the informant speaks is Kolombi, site of the only airstrip in the valley. Rudimentary even by highland standards, this strip is nevertheless an international terminal through which the inhabitants of the known world pass, "coming [from] and going [to]" outlying districts. "The plane makes the far near," bringing Enga, Huli, and "light-colored people" into the valley. The plane's "road" is a global road, one that traverses all known space and passes between sky and ground, going to "where the sun is" but also to "where women-men are." Today Paiela position the dead and other *yama*s not "inside the ground" or "in the forest," as in the past, but in the sky, where the Sun has gathered and "fenced" them lest they "return to see the living." In its transcosmic journeys, the plane "sees everything. With its mind it sees the dead and the living. . . . The plane goes where my eyes cannot see. [It is two-eyed rather than one-eyed.]" The most advanced tool contact has placed at the disposal of the Paiela is also symbol: a tangible mediator between sky and ground, a "platform" of elevation, a "road" or "path" to above, harbinger of the millennium.

The tangibility of this mediation is heightened by certain cargo beliefs.

The ancestor and other *yamas*, from their current vantage point in the sky, are thought to be manufacturing the items Paiela buy in mission-run trade stores. The plane ascends to the sky to acquire the cargo, then drops to the ground to deposit it. Though the wealth created by the ancestors stands "in the name" of the living as their gift to the living, most of it is nevertheless hoarded in the sky. (The Sun has "fenced" the ancestors.) The plane doles out this stash, but more awaits the living "when the ground ends." The dead and other *yamas* have obviously been reformed. They are friends, brothers, no longer themselves needy parasites but patrons of the relatively deprived. The belief that certain former enemies have been neutralized is made the more credible by the power of the white man's medicine. The *nili* especially ("nail," the penicillin injection) "chases away" spirits so effectively that the spirits do not "return," as they did in the past, even though pigs were sacrificed to them. The verb 'to be sick' is also the verb 'to die' (*oma*); and to the degree that Paiela enjoy better health, they experience themselves as (relatively) 'immortal' (*oma na pene*). "Before the white man came, we all died. Now that the white man has come, we take medicine and only a few of us die." Though Paiela employ a dual system of curing, alternating between medicine and sacrifice, sometimes using both, their abandonment of traditional rituals, at least to some degree, reflects their confidence in a history they themselves define and shape, not "culture fatigue" or, worse, cultural divestiture at the hands of dominant outsiders. As far as Paiela are concerned, Western technology *is* millenarian praxis.

The airstrip is called *bulu ama*, 'plane *ama*'; and like all *ama* it is kept weeded and flat. Along with the main mission and government stations in the valley, this *ama* is an *ama* all Paiela share. From "diverse" and "disconnected grounds" "to the side," Paiela come to this 'center place' (*yuu tombo ene ga*) to receive medicine, work on government and mission stations, attend school ceremonies, participate in the 'Christmas dance' (*kitimas mali*), buy and sell in a weekly market, assist in valley-wide building projects, "buy the plane," and purchase goods at the trade store (*pindu anda*, 'cargo house'). Insofar as all Paiela have "one *ama*," they also are "one *yame*." ("When everyone assembles at Kolombi, grounds become one; when they depart for home, grounds become multiple.") Unification makes Kolombi a "big ground," a term that somewhat deceptively evokes "development" but actually refers to the processes of centralization underway and their social and millenarian implications (Figure 15).

The airstrip, government and mission stations, and valley-wide public projects are hardly vehicles of centralization without the development of "infrastructural" personnel, for centralization depends upon the presence, moral guardianship, and galvanizing energies of big men. The plane has a pilot, the aid post an orderly, the school a teacher, the church a catechist or pastor, the trade store a "store boy." All of these are called "in between men." Those who speak the "white man's language" (Tok Pisin) and who "hold the white man's *mana*," eating and dressing "white," have "become white." Of course, they also remain black, mediators between the two communities. The model of the "in-between man" in this space-age epoch of one stone-age community is the government interpreter, the *tatima toko*. The term is a vernacularization of the pidgin phrase *tainim tok*, 'to turn the talk'. The word *tatima* has no meaning of which I am aware, but the word *toko* means 'bridge' or 'platform' (not 'talk') and suggests, as "road" does, conjuncture. All "in-between men," whatever their profession, and not just the government interpreter, are called *tatima toko*. They are, as the matter was put to me, "two-eyed, two-eared, two-armed, and two-legged": "on the one side" white, "on the other side" black, symbols and agents of coalition. The model is the model of cognation.

(Paraphrase and quotation) Whoever holds both the black man's and the white man's *mana* is white on the right side and black on the left side. The same is true of those who are in between their mother's and father's kin. On the right side they are toward the father; on the left side they are toward the mother.

Today the premier "in-between man" or "fight talk man" is the *kandole* or 'councillor', representative of the valley at the provincial level and heir to the *luluai* position of the past. During my stay in the valley, Paiela elected their first *kandole*. The election pitted an older and much-respected big man against a younger and also respected big man. The younger man won because he could "hear the talk of the white man" (though he could not yet speak it). He also could "hear" Engan, the most widely spoken language in the province. Far from evidencing the death of tradition, the election witnessed its perpetuation, for the election turned on the issue of how in-between (in language and custom) the incumbent of this key office would be. The *kandole*'s leadership is strictly millenarian. "The *kandole* stands on the ground, he stands in a center place, he stands in the sky, he stands on black ground, he stands on all grounds." He stands, in short, on one *ama*, Kolombi. The *kandole* was elected from among Kolombi candidates.

A neologism, borrowed from the pidgin but pronounced differently, names the *kandole*'s constituency *kanaka*, a word that in the colonial context reflects the paternalism and contempt of world-system agents but to the Paiela conveys what terms such as *yama* and "bad person" have always conveyed.

(Paraphrase and quotation) We have prohibited warfare. When *kanaka*s talk among themselves, speaking with a *kanaka* mind, they sometimes call for the resumption of warfare. But . . . when he [the *kandole*] comes, he encourages us to consider alternatives to war: paying homicide compensation or sending derelicts to jail. . . . When we are by ourselves, however, we [the *kanaka*s] say, "Let's fight."

The expressions "holding the *mana* of the *yama*s" and "holding *kanaka mana*" are today synonymous. The principal axis of the indigenous system is *the* axis of domination-subordination. Whatever "native" means to world-system agents, the global system, anchored as it is in the local order, is itself culturally encompassed at the point of its impact.

The Coming of the White Man

Local ambitions have always been global. Ground's end portends the creation of a single polyethnic community incorporating Enga, Duna, Huli, the Ipili speakers of Porgera, and (some even say) the semi-nomadic Hewa; and millenarianism has always been pursued through intermarriage and long-distance trade with these groups. Paiela now know that beyond the "saltwater" lies a hitherto-unknown land, the homeland of the light-colored people; and absorbing the white people is on today's millenarian agenda. Upon initial contact, the white man was classified as *yama* and enemy. Yet white and black now assemble on the same *ama* and exchange has been inaugurated between the two communities. Serving as an intermediary between the dead and the living, the white man and his plane stock the trade store; and across the counter, cargo and money move against each other. Cargo and money fall into the same category, *pindu*, a traditional category of valuables. *Pindu* has always been acquired through long-distance trade with neighboring groups. In attempting to finance their work, missionaries appeared to want to participate in the millenarian process under way. "The white man came cutting bush"; he "came" to "those who lived in the bush" (the *kanakas*), and he crossed water ("saltwater") to do so. Clearly he crossed the last border. His subsequent actions would open up the road that would unite black and white. From the local perspective, the history of contact is the history of peacemaking across an ethnic and racial boundary, the last such effort. Knowing of an interracial marriage occurring several decades before, Paiela plan to create world peace through an exchange of women with the white man. They have only to await the arrival of a critical mass of Europeans to set this plan in motion. Biding their time, they continue to enroll children in mission-run schools ("so that their eyes will shine"), thus artificially swelling the ranks of "in-between men"[18] in the absence of intermarriage. Cognation may take novel forms, but serial transformation remains.

Paiela learned the name Gote from the missionaries, of course. But as used the name serves merely to rebaptize the Sun—no longer Nai or Yakane, no longer the Enga's Guta, but Gote. "We used to have two names for the Sun. Now we only have one." Representations of Gote are transparently solar. Gote "looks around below," he "sits on the hills," he "does not see when it rains," he has an "eye" that "everyone can see," he "sees everything." Gote is a god of peace. His word is "fight talk"; all "fight talk" is inspired by him; and *ama*—the *ama* of government and mission stations and the *bula ama* or airstrip—is still the place where "fight talk" is spoken at midday. The Sunday "talk" of "talk men" (pastors and catechists) cannot compete with the prestige of "fight talk," spoken in its own time and place and for its own purposes. Pacification and not ritual is still the project, and of the two, the government and not the mission is the principal agent. It is said: "The mission is the mother; the government is the father."

With the disclosure of the Sun's true name, the final revelation is at hand: all will soon become true children of the deity and his creation will reach completion. As so many Paiela told me:

(Paraphrase and quotation) Gote says, "Now let there only be a center place. Let there only be a center place," he says. Long before there was only a periphery, only diverse, unrelated lands [the black and the white, for example]. Then Gote did not teach his *mana*. But now he is revealing it. Now Gote's *mana* is patent. When the ground ends, the *mana* will be patent. Before we did not see with our eyes, and our ears [literally: "ear roads"] were stuffed. Before Gote did not assemble everyone on one *yuu*. Now he assembles us. Before we had different talks, different minds [the situation of Figures 10 and 12a, prior to the *telos* of 12b]. Now he takes and assembles us, Gote. He assembles diverse grounds.

(Paraphrase and quotation) Before the white man came, we dark-colored people lived in the forest. Now that the white man has come, we live on *ama*. [What do you mean, live on *ama*?] We hear Gote's word. Gote has come and we say, "Let's stay on *ama*."

(Paraphrase and quotation) Before the white man came, we were all bunched up, not spread out. [In other contexts, this image represents something randomized by the presence of a contaminant.] Before there were both good and bad. Now there is only good; it is created ["made light"]. Before Gote dropped only a little *mana*. Now he drops big *mana*. With Gote's mind, we've cleansed ourselves of bad talk . . . ; we are only good. Our ground is now good; our minds are now good. We the body women-men are now good. Taking Gote's mind, we've discarded war, we've discarded the *mana* of the *yama*. Now we are spread out. [In this context, the spread-out image suggests the *telos* of Figure 12b.]

The white man came as the last divine emissary, as the messenger who would usher in the millennium. He is the "*tatima toko* between sky and ground"; he "comes to drop *mana*." Ironically, the personnel of government and mission tend to confirm this interpretation in the way they explain their presence in the valley. The Paiela, the *kanaka*s or 'natives', are "bad"; mission and government are "good"; and their purpose is to "take and invert the minds of the bad," to pacify and to baptize. "The *mana* Gote sent the mission and the government to drop are one. Gote wants to end the old ground; he wants to create a new ground." Given this contextualization of his arrival, the white man's position becomes hegemonic within the local political system. The white man, divinely inspired, talks to the *kandole*, the *kandole* talks to the *kanaka*s. The white man talks to the catechist or pastor, the catechist or pastor talks to the baptized. Thus and only thus is Gote now "near," not "far." The white man leads, subordinates all, not as colonial but as millenarian agent (Figure 19).

There is much in the European's material culture (not to mention his light complexion) to suggest this historical role. His kerosene lamps, flashlights, generators, and eyeglasses empower him to see in the dark —some even say to see in his sleep. "Gote gave us night but he gave the light-colored people day." His medicine safeguards him and makes him healthy. "He has no *yama*"; he does not die. His plane positions him everywhere, but then nowhere, postcosmically in the sky. "The Sun . . . gives the white man much thought. . . . He [the white man]

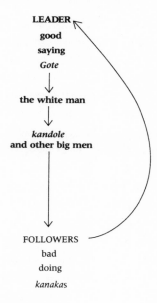

Fig. 19. The coming of the white man.

travels to the sky in the plane, then returns." He lives "far above with the Sun in the center"; he lives "near the Sun, fused with Gote." His affluence and entrepreneurial role in establishing, stocking, and running trade stores implies privileged access to the wealth stashed in the sky, an access Paiela themselves aspire to "when the ground ends." But the trappings of "civilization" (or, at least, advanced technology) are significant only to the degree that they are vested with significance by a very ancient millenarian discourse. Eliminate the white man's peacemaking and his political and religious rhetoric and he would today be classified as he initially was: *yama*. "The black talk is on the ground, far below, where the Sun dropped it. But the white man's talk is far away, undropped, above, close to the Sun." Hence, "fight talk men" looked at the sun along a spear shaft to acquire the white man's *mana*, Guta's word, in the mid-1940s.

If the Sun's true name is Gote and if the mission taught Paiela his real name, then perhaps the true account of ground's origin lies within the teaching of the mission as well. A myth Paiela allude to often, with nonchalance and by way of explaining the human condition in its entirety, will be familiar to readers.

Originally there was no separation between ground and sky. Then Gote created Atame (Adam) and after him Epa (Eve) so that Atame might have a companion. As created Epa had no vagina; and we must suppose that neither sexual reproduction nor the processes associated with woman exchange existed. The two lived on "good ground" (synonym for center place) in a garden Gote had fashioned. Gote stipulated only that the two not eat the nut of a certain tree. (The word translated here as 'nut', *dini*, means fruit or nut: the tree's offspring. In pidgin the term is *pikinini bilong diwai*, the 'children of the tree'.) This tree is the "source of good and bad," Gote said. He forbade the eating of the nut because he planned to "create well," not "incorrectly." Epa, as we all know, was tempted by an evil snake, who encouraged her to eat the nut. (The word translated here as 'tempt' is the verb *mandeke pii*, to 'try', to 'plan'.) She "ignored" Gote's *mana*. When Gote learned of Epa's breach of the taboo, he banished Atame and Epa from the good land, sending them "outside," and he cursed their descendants with sexual reproduction, labor, death, and, most importantly, warfare.

To punish the snake, Gote cut off his limbs and sent him to caves and tree roots to live. Ever after the descendants of Atame and Epa would trample him underfoot.

Despite its derivation from a Western Semitic tradition, this myth parallels in all particulars the indigenous myth of ground's origin. Atame and Epa were sent "outside," sky and ground separating. Though the *mana* the myth centers on—the ability to distinguish between edible and inedible, the observance of a food taboo—is trivial, local exegesis of the myth emphasizes instead the power of *moral* discrimination. Gote had been "planning" to "create well," but Epa ate "randomly [that is, without distinguishing the edible from the inedible, without observing the taboo]. Now Gote drops the bad along with the good." "Gote did not sort [purify] women-men. . . . [As a result] we hold two *mana*s . . . ; we hold good and bad *mana*."

Because Atame and Epa ate the nut, we act randomly and are defiled. Had they observed the taboo, we would not be defiled. He [Gote] gave us night when the ground originated. . . . Now we who hold bad *mana* labor with pain only. Had Atame and Epa not eaten the nut, Gote would have given us *mana* and we would have been sorted [perfect]. . . . Because Atame and Epa held bad *mana*, we continue to hold bad *mana*. Had Gote sent good *mana*, we would have been only good.

Conflict and warfare are characteristic of the "outside." Lest we miss the point, the cosmos, now split between sacred and profane sectors, originates complete with boundary. The snake is obviously a *yama*-like figure. Like the *yama*s Paiela claim occasionally to spot, he is deformed in appearance, all tail and no limbs. Punished, he is sent to live in secret niches: as forest totem, at the base of trees and rocks; as the underworld's primordial incorporeal occupant, underneath the feet of the descendants of Atame and Epa. From these vantages he may ambush the living; he may also be trampled by them. Each is the enemy of the other.[19]

Local exegesis extrapolates: The snake not only tempted Epa. With his long tail, he made her "road." She was now a woman who could profitably be exchanged. Thus her "sin": to eat the forbidden nut, to become fertile like the tree, a tree Paiela identify additionally as the tree of life and death. "The way of trees and the way of women-men are one. Trees are not lost. They replace themselves. Women-men also replace themselves." Death (like sleep) is the condition of the perpetuation of life. The cosmos originates as a spatiotemporal, stratigraphic order.[20]

But it also originates as an order to which the millenarian project is intrinsic. Woman exchange is the millenarian agent's tool. In the local version of the myth, Epa halves the nut and swallows her half, giving the other half to Atame. But the half-nut lodges in his throat instead of being swallowed. Ever since, men have had larynxes (and by implication the capability of revealing the word) and women have not. ("Women never say fight talk; they merely talk.") The principal cosmic axis, sky/ground, is then the principal *political* axis: virtuous male speakers dominating reprobate others (Figures 10–13). (Epa was tempted by the snake, not Atame; technically he violated no divine mandate; see Biersack 1984.) "Outside" originates as a zone of becoming, a *pre*-millennial order in which "descent" becomes serial transformation, a matter of "road"-making by dint of the woman's own "road."

Those who tend to expatiate upon the meaning of the myth add that it explains the difference in merit across the color bar as well. Atame and Epa were both dark-colored. One of them—and it is sufficient that it only be one—"said *no*" to Gote's law. "We the dark-colored women-men who ate the nut long ago hold two *mana*. We don't hold only good *mana*. We hold good and bad *mana*" (that is, we are *kanakas*). But the light-colored people "said *yes*" to Gote's law. They learned the father's *mana*! Consequently, the descendants of the white ancestor are entirely good, entirely pure. "The dark-colored people have two minds. There is a woman's mind [both women and men commonly say that women "have no mind"] and a man's mind. But the white man's mind is one. There is no difference between a woman's and a man's mind" (ibid.). Lest readers suspect that this man was trying to flatter me, he also said: "If we had heard Gote, we would not die. . . . Now we are outside. But you people [to me] are fused with Gote." ("You people are undescended, undropped from the sky. You are light-colored.")

Not really an explanation of the present so much as a reading of it, the myth vests the present with significance as the climactic moment

of a millenarian process. It testifies to the imperialism of local hermeneutical practices in the face of absolute novelty. Nothing seems to escape the imperialism of this hermeneutic, not natural fact (life, death,
sleep, the birds and the bees), not social fact, not historical fact. One
and all are made to signify a single body of religious truths: the human
being is morally corrupt but not satanic, evil but also good—capable
of self-transcendence, then, and imprisoned in time as the penalty of
that effort. Whether *yama* or god, the white man as historical figure
"is" what Paiela name him to be. He "is" a sign, historical metaphor
of a mythical reality (Sahlins 1981)—the cosmos of Figure 18, for example. Paiela are a people with a history they themselves write and,
in writing, make. If anything, it is the white man who has been rendered silent (cf. Wolf 1982).

World-System, Local Agenda

If Paiela boundaries were boundaries of containment, the white man
would have come as exogenous agent. But Paiela boundaries are the
sites of expansion and incorporation, and any agent who "comes" suc-
cumbs to the logic of the processes organized at these sites. Like the
world-system, the Paiela system is open, global in its ambitions. The
difference between the two lies not in the "hotness" of the one or the
"coldness" of the other, but in the agendas each promotes. In signifying
Western commodities as *pindu*, Paiela "act upon circumstances according to their own cultural presuppositions" (Sahlins 1981:67) and in
light of their own agendas. On their own side of the transaction, world-
system agents remain commodity-fetishistically committed to their own
projects of economic domination and cultural imperialism. The achievement of national independence in 1975 aborted one possible future
for the Paiela: the eventual disillusionment with the European that so
many other Papua New Guinea societies have experienced (cf. A. Strathern 1988) and that, here and there, has starkly manifested itself in
the vehement antiwhite sentiment of some cargo cults (see Worsley
1968, for example).

This account has been almost wholly preoccupied with the symbolism
and organization of human exertion, 'work' (*peape*). Not subsistence

labor—which, primarily female, is "small" and inconsequential—but the efforts of male millenarian agents and their followers constitute the most prestigious categories of "work," the "mind" cum "hand work" of this analysis (Biersack 1984, 1990). In relation to this "work," everything anthropologists are wont to call social structure appears as technology, means to an end. In combination with the cognatic rule, woman exchange strategically positions transactors in social space so that the "hand work" of exchange might eradicate the boundary that had enabled woman exchange to begin with. The rules exhibit an instrumental rather than a structural logic. Attention is thus diverted from structure to local history and its principal agents. As custodians of the society's agenda, big men keep the population ever mindful of the goal and the moral values it serves as they wed theory to practice in pursuit of a collectively chosen result.

Paiela society reveals itself to us through its rhythms and motions, not through its inertias, of which there are none. The Maker of Light "charters" an agenda and the means–end relationship of *mana* through which it is pursued. Of all the sociologies, Alain Touraine's "actionalist sociology" is paradoxically the most relevant. For Touraine, as Sennett explains in his introduction to *The Voice and the Eye* (1981:x), "structure is a property of activity. People do not act *in* a social structure, the structure of society is the structure of how a group moves; it has an identity only by virtue of its movement." The term Touraine prefers is "system of action," and he applies it to postindustrial society, which (he argues) is committed to transformation rather than reproduction (Touraine 1981:7).

The diacritical feature of postindustrial society is its "capability of acting upon [itself]" (Touraine 1977:18) so as to transform itself (ibid.:25). This capability is called society's "historicity" (ibid., 1981: 136). Society is thus a historical "self" or "subject" guided by its vision of itself and its image of its own ideal future.

Society produces itself, imposes a meaning on its own practices, *turns back upon itself*. It does not exist solely in nature; it does not possess a history only; it possesses historicity, which is the capacity to produce its own social and cultural field, its own historical environment (1977:16).

This capacity or historicity and the "field" or "environment" within which it operates derives from society's "cultural model," an "image of creativity and thus of historical action" (ibid.:66) that "governs the categories of social and cultural production" (ibid.). Through the cultural model "society 'reflects' upon itself by apprehending its own capability of action in a way that defines the field of social relations and . . . the system of historical action" (ibid.:19).

Society is not reducible to the laws that govern its functioning; nor is it governed by ideas . . . given as external to social practice. . . . It is constituted by itself—the social is explicable solely by the social—which is to say by its own means and its consciousness of acting on itself (ibid.:65).

Through the cultural model society becomes "first and foremost agent" (ibid.:4): operator within a historical field it itself specifies given its own "cultural orientations" (Touraine 1981:9). To know a society from within is to know its process of autogenesis and autoinvention and the practical and semantic values called into play.

Touraine calls the activity through which society transforms itself "work." "Historicity is neither idea nor material situation; it is the specific characteristic of social action, which constitutes its experience through the meaning it gives it" (1977:17). In this he takes issue with a materialism that privileges "base" and overlooks historicity, cultural in its foundations. Touraine wants to write a sociology that is intrinsically historical. "Rather than placing a society in history, we are talking about placing historicity in the heart of society as the organizing principle of a field of practices and relations" (ibid.:24). "Work," historicity, and cultural model together thus assume the analytical status structure has for societies where reproduction rather than transformation is the norm.

Paiela groups, *yames*, are said to have "one mind, one talk, one body, one *mana*, and one work"; they are purposing, acting, moral "selves" —macrosubjects—engaged in millenarian praxis (Biersack n.d.). *Yames* are self-conscious as well as conscious entities, organized reflexively around the leader-follower relation as an axis of "we, the good and the bad." In fact, all collective representations are reflexive, from the divine/diabolical polarity (ibid.) to gender (Biersack 1984) to the cosmos (Figure 18) itself. Utopian activity is pursued in the name of a higher, transcendent subjectivity. This reflexivity and its *philosophical* anthropology *is* the Paiela "cultural system."[21]

Anchoring culture in language, Geertzian "cultural analysis" and the hermeneutics it practices relativizes on the basis of phenomenological differences. In this framework action inscribes and objectifies thought; it is expression, not instrument. But Paiela are world constructors in a double sense. They live phenomenologically within a significant horizon, but they also live practically within a project-dependent horizon, one that fluctuates in accordance with the vigor and success of the millenarian effort (Figures 14 and 15) (see Biersack 1990). Saying and doing, signifying and acting, and local knowledge and local praxis are inextricably linked. The most important sign in the Paiela cosmos is motivational: the sun as an "image of creativity and thus of historical action" (Touraine 1977:66), emblem and source of the millenarian project itself. The sun is the sign of a new heaven, new earth, of a utopian future (see Burridge 1980).

The Paiela materials suggest another mode of relativizing, one that grounds cultural difference as much in praxis as in meaning. As Touraine has written:

The more one represents society as being built up through its work upon itself, the more one distances oneself from all forms of technical and economic determinism. The ideal of the production of society is contrasted to that of the society of production. It is not material activity that determines what happens to the remainder of society, primarily because technology forms part of a culture instead of being simply a material fact (Touraine 1981:49).

In this mode of relativizing, means become analytically secondary to culturally espoused ends, and categories such as technology and production become as underdetermined in their content as are other cultural categories—male and female, say.

The white man has a high level of technology, to be sure, but it is his purposes rather than his instruments that culturally distinguish him. He wants to go to the moon (and not the sun), and he has planes (not *bulu*) and spacecrafts to do so. He wants to accumulate capital and has industry and a commodity market (but no "shell" exchange) to do so. Paiela also have a technology, not merely the digging stick and stone axe but woman exchange, dispute mediation, and big-man leadership, all of which promote millenarian goals. Moreover, variations in goals and technology have variable implications for world construction. Paiela make themselves differently from the way the white man makes himself. As between Paiela society and postindustrial society there can be no evolutionary relationship because the relationship between these divergent means, ends, and worlds cannot be linear. Once we privilege agendas and historicities and not means per se, time itself becomes pluralized, another cultural product (cf. Sahlins 1985a). No longer outside culture, times ceases to be a neutral marker of cultural difference and becomes a pernicious instrument for orientalizing and othering those who cannot be positioned except on their *own* temporal scale (cf. Fabian 1983). The bond between world-system and local agenda—in the West but also among some of the Rest—privileges developmental schemes, ideas of progress, and master narratives (evolution, for example, or the Paiela cosmos as process) as cultural variables. From the native's point of view, the white man—with his planes and commodities—is indeed the atavistic *yama*, the ignoble savage, he was first named as being.[22]

Notes

Acknowledgments. The ethnographic present refers to the period from 1974 to 1978, during which I completed three years of fieldwork among the Paiela. Fieldwork was sponsored by predoctoral awards from the National Science Foundation, the Rackham School of Graduate Studies (University of Michigan), and the Center for the Continuing Education of Women (University of Michigan). The Wenner-Gren Foundation for Anthropological Research awarded a grant-in-aid for the preparation of the resulting dissertation. I gratefully acknowledge these sources of support. Thanks also to Bill Gammage and Jocelyn Linnekin for reading an earlier version. The center people were kind enough to tolerate my presence and to teach me.
   1. Most of the reporting here focuses on male rather than on female 'work' (*peape*). Each in his own way, the big man, the creator, and the white

man exemplify masculine agency. This bias in the essay's reporting is reflected in the androcentric character of its language. Though I do not explore the theme of gender explicitly here, I have taken it up in other writings (Biersack 1984, 1990), and I am giving it full treatment in a longer work I am currently preparing.

2. No contradiction is involved in arguing against deterministic models and in speaking of a cognatic rule. As will be shown, the rule merely creates the possibility of kinship Paiela-style, the condition of which is exchange.

3. The verb in the phrase *mandi yene*, 'the carried people', differs from the verb in phrases such as "to carry *mana*," which is *ai* rather than *mandi*. Used purely as verb, *ai* means 'to carry on the shoulder' and *mandi* means 'to carry in a netbag'. Men carry burdens on the shoulder and women carry burdens in a netbag. The word for netbag, *nuu*, also means 'womb'.

4. My fieldnotes are a mixture of vernacular text and paraphrases of informant statements. I use three kinds of block quotes: direct quotation, paraphrase, and a mixture of the two. Where the block quote is either a paraphrase or a mixture of paraphrase and direct quotation, I so note.

5. This distinction between "mind work" and "hand work," the thinking of the leader and the doing of the follower, is reminiscent of the contrast in functions between the chief (*ali'i*) and the talking chief (*tulāfale*) in Samoa. Shore writes: "While the *ali'i* may be seen as the repository of *pule* or authority, orators are commonly referred to as *faipule* (the activators of *pule* or authority), suggesting the distinction in power between its potential and kinetic aspects" (1982:241). He goes on to observe that "On important occasions, the *ali'i* merely 'sits' . . . , while the orator speaks for him and 'moves about' doing his bidding" (ibid.:242). As between the chief-talking chief and the leader-follower relationships parallels multiply: "The more highly ranked *ali'i* are known as *sa'o*, which literally means 'the straight one' or 'the correct one', while orators are described (although never formally or publicly) as *pi'opi'o* ('devious/meandering') and *kuluku* (from the English 'crooked')" (ibid.:243).

6. Many of my concerns in this section resonate with those of Marilyn Strathern in her "Discovering 'Social Control'" (1987).

7. The national motto of Papua New Guinea is *"Bung wantaim,"* a pidgin expression meaning 'meet together'. It suggests also a concatenation of otherwise independent, uncoordinated parts so as to produce a single whole. The emphasis is on the transformation of the fragmented and decentralized into the unified and centralized.

8. Since woman exchange shapes kinship networks and one is born positioned by marriage, "in-between," consanguinity itself is always achieved before it is ascribed.

9. "If we hear the fight-talk man's fight talk, then we take good mind and give a lot. If we do it with our own mind, then we don't give a lot and we act defectively. Through the fight-talk man, war is lost and we have good minds."

10. Paiela and the valley directly east, Porgera, share a single language. Gibbs (1977), who did most of his work in Porgera, reports these words for the sun there: *nitawe, nii, aluni, ewa,* and *onewa.* Here I capitalize the word *sun* when it refers to the deity but do not capitalize it when it refers to the natural object.

11. In *Works and Lives,* Geertz playfully writes of "author-ization" and the rhetoric of anthropological texts (1988:9). Here I play another way, by way of critiquing the objectivist bias of social-scientific reasoning.

12. Godelier reports an interesting parallel to Paiela cosmogony among the Baruya: "In the beginning, Sun and Moon were indistinguishable from the Earth. All was gray. Men, spirits, animals, vegetables lived together and spoke the same language. Men were not like men today, their penises were not pierced and women's vaginas were not opened. The genitals of dogs too were walled up. Then Sun and Moon decided to rise above the Earth and they did so by pushing the sky up above them. Once in the sky, Sun thought he ought to do something for the humans and he ordered Moon to go back down again. Moon went down and stopped midway. Since then, day and night, rainy seasons and hot seasons have alternated. Since then, the animals have separated from men to go and live in the forest, which is where the spirits, now hostile and malevolent toward men, have also gone. The language that everyone used to speak except that between men and dogs disappeared in the process of separation.

"But Sun also remembered that the man and the woman were not pierced. So he cast a flintstone into the fire, and the stone burst and pierced the man and the woman. Since that time they have been able to copulate and multiply. Later, the men, wishing to punish dogs for having spoken ill of them, shot arrows at them which pierced their sex. From that time on, dogs have ceased to speak and instead howl at night. Nowadays, men hunt the animals in the forest with their dogs. Nowadays, if Sun comes too close to Earth, he scorches it and devastates the gardens. If Moon comes too close to us, she engulfs everything in rain and darkness, and the crops then rot" (1986:66).

13. This man's simile is very clever. It combines what he has observed is true of reading (he himself is illiterate) with his awareness of the significance of the Bible (he himself is not baptized, but he does attend church services on Sunday).

14. Lest this be doubted, it is clear enough from the death state itself in its

social organizational dimensions. While still alive, a married person remains embedded in the matrix of relationships he and his parents together created. He "comes and goes" along the "roads" of the "ground skin," visiting and coresiding with affines no less than with consanguines, exchanging with one and all. Death restores the person to a prenuptial state in which transactional "roads" with affines are severed and exchange relationships are preserved, if only episodically, with consanguines alone. ("The spirits of the dead have no fathers-in-law and brothers-in-law.") The dead move in narrower social orbits than the living; their social milieu is retrograde. Interred, a dead person is repatriated to the "ground bone" that he, along with his consanguines, owns (see Biersack n.d.). The stratigraphy of the "ground bone" extrapolates the fact of death longitudinally, modeling the series of intergenerational transformations uncovered in the previous section.

15. The most intricate device for speaking of ground's end, also the one that remains the most opaque to me, exploits the semiotics of Paiela counting. The count is a body count with a base unit of fourteen, the sum tabulated on either side of the upper half of the body. The count begins with the digits of either hand, travels up the arm to the neck, and is completed on the head at the nose (the fourteenth count). To tabulate higher sums (the standard for bridewealth is twenty-eight pigs), the count "descends" the other side of the body, touching up to fourteen points for a total of twenty-eight. For higher sums still, the count begins again (see Biersack 1982). Though the count is most commonly employed in transactional settings to tabulate the scale of prestations, it is also used to trace cosmic and social history. The first count, at the small finger, represents "when the ground originated." All points up the arm are touched, then the neck, which divides the "body" proper from the "head," then the ear and the eye on the head. The ground ends at the fourteenth count, the nose. The commentary that accompanies the close of the count includes "hear" at the twelfth point (the ear), "see" at the thirteenth point (the eye), and "it will eat the nose, it will not descend" at the fourteenth point. Each point represents a generation, and the fourteen points together mark a passage of fourteen generations. Everyone I talked to positioned himself or herself somewhere "in the middle" of the count, though noticeably toward the higher rather than the lower end of the scale; and count fourteen was identified with the children's children's children's, the children's children's, or, in rare cases (the man who went to Port Moresby, for example), the children's generation. We may speculate on the imagery. The eye is the penultimate point: it symbolizes knowledge, lawfulness, revelation, and communion with the deity. The final point is the nose, which is the

only unpaired point in the counting system (even the neck has a right-
and a lefthand side); it is the boundary, the axis of duality, between the
two "sides" or "halves" (*pakisia*) of the body; and (to return to local categories), it is on the head, not the "body" (a term used only of the torso,
not the head). "At the nose" the count ends. Time is arrested and duality
overcome (the count will not "descend"); and it is the head (symbolizing
leadership, virtue, sanctity, and *mana*) per se that is associated with this
outcome.

16. Meggitt (1973:27) describes the ritual as being performed on dance
    grounds. Paiela dance grounds are *ama*, but the activities of *ama* are not
    restricted to dancing.
17. See Andrew Strathern's "Souvenirs de 'folie' chez les Wiru" for a different
    interpretation of "madness" in a contact setting.
18. Schoolchildren are preponderantly male.
19. The snake is a *puya* snake. The *puya* snake is said to be a "killer of men."
    "It breaks people's bones. It lies under rocks and goes to the house of
    the spirits of the dead."
20. According to Meggitt, the sun, for the Enga, is a symbol of the sky world
    (1965:108)."Long ago the land was uninhabited. The only quasi-human
    beings then living were the sun and moon, 'the father and mother of us
    all'. Eventually they had many children, 'the causal or originating people',
    who reside in the sky in conditions similar to those on earth" (ibid.:107).
    "Because of the behaviour of the sky beings in the past, it is the lot of
    the Mae to be gardeners and warriors. Men must toil to wrest the meagre
    livelihood from a harsh environment in which violent death is . . . an
    everyday occurrence" (ibid.:108).

    Brennan, a former affiliate with the Lutheran mission at Wabag, capital
    of the Enga Province, provides a fuller account.

    "The sky world of pre-existence provided for the forefathers of all clans
    existing today, a domain free of care and stress.

    "Sweet potatoes grew effortlessly and abundantly, and man lived peace-
    fully alongside his brothers in relationships of mutual respect, co-operation,
    and benevolence.

    "The reason for such a perfect state lay in the 'fountain of life' . . .
    which nourished all aspects of this existence.

    "The fountain brought abundance and wealth: to be nourished by this
    water, whether soil or man, meant to be given continued perfect life. . . .

    "But alas for man, his heavenly existence ceased. The myth relates that
    one of the sky beings one day began to travel, and in his wanderings he
    eventually reached the level of earth. Here he met woman and she bore
    him a child.

"At the infant's first cry, woman offered him the breast, and in that act—equivalent to a fall from grace—man was forever banished to the terrestrial plane. . . .

"On the plane of earthly existence, Original Man became the progenitor of a new generation. His children colonised earth, utilising their father's knowledge of culture and life style brought with him from above, but bereft of the fountain to sustain them.

"In this sad state, their only recourse was to people a realm characterised by tension, strife, and all of the antagonisms common to earthly existence" (1977:17).

21. Touraine recasts class conflict in posteconomistic terms, as a "struggle of social forces for the control of historicity and of the action of society upon itself" (1981:11). Society is "a cultural field torn apart by the conflict between those who take over historicity for themselves and those who are subjected to their domination and who are struggling for the collective reappropriation of historicity, for the self-production of society" (ibid.:62). Were antiwhite sentiment ever to surface and millenarianism to take an overtly cargo-cultic turn, it would be possible to apply Touraine's actionalist sociology still further, to "class" conflict within the world-system. In this attempt to establish autonomy from a once much-welcomed guest, there would be several issues: what kind of globalism (world peace or world domination and class war), what kind of center (secular metropolis or sacred *ama*), and what kind of valuable (commodity or cargo) would prevail. In short, the *quo vadimus* question of historicity and the significance of directionality would be raised (see Strathern, this volume).

22. In a recent book Grant McCracken (1988) has elaborated the thesis that consumption is a semantic no less than a material domain. The same, I am arguing, is true of production, within as well as without the West. (Biersack 1990).

References Cited

Babcock, Barbara, ed.
1978   *The Reversible World*. Ithaca: Cornell University Press.
Biersack, Aletta
1982   The Logic of Misplaced Concreteness. *American Anthropologist* 84:811–29.
1984   Paiela "Women-Men": The Reflexive Foundations of Gender Ideology. *American Ethnologist* 11:118–38.
1987   Moonlight: Negative Images of Transcendence in Paiela Pollution. *Oceania* 57:178–94.

1990	Histories in the Making: Paiela and Historical Anthropology. *History and Anthropology* 5.
n.d.	Word Made Flesh: *Mana*, Personhood, and Hierarchy in an Oceanic World. In *The Word*, ed. C. Jan Swearingen. Tucson: University of Arizona Press.

Blong, R. J.
1982	*The Time of Darkness: Local Legends and Volcanic Reality in Papua New Guinea.* Seattle: University of Washington Press.

Brennan, Paul
1977	The Enga and Their Enemies. *Post-Courier,* 16 December 1977, 17–19.

Burridge, Kenelm
1960	*Mambu: A Study of Melanesian Cargo Movements and Their Social and Ideological Background.* New York: Harper & Row.
1980	*New Heaven, New Earth: A Study of Millenarian Activities.* Oxford:Basil Blackwell.

Comaroff, Jean
1985	*Body of Power, Spirit of Resistance: The Culture and History of a South African People.* Chicago: University of Chicago Press.

Dening, Greg
1980	*Islands and Beaches: Discourse on a Silent Land, Marquesas 1774–1880.* Honolulu: University Press of Hawaii.

Fabian, Johannes
1983	*Time and the Other: How Anthropology Makes Its Object.* New York: Columbia University Press.

Feil, Daryll K.
1983	A World without Exchange: Millennia and the Tee Ceremonial System in Tombema-Enga Society (New Guinea). *Anthropos* 78:89–106.

Fortes, Meyer
1969	*Kinship and the Social Order.* Chicago: Aldine.

Geertz, Clifford
1988	*Works and Lives: The Anthropologist as Author.* Stanford: Stanford University Press.

Gibbs, Philip J.
1977	The Cult from Lyeimi and the Ipili. *Oceania* 48:1–25.

Godelier, Maurice
1986	*The Making of Great Men.* Cambridge: Cambridge University Press.

Goldman, Laurence
1983	*Talk Never Dies: The Language of Huli Disputes.* London: Tavistock Publications.

Jarvie, I. C.
1964   *The Revolution in Anthropology*. Chicago: Henry Regnery.
Kirkpatrick, John
1985   How Personal Differences Can Make a Difference. In *The Social Construction of the Person*, ed. Kenneth J. Gergen and Keith E. Davis. New York: Springer-Verlag.
Kracke, Ward H.
1978   *Force and Persuasion*. Chicago: University of Chicago Press.
Lawrence, Peter
1964   *Road Belong Cargo: A Study of the Cargo Movement in the Southern Madang District, New Guinea*. Manchester: Manchester University Press.
Lincoln, Bruce
1989   *Discourse and the Construction of Social Forms: Comparative Studies of Myth, Ritual, and Classification*. New York: Oxford University Press.
McCracken, Grant
1988   *Culture and Consumption: New Approaches to the Symbolic Character of Consumer Goods and Activities*. Bloomington: Indiana University Press.
Meggitt, M. J.
1965   The Mae Enga of the Western Highlands. In *Gods, Ghosts, and Men in Melanesia*, ed. P. Lawrence and M. J. Meggitt. Melbourne: Oxford University Press.
1973   The Sun and the Shakers: A Millenarian Cult and Its Transformations in the New Guinea Highlands. *Oceania* 4:1–37.
Ortner, Sherry B.
1984   Theory in Anthropology since the Sixties. *Comparative Studies in Society and History* 26:126–66.
Ricoeur, Paul.
1965   Work and the Word. In *History and Truth*, tr. C. Kelbley. Evanston: Northwestern University Press.
Sahlins, Marshall
1981   *Historical Metaphors and Mythical Realities: Structure in the Early History of the Sandwich Islands*. A.S.A.O. Special Publication no. 1. Ann Arbor: University of Michigan Press.
1985a   Other Times, Other Customs: The Anthropology of History. In *Islands of History*. Chicago: University of Chicago Press.
1985b   *Islands of History*. Chicago: University of Chicago Press.

Sennett, Richard
1981   Forward. In *The Voice and the Eye*, tr. Alan Duff. Cambridge: Cambridge University Press.

Shore, Bradd
1982   *Sala'ilua*. New York: Columbia University Press.

Strathern, Andrew
1977   Souvenirs de "folie" chez les Wiru (Southern Highlands). *Journal de la société des Océanistes* 56:131–44.

1981   *Noman*. In *The Structure of Folk Models*, ed. L. A. Holy and M. Stuchlik. A.S.A. Monograph no. 20. London: Academic Press.

1988   Satan's Mouth. Paper prepared for the American Ethnological Society annual meeting, St. Louis, Missouri.

Strathern, Marilyn
1972   *Official and Unofficial Courts: Legal Assumptions and Expectations in a Highland Community*. New Guinea Research Bulletin no. 47. Port Moresby and Canberra: New Guinea Research Unit, Australian National University.

1987   Discovering "Social Control." *Journal of Law and Society* 12:111–34.

Touraine, Alain
1977   *The Self-Production of Society*. Tr. Derek Coltman. Chicago: University of Chicago Press.

1981   *The Voice and the Eye*. Tr. Alan Duff. Cambridge: Cambridge University Press.

Wolf, Eric
1982   *Europe and the People without History*. Berkeley and Los Angeles: University of California Press.

Worsley, Peter
1968   *The Trumpet Shall Sound*. New York: Schocken Books.

7. Alejandro Mayta in Fiji

Narratives about Millenarianism, Colonialism, Postcolonial Politics, and Custom

Nicholas Thomas

Anthropology and history[1] both attempt to establish correct meanings at a distance. Ethnography's interpretive accomplishment is not simply an account of culture, but an account of a different culture, an interpretation of an alternate, distant field of practices and conceptions. On one hand, to the extent that the discipline's endeavor is explicitly or implicitly construed in these terms, the proper objects of study must be meanings that are "non-Western" and unfamiliar. On the other hand, what is borrowed from our culture or otherwise interpenetrated with it can only be analytically marginal or inconsequential: change and transcultural contact may often be acknowledged, but anthropological theory remains primarily about cultures that can be situated elsewhere. The discovery of alterity is the discovery of others' meanings, meanings that we take to be original rather than derivative.

For its part, history establishes a description of past circumstances, rather than the renderings of those circumstances in various past or present contexts. Authenticity is associated with an empirically secure account of a particular distant period or a particular sequence of distant happenings; what is proximate, on the other hand, is the telling and the writing, the production of a salient account. The orthodox historical imagination fails to acknowledge that versions of the past are always recreated for the here and now, are always politically inflected, partial, and interested.

Anthropology's synchronic depictions of the exotic might be historicized, just as history's authoritative narratives might be relativized. But anthropology can domesticate history by establishing that events are incorporated into a cultural order; and history can contextualize both events and narratives in "cultural systems" while neglecting the politically fractured and contested character of culture. Although the mutual borrowing that is well under way is clearly productive for both history and anthropology, it does not necessarily disable the distancing strategies of either discipline. Here I suggest that certain proximate meanings and distorted narratives are beyond the conventional vision of both anthropology and history but typify the invention of colonial and postcolonial indigenous cultures and subcultures in the Pacific. This political and cultural process is thus theoretically significant for anthropology and ethnohistory, but also has a more local importance in the understanding of the contemporary struggles about custom and tradition that arise in many of the region's postcolonial states, and that have produced two military coups and a constitutional crisis in Fiji. There, at least, it has become impossible to discuss "culture" as if it were unitary and uncontested.

Nothing seemed more pathetic than the sight of an individual Seventh-day Adventist sitting with a glass of water on the periphery of a kava circle. That struck me not long after I began fieldwork in the western interior of Fiji's big island of Viti Levu: a man appeared to be excluded from a customary ceremony, because Adventist taboos on alcohol were extended to the indigenous narcotic beverage. That personal reflection would however be justified by almost the whole corpus of anthropological literature on Fiji, rather than my own work. Kava drinking is visibly and manifestly a cultural practice, a ritual that is bound up with traditions, values, and social relations: in Fiji, as in Samoa and Tonga, it typically consists in a kind of sacrifice to the chief; the formal seating arrangements manifest a hierarchical order subsuming rank, age, gender, and contextual distinctions related to affinity and particular ceremonial events (see, for example, Toren 1988). In the formulas that are used daily, kava is "the water of the land" and "the chiefly kava"; the expression of pious religious (Methodist) sentiments in the context of these ritual utterances reinforces the explicit identifications among Fijian custom, a respect-structured kinship order, the way of the church, and the kava ceremony. Hence, although I was already aware that some Fijians abstained from drinking because of denominational laws, this visible marginalization seemed remarkable. How was it possible for people to take foreign religious prohibitions so seriously and eschew these crucial cultural values?

The extent to which Adventists set themselves off from the village society in other respects is very variable, but there is no doubt that a great deal is at stake: a senior man who might otherwise have been a contender for a chiefly title was deemed ineligible because he could not "take the cup," and changes in religious affiliation on the part of individuals frequently lead to acrimonious disputes. In one instance a chief excluded from his village several women who had switched to Adventism while working in town. Any denominational change is likely to be socially problematic, but the particular feature of the Adventist "sect" that has created tension in Fiji is the observance of the Sabbath on Saturdays, a correlate of which is taken to be an obligation to work on Sundays. This practice clashes with strict Fijian sabbatarianism[2] and the rhythm of villages that are organized as much around church occasions as other major communal feasts and ceremonies. The issue has also frequently been politicized: since chiefs were and are almost always Methodist, a change of church membership has usually entailed a challenge of some kind to the hegemony of the traditional hierarchy and what has in effect been the "official" church. Exclusion, or self-exclusion, from a ceremony may thus reflect some wider differences.

Without denying tensions internal to contemporary Fijian society, which are also expressed in the spread of newer denominations such as the Assemblies of God, it must be recognized that there is also a problem of recognition that is internal to anthropology. The essentialist pursuit of cultural structures that are distinctly Fijian can only entangle itself with codifications of hierarchy, chieftainship, and the customary order and will exclude, in a more or less categorical fashion, notions and practices destabilizing that ensemble. There is no sense in which the ritual speech of old men exchanging whale teeth in mortuary feasts or at traditional marriages and the ritual speech of old women in the Jehovah's Witnesses' hall can be equally Fijian from an anthropological perspective. And the issue is hardly restricted to Fiji. Ethnographers in Tonga, Papua New Guinea, and especially the Solomons have remarked (mostly privately) upon the "difficulty" of Adventist people and communities, upon their hostility toward custom—toward what we might take to be their cultural milieux—their taste for money, and their lack of openness toward ethnographers.[3] Whereas in the eighteenth and nineteenth centuries, the "real savages" were those most hostile to inquisitive white outsiders, it ironically seems that now those who have sacrificed and destroyed most of their own culture resist inspection and refuse the supreme gift of intercultural dialogue, and authentically traditional (if mainstream Christian) people are generally both hospitable and interested in being anthropologists' hosts.

How can cultural interpretation interpret this dissociation from culture? If the problem arises from a pursuit of the *correct names* for, or the *original meanings* of, other people's meaningful practices, then perhaps I can construct something else by beginning from the objectification and distortion of customs and names: we could thus regard historical anthropology as an inquiry into the inventive appropriation and recontextualization of culture, as a science of misnomers.

The particular investigation here is biographical, but the lives are those of narratives rather than of the individuals whose practices have been caught up and ultimately effaced by a number of competing renderings. The accounts discussed arose from a sequence of prominent politico-religious movements of the period between Fiji's cession to Britain in 1874 and the First World War.[4] Although the British regime in Fiji has been widely regarded as a protectionist system in which traditional authority and indigenous rights to land were enshrined, the colonial state in fact embarked on an extraordinarily thorough and systematic program of social regulation and taxation that was resented and opposed by many commoner Fijians. The administration and indirect rule system were generally supported by the chiefly hierarchy, but chiefs in marginal areas such as the interior provinces of Viti Levu, or those out of favor with the administration, were sometimes involved with commoners in protest and dissent—notably in Apolosi R. Nawai's broadly based Viti Kabani (Fiji Company), a politicized agricultural cooperative movement. Cross-cutting loyalties, official repression, and a variety of other factors restricted the effectiveness of most of these movements, so that rural society has been characterized by suppressed but enduring tensions rather than open conflict (Thomas 1990a, b).

Although I am partially concerned with how a number of important politico-religious leaders of the early colonial period are represented now, my focus is upon one of least consequence, a man named Sailosi (this being the Fijianization of Silas, and still now a common name) who was an inspirational priest of some kind from the Tavua area on Viti Levu's north coast (see Map 3). In 1918 he announced a set of

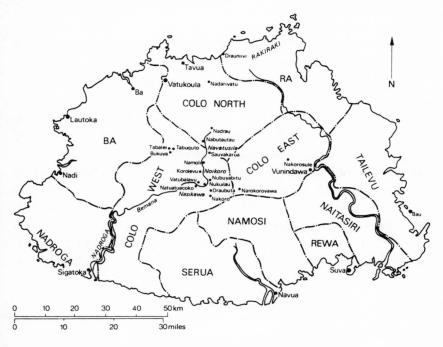

Map 3. Viti Levu, Fiji, showing early colonial provincial boundaries.

political prophesies and advocated reorganization of village society: wide interest was aroused in his area, and in neighboring interior provinces, but the movement was rapidly suppressed by the administration. My concern here is thus with an ephemeral outbreak, a trivial matter that might be considered beyond the margins of serious history. However, the present work has been rendered substantially more feasible by a prior reflection upon the investigation of such topics.

An extremely marginal and ineffective historical character also figures in a recent treatise on the methodology of history and biography, which has been cunningly disguised as a novel by the right-wing Peruvian politician Mario Vargas Llosa. *The Real Life of Alejandro Mayta* (1986 [1984]) amounts to an analogous attempt to fabricate the life of an unimportant dissident, his character being a Trotskyist militant who tries to escape from years of sterile political discussion in tiny, marginal groups through direct action. He cooperates with an enthusiastic but inexperienced soldier in an attempt to launch a Peruvian revolution from the Andes. The insurrection was of course always doomed to failure and based on total detachment from wider political realities. At the risk of introducing epistemological confusion, I may point out that the story is based on a real attempt initiated by someone with approximately the same name as the invented figure, although this basis in the factual is disclosed in critical commentary on the work rather than in the book itself (Dunkerley 1987:119–20).[5] Vargas Llosa's fabrication proceeds, rather like *Citizen Kane*, through a tight interpenetration of his reconstruction of the events leading up to the insurrection and the conversations in the present through which these are known. The dialectic of disclosure and suppression is thus constituted through a stylistically dazzling paragraph-by-paragraph and even sentence-by-sentence transposition of then and now, of the history and the dialogue. The reflexivity of the project is insisted upon, and many of those interviewed by the author-character question him about why he is engaged in the inquiry.

"What is it about Mayta that interests you so much?" Moisés asks me, as he uses the tip of his tongue to check the temperature of the coffee. "Of all the revolutionaries of those years, he is the most obscure."

I don't know how to go on. If I could, I would tell him, but at this moment I only know that I want to know, even invent, Mayta's story, and as lifelike as possible. I could give him moral, social, and ideological reasons, and show him that Mayta's story is the most important, the one that most urgently needs to be told. But it would all be a lie. I truthfully do not know why Mayta's story intrigues and disturbs me.

"Perhaps I know why," Moisés says. "Because his story was the first, before the triumph of the Cuban Revolution. Before that event which split the left in two."

He may be right, it may well be because of the precursory character of the adventure. It's true that it inaugurated a new era in Peru, something neither Mayta nor Vallejos could guess at the time. But it's also possible that the whole historical context has no more importance than as decor and that the obscurely suggestive element I see in it consists of the truculence, marginality, rebellion, delirium, and excess which all came together in that episode (1986: 44).

Vargas Llosa acknowledges to his informants that he intends deliberately and consciously to rework the past into "a faint, remote, and if you like, false version" (1986:66, cf. 81). Here I cannot recapitulate the course of inquiry and the history that was its object, but instead privilege the interested contrivance of representation, and intersperse two kinds of renaming that equally efface the historical fact of Sailosi's own motivation and action. I refer to the "distortions" of various perceptions of his movement and the constituted character of my own analysis. The claim behind this denial of any history outside recontextualization is not the relativist proposition that "we have different histories for different occasions" (Dening 1988:99) but that both the hands of others and one's own hand ought to be disclosed.[6] The cultural differences between different narratives emerge from political situations, from interests in particular constructions of the past. What confronts us is not merely a plurality of accounts, but a contested field. I do not put forward another history merely to add to those already in circulation, or to succeed those that have been forgotten, but to intervene in debate about the Fijian past. I would not write if I did not have an argument.

It would be impossible, anyway, to resort to any claim about the historical primacy of Sailosi's action—unlike Alejandro Mayta, he was certainly not the first Fijian to call for a revolutionary transformation of social relations—but I will argue later that aspects of contemporary Fijian culture and politics amount to a generalization of the political imagination of characters such as Sailosi and Apolosi R. Nawai. But I must proceed to situate the unoriginality of his protest in the history of opposition to the chiefly establishment based on the small island of Bau and the British colonial administration with which, from the time of Cession in 1874, the high chiefs were generally closely associated. Discontent was in fact something that distinguished his district and those of the adjacent upland interior. Drauniivi village on the Rakiraki coast had been the center of the Tuka activities, which were most conspicuous in the 1880s but had antecedents and many later manifestations.[7] Sailosi had some involvement in these activities and at some stage kept a notebook of ritual formulas, inexplicable hieroglyphics, and prophesies; in 1896 he was among those who made requests through provincial councils that those who had been deported from their villages to outlying islands be permitted to return, which in fact did not happen for almost twenty years.[8] But that is not what got him into trouble.

The distinctive feature of the British colonial regime in Fiji was the indirect rule structure, which ostensibly provided for government through the chiefs—"in the Fijian manner" as the officials imagined —although the neat administrative hierarchy of appointed village, district, and provincial heads[9] was of course essentially foreign. The problem with creating and circulating names is, of course, that the uses to which these are put cannot be easily controlled. Hence, it became necessary to ask the Buli Boubuco, the official district chief, whether he had any complaints against his *Ovisa*, his native constable.

Sailosi had apparently got into the habit of using the Buli's office, opening his mail, signing his name, "summoning the District Council on his own authority," and "doing a variety of other things in contravention of [the Buli's] office and dignity"—including, it seems, wearing his spectacles. On this occasion the Buli defended his subordinate and said that the allegations, which had been set out in a letter from his own son, and from an appointed village chief, were merely reactions to Sailosi's vigorous prosecution of his duty. The signatories were in fact tried for slander and each sentenced to three months' hard labor. However, less than a year later A. B. Joske,[10] the resident commissioner, found himself compelled to recommend Sailosi's dismissal. He was not immediately convicted of any charge, but there was further trouble, and he was incarcerated, first in the colonial hospital and then in the lunatic asylum, after he had allegedly been so indiscreet as to inform his nurse that, if so instructed by his guardian spirit, he would kill her, the chief medical officer, or anyone else.[11]

These occurrences echo something more elusive than an individual case of madness. As with Mayta, the excess and marginality are "obscurely suggestive" because they are emblematic of historical tropes, of a cultural structure of colonialism. Sailosi's acts seemed necessarily irrational; this kind of resistance typified the unmanageability of Fijians that haunted the British quest for orderly representation and control: I thus take the appropriation of official chiefly spectacles to epitomize the subversion of these hierarchical colonial relationships through the abuse of their own status markers and mechanisms for rendering texts and colonized places visible.[12] White officials generally reacted by writing off such political mimicry as the result of mental derangement or emotional instability. Joske, who seems to have had some sympathy for Sailosi, could only say that "he has by bad temper got himself into a false position in his own village."[13] The notion that there were "false positions" had wide application, but Joske also noted uneasily with regard to quite separate "disturbances" that the "turbulent" young chiefs of Nagonenicolo were "very intelligent & have an extraordinary knowledge of law & of parliamentary Govt."[14]

This was a rare admission that dissent did not always originate in misinformation. False assertions were certainly conspicuous when Sailosi, evidently discharged from the asylum, addressed a crowded meeting in the town of Tavua in March 1918. He informed those present that he had been on a mountaintop in Europe and had seen the king present a Fijian customary *soro* or gift of submission, together with an indemnity, to the kaiser; this meant that the government in Fiji was finished; there would be no more taxes, and that all the officials from the governor down to the village chiefs would be replaced by appointees from Apolosi R. Nawai's Viti Kabani (Fiji Company).[15] This was a powerful movement with an unmistakably political and antichiefly agenda: in songs[16] connected with raising money, Apolosi is sometimes referred to as *"na jivu ni bula ni Viji"*[17] ('chief of Fiji's life or health'). The odd use of the loan word *jivu* in lieu of the usual Fijian term for chief typifies the name-stealing characteristic of millenarian practice. In the case of Sailosi's new order, this centered upon the creation of a new church, the *lotu naba walu* or Number 8 Religion, which rather resembled the Number 7 Religion or Adventist church (*lotu ka vitu*).[18] The key shift was that Saturday was to be observed as the Sabbath and work engaged in on Sunday.[19] These proposals were adopted immediately but unevenly in parts of the generally disaffected interior provinces of Colo East, West, and North—"On Easter Sunday there was actually housebuilding and weeding in towns—which is indeed strange for Fijians," noted a district official.[20] A series of witnesses' statements confirmed that, in this story, Britain had been beaten on the 25th of March, that the government was abolished, and "the Wesleyan church & its sunday done away with—also the work in connection with it." One native minister was more specific:

This is the time that Fiji is to be at rest. There is no Government, no Governor, Roko, Buli, Turaga ni Koro, everything appertaining to the Government. The people who take their place are the Turaga ni Koros of the Fiji Company. . . . No taxes. No one is to pay his taxes. . . . Concerning the Church. No missionary meetings, or quarterly collections, or food for ministers. . . . Sunday is to be observed on Saturday. The present Sunday to be done away with. All these things have been told to me [i.e., Sailosi] by God. Know this also that Apolosi is like John the Baptist, I like Jesus, God has spoken to me & told me to free Fiji.[21]

Another witness reported that after the news had been announced

we were asked if any of us wished to enter the Freedom of Fiji—& if so to sign on the right side of the paper—& if we refused to sign on the left side. The touching of the pen was done—Rapuama wrote the names—he had one pen to write with—Onisimo took another pen which was touched by the people. They did not touch the pen which was used to write with as is the custom.[22]

I am not quite sure what "the custom" refers to, but the subversion of official practice evidently gave ritualized nominal rolls some force in other registers of dissent. In 1902, for instance, many Fijians signed petitions saying that they wanted to be part of New Zealand and have no local administration.[23]

Even at the time, Sailosi's narrative was consequential in locally modified forms. In the Noikoro area, the main proponent of the Number 8 Religion was a chief of secondary rank who had been engaged in a long-running struggle with the titleholder, Ratu Simione Durutalo, who was literate, was a staunch Methodist, had been employed in various capacities by the government, and also had written the traditional history of the "tribe" for A. B. Joske. This compilation of definite histories of chiefly families of course displaced the claims of certain lines. Sailosi's prophesies were absorbed into a more general litany of complaints concerning the local hegemony of this particular progovernment chief, his group, and the manner in which this dominance had been established at the expense of other chiefs and clans in the area not long after cession to Britain. To some extent these conflicts are difficult to discuss, because they are recapitulated in quite a specific manner by the descendants of protagonists on both sides and now have some connections with national political disputes. The general point is merely that adherence to the movement had different meanings and uses in different places, even right at the time.

It is not surprising that the administration and white establishment found it necessary to contain Sailosi's transgression. They did this not merely by arresting him, but also by writing about him in a particular manner. With respect to generalized rumors concerning British defeat by Germany, the *Fiji Times* speculated that these emanated "from natives who can read English in a parrot-like fashion and do not quite understand its purport."[24] Almost immediately, though, this explanation of falsity in terms of the misreading of a clear text by anomalously literate Fijians was displaced by quite a different story. Predictably enough, these reports got Sailosi muddled up with one Sakuisa or Sakusia and further deconstructed him as the author of the trouble. The Rakiraki "Fijian prophet" was "but the mouthpiece of a German white Fijian" who had been successfully persuading "the gullible kai Viti [that] Kaiser Bill is omnipotent and the Germans unconquerable."[25] The few sentences of these Fiji-English reports are replete with disputed and confounded identities.[26] The "prophet" was said to have been not a liar or political criminal but "deposed as an imposter"—in some sense because it had been revealed that he had been "tutored up to his assertions" by a German named Soderberg, who lived *vakaviti*, 'in the Fijian manner', "in the same district as the alleged prophet."[27] Just as there was much disquiet about half-castes and partially assimilated natives who appeared to be "bad imitations" of Europeans, the European who adopted a Fijian village life to such an extent that he would be described as a "white Fijian" could hardly represent anything other than an origin of disorder.

The head of the Methodist church also vigorously condemned Sailosi and specifically denounced the new religion "as political"—the objection thus being that the correct meaning of religion had been abused by the agenda of the Number 8 church. An editorial also expressed concern that "the native is becoming educated to the fact that it is possible to use religion as a cloak to hide a multitude of sins and ulterior motives."[28] The threat of disorder was thus closely connected to the circulation of language and the power that Fijians were thought to be just then acquiring over introduced signs.

Sadly, that imagined control could not save Sailosi, who was regarded as fit to plead guilty to being a lunatic at large: he was thus permitted a moment of reason in which he could acknowledge his own madness. And there is no paradox since, as was noted above, resistance could only occupy "false positions" in the colonial British imagination of the time. Our hero was dispatched to the lunatic asylum, where he ceases to be named but presumably persisted in being documented through the statistical reports of the *Blue Books*. These fully record the number of occasions upon which it proved necessary to physically restrain inmates and specify in each case what form of restraint was employed.

Outside official discourse, Sailosi's name was attached to the adjective *mad* and circulated in a few texts.[29] With enviably balanced judgment the historian Macnaught qualified this to "half-mad" (1982:99). Setting aside this reiteration of official classification, he must however be credited with having mentioned Sailosi at all, since it seems that all the other historians of Fiji share the view of the lunatic asylum itself: that those who circulate misnomers should have their own names suppressed.

This connivance in the policing of madness however represents bad historical practice in quite simple terms; as Macnaught noted, Sailosi's movement did have enduring ramifications for subsequent patterns of religious affiliation, which I will suggest are of broader significance still.

The Number 8 Religion had caused substantial defections from the Methodist church in parts of the eastern interior. The missionary Harold Chambers, who went up the Wainibuka Valley less than a month after Sailosi's arrest, found that some of those wavering had not broken with the church because of government action, but that in the villages higher up the valley, there were few who remained loyal. "Last year the people in crowds awaited me with smiling faces, warm was their welcome and joyous the services. This time a furtive sullen faced people slunk away at my approach or passed me with either none or but the scantiest response to my usual greeting."[30]

Of course, by this time legal action was being taken to suppress the movement and punish those who had been involved. In Colo West, twenty-nine cases were considered, and sentences of hard labor or fines imposed; those who had been village chiefs or other appointees were also of course dismissed.[31] Under these circumstances the Number 8 Religion could hardly be overtly adhered to, but the government's sense that it simply could not suppress religious choice permitted a transposition of the "original" theft of meaning: what had initially been the referent for subversive imitation became reconstituted and politically valorized as an extension of its own parody. This was already taking place as Chambers visited the Wainibuka villages, where a former Methodist teacher, Pauliasi Bunoa, had been holding meetings.

Of late days the position has been complicated by the pushing in of Pauliasi the 7th day Adventist bummer. The wily Sailosites saw their chance and thinking to throw dust in the eyes of the Government professedly accepted the cloak offered them by the 7th day Adventists while they hold the doctrine of Sailosi secretly and await for his statements to be justified. . . . Pauliasi wrote . . . that he had won 330 converts in his district. I think the number fairly correct but they are no more Lotu ni kavitu than I am. To the marrow of their bones their leaders are No 8 and the rank and file are "veimuri-muriga" [followers].[32]

Pauliasi's speeches had allegedly consisted of diatribes against extractive Methodist fundraising and praise for Sailosi's knowledge and energy (*"Au sa dokai Sailosi vakalevu"* ['I respect Sailosi very much'], and so on). The consequences were permanent: these settlements have been Adventist ever since.[33] In Colo West, essentially the same swift defection occurred, but the bitter opposition of the chief and prompt action on the part of a district officer made it possible to expose the "political" motivations beneath the religious cloak. Intervention thus resorted to a distinction between "genuine" and "false" conversion, and one Noikoro man was considered a "sincere" Adventist. Again, there is a curious sense of displacement of the authorship of dissent: a figure identified at one point as the source of trouble is shown to have been put up to it by others, who predictably occupy "false positions." The unruly character of one of those blamed, a dismissed native stipendiary magistrate, was manifest in his detachment from his own home village: he had arrived in Noikoro after having been ejected from another district "for causing trouble there." In colonial discourse, the legibility of Fiji depended very much on its partitioning and proper ordering: wandering individuals and attempts to establish new or outlying settlements constituted "irregularities" to be regarded with extreme suspicion (cf. Thomas 1990a).

In 1918 the chiefly Methodist hegemony in Noikoro was reasserted, and those who had attempted to install the Viti Kabani and a competing chiefly clan were obliged to make customary apologies. Though the district official recognized that the people were in "a very sensitive state," he appeared confident that their promises never again to "have anything to do with the S. D. Adventist religion" would be kept. However, the families of most of those listed as party to the defection are now Adventists and on the basis of oral information seem to have gone over in about 1930. Some later and distinct disputes also seem manifested in the patterns of contemporary affiliation, and of course some of the older conflicts have become irrelevant. As the *Fiji Times* feared, the "cloak" of religion would inevitably be exploited.

There are some things I know about Sailosi that I have not included here. There are other things that I will never know and perhaps should have mentioned. I could have conveyed something more about the man, about the look of his village, about his own physique, about the eloquence or magnetism that made his heresy persuasive. That "fleshing out" would have enabled an understanding of the causes of the events that I have described in an individual's actions: there might have been a counterpart to the rebellious delirium of extravagant prophesies in a figure composed of personal idiosyncracies. In fabricating such a historical character, I could even have suggested that Sailosi's sexuality manifested the same transgression and deviance as his cultural mischief: I could have taken some of the cases that came before provincial courts concerning sexual irregularities and placed Sailosi's name amongst those of the accused. And it was in fact the case that the colonial state policed the "false positions" of both bodies and religions.

But what if, at some point in these inquiries, I had met the man, or one of his relatives or descendants, and felt drawn into some dialogue of confession and concealment about what I had done—what I am doing—with these narratives? Would I have felt as awkward as Vargas Llosa did when he finally encountered Mayta and half-discussed the events and his versions of them with him?

"The character in my novel is queer," I tell him after a bit.
He raises his head as if he's been stung by a wasp. Disgust twists his face. He's sitting in a low armchair, with a wide back, and now he seems to be sixty or more. I see him stretch his legs and rub his hands, tense.
"But why?" he finally asks.
He takes me by surprise. Do I know why? But I improvise an explanation. "To accentuate his marginality, his being a man full of contradictions. Also to show the prejudices that exist with regard to this subject among those who

supposedly want to liberate society from its defects. Well, I don't really know exactly why he is" (1986:301).

My account parallels Vargas Llosa's in the sense that a farcical rebellion unworthy of serious historical notice is made resonant of a conflict-ridden history. But unlike Vargas Llosa, I have refrained from imagining a character who personifies political irrationality, perversity, marginality, and excess. It may seem inconsistent to emphasize (in opposition to conventional history) the multiplicity of inventions and the creativity of history making while refraining myself inventing a history: these stories have detoured around the absent space of their character. I hesitate to adumbrate Sailosi because he can only be imagined as a character through sources that reflect the official perspectives of both colonial and indigenous hierarchies and that necessarily distance him from rationality and emphasize his false positions. For this reason, I have imagined a succession of narratives rather than the creations of actors. Sailosi's understanding of his own actions remains beyond the vision of this account, just as it has always remained beyond the logic of the colonial schemes, which sought to legislate and discipline indigenous dissent.

Let me now make a long temporal jump to consider a story, or rather a set of observations implying a story, which has some currency in Noikoro. I do not claim that all Fijians, even there, see things in the terms described; if the military coup had a single positive consequence, perhaps it was that it made it impossible to refer to "the Fijian view" in such a unitary and politically decided manner.

Noikoro people do not, so far as I have established, tell stories about Sailosi and the Number 8 event particularly. It must be recalled that this was merely one of a long sequence of "disturbances" and revivals of proscribed ritual activities and among those that were most rapidly suppressed. Proscribed "heathen practices" are now understood to belong essentially to one class, whereas the individuals referred to are mainly much more prominent leaders such as Navosavakadua, the Tuka priest, and Apolosi, the leader of the Viti Kabani mentioned above.

The political and anticolonial aspect of their practices scarcely features in most accounts—which is not surprising, because the colonial presence itself is scarcely present in any local historical understanding. Although these facts of Fijian history are well known through school education as well as other contexts, neither Fiji's cession to Britain in 1874 nor independence in 1970 are often alluded to. So far as the latter is concerned, this is understandable, because the postcolonial state has only sustained the inequities of resource distribution and representation that developed earlier: there is a sense of continuity over the whole postwar period rather than any great change around 1970. On the other hand, the earlier social transformation from pagan warrior society is represented exclusively as a consequence of "taking the *sulu*"—that is, conversion to Christianity—which, as the phrase and certain narratives indicate, is seen to have been an uncompelled voluntary act. Associated changes over the same period—such as the concentration of settlements —are represented as outcomes of positive local choice rather than external imposition (Thomas 1990a).

The elements of a story adduced here arose from a number of conversations in Korolevu, in the Noikoro District, but I have particular reason to recall a very long discussion that took place on the cement verandah of one of the village's few concrete block houses. This was a male group, and as usual we were drinking kava. I think it went on until 4:00 A.M., and normally that sort of thing numbed my brain to such an extent that I could hardly listen to what was said in a language in which I was in fact semifluent. But on this occasion I was so intrigued by the renderings of a ritual system that had supposedly been displaced 113 years earlier, and some other matters, that I felt alert and scarcely tired at all.

We had begun by discussing religious practices among Malays and Australian Aborigines. The Noikoro men were interested in the latter because I had given people some picture books featuring the Australian *taukei*, or 'indigenous owners of the land';[34] knowledge of the former arose from some men's experience in the campaign against the Communists in the 1950s. One man had in fact seen a few Aborigines while briefly at an airbase in Queensland en route to Malaya, as it then was, but he claimed that the Aborigines had been so terrified of the Fijian soldiers that they ran away. A direct analogy was made between the situations of ethnic Fijians and indigenous Malays: the latter also have a strong hold on custom but are weak in the path of money. These comparisons depend upon a perception of a proportionate relationship between customary strength and inability in commerce, which carries a heavy political burden in Fiji (cf. Thomas 1990b).

The stories that emerged concerning Navosavakadua, Apolosi, and certain more local prophets were variations upon those widely told in Fiji, or at least on Viti Levu, and dealt with miraculous acts, some of which had close Christian parallels. The fish bones Navosavakadua left over turned into whole fish; his taro leavings turned into whole tubers. There were many attempts to kill him. At Rotuma the king heard that attempts to get rid of him had been unsuccessful, so he called Navosavakadua to his house. As Navosavakadua stepped across the threshold, the king fired a pistol directly at his chest. When the smoke cleared, Navosavakadua, unhurt, said, "Yes? What did you want to see me about?" The sense of some of these stories turns purely on the miraculous. At Nukuilau, Apolosi once took a machete and cut a cat in half; the head was here and the back legs and tail there. Then he put it back together and it ran off, alive as before. He could also kick over a full kava bowl and it would be full again when it was placed upright. The power of these men was such that the possibility of their still being alive is widely entertained. Navosavakadua is said to have gone to rest. He was dressed and wrapped up in mats and placed in a coffin, and the house was then sealed for three days. When it was opened for his burial, the people found the coffin broken open and the mats scattered; the priest had vanished. Of Apolosi it is also said, "*si cola tu e kia*," 'he lives still'.

It would be surprising, of course, if names like these were not drawn into stories about singular power, but the motivation of these narratives seems somewhat more specific. The fact that the capacities that are alluded to are distinctly mystical and indigenous becomes explicit in comparative statements concerning ritual activities at *nanaga* sites:

White people could fly with machines, but up at that place the old people [*na tuqwaqwa*] flew without machines. That was where the priest gave the warriors the *mana*. If you were sitting by the river and there was a mango right up there in the tree, your arm would detach itself, fly up and pick it, and then be joined back to your body.[35]

A similar contrast between powers is sometimes manifest in statements concerning healing: prayers said over kava in the spirit house[36] had the same efficacy as the technical medicine of white people and are represented as a direct indigenous equivalent to it. Now, however, because the church is strong, these activities, and undesirable counterparts such as sorcery, cannot persist: "now everyone respects machines."

These people thus portray themselves as having moved from a condition of former parity with whites, based on qualitatively different kinds of power, to a situation of asymmetry. The transformation has both positive and negative features: the mutual implication of the church, kinship, sentiment and hierarchy is—for the majority—unambiguously good, and in fact such institutions are central to Fijian ethnic pride and the conviction that their customary sociality embodies more mutual care and practical Christianity than the way of life of white foreigners. On the other hand, the people of Viti Levu interior have a strong sense of their own poverty with respect to foreigners, Indians, and certain other Fijians. Whenever one is engaged in repetitive kinds of work connected with cash crops, people remark upon the laboriousness of weeding or planting by hand—"Overseas you have machines to do this. Here our machines are our hands!"

This may appear to take us some way from the question of the representation of figures such as Sailosi and Apolosi and the movements with which they were associated, and I have in fact argued that there are disconnections in contemporary historical consciousness. But just as stories about *mana* are recontextualized specifically as expressions of endogenous Fijian vitalizations of divine power, the political movements need not be conspicuous in contemporary views because their force has been transposed to another domain. I noted above that the commitment to custom—which is paradigmatically expressed in very costly ceremonial feasts and presentations connected with marriage, death, and so on—is understood to be directly related to weakness in the field of commerce. On one occasion in the midst of a ceremony a man remarked to me on the splendid abundance of exchange valuables—pots, mats, and so on—and in the next breath said, "In Fiji for us it is difficult. We are poor." The point is also established, so to speak, by the stereotypical perception of Fiji-Indians as individualists without real kinship but as efficacious in business. The political resonance of the polarity however also emerges in disputes between Fijians about custom and commerce; at a cultural level, it clearly makes possible a reversal of values and a rejection of what is selectively identified as custom, as I shall show.

The most extreme example of this was the Bula Tale ('Live Again') movement of the early 1960s, led by Apimeleki Ramatau Mataka, a former medical clerk. This was represented as a "Communist" movement, although its striking feature was a precise reversal of all of the key symbols of the Fijian customary system. The use of kava and presentations of whale teeth in marriages and mortuary ceremonies were abolished; large-scale marriages and betrothals, which are now elsewhere absolutely central to the perception of the way of the land, were replaced by a strictly private exchange of vows—"there should be no feasting." Even internal domestic hierarchy in eating—which, as Toren (1988) among other anthropologists has pointed out, is central to the daily spatial and experiential recreation of hierarchy—was rejected: "everyone eats together in a common dining house . . . everyone eats the same sort of food" (*Fiji Times*, 12 August 1961; see the appendix, this chapter). And although village people in 1988 were conspicuously reluctant to use clinics and hospitals in the absence of a real emergency, Apimeleki said that "when a member is ill, we don't tinker with Fijian cures but send him or her to hospital for treatment" (ibid.).

This can be understood as a manifestation of the broader process of objectification and codification of culture in the form of *kastom* or *kastam* ('custom' in Solomons pijin, Vanuatu bislama, and New Guinea Tok Pisin) in the Solomons and Vanuatu, and the local variants of the "Pacific way" in Tonga, Samoa, and elsewhere (cf. Thomas n.d.).[37] "Customs," "traditional culture," and related labels do not refer merely to a set of beliefs and practices that happens to have persisted over a long period, but to a selective construct defined partly in opposition to foreign ways or intrusions.[38] Particular customs, such as widow strangling in Fiji or *suttee* in India, may acquire novel significance as emblems of a resistant non-Christian or anticolonial regime. The practices or attitudes that become significant may obviously not be "traditional" at all in the sense of being continuous with past practice. Codifications of this kind have frequently been central to affirmations of national or local identity, but it is not necessarily the case that objectified cultures are positively upheld as resources to be preserved and employed. Once a set of practices and institutions has been named, the name can be displaced or rejected.

The Nadroga movement was not a bizarre exception but merely a strong expression of something inevitably generated within neo-traditional Fijian culture, which is manifested all the time in more or less conspicuous and significant forms. For instance, an Assemblies of God woman whom I met on a bus attributed the fact that her marriage had broken up to its traditional "arranged" character (as she put it in English). It hardly needs to be reiterated that such an observation depends upon the naming of customs that did not formerly signify totalities of any kind, let alone a restrictive communal order.

It is rather surprising that one review of *The Real Life of Alejandro Mayta* saw the book as "strip[ping] bare self-indulgent insurrection and show[ing] its descent into squalid criminality" (Pickering 1986:30). Although the essentially self-parodying character of Trotskyist sects can hardly pass undisclosed, there is rather an insistence upon the point that Mayta's action has undergone a historic if not a moral vindication. That is, the transformation of circumstances reveals in what was essentially marginal and politically unrealistic the germination of political reactions and disputes that now surround us. Vargas Llosa constantly refers to the fact that Mayta was trying to act as if the world then was the way it has become: then "the things that are happening now would seem impossible"; "Mayta was twenty-five years too early with his plans" and so on (1986:152, 169, chs. 6 and 7 passim). In the same sense, before 1987, this essay would have lacked the truth it now possesses. How could I have imagined when I first began to research this that someone actually would change the name of the governor, that all political definitions would be contested, that Fiji, or at least urban Fiji, would become one of those tense places where soldiers are constantly seen but where violence ceases to be policed, where it has instead become an undefinable fact of daily life. There is an unknowable incidence of overt political harassment and assault, which is perhaps relatively small, but also a marked increase of violence that is merely criminal in one sense but entirely enabled by new political circumstances and categories in another. The climate in Fiji is quite revolutionary in that many poorer men simply no longer accept the constituted distinctions that restrained them from seizing property in the past. This is not to suggest that the present wave of urban violence and sexual violence is in any sense politically productive or progressive, but merely to point out that order, hierarchy, and class privilege are contested to an unprecedented degree.

One claim about the historic significance of movements such as the Tuka and the Viti Kabani, as well as later cases like Apimeleki's Bula Tale, has been made by sociologists supportive of the Fiji Labour party, which was formed in 1985, elected in coalition with the Indian National Federation party in April 1987, and overturned in a military coup on 14 May that year. The argument concerning the past and future basis for its support has been that there has been a tradition of dissent from the conjuncture of chiefly and colonial rule, and its transformation into the Alliance government, that was dominated by chiefs and marked by a strong probusiness orientation. In this view, various earlier movements stand as the precursors to a class-based multiracial protest that comes to fruition in the formation of the party and its political triumph: the coup represents essentially a reaction on the part of an embattled elite that refused to surrender power.[39]

There is clearly much truth in this, as a history for the present; but it is important to recall that the reasons why the coup was perpetrated by a certain group cannot be identified with the reasons why it was generally supported. This permits disclosure of another way in which the present is prefigured in the millenarian narratives.

The early twentieth-century movements certainly did entail commoner protest, but this often took a nationalist form. One of Sailosi's prophesies was that Europeans and Indians alike would be expelled from Fiji;[40] this is echoed in much more recent marginal charismatic churches, such as the Congregation of the Poor (Rokotuiviwa 1985: 182), and rather disables any link with a politically sophisticated struggle based on a common front. The recontextualization offered here stresses that some people were positive about both Colonel (now General) Rabuka and deposed Prime Minister Bavadra; they saw positive elements in Labour and in the coup that was seen to displace both the Alliance and Labour. And at certain times, such as around the second coup, it actually was the case that the old Alliance leadership was completely marginalized by a coalition between the military and (nationalist) Taukei movement people, who had either never been part of, or were alienated from, the Alliance and the old government.

This reaction is explicable if the significance of dissent from tradition is appreciated. "Tradition" represents a social order having a range of extremely desirable features, but is proportionate with Fijian poverty. The dichotomized view does not map at all directly the complex interpenetration of ceremonial activities and cash cropping but has motivated a very extensive discussion since the coup about the necessity, and difficulties, of bringing Fijians into commerce. This debate, which has actually been far more important than argument about constitutional and juridicopolitical restructuring, has featured an enormous amount of contradiction and ambivalence, and the extreme anticustom option—which I have traced through certain adoptions of Seventh-day Adventism, and which was most conspicuous in the Bula Tale case— does not necessarily have an especially wide following.[41]

The present thus amounts to an expression and enlargement of the Fiji that was manifested in Sailosi's and Apolosi's political theater much earlier this century. In its stronger form this conception seeks a recovery of power on the part of indigenous people and their priests against the foreigner-chiefs who abuse colonial or bureaucratic privilege and a range of actual foreigners, including Indians. Because there is at once a commitment to custom and an interest in material prosperity, which is perceived to be disabled by it, few can opt for the categorical rejection of hierarchy with which real economic advancement might be identified. But there is above all a sense that the tensions of the neotraditional order cannot be contained. Hence, though figures such as the high chief and administrator Ratu Sukuna are represented as the visionary architects of social compromise and the modern Fijian nation in official history, Apolosi and Sailosi perhaps always had a sharper sense of the fractures in the edifice.

As a genre, biographies inevitably establish or restate the importance of their subjects. That is a convention that I do not resist here. But the story of Sailosi is intended to do more than disorient the conventional histories and anthropologies of Fiji. In *Crime and Custom*, Malinowski noted that the binding force of customary reciprocity was sometimes illustrated inversely in the ostracism of partly assimiliated natives: "Test cases are supplied nowadays, when a number of natives through laziness, eccentricity, or a non-conforming spirit of enterprise, have chosen to ignore the obligations of their status and have become automatically outcasts and hangers-on to some white man or other" (1926: 42). I have already noted that the neotraditional codification of culture in forms such as *kastom* or the Fijian way always permits certain forms of selective rejection, which often embody precisely a "non-conforming spirit of enterprise" of the kind mentioned. But this kind of cultural perversity has been engaged in by too many communities and is too closely connected with cult activities and prior social divisions for it to be regarded as an idiosyncratic nonthing, an exception proving the rule. From an anthropological perspective, the fact that a young Fijian man might say to me in a bar in town that "tradition is a lot of shit" means almost nothing; the complaint of the Assemblies of God woman about arranged marriage means almost nothing; such people are educated, speak English, and are not Fijian to the same extent as the old men in the village who told those other stories I have used. But the associations between these statements could lead to a different investigation, which deals precisely with this sort of abuse of the idea of culture. The forms of renaming discussed here at once permit the codification and subversion of hierarchies and customs, and the parodying and appropriation of new religions. That is the process through which the cultural history of the present is being invented and contested.

Appendix

The Bula Tale Movement

This reproduces a 1961 newspaper article concerning this movement, which expresses particularly clearly the manner in which dissent and sociopolitical innovation depend upon the selective constitution and rejection of "Fijian customs."

NEW WAY OF LIFE IN FOUR VILLAGES

Four villages in Nadroga have formed a co-operative society under the leadership of Apimeleki Ramatau Mataka, a former clerk in the Medical Department. Among other things, they have done away with traditional Fijian customs and with orthodox Christianity.

Apimeleki told a *Fiji Times* reporter that the co-operative was a "government of its own" and all laws were made by the management committee. He criticized Fijian laws and said that most of them should be abolished. Apimeleki said that members of the co-operative society still believe in Jesus Christ, but they have stopped the "practice of worshipping."

The village church at the headquarters of the group, Emuri, has been converted into living quarters.

Other villages in the society are Togovere, Kabisi, and Vagadra. The use of the tabua and yaqona and feasts in connection with weddings and deaths have been abolished. Apimeleki said that some people had called him a Communist. "I am not ashamed of my actions," he said.

NAME CHANGED

The name of the co-operative society, which was previously Dranilami (Lamb's Blood), has been changed to Bula Tale ['Live Again']. Apimeleki explained that when a couple wished to marry it is their doing, and only their parents should be there. When vows are exchanged they go home and live together. There is no feasting. Yaqona drinking and the presentation of the root in ceremonies have been abolished.

"I am the only man in the co-operative society who is allowed to touch yaqona, because I travel from place to place on business and sometimes have dealings with chiefs," he said.

"When a member is ill, we don't tinker with Fijian cures but send him or her to hospital for treatment," he added.

SOCIETY'S PRINCIPLE

The principle of the society, he said, was to live equally.

"What I eat, my wife and children must also eat.

"In the Fijian custom the man of the house eats first and eats the best of the food. Whatever is left over is eaten by his wife and children.

"The system employed in the member villages at present is that everyone eats together in a common dining house."

"The cooking is done by turn, and everyone eats the same sort of food."

CO-OPERATIVE STORES

"Nobody buys anything. We have co-operative society stores in each village and if any one requires anything like toilet gear etc, he just goes to the store and asks for it," Apimeleki said. When a lali is sounded at 6 AM each day the men go out and clean up the villages. The villages' activities begin at 6 AM and end at 9 PM, the official bedtime. The men work in the plantations during the day. The produce is sold at the society's various markets which are in the various centres in the north-west. Early this year they bought a lorry to cart the produce. Apimeleki said that the minimum return after produce is sold on Saturday is £50, but they have received as much as £89.

TWO PARTS

"The money is split into two parts in the first instance. One part goes to the bank and the second part is distributed equally among the four member villages," Apimeleki said. "This money is also used for emergencies like sickness."

He said he has stopped members of the society from taking part in communal work, like building bures in villages. "We contribute our share in money," he said. "That is one reason why I have been called a Communist. It does not worry me. All I am interested in is the success of my members."

Apimeleki has plans for the society's own school, dispensary and clinic. These, when they are built, will be open to the public as well, he said.

(*Fiji Times*, 12 August 1961;
reproduced with permission)

Notes

Acknowledgments. This paper draws upon research in the National Archives of Fiji; the Mitchell Library, Sydney; in Korolevu village, Nadroga-Navosa province; and discussions with many others in various parts of Fiji. I am indebted to all those who helped, and to Margaret Jolly and Aletta Biersack for suggestions. Klaus Neumann's work has been an inspiration.

1. Both these discursive entities are obviously very diverse. What is said claims to reflect the form of conventional work in both disciplines but must necessarily be uncharitable and inaccurate with respect to various innovative and subversive perspectives. The generalized polemic engaged in here might however be defended on the grounds that a succession of dramatic paradigm shifts have not in fact altered underlying features of anthropological rhetoric (for partial justification see Thomas 1989a). A similar proposition would probably be less true of history.

2. This has been especially contentious since the military coup in 1987, when an interim administration attempted to impose strict observance by decree. Shifting government opinion and pressure from the churches themselves later led to this being relaxed, but an intransigent faction within the Methodist church then set up roadblocks in an attempt to restrict movement and preclude any commercial activities on Sundays; the defiant attitude of certain prominent church leaders and their numerous supporters came close to creating a crisis of state authority. The decree was initially directed mainly against Fiji-Indians, but the subsequent dispute was essentially intra-Fijian and did magnify old tensions between Adventists and others.

3. The only ethnography I am aware of that was actually based upon work with Adventists is Hviding 1988. This fails to substantiate the notion that Adventists are money people with no culture.

4. Dissent was not, however, restricted to that period. More localized protests and "revivals" of non-Christian religious practices have appeared sporadically in many parts of Fiji since, and earlier manifestations of syncretistic and inspirational religion may be regarded to some extent as historically continuous with contemporary urban charismatic sects.

5. On that point, this essay inverts the novel by sustaining through the contrivances of scholarship the claim that this is history and leaves it to critics to circle it off as mere fiction.

6. In an innovative and reflective analysis of history making the Tolai (Papua New Guinea) case, Neumann also argues for the displacement of "History" by "many histories" but conceives of this politically and critically rather than relativistically: "This is not a mind game. It is an attempt to explore

what lies beyond the reconstruction of the past as practiced by mainstream historiography" (1988:223).

7. This became one of the textbook cases for comparative cult studies (Worsley 1957), although the "cargo" element, allegedly characteristic of many Pacific movements, was virtually absent. For a reappraisal, see Kaplan 1988.

8. Colo North Provincial Council Minutes, 15 April 1896 (National Archives of Fiji. Except where otherwise noted, all source material cited below can be found in the National Archives of Fiji).

9. These were *tūraga ni koro*, *buli*, and *roko tui*, respectively.

10. Joske later changed his name to Brewster because of fears concerning anti-German sentiment; he was the author of a book of reminiscences and ethnography concerning the "hill tribes" with which he had worked (Brewster 1922); this is one of few accessible sources for the anthropology and history of the area.

11. Colo North Provincial Council Minutes, 20 May 1897; CSO (Colonial Secretary's Office Minute Paper) 1460/1898; letter from A. B. Brewster (Joske) to Spence, 26 April 1918, Fiji Museum, document 24 (bbb); Brewster 1922:253–54.

12. Many elements of the colonial project—descriptive specification through censuses, codification of customs, village regulation and consolidation— were motivated by a symbolic effort to make Fijian society as a totality visible. For elaboration, see Thomas 1990a and 1989b:48–52.

13. CSO 1460/1998.

14. CSO 4625/1902.

15. CSO 2018/1918, 6336/1918; Willis to Small, 25 March 1918, F/1/1918.

16. Transcribed in Sauvakarua, Navatusila District, in 1988.

17. Most of the Fijian words quoted in this article are in standard Fijian (derived from the Bauan dialect). Viji is a western interior equivalent of Viti (Fiji).

18. The Fijian term is actually ordinal: "the Seventh church."

19. It is not clear whether the food taboos and prohibitions on drinking and smoking, which distinguished Adventism, were also adopted.

20. CSO 6336/1918.

21. Ibid.

22. Ibid.

23. See, for example, Colo North Provincial Council Minutes for 1902, CSO 5837/1902 and CSO 5471/1902, in which particular emphasis is placed by the witness and prosecution alike upon putting "down the names of people."

24. *Fiji Times* (hereafter *FT*), 27 March 1918.

25. *FT*, 28 March 1918.

26. On the extensive use of Fijian words in English discourse in the colony, see Siegel 1987, especially appendix C.
27. *FT*, 27 March 1918.
28. *FT*, 10 April 1918.
29. For instance, the Catholic Fiji-language history referred to him as *edua na tamata ulu ca* (Anon. 1936:302).
30. Chambers to Small, 25 May 1918, F/1/1918.
31. CSO 6043/1918.
32. Op. cit., Chambers to Small.
33. A recent official Adventist history celebrates Pauliasi's role in obtaining conversions, and noted that "the European missionaries . . . were quick to realise that the key to the spread of Seventh-day Adventism in Fiji was the indigenous worker" (Dixon n.d. [1985]:202). This was perhaps even more true than the writer realized. The spread of the SDA in Fiji can be traced through the religious statistics in the *Blue Books*: it was not mentioned at all before 1909, but between 1909 and 1917 it claimed between five and six hundred adherents. In 1918 the effect of the defections was that this rose to just under seventeen hundred; around two thousand were claimed between 1920 and 1930. Catholicism was also an option for those who aimed to express some kind of protest, and chiefs often complained about the activities of Catholic teachers or priests (e.g., CSO 2973/1889). A connection with dissent and millennial activities was often also manifest: "Samuela has gone over because he considers Roman Catholicism antagonistic to the Government and consequently so to his chief and because he has a grudge against the Wesleyans for giving information in the recent Tuka prosecutions" (CSO 1011/1892). Although the government did not feel it could do much to prevent people changing denominations, missionaries required passes to move around; and in discontented areas such as Colo North, these seem to have been generally denied (e.g., CSO 1956 /1892).
34. The word used in this context was *taukei*, 'owners of the land'. This refers contextually to the occupants of an area as opposed to a group of visitors (and often the hosts versus the receivers of a feast); but since the political instability just before the May 1987 coup, the word has been politicized as an ethnic category equivalent to "Fijian," especially in the nationalist rhetoric of the now-fragmented Taukei movement. Parallels between indigenous Fijians and other 'native owners' such as the New Zealand Maori have been made and disputed.
35. This paraphrases several statements. Apart from those made on the occasion discussed, these were often reiterated in explanations of former activities at the *nanaga* ritual sites and in spirit houses.

36. *Beto*; elsewhere *bure kalou*.
37. This term, meaning 'custom', is used in all the pijin languages of the South Pacific (Bislama, Solomons Pijin, and Tok Pisin). For a series of analyses, see Keesing and Tonkinson, 1982. Note that I do not claim that things such as *fa'a Samoa* ('Samoan way') are merely consequences of colonialism. It is well established historically that certain conceptions of distinct Tongan, Fijian, and Samoan customs existed earlier—as they must have, in some form, for as long as these closely related societies have interacted. However, I would insist that the modern constructs carrying these labels have been completely revalorized around meanings that are mostly specifically in opposition to "foreign" values (themselves selectively understood and substantivized [Thomas n.d.]). In the Fijian case, the oppositional structure is of course implicated in the difficult relations with Fiji-Indians.
38. For a useful discussion of objectification in quite a different context, see Cohn 1987.
39. See especially Robertson and Tamanisau (1988); but for an important earlier discussion, see Durutalo (1985), which contains extended discussion of various protests and the Nadroga movement.
40. Willis to Small, 25 March 1918, in F/1/1918.
41. Dissent of some kind from the dominant chiefly Methodist Fijian hierarchical order is reflected in present patterns of religious affiliation: according to the 1986 census, of 329,305 Fijians, 244,381 were Methodist, 45,385 were Catholic, 13,269 were Seventh-day Adventist, 12,814 were Assemblies of God, and 9,713 were "other Christians," which must include Jehovah's Witnesses and various local charismatic sects such as the Congregation of the Poor. It is certainly not to be assumed that all or even most non-Methodists are in some sense opposed to the chiefly system and the official constructions of Fijian custom; but substantial numbers of Assemblies people, Adventists, and "other Christians" could be expected to be following another path. There are also a few hundred Fijian Hindus and Muslims (Population Census 1986, Parliament of Fiji, Parliamentary Paper no. 4 of 1988, 1:100).

References Cited

Unpublished works, theses, etc. are cited in the Notes. All of these archival sources are in the National Archives of Fiji (Suva) unless otherwise specified.

Anonymous
    1936   *Na Ekelesia Katolika mai Viti*. Lyons: Emmanuel Vitte.

Brewster, A. B.
1922   *The Hill Tribes of Fiji*. London: Seeley, Service & Co.

Cohn, Bernard
1987   The Census, Social Structure and Objectification in South
     Asia. In *An Anthropologist Among the Historians and Other Es-*
     says. Delhi:Oxford University Press.

Dening, Greg
1988   *History's Anthropology: The Death of William Gooch*. A.S.A.O.
     Special Publication no. 2. Lanham, Md.: University Press of
     America.

Dixon, R.
n.d.[1985].
     The Pacific Islands. In *Seventh-day Adventists in the*
     South Pacific, 1885–1985, ed. Noel Clapham. Warburton,
     Australia: Signs Publishing Co.

Dunkerley, J.
1987   Mario Vargas Llosa: Parables and Deceits. *New Left Review*
     162:112–22.

Durutalo, Simeone
1985   Internal Colonialism and Unequal Regional Development:
     The Case of Western Viti Levu, Fiji. M.A. thesis, School of
     Social and Economic Development, University of the South
     Pacific.

Hviding, Edvard
1988   Sharing Paths and Keeping Sides: Managing the Sea in
     Marovo Lagoon, Solomon Islands. Thesis, University of
     Bergen.

Kaplan, Martha
1988   Land and Chiefs and the New White Men: A Reconsidera-
     tion of the Fijian Tuka Movement. Ph.D. dissertation, De-
     partment of Anthropology, University of Chicago.

Keesing, Roger, and Robert Tonkinson, eds.
1982   Reinventing Traditional Culture: The Politics of Kastom in
     Island Melanesia. In, Reinventing Traditional Culture: The
     Politics of Kastom in Island Melanesia, ed. R. M. Keesing
     and R. Tonkinson. *Mankind*, 13.

Macnaught, Timothy J.
1982   *The Fijian Colonial Experience*. Canberra: Research School of
     Pacific Studies, Australian National University.

Malinowski, Bronislaw
1926   *Crime and Custom in Savage Society*. London: Routledge.

Neumann, Klaus
1988   Not the Way It Really Was: Constructing the Tolai Past.

Ph.D. dissertation, Department of Pacific and Southeast Asian History, Research School of Pacific Studies, Australian National University.

Pickering, P.
1986   A Closet Revolutionary [review of *The Real Life of Alejandro Mayta*]. *New Society*, 3 October 1986:30–31.

Robertson, R., and A. Tamanisau
1988   *Fiji: Shattered Coups.* Sydney: Pluto Press.

Rokotuiviwa, Paula
1985   The Congregation of the Poor (Fiji). In *New Religious Movements in Melanesia*, ed. C. Loeliger and G. Trompf. Suva/Port Moresby: University of the South Pacific and University of Papua New Guinea.

Siegel, Jeff
1987   *Language Contact in a Plantation Environment: A Socio-Linguistic History of Fiji.* Cambridge: Cambridge University Press.

Thomas, Nicholas
1989a   *Out of Time: History and Evolution in Anthropological Discourse.* Cambridge: Cambridge University Press.

1989b   Material Culture and Colonial Power: Ethnological Collecting and the Establishment of Colonial Rule in Fiji. *Man* (N.S.) 24:41–56.

1990a   Sanitation and Seeing: The Creation of State Power in Early Colonial Fiji. *Comparative Studies in Society and History* 32: 149–70.

1990b   Regional Politics, Ethnicity and Custom in Fiji. *Contemporary Pacific* 2:131–46.

n.d.   Substantivization and Anthropological Discourse: The Transformation of Practices into Institutions in Neotraditional Pacific Societies. In *Tradition and History in Melanesian Anthropology*, ed. James W. Carrier.

Toren, Christina
1988   Making the Present, Revealing the Past: The Mutability and Continuity of Tradition as Process. *Man* (N.S.) 23:696 –717.

Vargas Llosa, Mario
1986[1984]
      The Real Life of Alejandro Mayta. Translation of *La Historia de Mayta*, 1984. London: Faber & Faber.

Worsley, Peter
1957   *The Trumpet Shall Sound.* London: McGibbon & Kee.

8. New Ireland Is Shaped Like a Rifle and We Are at the Trigger

The Power of Digestion in Cultural Reproduction

Roy Wagner

Production, like reproduction, only makes sense when counterpoised against some form of termination: obsolescence, consumption, death. Otherwise, as Gregory Bateson eloquently observed, "the shit comes up the floor" (Lipset 1980:301). And perhaps because our own capitalist ethic has put us up to the ears in the stuff, in one analogous form or another, or has made us, so to speak, consume it, it is interesting to consider whether the issue of cultural reproduction can be negotiated in reverse, in terms of consumption and death. These are conflated in the mortuary feasting of the Usen Barok of south-central New Ireland, a performative enactment that serves as the constitutive core of the ethic that they call *kastam* and that has provided a brilliantly successful format for cultural reproduction.

Kastam is the term, obviously adapted from English and in fact widely disseminated by official encouragement, that Usen Barok use for their traditional culture. Although it may be used somewhat indiscriminately in reference to traditional usage, its more pointed and specific reference is to the taboos and protocols involved in kin relations and feasting. Cultural reproduction concerns the manner and means by which the concepts and usages of a culture are carried forth in time and reconstituted. I shall argue here that it is *kastam* in the specific sense of mortuary feasting—negotiation through consumption and death—that fosters cultural reproduction, as it serves as the principal means for the validation of claims.

Usen speakers constitute the less numerous of two Barok dialects, perhaps six or seven hundred among some two thousand Barok. The language is Austronesian, and the Usen are its southernmost speakers, situated just north of Namatanai at the narrowest part of New Ireland. They would like yams to be their staple food, in fact grow and eat more sweet potatoes, but subsist largely on the cash cropping of coconut. Usen speakers maintain that they are the true Barok, because they keep *kastam* rigorously and are relatively unaffected by the tide of alcoholism and social dancing sweeping down from the north. This claim is not always contested by speakers of the northern, or Nabo, dialect.

Usen have largely readopted the traditional settlement pattern of small hamlets, with an average of about fifteen inhabitants per hamlet (Wagner 1986:17–19). Six or seven of these hamlets make up a village. A hamlet is invariably centered upon one or more men's houses, *tauns*. A *taun* is sponsored and built, or reconsecrated, by a man (in rare cases a woman), who acquires some claim to the title of *orong* ('big man') in the process. Membership and service in the *taun* is determined according to an ideology of matrilineal descent, which also provides the rationale for linking *tauns* and their memberships into clans, *bung marapun*, and the clans into two exogamous moieties, Tago, or sea hawk, and Malaba, sea eagle. Barok will generally identify themselves through this formal affiliation.

I have approached the issue of social structure in this way advisedly, for the *taun* seems to be the constitutive element in establishing the authority and claims of the local 'branch', *agana*, of the clan. Besides a common name, a clan defines itself by three elements: its *tauns*, and especially the *taun* of its *orong*; its assemblage of *mangin*, the traditional shell-disk wealth, used in marriage; and its *tadak* or *masalai*, a tutelary spirit that has the power to change appearance and is thus immortal. Some, or all, of these elements may be individuated at the *agana*, or lineage, level, so that the distinction between lineage and clan is often blurred. In addition, local branches of clans belonging to the same moiety may enter a relationship of symbolically "pooling" their *mangin*, forging a formal link of identity between them.

These are, of course, symbolic or conceptual characteristics of the clan; and a clan in this sense is a kind of meaning, or a way of talking about things. So, too, is cultural validation, and in fact the manner in which Barok *kastam* achieves validation is intrinsically a matter of meaning, though it emphasizes the perceptual and experiential more than the verbal (Wagner 1986:153–54). Although it has likewise dealt with meanings, social anthropology has traditionally focused its attention on the *group*: a set of people who hold some sort of property corporately. Its interests, that is to say, have been institutional, political, and sociological. But there are reasons, apart from my attention to symbolism and validation, for why the "group" proves inappropriate as a focus here. First of all, a clan is rarely a group—it is typically dispersed among many villages or even among linguistic groupings, though it may assemble for an important feast. Secondly, the viable "group" that inhabits a hamlet and manages a *taun* is quite small—usually a sibling set or two. And although this is the level of political motivation and effective property disposal, it is also a level at which patrilateral inheritance is as distinctive and significant (a sibling set, in this region of virtually nonexistent polygyny, shares a father and a mother) as matrilineal. Thus the level at which corporateness counts most is also the level at which unilineality counts least.

The ideology of clan and *taun* is matrilineal and viripotestal; that of postmarital residence and family is virilocal and viripotestal, though statistically viri- and uxorilocality are about evenly divided (Wagner 1986:18–19). Landholdings, in the largest sense, are the concern of clans, but local holdings are managed and in many cases claimed by the lineage. The lineage is the locus of political interest, and the clan of lineal identity.

It is the moiety contrast that is generative of production, in the domestic mode, and of reproduction. The matrimoieties are exogamous, and the breach of exogamy is sanctioned by the declassing of offenders from kin designations and from polite society. Members of the respective moieties relate in three ways: affinity; in the *naluwinin* relationship between a man and the males of his father's matriline, marked by heavy joking and property confiscation; and as "fathers" (male and female) and the offspring of men (*nat*). It is the third of these, however, that gives the relation its ideological character and that colors the other two.

Each moiety claims its own matri-descendents and identifies their place in society, but it also claims paternity and inception of the other moiety. Your mother's people bore you and thus have a legitimate claim to authority over you, they say, but your father's people created and animated you, and that is something more, because they were under no obligation to do so. The relation to father, and especially his sisters, is emotionally charged and often sentimental; whatever a father deeds over to his children, their *nat-lo*, is inalienable. In effect, the claims of a moiety are a variant of the time-honored "what's mine is mine, and what's yours is negotiable." Marriage is frequently phrased in terms of a patrilateral idiom, as marriage with the father's sister or her daughter (though this is not realized in a genealogical sense; see Wagner 1986:92–97); the fierce *naluwinin* relationship involves those who stand in a potential holder–heir conflict over matri–patri-inheritance. In ethical terms, the relation of the moieties is summed up in the concept of *malum*. This is the ethic of forebearance: whatever is done to you by the father's people must be borne with easy grace and good humor, out of consideration for the selfless acts of paternal animation and nurturance. In the more general sense, moieties exist through the mutual nurturance of fatherhood; even in honoring its own substance, a mourning clan is implicated in *malum*, and so it becomes the generic ethic for mortuary feasting.

If the relation between moieties is the prime locus of engendering, the feast in the *taun* is generative of cultural validation. Every major change of status or transferal of property must be constituted by feasting; every step in *taun* construction must be marked by a major feast, with the killing of pigs, and every day spent in the *taun*'s cleaning or refurbishment, or spent in preparation for a major feast, requires the formalities of at least a perfunctory feast. The overall format of the feast is epitomized by the mortuary feast, and all elaborate feasts follow the mortuary protocol. The planting of the V-shaped entry stile, the *olaǧabo*,[1] or 'gate of the pig' (see Figure 20), is said, for instance, to be a burial, because the lower portion is interred in the ground.

A *taun* is ideally open and free to any male of any degree or affiliation; any man may shelter and sleep there as long as he wishes and will be fed. Any male is entitled to an equal and lavish portion of any feast held in the *taun*, and an atmosphere of easy fellowship and lack of

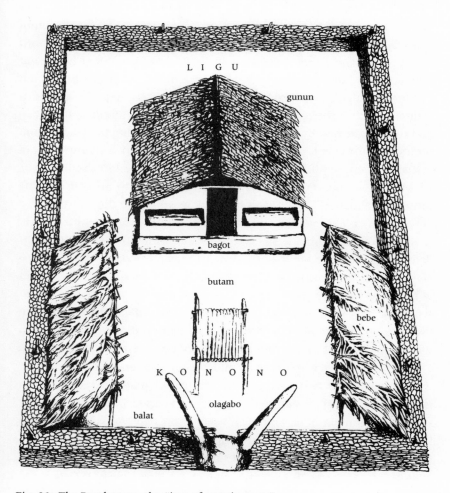

Fig. 20. The Barok taun, *the "icon of containment."*

strife is enjoined on pain of heavy fining and disgrace. Every object and space in and around the *taun* is subject to taboos or considerations of respect, and every stage of the feasting itself is the subject of a strict protocol and of careful, critical scrutiny by the participants. A feast progresses through a series of known stages, beginning with the display of its courses in the center of a containing square of feasters and proceeding through distribution and consumption of the first course of "refreshers," the purchase, cutting, and distribution of the pigs, with tubers. At the conclusion, the heads of the pigs are offered and presented to visiting big men, and cooked delicacies are awarded and sent to other *tauns*. A fine decorum prevails throughout, young men serving the diners on leaf plates, then removing the refuse, with studied briskness. Between the "refresher" course of green coconut and areca nut and the main course, and before the purchase and cutting of the pigs, a formal speech is made by the *orong* announcing the intent of the feast, and this is followed by volunteered speeches criticizing the staging and protocol of the event, generally scathing in their intent and implication.

It would not be difficult, even for someone steeped in the literature on Melanesia and versed in the lore of symbolism, to misconstrue the sense of "validation" as it relates to Barok feasting. For the "symbolism" at work here is experiential and performative rather than representative. A Barok feast is *not* made to "celebrate" or "formalize" the thing validated, as we might do in the case of a birthday party or on Thanksgiving Day. It is rather that the actions of the feast are themselves *constitutive of the thing validated*, that the validation is realized rather than represented. If this were not the case, it would be difficult to account for the painstaking attention to protocol, an attention that recalls the original sense of the (North American) Northwest Coast potlatch (Walens 1981:87–96). The easiest way to understand this sense of "validation" is to consider the two very general motifs or "matrix concepts" that Barok *orong* say are replicated endlessly in every aspect of their lives: *kolume*, or 'containment', and *gala*, 'elicitation'. *Kolume* is evidenced in the containment of a corpse in its ancestral ground, of an embryo in the womb, of a person in his or her moiety and clan, and, ritually, of a *taun* as the "icon of containment" (Wagner 1986: 153–54). *Gala* is exemplified by a thorn or erect penis, an angular tree-limb bearing fruit, the knife with which the festive pig is cut, and, ritually, by a rooted, nurturant tree.

The tendency to reduce these very general concretivities, parts of experience, as the Barok would have it, to representative symbols is the object of the most frequently voiced Barok adage: "words trick you." *Kolume* is *not* "female," *gala* is *not* "male," though gender, like lineality, counts among the many effects of their interaction. It is not difficult to find examples of male *kolume* (the *taun*) or of female *gala* (the taproot of a tree, downward pointing *gala*, is identified by Barok as the apical ancestress of a clan). But the unglossable character of these motifs merely serves to underline a much more important point: that their effects are to be realized perceptually and constitutively. The correct mode of elicitation is the *gala* of feasting, which "opens" the *kolume* of self-contained iconography experientially.

The nonrepresentational format of the *taun* is another instance: were the structure intended to "symbolize" a womb, a stomach, a tree, etc., nothing would have been simpler than to shape its contours accordingly. *Kolume* is a more comprehensive notion (*not* more "abstract," for its very essence is the imagistic *sense* of containment, exemplified in any form but the verbal). A *taun* consists of a stylized, single-room house, *gunun*, located roughly in the center of an imposing dry stone wall, *a balat*. The forecourt of the *taun*, framed by the carved tree-limb gate (*olaĝabo*) and the threshold log of the *gunun* (*a baĝot*), framed by *gala*, is the feasting area, *konono*. It contains the benches for the feasters and the half-pitch roof shelters, *bebe*, as well as the *butam*, the central table where food is arrayed. The rear court, *ligu*, is the "unmarked" *kolume* of burial; it has no gate, and the rear of the *gunun* has no door. The *gunun* itself, at the intersection of the two spaces, contains traditional heirlooms, shell wealth, and the trophies of previous feasts. The dead are sometimes buried beneath the floor, and the benches within the *gunun* are the preferred seating for the visiting *orong*. Thus the *taun*, within its stone enclosure, contains both the feasting and the dead, *gala* and *kolume*.

The *gala*, elicitative nurturance of feasting, is metonymized in Barok as *bet lulut* or *kurubo*, 'cutting pig'. It "opens" the iconography of *kolume* by imposing a temporal order, which is the order of experiencing or realizing this iconography as *a lolos*, 'power'. The order is the succession *kolume gala*-conflation of the two: it underlies the form of the individual feast as well as that of the order of the mortuary cycle itself. The individual feast, in each of its courses, begins with the display of the comestibles, surrounded by the feasters, leads to the cutting and/or distribution, and concludes with the consumption, the "nurturance that is containment."

Although Barok recognize many named varieties of feasts, differentiated for the most part in minor details, in terms of the iconic use of space three basic forms can be distinguished. These, in their temporal order as well as their content, correspond with the format for the individual course/feast, and their succession is that of the mortuary cycle. The first, which I shall call the "closed feast," is held on the day of death and up to the point of burial, when the body is entered into the containment of the ground. In the closed feast the food is provided by the moiety opposite to that of the *taun* (and the deceased). No food may be removed from the *taun*; even those who inadvertently leave while chewing will be fined. The cooked pigs are arrayed in the *konono* facing inward, toward the rear of the *taun*, and the distribution of the food must begin at the front and proceed inward. These feasts manifest *kolume*; the *taun* as a whole becomes *ligu*, as it were—food is received from the paternal moiety, as the deceased was nurtured by them, and this preferred nurturance is contained as the moiety's own.

The second form of feast, which manifests *gala* and is in fact called *goǥorup*—the 'cutting' or 'cutting the graveyard'—may ideally only be held after the corpse has decomposed. The food is provided by the host moiety, and food may be removed from the *taun* after the feast. Cooked pigs are arrayed facing outward, and the distribution of food proceeds from the rear forward. In the *goǥorop gala* is manifested, as the *kolume* of the *taun*, replete with the nurturance of the paternal moiety, now turns to its nurturant and begetting role.

The third and final form of feast turns from the *kolume* of the *taun* to the *gala* of the tree as its definitive icon; rather than being contained between the *baǥot* and *olaǥabo*, the "tree" of the *konono* portion of the *taun*, the feast now surrounds and contains the tree. Made to "finish all thought of the dead," the *kaba* is held at widely spaced intervals for cumulative numbers of the dead, or for very distinguished individuals. A *kaba* involves years of planning and extensive preparation; as we might suspect, there are two forms of *kaba*, the lesser (*gala*), or 'tree-branch' (*agana ya*), and the greater (*kolume*), or 'tree-base' (*una ya*). It is the latter form, associated with the installation of *orong*, that enacts the definitive conflation of *kolume* and *gala*. To understand how it does so, it is necessary to return to the nonspecificity of *kolume* and *gala*. For the two icons, *taun* and tree, exemplify respective horizontal and vertical alignments of the same image (a transformative schema that is found also in the *malagan* tradition practiced to the north of the Barok). The definitive transformation of the *una ya kaba* is to *invert* the tree, burying its upper (*gala*) half in the ground, and making use of its lower (*kolume*) half, or rootstock, as a feast table.

When the proper kind of tree is located, it is cut off about 6 feet from the ground, and the roots are followed and dug out of the ground, one by one. A feast is held as each major root is unearthed, and a large feast when the taproot is cut. The roots are trimmed to form a circle 6 feet or so in diameter, and the tree is then pulled into the village, with much ceremony and feasting, and set up. After much decoration and additional preparation of the tree, accompanied by daily feasting (the tree may be embellished with carving, and is festooned with strings of shell money), the image of the *kaba* takes form. Dead pigs for the feast are arrayed on top of the roots, with the neophyte *orong*, or *winawu*, standing atop the pigs, *in the position of the* (now severed) *taproot*. Around the base of the *kaba, at the place where the* (imaginary) *buried branches would break the surface of the ground*, nubile young women (*dawan*) sit on stylized tree forks.

Thus a *young* man, the neophyte *orong*, replaces the apical ancestress, whereas unmarried young women, the *dawan*, are imaged as "tree fruit" dangling upward from the inverted branches— in a position analogous to that of married men, who are spoken of as "tree fruit" nurturing other clans. The conflation of *kolume* and *gala* is complete: a contemporary "big man" is as much the "container" of his line as its original ancestress; young brides "nurture" other lines with their gift of containment. The containment of elicitation is the elicitation of containment.

If, in other words, gender, moiety, and moiety function are but *effects* of *gala* and *kolume*, a different disposition of *gala* and *kolume* can produce different effects. The "nurturance" of an *orong* as feast giver can contain the clan from a contemporary (rather than an ancestral) position; the containment of young women can be a gift, "nurturance" of the *nat* of other lines. Hence if, through the power of image transformation (*a lolos*) evidenced in the *kaba*, *kolume* and *gala* can be shown to be identical, the distinction between genders, moieties, and moiety functions collapses. The distinction is shown to be *controlled* by the *kaba* and by the feast giver, who thereby validates his position and power.

It would be difficult indeed to make an argument for the enactment of *kastam* as the workings of a "cold" culture, assimilating "event" to a timeless "structure." For the *kaba* itself is an event that dissolves the differentiation of "dual division" and any other kind of structure. Moreover, if we were to isolate a single point or "moment of truth" as the essence of the *kaba*, that point would hardly be a moment of frozen or suspended rational order. It would have to be the single instant of transformation, *diachrony* condensed to a point, instantaneous "history."

Now if fatherhood, *nat*, were primarily a matter of shared substance among the Barok, the demonstration of this tranformation, however experiential, would have little to do with it. But if we look closely at the father's role in procreation and nurturance, "substance" itself is rather peripheral. The term for semen (*a pege*)is largely used in contexts of blame or derogation: "look at what *your semen* (*a pege te nongon*; that is, 'your issue') just did!" Likewise a woman's menstrual blood is considered "dirty" and said to play no role in procreation. What is needed is "clean blood" (Wagner 1983:79). This is created through serial acts of intercourse, whereby the semen of the father acts upon the vaginal secretion (*a pege a une*, 'female semen'), to enact a transformation into clean blood, the conjoint product that forms the fetus. Hence it is that the father's contribution, like the mother's, is spoken of simply as "blood." A father begets by means of *gala*, eliciting his wife's *ability* to reproduce children, and hence eliciting the children. And the father's nurturance in providing food for his offspring has nothing to do with any imagined transferral of his substance; it is a matter of eliciting the containment (*kolume*) of the mother and her moiety.

Thus procreation is, for Barok, a further instantiation of the transformation met with in the *kaba*. And if an *orong* can be demonstrated to be equivalent to an apical ancestress, *gala* to *kolume*, then we can understand something of the force of *nat-lo*. For it is the *meaning* of the *kaba* that demonstrates that the elicitation of containment equals the containment of elicitation. Considering the exacting precision with which feasting is carried on, and the ethic of shame that sanctions it, the enactment of the *kaba* is rather like burning the Declaration of Independence and dynamiting the Washington Monument at the inauguration of a new president. In terms of our interest here, the *kaba* is the affirmation and enactment of antiproduction, the termination by which Barok negotiate cultural reproduction.

If the *kaba* were the only instance of such negation, we might well be justified in considering it a kind of captive denial, like Gluckman's rituals of rebellion, and the scalp of Durkheim, as well as the juridical wigs of British social anthropology, would be saved. But it is not. For it seems that the *taun*, that grounding point of validation and local settlement, icon of moiety, kinship, and social ideology, can be and often is alienated from the lineage, clan, and moiety whose dead it contains, at the whim of its sponsor.

A Barok *taun* is generally sponsored, that is, built or cared for, through the resources of one man, perhaps the eldest of a set of siblings. It is thus held somewhat more individually than land, which, if a traditional holding, is collective clan property. Owen Jessep, who has studied land tenure among the northern (Nabo) Barok, deals with land inheritance in terms of exchange. Usufructuary rights in the father's land among the Nabo may be obtained by a person's making a payment (*milenien*) to his father's matriclan upon his death, to compensate for the nurturance received from him. It is also sometimes possible for the Nabo Barok to acquire permanent rights by killing pigs at the father's mortuary feasts in a practice called *sebolep* (Jessep 1978:262 ff.). *Sebolep* is not practiced among the Usen, *milenien* payments are smaller and less formal (in fact, they are payable on the death of *either* parent; cf. Wagner 1986:65–66), and traditional land remains a difficult thing to alienate.

Not so a sponsored *taun*. A man among the Usen can deed over his *taun* to his begotten children as *nat-lo*, and as such it is incontestable. This had happened in 1974 to the *taun* at Bakan village with which I was later affiliated, was planned for another Bakan *taun*, and had occurred numerous times in nearby villages. It alienates many thousands of hours of labor from the founding matrilineage, over and above any *milenien* that might be paid, and alienates them from the incremental prestige of the site, its feasts, and its interred ancestors. All that is necessary is for the transference to be validated by a feast in the *taun*.

What this means is that the *taun* and the symbology of feasting, although they embody iconically the nurturance and containment of moiety, clan, and lineage, cannot be understood as merely a symbolic affirmation of social wholes or forces, matrilineal descent, or the corporate group. Ancestors exist in the generic; they ground and guarantee the *taun*, not the clan or moiety. It would seem that *kolume* and *gala, as generic powers*, are at once the means and the products of the *taun*, that validation constitutes this generic power for its purposes, that it is the social, rather than the power, that is contingent. What this means in broader terms is that Barok *kastam* is not bound to an archaic, frangible social order, mired unyieldingly in something called the "Stone Age." It is doing quite well in the twentieth century, managed and maintained by contemporaries.

Laboring under the tutelage of Durkheimian sociology, and beyond that of Rousseau's idea of the "social contract," anthropology has been largely content to limit its conceptualization to the power *of* society. Like the governments that sponsor them, with their slogans of "the just consent of the governed" or the Marxian power of the labor force, social scientists often confine their object of study to what we would call its own "center of gravity," the power of society to be what it is. The power *over* society, moving the "social center of gravity" from a point beyond its limits, is, however, foreign to this tendency, neither mysterious nor mystical. Analytically, it is achieved through a negation of the cultural meanings or categorizations that ground social life; the transformation witnessed in the *kaba* is a controlled and contained form of this negation.

In the experiential terms through which Barok prefer to deal with it, the negation is a power (*a lolos*), that of image transformation. Since all we can ever own of the world is its images—the appearances, sounds, smells, textures, and movements through which we apprehend it—*a lolos* becomes a power over reality. Barok recognize this power as occurring autochthonously in the world as *a tadak* (Tok Pisin *masalai*), 'form-changing place-spirits'. The *takak* contains transformative power *outside* of human society, though it may elicit its force in human beings through a kind of tutelary rapport with the *orong* of a clan.

A *tadak* is itself formless and is defined by its power of changing form; it is known and grasped by habitual appearances in certain named forms (usually a human being, a python, and a shark) and in relation to certain known places, *goron tadak*. The known forms assumed by a *tadak* are called its *masoso*, and the list of *masoso* for a given *tadak* may be extensive, including trees, rocks, shore birds, hydrocephalic children, mermaids, and even cave paintings.

A thorough investigation of the *masoso* of a given *tadak* will turn up some interesting things. Frequently one finds that many of the *masoso* and *goron tadak* associated with any one clan spirit are those that formerly belonged to spirits of clans that are now defunct, and whose lands, *taun, mangin,* and other attributes have been incorporated within the present unit. Small and obsolescent clans will be taken under the protection of larger ones and gradually digested by them. In one recent case, the sole (male) surviving member of a defunct clan was "purchased" for one string of *mangin* by a leading clan of the village where I resided; when the man dies, the clan will perform his mortuary feasts and inherit an acreage equivalent to that of a medium-sized Texas ranch. It matters not at all that the incorporated clan will belong to the moiety opposite to that of the incorporating one.

There is one more fact about *tadak* that may be helpful to us. This is that a clan member may victimize those of other clans by smearing mud and debris from his *goron tadak* surreptitiously on their canoes; the *tadak* will cause a shipwreck and swallow the victims. But those who are swallowed by a *tadak* do not die; instead they live forever "within the *tadak*" and do its bidding. There are techniques by which a sorcerer may strike a rock at the *goron tadak* and "see everything within the *masalai*." A *tadak*, in other words, not only assimilates spirits of defunct clans but also human beings. What is interesting here is that clans do the same thing. Because of nearby coconut plantations, there has generally been a plethora of itinerant laborers in the Barok area, most often from the southern highlands or the Sepik. Many of these will have defected from labor contracts. These youths, frequently out of pocket and hungry, will be approached by a clan and offered adoption. They will be formally adopted within the clan, offered bed and board within the *taun*, and given a clan name. But the other side of this particular "king's shilling" is that from then on they will be exploited, doing free labor for the clan from dawn till dusk—they will live within the clan forever and do its bidding.

Adoption is also offered to non-Melanesians, and I knew of only one European within the area (excepting plantation managers), the Catholic father at Namatanai, who was not so adopted. Since I could read, write, and cipher, it was explained to me, my job was to clerk in the lineage store, count the proceeds, and bank them in Namatanai. And so I got a sorcerer's view of everything that lived within this particular economic *masalai*. It was very simple: slowly profits and proceeds from hiring out the lineage truck would accumulate until money was needed for something—restocking the store, fixing the truck, or holding a mortuary feast. Then all the money was withdrawn for the purpose, and the account started from scratch again. No distinction was drawn between practical and ritual uses of the money, nor was there more than one account: it was all the same thing.

The "thing" I am talking about can manifest itself as clan or lineage, although these distinctions, as well as that between moieties, are frequently, as we have seen, blurred over. It is enacted and prefigured in the *taun* and in *kastam* generally, the model of and the model for its operation, in Geertz's terms. It is not in any sense the "content" of any symbolic category or ideology, neither production nor reproduction, neither matrilineality nor patrilineality; it is the conjoint product of *kolume* and *gala*. It can be used, in the transmission of a *taun*, to alienate a matrilineage from its own production and its dead, and it can be utilized, in the *kaba*, to nullify the principles of gender and moiety, in whose terms production and reproduction are generated, in the interests of successorship. But the transformation itself is never nullified, because the *taun* must be used to effect its own transmission, and because the *kaba* negotiates the containment of the *taun* by the feast. As a pragmatic operator, it provides the Usen with the basis for what I could call gastroenterprise, a format for the digestion and incorporation of the new as well as the old, of capital as well as labor.

For whatever reason, the Usen Barok have been inordinately successful; they are quite wealthy by Papua New Guinea standards and have done well politically. At the time of my fieldwork, the premier of the province, head speaker of the provincial assembly, finance officer of the province, and a cabinet minister of the national government all hailed from the tiny Usen area, the latter two from the village where I resided. As one of my informants put it, "New Ireland is shaped like a rifle, and we are at the trigger." Identification with the trigger may or may not explain the immense popularity of Roy Rogers in the Namatanai area; Barok did not like *Deep Throat* ("These people live like dogs, how can they be happy?"), and when I queried them about John Wayne, they replied, "We know about John Wayne, he's tough, but Roy is *tricky*." Liberated sex and moral machismo have nothing on facile, lariat-swinging success, and maybe a little singing afterward.

Of course, if Roy Rogers were as tricky as a *masalai*, he would be immortal in real life as well as, perhaps, on the silver screen. But what kind of history does an immortal have (besides a very long one), or anything, for that matter, that is capable of transformation? In the case of a *tadak*, it would have to be a private autobiography (who else would know?), for it is the *subject* of its own history.

The *objects* of history turn out to be (authentic or imagined) constant identities: empires, roles, principles, institutions, ideals, peoples. Transformations, when they do not slip through the meshes entirely, are at best a headache. Did the Roman Empire "turn into" the Byzantine, the Byzantine Empire "emerge from" the Roman? Did something magical happen at the point in time when Romans stopped feeding Christians to the lions and started lionizing them instead? The full picture of the empire at a given moment might give us a clue, but the transformation was a temporal process.

What we call "history" is the two-sided conundrum of literate, rational (that is, verbal) order; if the order of placing words, or thoughts, end-to-end is made use of to account for the simultaneity of many things happening at once, the sequence of events is left out. And if the verbal order is used to take account of the sequency, the force of context in all its intensity is put by. Words are "tricky," like Roy Rogers. And so the Barok expedient is to watch the "flicks," leave the *words* out. This is of course an abrogation of verbal responsibility for "what happened," either in its polyphonic presence (context) or its narrative flux (sequence). For what happened is contained (*kolume*) in the images that circumscribe (but do not *describe*) it and is elicited (*gala*) in the presentation of those images. History is then a matter of how the images happen to *you* (as it perhaps always is anyway), a subjectivity that does not need verbalization.

Temporal alienation, other times that sit oddly in our present and do their best to try our credibility, become "history" when rationalized and described or interpreted, worked into the frame of reference that Western tradition insists upon. But if one begins, like the Barok, from the position that *present* experience is a *pidik*, a 'trick' or mystery in which knowledge is only won by undergoing an intuition-estranging revelation, the alienation takes on a different composure. One is disposed to revel in the disorienting strangeness of myths and recounted experiences, to anticipate the bizarre and the devious. One Barok acquaintance confessed to me his suspicion that Pearl Harbor was bombed by *Australian* aircraft disguised with Japanese markings, so as to bring the United States into the war!

Is this so very different from the way in which we, in many cases, "do" history? One can imagine the New Ireland best-seller, *Surprise from Down Under*, with its garish dust jacket of ground crews in digger hats painting up their Wirraways to look like Zekes and Kates. There is a certain strain of historical writing, not all of it "popular," that resembles nothing so much as that speculative literature regarding human origins, in which every emergent quirk of human behavior or anatomy is represented as *the* giant step in the transformation of "natural" into cultural being. All of it is written about that most elusive of beasts, the *masalai* of transformation in human history. Transformation is the relativity, the "other side" of history, and those who do not control their transformations are condemned to look for them in history, to see them as history.

To say that history exists at large and independently in the world is rather like saying that science, or art, or theater does. Phrases like "the biology of a forest" or "the physics of a star" are projections, mystifications that carry much of the freight of scientific "objectivity." The recognition, writing, and hence creation of history is no less an intended and contrived act than the enactment of a Barok *kaba*, something produced by human beings. Written history is a veritable Rube Goldberg device of rhetorical levers, wheels, and pulleys, ritual paraphernalia to "make an effect." That effect, which does not and cannot exist at large and independently in the world, is what we project generically upon the world and imagine as "history."

Successful histories, then, are the ones that allow us to make this projection easily enough that a sense of objectivity is fostered; they disguise the "effect" as that of the factuality itself, of how it works on and through the imagination of the historian. What is tranformed, the "ritual" of history, is the set of words and verbalized identities; what is left to the imagination is how these tropes and their implied transformations could possibly take place without words. Thus history, concealing its ritual transformations behind the facade of an overarching factual reality, is the very opposite of the Barok *kaba*, which articulates its artificial transformations publicly and openly to illustrate the deception that lies beneath the surface of everyday appearance. If this serves to qualify the Barok as a "people without history," then we might grant them the right to ask in their turn whether this is not better than to have a history without people.

Note

1. Here the voiced velar fricative, guttural in sound, is transcribed as ǵ.

References Cited

Jessep, Owen D.
1978   Land Tenure in a New Ireland Village. Ph.D. dissertation, Department of Law, Research School of Social Sciences, Australian National University.

Lipset, David
1980   *Gregory Bateson: The Legacy of a Scientist.* Englewood Cliffs, N.J.: Prentice-Hall.

Wagner, Roy
1983   The Ends of Innocence: Conception and Seduction among the Daribi of Karimui and the Barok of New Ireland. *Mankind* 4: 75–83.

1986   *Asiwinarong: Ethos, Image, and Social Power among the Usen Barok of New Ireland.* Princeton: Princeton University Press.

Walens, Stanley G.
1981   *Feasting with Cannibals: An Essay on Kwakiutl Cosmology.* Princeton: Princeton University Press.

9. A Poetic for Histories

Transformations That Present the Past

Greg Dening

Poetics are not poetry, but the suggestion that they might be is left with the breath of the word. I would not in any case be embarrassed to be thought in this to be writing a poem for history as well as a poetic for histories. There is much of life and living in history. Being a humanity is one of history's many graces. Poetics and poems are both concerned with the authenticity of experience rather than the credentials of the observer. In a poetic for histories, I mean to free our discourse on history from any claim or presumption by historians or anthropologists that by our expertise we are directed to seeing history as having one form or another.

The histories I write of are mainly a human characteristic, not a technique of inquiry. They are the vernacular of our cultural and social systems. We all make histories endlessly. It is our human condition to make histories. No sooner is the present gone in the blink of an eye than we make sense of it as past. We tell stories about it. We inter-

347

pret the meaning of gestures made, of words spoken, of actions done. We make a narrative of the past in our mind, in our conversations. We record it in some way—in a diary, in a letter, on a certificate, in a tax return.

Poetics are a serious business, a critic has told me. "Use the word with respect for those who refined it." I do. But I do not mean to puzzle over Aristotle's famous distinction between poetry and history. And Hayden White does not need my compliments for destabilizing the Anglo-Saxon tradition in reflective history. Structuralists and literary critics expecting additional precision to their discourse on poetics can stop here. By *poetic* in "poetic for histories" I simply try to discover the most generous way to describe a reflective discourse on all the hermeneutic dimensions of histories as cultural artifacts. Poetics, like prose, are something we are always practicing. Poetics are the relationships we have with the texts that suffuse our lives. Poetics are the facility with which we relate the systems of meaning in these texts to the occasions of their reading. In the poetics that I practice here, I pursue what Richard H. Brown has called "symbolic realism" (Brown and Lyman 1978:14). In histories, object and subject, the known and the knowing, the said and the hearing, I and Thou and It, all are bound together. Our science will need an aesthetics to discover them all.

It is unimaginable that someone—"primitive" or "civilized"—has no past; it is unimaginable that someone does not know some part of that past. *Memory* is our everyday word for knowledge of the past, but memory suggests some personal or institutional immediacy in the connection between the past and those who experienced it. We need a word that includes memory but embraces all the other ways of knowing a past. We do not have such a word; but in this poetic for histories, let me declare that word to be *history*.

History by this is public knowledge of the past. Being public, it is expressed in some way. Being expressed, it will always be possessed of some system. Being communicated, history's systems will always hold the ambivalences of circumstanced exchange: the systems will always be modified by being expressed and heard.

History is a human universal. Knowledge of the past is expressed by all human beings according to their different cultural and social systems. History is a generic form of consciousness in which the past experience of oneself or of others in an environment outside oneself is transformed into symbols that are exchanged. Let us say there is history —like culture, a methodological abstraction for talking about a perspective on human behavior. There are histories, like cultures, that need an ethnographic description for their forms and structures and functions. A poetic for histories is that ethnographic description.

We each, no doubt, have a thesaurus in our mind of the different ways in which we and others make sense of the past—reminiscence, gossip, anecdote, rumor, parable, report, tradition, myth. We could probably fill a crossword puzzle with histories of different sorts— saga, legend, epic, ballad, folklore, annal, chronicle. We would recognize the distinctiveness of these ways of knowing the past, even if we would probably argue over what precisely the distinctions should be. That is, we have a practical sense of their different poetics. We know the different meanings we abstract from their different forms. We know how to behave on the different occasions of their expression. Maybe you are suspicious at this moment that I should collect all of these under the one analytic concept of history and call them all histories. You know history as something different and as yet owe my definition no deference. Hold your suspicions for a while. I am going to try to persuade you that your having them will lead to a discovery of how powerful poetics are.

Histories, transformations of the past into expressions, clothe, constitute, *are* a present social reality. Histories always have this double entendre. They refer to a past in making a present. The knowledge of the past that re-presents the past in story or account makes the structures of the present—such as class or identity—in the expressing. So histories in our poetic are not just the stream of consciousness about the past but that knowledge made dramaturgical in its forms of expression. Histories are fictions—something made of the past—but fictions whose forms are metonymies of the present. Histories are metaphors of the past: they translate sets of events into sets of symbols. But histories are also metonymies of the present: the present has existence in and through their expression. The present—social reality, the structures of our living—has being through re-presentations of the past in coded public forms. We read or hear histories in this double way. We know in them both a present and a past.

This should not be a disturbing statement. But it sometimes is. It is sometimes seen to plunge us into subjectivity and relativism. It is sometimes seen to leave us with the appearances of things and no underlying reality. But it was the young Karl Marx who said in *The German Ideology*: "Consciousness can never be anything else than conscious existence, and the existence of men is their actual life process" (Feuer 1969:288). He puzzled how the most powerful structures have trivial, particular expression. I do not see myself as doing something very different from him. To write the grammar by which the past is transformed through histories, one need not do something new, only hold the middle ground between poles of every kind.

The founding fathers of sociology and anthropology did their sciences a disservice when they confused historical explanation with history and histories. In seeking their independence and separation from other sciences, they looked for ways other than historical to explain human events and actions. Their exclusivity distracted them from the discovery of how histories as everyday experience construct social reality. They equated a method of argument with a mode of consciousness and by that were unable to discover a fundamental postulate about human social reality: it is experiential; it is constituted in and by the presentations of the past. Put another way: praxis is histories. Histories are "sensuous human activity" that make and unmake the structures of living.

Such declarations are solipsistic and not a little gnomic. I write a solemn little convention to myself that histories are public knowledge of the past that make a present. But we have everyday usages of words like *history*, and these are not changed by any definition of mine. In everyday usage *history* is sometimes an account of the past and sometimes the actions and events of which there is an account. "That's history," we say, meaning something is done with and is no longer relevant. "Making history" is a phrase we use comfortably and ordinarily. Someone who has done something first, registered a record, been notably unique or inventive has "made history," we say. Or something is said to be "historical fact." There is no doubt that it happened.

Now I, wanting to persuade you to my conventionality, can point to all these everyday phrases and show how they hold a distinction, clear on reflection, between history as expressed knowledge of the past and the past as something that happened. The careless presumption of everyday life, however, is otherwise: the past and history are the same. Or given the impact on our culture of one-and-a-half centuries of higher education, the presumption of everyday life could be that history is a special sort of activity belonging to "historians."

Perhaps by the end of this essay I will have persuaded you to enter my conventionality. The likelihood, however, is that we will talk past each other. "Real" and everyday meanings will constantly reassert themselves. Unless I invent some algebra—"X is ways of knowing the past"—critics of my conventionality will be distracted by the fact of it and fight my idiosyncrasy. Discourse never begins because we can never strike a bargain to agree as if *history* means this or *history* means that. We lack the discipline or social contract to see *history* as if it meant something other than our taken-for-granted interpretation of it. Surrender to conventionality is always a socializing process. It is then that our "as ifs" are real.

Surrenders to conventionality are what disciplines are. The disciplines are social systems that raise their partial "as if" perspectives from mere conventionality to mythic proportions. In the language of semiotics, their models move from being symbols to being signs. They move from metaphor to metonymy. From being known to be conventional and partial, they are understood to be real and whole. All the boundary-making rituals of everyday life in which the conventionalities of class and sex and race and sect are transformed into social realities are the same rituals that make for the powerful ethnocentricity of the disciplines.

We will find them all, these rites de passages, in examinations, in selection, promotion, and establishment, in the residence rules of departments and schools, in the special languages, in the professional ta boos. These are ways of making a blinkered view of the world seem mythically true. No matter that every science properly protests its rationality, the mood and sentiment created by each science's social relations make the artificiality of its perspective as natural as good and bad manners. As social and cultural systems, disciplines move from their sense of the conventionality and metaphoric quality of their models to a sense of their naturalness and reality. Their models become signs of the whole of reality, not just symbols of its parts.

With the rise and fall of their political and social power, disciplines transfer their own models to their culture's mythic understanding of the environment. "Supply and demand," "id and ego," "survival of the fittest" move from being recognized analytical contrivances to being objective descriptions of what actually happens and reliable predictions of what will happen as the models gain the strength to have an undeniable and cosmological value in the culture at large.

Let me put a thesis about the discipline of history. Our everyday usage of *history* as equivalent to the past comes from the small hegemony that the "as if" models of the discipline of history have had. A history of the concept of history inevitably focuses on the development of national identities and bureaucratic mass societies and the institutionalization of politics, religion, and the economy in the civilizing process in the nineteenth century. All these processes demanded the ideology of the factual. Just as the myths of psychologists, sociologists, economists, and now, perhaps, of geneticists have become the myths of our culture, so previous to that the myth of historians that their history was the factual past has given a blinding clarity to our perceptions. It has been the myth of historians become the myth of our culture that the past is discovered objectively and factually by our being accurate about it. One symptom of that belief is the statement that "primitive" societies have no history. That statement should be: "primitive" societies do not have the systematic conventionalities—rules of inquiry and evidence—that allow them to historicize in ways recognizable and persuasive to us; nor do they have the infinitude of institutional support systems (from archives to *The Guinness Book of Records*) to persuade them that accuracy is the truth, that history is the past. I trail my coat. Let me show that being accurate is a fetish of a very special sort of history. A poetic for histories will show histories' more varied concerns. Let me show also that an ethnography of history as a mode of consciousness is history's anthropology even as it is anthropology's history. Historians cannot escape a theory of how the past is in the present any more than can anthropologists.

Histories are ways of knowing what happened in the past. The qualities of histories are different from the qualities of the past. On one hand, ways of knowing are described by their systems of expression, their processes of communication, their relationship to shared experience. Ways of knowing can be called among other things "objective," "metaphoric," "romantic." On the other hand, all that has happened is almost indescribable. The moment we give it distinguishable characteristics, we transform it, we know it, we make of it a history. Yet in our culturally mythic view of it, this past of which we make a history has two characteristics: it happened independently of our knowing that it happened—we are not its creators—and it happened in a specific way, in specific circumstances—its specificity is its objectivity, independent of the narrative or the meaning we make of it.

We cannot describe the past independently of our knowing it, any more than we can describe the present independently of our knowing it. And, knowing it, we create it, we textualize it. That is the circle, hermeneutical if you like, of our human being. Nonetheless, we have a sense that the past is textable. The past is everything that has happened—every heartbeat, every sound, every molecular movement. This totality is both objectively specific (it happened in a particular way) and infinitely discrete (the happenings are not connected). Mozart writes a sonata on a cold day in a spiteful mood; Pomare, high chief of Tahiti, at the same moment distractedly "eats" the eye of a human sacrifice. Yet we have a commonsense confidence that the "real" past, like the "real" present, is much more connected and ordered. We have a confidence that the past is ordered in itself in such a way that we can make a narrative of it. It is textable. We are confident that our selection is an exegesis of an order already there. It is the same commonsense confidence we have in the cultural systems of our present.

This mythic confidence in a textable past is the ambience in which histories are made. The past itself is evanescent: it has existence only in histories. Histories are the texted past.

What happened in the past inevitably leaves sign-bearing relics: in personal memories first of all, but, more importantly, in memory translated into its public social forms—gossip, legend, story, myth, anecdote, parable, sermon, speech. It leaves relics as well in transcriptions of all kinds—in memory written down, in the registers of institutions, in illustrations and depictions, in all the material things of the cultural environment. These oral, literary, and material relics are extraordinarily complex in their sign-bearing characteristics, although there is an everyday commonsense prejudice that they are simple. The oral and the literary relics bear a message; they inscribe language; they convey information. Inevitably the inscribed language is stripped of the context of speech, the eye-to-eye exchanges that catch the mood, the nuances, the tropes that condition the signs. Already the relics of the past in their messages are transformed simply by being read. Already the past is as much created as preserved by readings, which must invent the circumstances that give meaning to words. Our ordinary histories, double texted as they usually are, contain all the inventions of readings divorced from immediate experience.

Most relics hold a message; they all hold a code. They all encapsulate their cultural forms. Precisely because they are cultural artifacts, they hold within themselves their ordinary significance as things that are beautiful or sacred or useful or precious or manufactured. Those who use these artifacts know them in their ordinariness. They know when and how to use them and with what proprieties. These cultural things make a symbolic environment that shows sex in a color, status in a type of wood, class in a design. Even those relics that we would count more traditionally as documents—diaries, letters, logs, books—are cultural things as well and have encoded in their forms, materials, and shapes expressions of meaning beyond their messages.

The complexities do not end there. Relics of what happened in the past are cultural artifacts of the moments that produced them, but they also become cultural artifacts of all the moments that give them permanence. In a familiar Pacific metaphor, the relics of the past are always cargo to the present. Things that cross cultural boundaries lose the meaning encapsulated in them and are reconstituted in meaning by the cultures that receive them. Relics of the past cross all the cultural boundaries that lie between past and present, and when they do they are reconstituted in the relations and means of production of each cultural zone they enter. We say that relics of the past "survive the accidents of time," but it is only the destruction of these relics that is accidental. Their preservation is cultural. I think of institutions: archives and museums are mirrors of power and cosmologies. I think of roles: bards, priests, and journalists protest that they convey what is given them by inspiration, God, and events; but they make their news anew nonetheless. I thing of class and sex: they own both the past and the present who own the means of preserving what has gone. I think of souvenirs and memorabilia, national trusts and heritage commissions. I think of Daughters of the American Revolution, conservationists, and environmentalists. Relics of the past come directly from the past, but they are reconstituted in their meanings by all the cultural systems that give them meaning. They gain meaning out of every social moment they survive.

The past, which we are mythically confident is knowable as such, is only known through symbols whose meaning is changed in the reading of them and in the preserving of them.

Histories are the product of that dialectic between discovery and invention. That does not make histories different from everyday experience. Everyday social reality is a product of the dialectic between the given of its systems and the creations of our interpretations. We are not the less realists for accepting histories' processual fictions any more than we are relativists for seeing that human culture is a balance between the predictability of socialization and the creativity of interpretation. Even in the most mundane circumstatnces, we are forced to invent because our rules never quite fit the idiosyncrasy of the circumstances, because the circumstances are always changed by our previous interpretations. The ordinariness of everyday life is always disturbed by the extraordinariness of a misread cue, or a bon mot become faux pas, or a novel combination of personality and role. I would say that every day we are confronted by some otherness that teases us to interpretation. When that otherness is outside our cultural system, we call those moments of interpretation "ethnographic moments." But we have those moments within culture as well. In times of conflict or social ambiguity, we make a ritual of interpretaion. We carve out a social space, make boundaries around it with language and protocol, the better to convey the simplicities of our interpretations. I think these teasing moments are made for histories. Anyway, that is my thesis. In the strangeness or novelty of the circumstances, we are teased to understand, to rationalize, by looking back. We present ourselves by making histories.

Past and present are bound together in an interpretive act we call "history." The character of that interpretive act and its varieties we will return to later in this poetics. How social reality is constructed by and in these interpretive acts is an anthropological concern. Speaking now of the special conventionality of academic history, I have to say it is also a historian's concern. What anthropologists do of present cultures, historians do of past cultures. They ask how the past is in the present. French revolutionaries make a revolution looking backward. Reformations are re-formations. Whatever the differences of methodology and evidence between anthropology and academic history—and they are only differences of degree, not of kind—they each cannot describe the other or the past without asking how the praxis of culture is made up of interpretive acts. Now I call discourse on that shared concern "ethnohistory."

Ethnohistory is the focused conversation we have about the ways in which historical consciousness is culturally distinct and socially specific and how, in whatever culture or social circumstance, the past constitutes the present in being known. Ethnohistory, anyone who reads this will know, has had other meanings. Ethnohistory has meant "history of primitive or traditional cultures"; it has meant the "anthropology of past primitive or traditional cultures." But "ethno-" does not mean "primitive" any more than "anthro-" does, and I have objections to being thought to do ethnohistory of the "primitives" and history of the "civilized."

I do the history and the anthropology of "primitive" and "civilized" alike; and insofar as there are those who would join me in understanding the nature and function of historical consciousness, I do ethnohistory both of "primitive" and "civilized" and of cultures in the past and in the present. So I think I am "doing" ethnohistory and inviting my students to "do" ethnohistory when we ask why it is that Australian schoolchildren are likely to say that the aborigines killed Captain Cook. We are curious how the history of the death of a hero has become entangled with a fear of what is strange and dark. I think I am doing ethnohistory when I puzzle why sailors might think that the mutiny on the *Bounty* was caused by Bligh's bad language, whereas admirals thought it was because he was not a gentleman. Sailors make history out of their experience in total institutions and know what sort of impersonal language gives them privacy and what sort of personal language exposes them. Admirals know that anyone who has to say he has authority has not got it, and they see how a gentleman is born to it in his deportment and etiquette. They write their reflective histories telling stories at the wardroom table about the gaucheries of non-gentlemen. I think I "do" ethnohistory when I try to describe strangers in contact with natives and natives in contact with strangers, interpreting what is new in the light of what is old and, in that, remaining the same and changing. Indeed, I do ethnohistory wherever the ethnographic moments of everyday life make cultured being.

As it happens, however, I find that ethnographic moments are never so piquant for a poetic of histories as they are in the contact of natives and strangers. The compounded nature of histories, the self-images in the cartoons of the other, the processes of culture and expressed structures, are simply writ large in circumstances of extravagant ambiguity.

It is an old joke that the world will not end with either a bang or a whimper. It will simply sink under the weight of old *National Geographic* magazines. The cargo of even that small universe of ethnographic experience is large. The sum total of the cargo of all the interpretive encounters of our world is immense. One lifetime would not be enough to read all the interpretations that were the product of ethnographic moments in Polynesia alone. One could write of the Pacific what Edward Said wrote in *Orientalism* of the Orient. Europe invented the East in its ethnographic encounter and then, possessing the inventions, added invention on invention. European inventions of the Pacific, to be discovered wherever there is an academy or an archive or a museum or a library, are beyond measure. And one must add to them all the living inventions not written down but which survive in lore, in shared images, in cannibal jokes, in fantasies about sarongs. It would be a brave man who would say he could write the ethnohistory of these encounters and have reflected on all the inventions of native Polynesians as well as European strangers. Let me, in an effort at practical hermeneutics, offer a sample.

The British took possession of Tahiti in 1767 with ceremonies of "turfe and twygge" and by putting a flag on a pole. Their ceremonies of possession were directed at themselves. They did authoritative acts with such propriety that they "made history," which they expected Spaniards and French to read and note. The British gave their transient rituals permanence and continuity by establishing an institutional memory of them —in official logs, in constant restatements of their privileged position as discoverers, by treaties and proclamations, by archives and public records offices. They made historical proof of their possession by their bureaucratic capacity to retrieve the documents. The Tahitians for their part possessed the British, by taking down the British flag and incorporating it into their own symbol of sovereignty, their *maro ura* or feather girdle, by making an institutional memory of the flag in putting it in the museums of their sacred places, and by "making history" of it in every ritual moment celebratory of the establishment and/or continuation of their own power. Right opposite the passage of entry of the *Dolphin* to Matavai Bay, the Tahitians built a *marae* to 'Oro in which they kept the flags, a portrait of Captain Cook, the skulls of two *Bounty* mutineers, the red hair of another mutineer, the drums and spears the mutineers had brought back from Tubuai, together with all their most sacred paraphernalia of sacrifice and sovereignty. I have no doubt that I could persuade you that *both* British and Tahitians knew themselves best through their interpretations of the other. They also gave continuity to their ethnographic experience of each other in institutions making cultural artifacts of that transcribed experience.

I believe I could persuade you as well that I cannot tell you the story of the British and Tahitians mutually possessing one another, nor make my own history of the natives' and strangers' past, without making fictions of all the fictions that have intervened between then and now. Not all our confidence in the continuity of culture, not all our certainty in rejecting a doctrine of fatal impact, can change the fact that the natives' past is unreachable except through strangers' eyes. Even more, this particular event of a native past is inexpressible, except in terms that lie outside the experience of contact. I could not tell what else intervenes. My own fictions have a genealogy that begins with Douglas Oliver, Colin Newbury, Niel Gunson, Henry Adams, Teuira Henry,

Jacques Moerenhout—all heroic in their scholarly knowledge of Tahiti. My fictions about the past are filtered through all the ways in which interpretive experiences have been made into cultural things—books, articles, papers, diaries, letters. The native Tahitians and European strangers constituted their present moments by making history. I do the same when I make history for you. They made history out of their ethnographic moments. I do too, although I would be hard put to give you a hermeneutics of the ambiguities that drive me to make history for you—but every historian lives with the certain knowledge that if he or she cannot write an autohistoriography, someone is coming who will do it. Someone is coming who will tell what we really meant when we wrote of something else. Someone will discover that our histories of the "other" are really parables about ourselves. Native Tahitians and European strangers made their history not by leaping from their present to a past cut off and independent. They made history by the bridge of the museums of their social memory, which preserved the cargo of the past and constantly made it new. I do too.

I like the metaphor of cargo. The relics of the past, the only ways in which the past survives, *are* cargo to all the present moments that follow. We all stand on the beaches of our present and make of our past, even of our past person, an object. The past is me; the past is it. Probably every person who reads this will be actively involved, individually or institutionally, in preserving some of that cargo. Like myself you might have a souvenir of an ethnographic experience, an artifact, the proof of some fieldwork, a memory of boundaries crossed. It might be a statue, a bowl, a stone adze that was the cultural currency in one symbolic system translated now into an instrument of teaching, a status symbol, a badge of anthropological interest. Like myself, you will be on some committee to discuss the cost of conserving somebody else's souvenirs or to discover the institutional will to keep something or to throw it away, to fathom the morality of owning the loot of ages. All relics of the past, even if they disappear with the note of a song or the sight of a mime, have a double quality. They are marked with the meanings of the occasions of their origins, and they are always translated into something else for the moments they survive. Historical consciousness is always built out of that double meaning. History is always the past and present bound together in the sparse and selected symbols that time throws up.

James Boon began some years ago, and then left off, consideration of "cultural operators" (Boon 1973:15). He was curious about the mechanics of interpretation in which we *know* the simple point of complex actions laid out for us in a sequence of time in drama or in opera. We catch the moment around which all else seems to turn. We entrap the whole in an instant. Imagine that we go to the theater to see *Death of a Salesman*, a part of life and life's relationships and structures, set out, like life itself, in a series of conversations. We hear the sentences of the conversation on the stage—about baseball, about dingy hotel rooms, about careless children and too careful wives—and we transform all the sentences, reduce them to one principal significance. We know the sentences to be saying something other than their simple meaning. We know the sentences in their unity to be concerned with coping or not coping with the emptiness of public presentations of self. Let us say we go to the theater. The curtains are pulled back. There is Arthur Miller sitting on the stage. *"Death of a Salesman,"* he says, "is about Everyman, Willy Loman, in an entrepreneurial society, and Everyman's inability to cope with the emptiness of the public presentation of self. That will be $10.00 please." We would not *know* it at all. We would not be entertained by it. The medium of most of our living is conversation, of texted narrative. The clothing of our structures is the trivialities of everyday existence. We nonetheless have the poetics to make such theater of this "sensuous human activity" that captivates us, not by its parts but by its whole.

I want to say that in history we are *entertained* by the meanings we put on the past. And strangers are entertained by natives.

Entertainment may seem a frivolous word. Clearly we are often more than amused or agreeably engaged by the past. Indeed, no matter what hegemony the entertainment industry has given to its meaning of amusement, *entertainment* still keeps its more primary meaning of being engaged, having attention focused, being held to something. We entertain or harbor a thought. We entertain or accommodate a guest. Victor Turner attracted me to the word (Turner 1977), but Clifford Geertz (quoting Northrop Frye) attracted me to the notion. We do not go to

Macbeth to learn the history of Scotland; we go to see a man lose his soul for the sake of a kingdom, Frye says—and Geertz approves (Geertz 1975:450). In entertainment—on the stage or in our mind—we set up conditions to distill meaning. Out of complexities we make simplicities. We put round a boundary, we hold varied words and actions within a convention. Out of conversations on a stage, we abstract a dramatic unity. Out of images on a screen, we draw significance. In the theater, of course, we are conditioned to act as interpreters. We are cut off from our ordinary social acts to enter the conventionality of being an audience. We are cued to the beginning and end of the drama with lights and curtain and silence. The noise of ordinary life is quieted so we hear the sound of play. We will weep or laugh in the space of the theater, as we pray or know a presence in the sacred space of a church. We are unfettered by the ambience, by the rubrics, by the expectancies within us to respond.

I suspect we all can write the poetics of the theater: we are all theologians of our own entertainment. We are participant-observers of the action on the stage and of ourselves as audience. In the foyers we discover we were "only entertained" because we discover the conspiracies of directors and actors to make "as if" what we saw was real. We do not play the critic so readily in ordinary life. It is another quality of the hermeneutical circle that ordinarily there is the difference between entertainment and reality.

I argue in what follows that historical consciousness finds expression in different forms of dramatic unity, that those forms have different conventionalities, that they make the past meaningful both in the conventionality of their textual nature and the conventionality with which they are received and heard. The past is constitutive of the present in the entertainment that histories give. Histories are the theater of this entertainment. Rather, histories are the varied theaters of this entertainment. That is, histories are not just the content of a story or an interpretation of the past. Histories are not just a message. Histories are the mode of the story's expression, the public occasion of its telling. That is why histories are an anthropological concern. Ordinarily, one would call this understanding of history hermeneutical and acknowledge the influence of giants like Dilthey, Collingwood, Weber, and all the commentators on them. But inevitably, in the formalist hermeneutics of the likes of Ricoeur and Gadamer, history is reduced to a sort of "high history" that is the practice of historians, set apart like priests to do something special. Anthropology has the patience that hermeneutical philosophers do not have to see and describe the everyday nature of special histories and the historical nature of everyday life as well.

The forms and structures of histories differ with different expressions. A history recounted at the family dinner table is different from a history told in religious ritual. A history recited in political parable is different from a history written in a doctoral dissertation. Each type of history will have its own social rules of expression, its own criteria of objectivity. Each type of history will balance past and present in different ways. The participants in each entertainment will know fairly exactly the reactions expected of them. There will always be some claim that one type, say academic or sacred history, is "real history." There will always be some jockeying for the exclusive use of the ordinary word *history*. Sometimes some social group might win or nearly win and "history" is declared in some fundamentalist way to be only this or that transformation of the past. But such definitions are rarely descriptions of what is, only declarations of territoriality claimed.

The transformation of the past that is a history is always made in social circumstances. Take the story told at the family dinner table, no doubt repeated a thousand times, leached in the telling to its essence, creating laughter and tears in the hearers in its almost coded phrases. What it loses in accuracy it gains in truth. Its truth concerns the bonds of familiarity. Insiders know their closeness in the shared humor at a social disaster or impropriety. The circumstances of its telling—acceptance, affection, expectancy, openness—make a boundary about the group and intensify their understanding that the story about the past describes the present. Maybe someone will correct an inaccuracy about a date or a place or a person, but usually so as to enlarge the meaning with a savored relevance, not in the name of facticity per se. Response and reaction is almost studied, as in a script, especially if some outsider is present to whom the family performs. They will bow to the one who "tells its best"; they will groan with exaggerated boredom at yet another repetition of the story; they will interject on cue. It is an invitation to see family members as they "really are," with their social screens lowered and their proper social selves put aside, confident that their bonds will not be loosened by a peep at their ignorance or their gaucheness or their social peccadilloes. These are the rituals of transformation. The past is thus made over into the present. The history cannot be divorced from the circumstances of its telling. The very pointedness of selection in the story, the caricature of its exaggerated drama—all the marks of its inaccuracy—are what make it true for what it does in representing the family as they "really are."

Take sacred history read in religious ritual—"the Gospel according to St. Matthew," "the Epistle of Paul to the Romans." There is never so strict a fundamentalism that accuracy is not subservient to truth. If one made an ethnography of a Christmas service, how would one describe the reading of the gospel? The "Infancy Narratives" of the Gospels have been subjected more than any other passage of Christian sacred scripture to reformed reading and modernist scrutiny. They have also been overlaid with apocrypha and nearly two thousand years of cultural interpretation. They are now texts that contain overlay upon overlay of metaphor and mood that would be impossible to describe fully. Painters, poets, musicians, cribmakers, and house decorators have imprinted myriad images on our cultural consciousness, let alone preachers and theologians. What happens in time in culture happens in time in a person. There is no easy shuffling off of the fundamentalism concerning cribs, angels, animals, and snow with which one was indoctrinated as a child. Standing in a Christmas service listening to the gospel read, an adult believer will be touched by the moods engendered by childhood fundamentalism even if he or she hears the reading with a modernist ear. As believer, his or her credulity will not be strained by the realization that angels' messages to shepherds, kings following a star, even virgin mothers, are metaphors for the deeper, more mysterious truths the sacred history contains. They do not need the sophistication of the scripture scholar to move deftly between a demand that things be "historically" accurate and an understanding that the mythic clothing of truth can be contradictory and even "untrue." As parents, they will happily convey a literal truth to the child at their knee and not be disturbed at their own divided understanding that angels, kings, and virgin mothers might really mean something else. The firmness of faith binds them not to the historicity of detail but to the meaningfulness of the whole.

I make no point that this imagined believer is typical or that all of us are relativists now. I make a point about the rituals of the transformation of the past. Sacred history, especially, but all history as well, is no inert text. The past is transformed not once and for all, in a simple act of historical expression. The meanings in the expression are never stable or frozen at their moment of expression. They are always added to and embroidered by the very continuity and preservation of the text. Their continuity and preservation is always a cultural act in itself, done in institution and ceremony, done in technology, done in the very forms and structures of the text as a cultural thing. But the transformations are more multiple than even in their expression and their continuity. Our imagined Everyperson at the Christmas service, however slightly touched with the fire of the great contemplatives, will have made his or her own distracted meditations on the "Word made flesh." The meanings he or she will see in the text will come from self as much as from text, but never just from self or just from text. The hermeneutics of such a transformation have long been a science. I think of Ignatius Loyola and his *Spiritual Exercises*; I think of John Wesley. The essence of that science surely has been to discover both the spur and the curb of enthusiasm. The spur has been to see the timelessness, the eternally renewed relevance of the sacred work. The curb has been to see that meaning has nonetheless some authoritative, institutional definition. If we would understand the transformations of the past that histories are, then we must describe as well the tension between the creative thrust by which personal meaning is implanted in the text and the authoritative demand, whether sacred or secular, that the meaning be public and conventional. Sacred history is entertainment in its essence. The text is neither totally inside nor totally outside the reader. The meaning is both changing and unchanging. The reader will be fully absorbed in the particularities of its expression and know it in its reduced simplicity. The history is received and made at the same time.

Political parables recite history for the lessons it contains. I think of election speeches, party nominations, manifestos, celebration of some public metric moment. Hearers are invited to bridge the past and present in the identification of similar conditions or motivations. The thrust is to put aside the differences of time, the nuances of change, and to motivate the hearer with clearly perceived similarities. There is little effort to persuade to the truth of the interpretation of the past: the truth of the interpretation is presumed. The effort is directed at evoking mythical metonymies, likenesses that are seen immediately to be true and are sustaining not because they are new but because they are old. They call on the way the world is known to be from some perspective of class or race or sex. To be a cliché is a virtue. Given the right circumstances, this clichéd history gets renewed meaning, just as a national anthem gets its strength from the circumstances in which it is sung. The goal of history in political parable is mood, sustained righteousness or anger or pride. The understanding it gives has the completeness and indivisibility of an emotion and comes from the ambience of experienced signs in the medium, not the reasoning in the message. Hearers are expected to make their rationality subservient to a *Realpolitik*. To question whether the history is correct, to quibble about its certainty, would be like giving a medical report in answer to the everyday question of "How are you?" The history in political parable is sacramental: it makes the reality in its signs.

One has to understand that "scientific history" or "academic history" is as cultural and as social as a dinner-table story or scripture or a political parable. The rhetoric about these logical systems of "academic histories" and the declaratory definitions of what they are and are not sometimes hide what disciplines share with everyday cultural phenomena. Indeed the vested interest in making them seem different and above culture is the very quality that makes them the same. The most remarkable development over the last century in Euroamerican cosmological systems has surely been the evolution and division of innumerable sciences. Each one claims to be distinct from all the others; each proclaims its difference from common sense; each is jealous that its partial, unreal bit of reality should belong to somebody else. My own university, established in 1854 in a raw colony fired to some delusions of grandeur by the discovery of gold, created four founding chairs—of Modern History, of Classics, of Law, of Literature and Language. It was a fair, if compromised, map of an educated man's cosmology. Now the university has 117 departments. For 136 years it has boiled like some symbiotic brew, primed by the politics of knowledge to divide and subdivide. The process at the University of Melbourne by which groups of men and women (mostly men) grabbed this or that bit of the human anatomy and the physical environment and said it was theirs is only a tiny part of the fractionalization of systematic knowledge. One almost needs an ethnoscience to see the categories of the world as "scientific man" sees it. The begetting of science by science produces as many kinship and residence rules and boundary-maintaining mechanisms as any clan or moiety. The rites de passage that give entry and status in the discipline mark the mind as circumcision marks the body, so that historians do not "understand' sociologists, for example, and each enjoys its caricatures of the other. The reifications by which some object is separated out of the continuity of experience—say, a gene or a neutron or a psyche or even a "Renaissance"—are established as so really distinct from everything else that it needs a different language to describe it, a different system of evidence and discourse to analyze it, a special sensitivity to see it. Virtually as much social energy is put into the support of differing reifications of the sciences as is put into the central reifications of our local system, such as the law, the state, the church. We are socialized to their real distinction by examination, promotion, residential requirements, associations, conferences, publications. C. P. Snow was satisfied to discover two cultures. At the University of Melbourne, he might have discovered 117 if his measures were those we make for race or class or sex.

The transformation of the past in "academic history" is set in different social circumstances and performs functions different from other sorts of transformations of the past. That it does have a social set and performs social functions needs to be explored a little, because many academic historians would be uncomfortable with the notion. The very idea of "scientific" or "academic history" would seem to take that sort of history out of the social circumstances that relativize it. Indeed, nineteenth-century Euroamerican society invested extraordinary social energy in inventing a history that was supposedly divorced from its social circumstances. For a brief span in the middle of the century, when philosophy and religion had lost some of their cosmological hold, "academic history" took their place. The growth of nations, the development of mass society and of massive institutions to control it, and the bureaucratization of empires encouraged a faith in a science that told "what actually happened." Scientific history was seen to be different from romantic legend, sacred text, and political manipulation of the past because it demanded accuracy. It also defined what accuracy was and provided an open discourse in which accuracy was measured.

Scientific history was admirably suited for government, law, education—everywhere where the transformation of the past had to be seen to be reliable, measured by the same criteria, true. The rub, of course, was in being true. Scientific history, by definition, was accurate. The opening of national archives, and then of special collections, the growing cultural realization that the ordinary national and political past as distinct from the cultural past of classical antiquity was worth observing, the emergence of new histories out of new sources, the creation of reviews in which the amateur was flogged into line for his faulty references and the professional waited in terror for the recluse who knew it all and had not told—all gave practical definitions to what was accurate history. Accurate history was what could be attested to by appeal to some "primary source." Inventiveness and imagination in discovering new primary sources became a mark of a historian's genius and good luck. In a joined-together world of historical societies, academies, publishers, libraries, archives, and reviews of all sorts, a historian's finickiness toward accuracy was a public possession. Under the circumstances it is not surprising that being accurate became equated with being true and that history became equated with historical facts.

It would be difficult to exaggerate our own Euroamerican culture's preoccupation with the past as historical fact. Every minute in the world some athlete "makes history" somewhere in the world with another record. The industry of revising the past by the discovery and publication of some "startling fact" is, beyond measure, huge. We are bombarded with quizzes, with calendars of people and events, with celebrations of metric moments. We are entertained by our own historicity: accuracy is truth. I remember a newspaper reporter who, goodwilled and wanting people to hear me lecture but frustrated by my reflexivity and my bland relativism, did his best with me with a headline: *Bligh, A Real Nice Guy*. It was up to me to make history news with an "exposure," a "revelation." The past entertains us, romantic positivists that we are, by being rendered ever more accurate.

It should be clear that in calling academic history "entertainment" I do not mock the seriousness or the good intentions of the pursuit of meaning in disciplinary ways. I only mean to indicate that pursuit of meaning never was a privileged position outside of culture and society. I equate different types of meaning pursuits—from gossip to the recitation of myth to systematic inquiry—in their dramaturgical quality. I do not equate them for what they are or what they do or for the worth of investments we put in them. We are entertained by the past in our different histories under their different conventionalities. No one form of these histories is truer that the others *because* it is unconventional. Our poetics for all of them allow us to read the "truth" in all of them. Objectivism and relativism are both unreal, unhuman perspectives if being objective is thought to be unconventional and being relative is thought to be maverick. Our poetics allow us to share our entertainment by the past under different conventionalities.

The conventions of that dramaturgical entertainment include not just the text and its structure but the reading and the cultural rules of reading as well. The presentation of "academic history" and the reading of it —that is, the living discourse that is the response to the written-down text and the then-continued tradition that is the context of reading— these correspond to my notion of "entertainment." I should add, without wanting to raise another hare, that the seriousness of the intent of the author of a text does not preclude an audience being amused by it, and being amused, like having a joking relationship, can establish realities in turning them around.

It should be clear by now that this essay will not offer a poetic of "Polynesian" historical consciousness, nor indeed of the historical consciousness of native Polynesian and stranger European, each in the environment of the other. The "ifs" and "buts" of such an exercise offend my sense of economy for this piece. I have tried it elsewhere and I invite you to taste its ambiguities there. The truth is that I have been so preoccupied with the dead Polynesians of the past that I have little expertise to talk of a poetic of historical consciousness of the living Polynesians of the present. I watch with interest the efforts of the new nations of the Pacific to produce their own histories, and I note the pressures on them from their own institutions of power to produce histories in an acceptable Western idiom. I watch the movements for ethnic and cultural identity in the various Polynesian islands, and I note in the poetic of their histories their distrust of their processual selves, as if they think being Hawaiian or being Tahitian is some positive, unchanging essence that is now lost but is somehow recoverable. I watch the ever more self-conscious dialectic between living cultures and ethnographic descriptions of their past. I think of Mead/Freeman and the "Samoans." But all around the Pacific it is the same. Cultures cannibalize their own images. It has happened often enough in our own culture, this dialectic between living and reflections on life, but it is happening all around the Pacific starkly now. What a complicated two-way "Mirror for Man" anthropology has turned out to be once we understand the poetics of an ethnographic moment.

A poetic for histories of the dead Polynesians will overwhelm anyone who tries to do it unless he or she has a pragmatic confidence in only doing what can be done. The relics of the native Polynesian past have all been transformed into relics of the stranger European past. There is nothing—not a written-down experience, not myth or a legend, not a material artifact, not an archaeological site—that does not, by the expressions of it, by the collection and preservation of it, and/or by the interpretation of it and inclusion of it in a stranger's discourse, re-quire critical reading to separate the stranger's cargo from the native's past. There is no need, because of that, to adopt a know-nothing silence about a poetic of histories of past Polynesians. Both European strangers and Polynesian natives of the past are distant from us now. At a dis-tance, history's ironies are to our advantage, and we can catch a glimpse of their different taken-for-granted worlds.

Roy Wagner has offered us the disturbing notion that culture belongs to the stranger's eye—to the professional stranger, if he or she be an anthropological observer, say, or to the person who is distanced by reflection or role from what happens around him or her (Wagner 1981).

Culture is a stranger's invention: it is the sense of wholeness and integration an outside-outsider or an inside-outsider develops. In a poetic for histories, one has to describe this same invention of the past. Whatever the different social expressions of historical consciousness, they are all born of the irony that things are never what they seem. Irony is history's trope. In the space between the meaninglessness of the present and the unknowable past is the entertainment of history. The artifice of history's words is to give historians, whoever they are—gossips, priest, academics—control over the past in a way participants could never control their present. Historians—again, whoever they be—are outsiders. They always make a drama out of what the participants experienced as one damned thing after another. Historians always order the chaos of chance and circumstance to give it meaning. They always see the past from a perspective the past could never have had. They are like meteorologists predicting yesterday's weather today. They get their certainties from consequences.

Let me end with an invention and an entertainment of my own. I wrote above that I was puzzled to describe the mechanisms by which the ethnographic moment between native and stranger became culturally significant to them both. In 1785 there was a Christmas pantomime at Covent Garden to celebrate the discoveries in the Pacific and the apotheosis of Captain Cook. The pantomime was called *Omai or a Trip around the World*. That it was a pantomime was important. It was a highly conventionalized idiom of the fantastic adventure voyages of Harlequin, Columbine, Pantaloon, and Clown. It was a vaudeville of magic and trickery with no plot save lovers fleeing authority or jealousy, in the end to triumph. In *Omai*, the lovers were Londina, Britannia's daughter, and Omai, heir to the Tahitian throne; and they fled from the Spaniard, Don Struttolando, who pursued them to Kamchatka, the Ice Islands, Hawaii, Tonga, and Tahiti. In the end, in the great bay of Matavai, Omai received his crown and his Londina, and there was a procession of all the nations Captain Cook had discovered. As they sang their homage to Cook, a huge painting of him in glory, crowned by Britannia and Fame, descended onto the stage. The pantomime played fifty-eight times. George III went to see it many times, and the critics wrote of it that it was a "school for the history of man." It is a puzzle how so fantastical an entertainment could have been thought a "school for the history of man." But under the absurdities and magicals the audience thought they saw something real. John Webber, Cook's artist, was consultant for the scenes and the costumes. William Shield, the composer, made "realistic" imitations of "savage" music. Above all, Phillipe de Loutherbourg, a brilliant stage innovator, used all his genius to combine the recognizable realism of Plymouth Port and Margate Pier with the unfamiliar realism of native custom and native environment.

The audience sat enthralled at Loutherbourg's brilliance in presenting flying baloons, not two years invented, sailing ships, thunderstorms, and penguins on icebergs and knew they were being entertained to understand the native because they were being entertained to see the genius of the civilized. When they, the civilized, made a god of Captain Cook, the critic's only complaint was that just lowering a portrait was a little unspectacular. There was nothing unreal, however, in the history that came through the lyrics as the nations of the Pacific raised their voices: "Cook taught mankind how to live. He *came* and he *saw*, not to *conquer* but to save." I suspect they knew precisely who they were in knowing the other so realistically. Such a past invented out of such an ethnographic moment entertained them no end.

For more years than I care to remember I have read and written about the relationships of history and anthropology. I, who thrive on anthropology's generous spirit of discourse, sit in a chair of history; and in a university that has had no anthropology, I have been the anthropologist. Beached in this way by the politics of knowledge, I have a jaundiced view of the boundary disputes of disciplines, and I would turn reflection on history and anthropology away from them. I see the cartoons and caricatures disciplines draw of one another as symptoms of a territoriality that is human enough, but dangerous when its masks a claim for power based on the partiality of each discipline's view. Kings as philosophers amuse me, but philosophers as kings frighten me. Now that my liberalism is more radical and my pragmatism more certain, I have little patience when the question "Who are you who say that?" precedes and precludes the question "What is it that you say?" Yet

I am impatient, too, with the false consciousness that separates ways of knowing from ways of being. This is why I have written of a poetic for histories.

In a period now when anthropologist-historians such as Clifford Geertz, Marshall Sahlins, Renato Rosaldo, Rhys Isaac, Barney Cohn, Natalie Zemon Davis, Valerio Valeri, James Boon, and Richard Price have consciously blurred genres, my old concerns are somewhat dated. Maybe. Boundaries, I suspect, like the poor, are always with us.

Back in 1966, feeling professionally competent as a historian but in the middle of the torturing initiation rites of being an anthropologist at Harvard, I wrote "Ethnohistory in Polynesia" (*Journal of Pacific History* 1:23–42) to make two pragmatic points: a priori definitions of what could or could not be done in history and anthropology were irrelevant; each inquiry stood on its own persuasiveness as to what could be done. And, since the history of Polynesian cultures could only be written out of sources that were European, one would always have to know who the Europeans were before knowing the Polynesians. I was disturbed at what I thought was a flaw in Pacific anthropology. It was ahistorical, it pursued the Polynesians in a time out of time. It was not truly ethnographical of the present nor of the past. Even in the fieldwork of the 1920s to the 1950s, the cultures described were not so much what was observed as something that belonged to an imagined moment before the Europeans came.

Twenty years later, I am not comfortable with the term *ethnohistory* if it is thought to be a special sort of history that one writes of non-Western societies. I now think of myself as an ethnohistorian only when I am distinguishing systems of historical consciousness across cultural time and space and when I am describing the ways historical consciousness creates present cultural moments. The realization in Pacific studies that "fatal impact" is an unhelpful analytic concept in describing cultural processes has reinforced my earlier postulate that the relationship between native Polynesians and intruding Euroamerican strangers has been symbiotic.

In 1973, I wrote an ethnography of the demarcations of disciplines ("History as a Social System," *Historical Studies* 15:673–85). Philosophers had usurped discussions of the disciplines and what they said about the logic of explanations was of little relevance to what actually happened in the systematization of knowledge. Scholars were divided, I argued, by their tropes of understanding, "prudence" on the historians' part, "scanning" on the sociologists' and anthropologists'. They were all socialized to the acceptance of the limitations of their own tropes and the foreign qualities of others' tropes by all the ways social boundaries are made. For some time I had engaged my history students in ethnographic descriptions of their own and present social milieu, the better to interpret and the better to sense how sparse and disembodied of context were relics of the past. "History as a Social System" flew the kite that trailed the banner "History is ethnography."

In 1974, I edited the *Marquesan Journal of Edward Robarts 1797–1824* (Canberra: A.N.U. Press). The journal had been written by a beachcomber who had lived seven years in the Marquesas at the end of the eighteenth century. Robarts's account was a remarkable ethnographic moment become cultural artifact. In his personal experience, Robarts showed how the native Marquesans were invented and then possessed by stranger-societies and stranger-scholars once the inventions were written down. There was an extraordinary osmosis, which I cannot describe here but only wonder at, whereby one small man's personal experience was registered in the experience of explorer-visitors, raised through them into literature in Herman Melville's *Typee*, and came to affect and condition twentieth-century anthropology of the Marquesas. Everything I have said in "A Poetic for Histories" is exemplified in Robarts's journal.

There was a more important point conceptually to which I was led in editing Robarts. Robarts's journal described the actuality of Marquesan society: it told of Marquesan persons doing things, conditioned in their roles and their obedience to their cultural roles by their personalities and by the chance and circumstances of living. Against a structured view of what he thought the Marquesans thought they *should* be doing typically and culturally, Robarts also told whom they actually married and with whom they were in conflict and why. It is in describing what actually happened that I find history (the discipline of history) and ethnography joined. I see a distinction between actuality and reality. By "actuality" I mean what happened as it is known in its balance of the circumstantial and the determined, in its typicality as well as its particularity, known for its multivalent meanings. By "reality" I mean what happened as it is reductively known, by its determinants, known in its simplicity of meaning, set in some hierarchy of acceptability. History and anthropology are joined by the common humanism of their interest in the actual. They both deny themselves the fundamentalism of reality-construction. Their tolerance in seeing and describing things as they actually are is self-denying of the power to make things really something else. I like the shared poetry of their vision: they know their own ambiguities and cannot see reality for its ironies.

In 1978, I wrote an ethnographic history of a school—*Xavier, A Centenary Portrait* (Melbourne: O.X.A. Press). It was a long way from the Pacific, but not from "primitive" cultures. Schools are as good a place as any to describe the dialectic between *langue* and *parole*. They are marvelous places to see the symbolic environment that histories make. In itself, the celebration of a centenary, the writing of a school history by a socially prestigious "old boy," the decisions that needed to be made as to the style of entertainment a school history should be, and the debates that were raised around breached conventionalities—all made for a personal experience of the public nature of historymaking. Susan Sontag ended her essay *Against Interpretation* with a call for an erotics (in place of a hermeneutics) of art. Certainly ethnography is a celebration of the pleasure of being and history will never entirely escape its own antiquarianism. But then again, I do not think that being a guardian of the signatures human beings make on life is antiquarian at all.

Xavier—and the erotics of writing history—liberated me to write *Islands and Beaches: Discourse on a Silent Land, Marquesas 1774–1880* (Honolulu: University Press of Hawaii, 1980). I felt liberated from the need to disguise the pasts of Marquesan natives and European strangers "as if" they were free from each other or from me or from all that intervened between me and them. As strangers and natives were bound together, so were present and past. *Islands and Beaches* was an effort to show what that binding-together actually was. It was anthropological history in that "I" the author enlarged the past by being enlightened by the snatches of anthropological discourse I had caught. It was historical anthropology because it reflected the ways in which historical consciousness constituted the present moments of 1774 to 1880 in the Marquesas as well as the ways in which historical consciousness constituted all the present moments that joined the then of 1774 to 1880 to the now of 1974 to 1980, the period of my writing. Writing history is inevitably an exegesis of an exegesis. I speak of what I thought I did. What I did is to be found in all the varied readings of *Islands and Beaches*.

I have been teased in recent years by how one could better do this anthropology of the past. I cannot escape the consequences of the directions I have already taken. Anthropology's vision is built not on the "primitiveness" of the native but on the advantage of the dialectic between distance and familiarity. The symbolic environment of an eighteenth-century missionary chapel is as revelatory of the nature of religion as the symbolic environment of an eighteenth-century Tahitian *marae*. The triangle of distances and lines between strangers and natives and between now and then is still the advantage and the frustration of historical anthropology.

In recent years I have tried to narrate these abstract theoretical issues through anthropological histories of particular events. In 1983, in "The Face of Battle: Valparaiso 1814" (*War and Society* 1:25–42), inspired by Jack Keegan and Paul Fussell, I attempted an ethnography of men in battle. The narrative remarks on the ways history, interpretation of what has happened, feeds on itself to make a present. An absurdity —the slogan "Free Trade and Sailors' Rights"—became a faith by which men died as their historymaking lessened their options by the minute. It was a small but awful example of culture as process. In "Sharks That Walk on the Land" in 1982 (*Meanjin* 41:427–37), I had mimicked Marshall Sahlins's admirable *Historical Metaphors and Mythical Realities*. There were two histories in his "structures of the conjuncture": the Hawaiian and the British. It seemed to me that the British discovery in their histories that Cook was a hero was not very different from the Hawaiian discovery in their histories that he was a god. In presenting Cook as hero and as god in their histories, British and Hawaiians mirrored themselves. "Possessing Tahiti" (*Archaeology in Oceania* 21:103 –18) in 1986 was a reflection on all the different ways in which Tahiti has been possessed—by empires, by Tahitians, by scholars, by me. One only has to try to discover the roots of one's knowledge to be persuaded of its many moments of invention.

I do not believe that I have moved far from my initial belief that in academic history and anthropology it is better to do what can be done than to declare what cannot. Several years ago I published a small monograph called *History's Anthropology: The Death of William Gooch* (A.S.A.O. Special Publication no. 2, Washington, D.C.: University Press of America, 1988). I do not believe we can escape Picasso or Einstein or Roland Barthes or Michel Foucault any more than we can escape Jesus Christ or Buddha. What they have spoken cannot be unspoken. We are all plagiarists on life and living. *History's Anthropology* is ultimately an ethnography of a historical act—mine and all those that made the life and death of William Gooch. All writers, all scholars, must make some surrender to the systems that allow their thoughts and images to be shared. I wish now of *History's Anthropology* that I had plagiarized the courage of Picasso or Einstein or Barthes or Foucault to test the vulnerability of these systems a little more. There is much of the liminality of ritual in writing. It has an in-between quality that I value most as a professor of history, a declarer of histories. It is a space for knowing oneself, bonded and free at the same time.

Any reader of this essay will have entered on a familiar discourse. Any reader will see that I have written what Clifford Geertz has written, and Victor Turner, Hayden White, Marshall Sahlins, Sally Falk Moore, Roy Wagner, Richard H. Brown, Jonathan Culler. And young Karl Marx is there, mediated by Georg Lukacs and Shlomo Avineri.

Experience out of discussions of the issues in this essay tells me that there are a few points at which a reader might balk. The word *public* is one. History is public knowledge of the past, I say. *Public*, however, is heard as institutional, even governmental. But *public* is only a word I use to describe the shared and systematic character of histories. Even the most personal and unique understanding of the past is public insofar as it is expressible to oneself and to another. Who can express an "I" without making a "Me"?

My emphasis on process rather than structures and my insistence on the inventiveness of our historymaking have encouraged some to call me an optimist. I think maybe I am, if by that is meant that I believe human beings to have the potential to change their world, and that irony is an instrument of such nonviolent change. But one cannot write the history of natives and strangers without being aware of how alien the past is and how burdensome histories can be. The pain histories cause does not go away by stressing the dialectic of subjection and contrivance that histories are. However, a moralism that stresses that the only thing we can change is the present is less self-indulgent than one that lambastes the past for not having changed itself.

That part of our symboling life in which we collate signs and hold them up for consideration by giving them some dramaturgical or narrative unity I have called "entertainment." To *inter-tenēre* ('hold between'), entertain, is a serious activity. We are astute participants in our everyday dramaturgies. We stage our performances between markers that allow us to read their meaning clearly. If *entertain* is a word with too many distracting connotations, what other word should we use?

Selected Readings

Arpad, J.
     1977   Immediate Experience and the Historical Method. *Journal of Popular Culture* 11:141–54.
Avineri, Shlomo
     1968   *The Social and Political Thought of Karl Marx*. Cambridge: Cambridge University Press.
Barthes, Roland
     1977   *Roland Barthes by Roland Barthes*. New York: Hill and Wang.
Berger, John
     1972   *Ways of Seeing*. London: Pelican.
Berkhofer, Robert F.
     1973   Clio and the Culture Concept: Some Impressions of a Changing Relationship. In *The Idea of Culture in the Social Sciences*, ed. L. Schneider and C. Bonjean. Cambridge: Cambridge University Press.
Boon, James
     1973   Further Operations of Culture in Anthropology. In *The Idea*

of Culture, ed. L. Schneider and C. Bonjean. Cambridge: Cambridge University Press.

1982   *Other Tribes, Other Scribes*. Cambridge: Cambridge University Press.

Brown, Richard H.

1977   *A Poetic for Sociology*. Cambridge: Cambridge University Press.

Brown, Richard H., and Stanford M. Lyman

1978   *Structure, Consciousness and History*. Cambridge: Cambridge University Press.

Canary, Robert H., and Henry Kozicki, eds.

1978   *The Writing of History*. Madison: University of Wisconsin Press.

Chesneaux, Jean

1976   *Pasts and Futures*. London: Thames and Hudson.

Crick, Malcolm

1976   *Explorations in Language and Meaning*. London: Malaby Press.

Culler, Jonathan

1975   *Structuralist Poetics*. Ithaca: Cornell University Press.

Feuer, Lewis S., ed.

1969   *Marx and Engels*. London: Fontana.

Fox-Genovese, Eugene, and Elizabeth D. Genovese

1976   The Political Crisis of Social History. *Journal of Social History* 10:305–19.

Fussell, Paul

1975   *The Great War and Modern Memory*. London: Oxford University Press.

Gadamer, Hans-George

1982   *Truth and Method*. New York: Crossroad.

Geertz, Clifford

1975   *The Interpretation of Cultures*. London: Hutchinson.

1983   *Local Knowledge*. New York: Basic Books.

Graham, Loren, Wolf Lepevies, and Peter Weingart, eds.

1983   *The Function and Uses of Disciplinary Histories*. Dordrecht: Reidel.

Haskell, Thomas L.

1977   *The Emergence of Professional Social Science*. Urbana: University of Illinois Press.

Henige, David

1982   *Oral Historiography*. London: Longman.

Judt, Tony
1979   A Clown in Regal Purple: Social History and the Historians.
                History Workshop 7:66–94.
Keegan, John
1977   *The Face of Battle*. New York: Cape.
Moore, Sally, and Barbara G. Meyerhoff, eds.
1976   *Symbol and Politics in Communal Ideology*. Ithaca: Cornell
                University Press.
Parkin, David, ed.
1982   *Semantic Anthropology*. London: Academic Press.
Price, Richard
1983   *First Time*. Baltimore: Johns Hopkins University Press.
Prown, Jules D.
1982   Mind in Matter. *Winterthur Portfolio* 17:1–20.
Sahlins, Marshall
1976   *Culture and Practical Reason*. Chicago: University of Chicago
                Press.
1981   *Historical Metaphors and Mythical Realities*. A.S.A.O. Spe-
                cial Publication no. 1. Ann Arbor: University of Michigan
                Press.
1985   *Islands of History*. Chicago: University of Chicago Press.
Said, Edward
1978   *Orientalism*. New York: Random House (Vintage Books).
Samuel, Raphael
1981   *People's History and Socialist Theory*. London: Routledge and
                Kegan Paul.
Sontag, Susan
1967   *Against Interpretation*. London: Eyre and Spottswoode.
1979   *On Photography*. Harmondsworth: Penguin.
Tillinghast, Pardon E.
1972   *The Spacious Past*. Reading, Mass.: Addison-Wesley.
Turner, Victor
1977   Process and Symbol: A New Anthropological Synthesis.
                Daedalus 106:61–80.
1982   *From Ritual to Theatre*. New York: Performing Arts Journal
                Publications.
Wagner, Roy
1981   *The Invention of Culture*. Chicago: University of Chicago
                Press.

White, Hayden
    1973   *Metahistory: The Historical Imagination in Nineteenth-Century Europe*. Baltimore: Johns Hopkins University Press.
    1980   The Value of Narrativity in the Representation of Reality. *Critical Inquiry* 7:5–27.

Yovel, Yitmiahu, ed.
    1974   *Philosophy of History and Action*. Jerusalem: Reidel.

Zinn, Howard
    1970   *The Politics of History*. Boston: Beacon.

Contributors

ALETTA BIERSACK is associate professor of anthropology at the University of Oregon and has done fieldwork in the Papua New Guinea highlands (Paiela) as well as in Tonga. Her articles concentrate upon gender, historicity, religion, and political systems. Currently she is preparing a monograph on gender, time, and cosmos among the Paiela. In 1974 she was awarded the Curl Bequest Prize by the Royal Anthropological Institute.

The anthropologist GREG DENING is Max Crawford Professor of History at the University of Melbourne. Well known for his reconstructions of the cultural systems of the past, particularly as these come into play in historical intercultural encounters in the Pacific, Dening is the editor of the *Marquesan Journal of Edward Roberts 1797–1824* (1974), *Islands and Beaches* (1980), *History's Anthropology* (1988), and *The Bounty* (1988). In 1988–89 he was at the Institute for Advanced Study at Princeton.

JOCELYN LINNEKIN is associate professor of anthropology at the University of Hawaii at Manoa. Her writings concern questions of cultural persistence and change, women's status, and identity formation in the contemporary Pacific. She is author of *Children of the Land* (1985) and *Sacred Queens and Women of Consequence* (1990), and she is the co-editor of *Cultural Identity and Ethnicity in the Pacific* (1990). Linnekin is currently conducting an ethnohistorical study of money and ceremonial exchange in the two Samoas.

MARSHALL SAHLINS is Charles F. Grey Distinguished Service Professor of Anthropology at the University of Chicago. His research and publications have centered on Pacific ethnology and cultural theory with particular attention to the ethnography and history of Hawaii and Fiji. His books include *Social Stratification in Polynesia* (1958); (with E. R. Service) *Evolution and Culture* (1960); *Moala* (1962); *Tribesmen* (1968); *Stone Age Economics* (1972); *Culture and Practical Reason* (1976), which was awarded the Gordon F. Laing Prize by the University of Chicago Press in 1978; *The Use and Abuse of Biology* (1976); *Historical Metaphors and Mythical Realities* (1981); and *Islands of History* (1985). He has held visiting professorships at the University of Adelaide, the University of Hawaii, Beijing Foreign Studies University, and the University of Tokyo. His honorary lectures include the Marc Bloch Lecture (Sorbonne, 1981), the Sir James Frazer Lecture (University of Liverpool, 1982), the Distinguished Lecture of the American Anthropological Association (1982), the Westermarck Lecture (Helsinki University, 1983), and the Radcliffe-Brown Lecture (British Academy, 1988).

Native of Scotland, ANDREW JAMIESON STRATHERN has spent a large part of his professional life in Papua New Guinea, where he has nurtured an interest in anthropology and made a contribution to that new nation. In 1987 the Papua New Guinea government awarded him one of its Tenth Anniversary of Independence Medals. In 1968, he was awarded the Curl Bequest Prize from the Royal Anthropological Institute, and in 1976 he received the Rivers Memorial Medal for fieldwork from R.A.I. He continues to conduct long-term research among the Melpa and the Wiru. His monographs and essay collections include *The Rope of Moka* (1971), *One Father, One Blood* (1972), *Ongka* (1979), *Inequality in New Guinea Highlands Societies* (1982), and *A Line of Power* (1984). Currently Strathern is Andrew W. Mellon Professor of Anthropology at the University of Pittsburgh.

NICHOLAS THOMAS was a research fellow in cultural anthropology at King's College, Cambridge, 1986–89 and is now Queen Elizabeth II Research Fellow, affiliated with the Australian National University. He has conducted archival studies on eastern Polynesia, Fiji, and the Solomons and has done fieldwork in the Marquesas and recently in western Fiji. His interests include cultural dimensions of colonial history, gender, exchange, and eighteenth-century anthropology; his publications include *Out of time* (Cambridge 1989) and *Marquesan Societies* (Oxford 1990), and he is a co-editor of *History and Anthropology*. He recently completed a book on indigenous exchange and transcultural movements of objects in the Pacific and is now working on colonialism and objectification.

Professor of anthropology at the University of Chicago, VALERIO VALERI's main research areas are Polynesia and eastern Indonesia. He is the author of *Kingship and Sacrifice* (1985) and various papers on alliance, exchange, dual organization, and gender in Polynesia and eastern Indonesia. Currently he is preparing a monograph on the Huaulu of Seram at the Institute for Advanced Study at Princeton.

ROY WAGNER has conducted research among the Daribi of the Papua New Guinea highlands and the Usen Barok of New Ireland. His ethnographic and theoretical writings are closely intertwined, both centering on symbolism, symbolic production, and human creativity as culture's source. His monographs include *The Curse of Souw* (1967), *Habu* (1972), *The Invention of Culture* (1975, 1981), *Lethal Speech* (1978), *Symbols that Stand for Themselves* (1986), and *Asiwinarong* (1986).